Abortion and the Christian Tradition

Abortion and the Christian Tradition

A Pro-choice Theological Ethic

Margaret D. Kamitsuka

WESTMINSTER
JOHN KNOX PRESS
LOUISVILLE • KENTUCKY

First edition
Published by Westminster John Knox Press
Louisville, Kentucky

19 20 21 22 23 24 25 26 27 28—10 9 8 7 6 5 4 3 2 1

Except where otherwise noted, Scripture quotations are from the New Revised Standard Version of the Bible, copyright © 1989 by the Division of Christian Education of the National Council of the Churches of Christ in the U.S.A., and are used by permission.

Book design by Sharon Adams
Cover design by Lisa Buckley Design

Library of Congress Cataloging-in-Publication Data
Names: Kamitsuka, Margaret D., author.
Title: Abortion and the Christian tradition : a pro-choice theological ethic / Margaret Kamitsuka.
Description: Lousiville, Kentucky : Westminster John Knox Press, [2019] | Includes bibliographical references and index. | Summary: "Abortion remains the most contested political issue in American life. Poll results have remained surprisingly constant over the years, with roughly equal numbers supporting and opposing it. A common perception is that abortion is contrary to Christian teaching and values. While some have challenged that perception, few have attempted a comprehensive critique and constructive counterargument on Christian ethical and theological grounds. Margaret Kamitsuka begins with a careful examination of the church's biblical and historical record, refuting the assumption that Christianity has always condemned abortion or that it considered personhood as beginning at the moment of conception. She then offers carefully crafted ethical arguments about the pregnant woman's authority to make reproductive decisions and builds a theological rationale for seeing abortion as something other than a sin"— Provided by publisher.
Identifiers: LCCN 2019021677 (print) | LCCN 2019981609 (ebook) | ISBN 9780664265687 (paperback) | ISBN 9781611649734 (ebook)
Subjects: LCSH: Abortion—Religious aspects—Catholic Church. | Women's rights—Religious aspects.
Classification: LCC HQ767.3 .K36 2019 (print) | LCC HQ767.3 (ebook) | DDC 241/.6976—dc23
LC record available at https://lccn.loc.gov/2019021677
LC ebook record available at https://lccn.loc.gov/2019981609

Most Westminster John Knox Press books are available at special quantity discounts when purchased in bulk by corporations, organizations, and special-interest groups. For more information, please e-mail SpecialSales@wjkbooks.com.

Contents

Acknowledgments   vii

Introduction   1

PART 1: CRITIQUE OF PRO-LIFE ARGUMENTS

1. The History of Abortion: Neither Univocal nor Absolute   17

2. Biblical Arguments for Personhood   49

3. Fetal Personhood and Christ's Incarnation   71

4. Christian Philosophy and Fetal Personhood   97

PART 2: CONSTRUCTIVE PRO-CHOICE PROPOSALS

5. Maternal Authority and Fetal Value   121

6. Gestational Hospitality and the Parable of the Good Samaritan   155

7. Motherhood Choices, Abortion Death, and the Womb of God   193

Selected Bibliography   225

Index   241

Acknowledgments

This book is the product of years of grappling with the abortion issue in conversations with many colleagues, current and former students, and pastors. Students in three of my courses at Oberlin College, "Theologies of Abortion," "Abortion and Religion," and "Mothering and Religion," were lively interlocutors on all aspects of women's reproductive lives, and I am grateful for our interactions. Several conferences provided settings for important critical and constructive feedback on my ideas: the Constructive Theology Workgroup meeting in Nashville, Tennessee (2008); the Duquesne University Women in Philosophy conference, "Critical Philosophies of Life" in 2017; and the 2018 Societas Ethica conference, "Feminist Ethics and the Question of Gender" in Louvain-la-Neuve, Belgium. My thanks go to the anonymous reviewers of two essays whose comments helped me to refine my thinking: "Feminist Scholarship and Its Relevance for Political Engagement: The Test Case of Abortion in the U.S.," *Critical Issues in the Study of Religion and Gender* 1, no. 1 (2011); and "Unwanted Pregnancy, Abortion, and Maternal Authority: A Prochoice Theological Argument," *Journal of Feminist Studies in Religion* 34, no. 2 (Fall 2018).

I am grateful to Oberlin College for research support through the Francis W. and Lydia L. Davis Chair fund. Several colleagues deserve a special word of thanks. Mara Brecht, Cindy Chapman, Linda Mercadante, and John Thiel generously gave of their time to read long, early drafts of parts of this manuscript, and their thoughtful comments were invaluable in helping me move forward. Robert Ratcliff at Westminster John Knox was not only an instrumental editor for the whole project but also an insightful commentator.

I thank my family, who supported me through the years of ruminating and writing this book. Encouragement to pursue this project came from my mother, Shirley Despot (1919–2012)—educator, quilter, and volunteer "grandma" at the neonatal intensive care unit—who took seriously being what she called a card-carrying member of Planned Parenthood. My sister, Katy Despot, a midwife for over thirty years, provided not only medical expertise but also important insights about a diversity of pregnant and birthing women's experiences. My sons have come of age while this book progressed, and it was a joy for me to discuss these vital issues with them as they enter adulthood. My deepest thanks go finally to my husband, David Kamitsuka, with whom I discussed innumerable drafts, and who believes, alongside me, in the vital importance of articulating a pro-choice Christian argument for today.

Introduction

How can theologians and ethicists defend a pro-choice stance on abortion today? *Abortion and the Christian Tradition* attempts to answer that question against the backdrop of a cultural environment, in the United States especially, where Christian pro-life discourse commands most pulpits and inundates all forms of the media and public spaces, from blogs to the sidewalks in front of women's health centers to the halls of Congress. This vigorous, well-organized, and articulate popular pro-life movement is paralleled in academic circles. Biblical scholars, theologians, and Christian bioethicists and philosophers disseminate a pro-life message that, they claim, has deep roots in the history of Christianity and is supported by Scripture, the church's creeds, and moral philosophy—namely, the unborn are persons from conception, who have a sacred right to life and, therefore, abortion is a heinous sin. On every point, my research tells me, pro-life claims are biblically weak, conceptually misleading, theologically mistaken, and even dangerous. Church history tells a more complicated story about abortion, and pro-life biblical, doctrinal, and philosophical arguments for fetal personhood fail to come close to making a compelling case that would justify removing or curtailing the reproductive rights that women currently have in most of the world. That pro-life rhetoric has proved successful in finding a committed pro-life constituency does not mean that they have faithfully represented the Christian tradition on the issue of abortion. To the contrary. They have distorted the central symbols and stories of the Christian faith, including creation in God's image, the doctrine of the incarnation, Mary's role at the Annunciation, the parable of the good Samaritan, and others. This book endeavors to reclaim these symbols and stories in support of women's moral conscience and decision-making authority over their reproductive lives.

While Christian pro-choice voices exist, their numbers appear to be fewer and their influence is less widespread. Only a handful of book-length scholarly texts have been published over the past decades giving a defense of abortion rights from a Christian perspective—the late Beverly Harrison's well-known manifesto of feminist ethics, *Our Right to Choose: Toward a New Ethic of Abortion* (1983); Kathy Rudy's more moderate *Beyond Pro-Life and Pro-Choice: Moral Diversity in the Abortion Debate* (1996); oriented to a Roman Catholic audience, *A Brief, Liberal, Catholic Defense of Abortion* (2000), by Daniel Dombrowski and Robert Deltete; and recently, Rebecca Todd Peters, *Trust Women: A Progressive Christian Argument for Reproductive Justice*.[1] A very few pro-choice books geared to a more general Christian readership have been published by writers willing to face the backlash.[2] A number of important feminist pro-choice essays have been published in recent decades on select aspects of the abortion debate in Christianity; however, as we will see in later chapters of this book, differences exist among some of their positions, especially regarding when and under what conditions abortion is morally justifiable. The combination of a paucity of in-depth pro-choice writings using Christian sources, and the lack of consensus among pro-choice advocates on the ethics of abortion, have left scholars, pastors, and ordinary believers without the tools to see pregnancy and fetal life from a perspective other than that promoted by the pro-life movement. I offer both a comprehensive critique of recent pro-life scholarship and, even more importantly, a constructive theological and ethical defense of women's reproductive rights based on authoritative texts in the Christian tradition.

The abortion debate is important to discuss not only because it continues undiminished but, even more significantly, because most women will face difficult reproductive choices at some point in their childbearing years.[3] What

---

1. Beverly W. Harrison, *Our Right to Choose: Toward a New Ethic of Abortion* (Boston: Beacon Press, 1983); Kathy Rudy, *Beyond Pro-Life and Pro-Choice: Moral Diversity in the Abortion Debate* (Boston: Beacon Press, 1996); Daniel A. Dombrowski and Robert J. Deltete, *A Brief, Liberal, Catholic Defense of Abortion* (Urbana: University of Illinois Press, 2000); Rebecca Todd Peters, *Trust Women: A Progressive Christian Argument for Reproductive Justice* (Boston: Beacon Press, 2018).

2. See Anne Eggebroten, *Abortion—My Choice, God's Grace: Christian Women Tell Their Stories* (Pasadena, CA: New Paradigm Books, 1994); Kira Schlesinger, *Pro-Choice and Christian: Reconciling Faith, Politics, and Justice* (Louisville, KY: Westminster John Knox Press, 2017).

3. In this book I use the term "woman" to mean a cisgender woman, or a person assigned female at birth and identifying as female. Statistics are only beginning to emerge about transgender people seeking abortion services; see L. Abern, S. Nippita, and K. Maguire, "Contraceptive Use and Abortion Views among Transgender and Gender-Nonconforming Individuals Assigned Female at Birth," *Contraception* 98, no. 4 (2018): 337. However, it is uncontroversial to state that transgender people also are affected by reproductive stresses. This book will not address

does it mean to be a woman of reproductive age in America today? One Gutt-macher Institute study finds that "on average, U.S. women want to have two children. To accomplish that goal, a woman will spend close to three years pregnant, postpartum or attempting to become pregnant, and about three decades—more than three-quarters of her reproductive life—trying to avoid an unintended pregnancy."[4] While the rate of abortions has fallen in recent years, it is estimated that about "one in five U.S. pregnancies ends in abortion."[5] Given that about half of women in America who have abortions self-identify as Christian,[6] there is a disconnect between the rhetoric and claims of pro-life proponents and the actual lives of the many believing women who are getting abortions—quietly, secretly, and in substantial numbers. These women not only face the often agonizing decision to terminate an unwanted pregnancy, but they do so mostly in isolation and burdened by the onslaught of extreme anti-abortion accusations that women who abort are murderers. Even more moderate pro-life rhetoric that aims only "to stigmatize [so-called] casual abortion," in effect, shames any Christian woman who has an abortion.[7] An updated and comprehensive discussion of abortion—one that supplies a coun-terargument to pro-life fetal personhood claims, speaks to the burdens and risks of pregnancy, and attempts to alleviate the stigma that Christian women who abort are made to bear—is long overdue and much needed.

Since Christianity is a historically expansive and diversely lived tradition, the abortion question can never be answered definitively for all Christians. I enter into conversation with representatives from many different branches and denominations of Christianity, a range of academic and unaffiliated pop-ular writers, as well as ordinary Christian women, whose views on abortion would probably never be known had they not been interviewed by research-ers. My attempt to assess a gamut of current pro-life views has taken me to online sites ranging from moderate pro-life blogs to the Web pages of extremist anti-abortion groups that would appropriately be called domestic

the reproductive justice needs of the latter group, though some of the discussions here may be relevant for transgender and gender nonconforming people who can get pregnant and for whom Christian faith is a factor in their identity. For transgender reproductive issues, see Laura Nixon, "The Right to (Trans) Parent: A Reproductive Justice Approach to Reproductive Rights, Fertil-ity, and Family-Building Issues Facing Transgender People," *William and Mary Journal of Women and the Law* 20, no. 1 (2013): 73–103.

4. "Unintended Pregnancy in the United States," *Guttmacher Institute* (September 2016; updated January 2019), https://www.guttmacher.org/fact-sheet/unintended-pregnancy-united-states.

5. Rachel K. Jones and Megan L. Kavanaugh, "Changes in Abortion Rates between 2000 and 2008 and Lifetime Incidence of Abortion," *Obstetrics & Gynecology* 117, no. 6 (2011): 1358.

6. See Jenna Jerman, Rachel K. Jones, and Tsuyoshi Onda, "Characteristics of U.S. Abor-tion Patients in 2014 and Changes since 2008," *Guttmacher Institute* (May 2016), https://www.guttmacher.org/sites/default/files/report_pdf/characteristics-us-abortion-patients-2014.pdf.

7. David P. Gushee, *The Sacredness of Human Life: Why an Ancient Biblical Vision Is Key to the World's Future* (Grand Rapids: Wm. B. Eerdmans Publishing Co., 2013), 360.

terrorism groups—the latter being the ugly underbelly of anti-abortion fringe Christian activism. I insist on the importance of both distinguishing the moderates from the extremists in the pro-life movement, as well as exposing how the former can, inadvertently, provide fodder for the latter. While the source material I use is predominantly Christian, I enlist Jewish ethical viewpoints at important points. I give some mention of other religions, and pro-choice proponents in those traditions may be served by some of the analyses offered here. Many secular and post-Christian feminists write off the Christian tradition as irredeemably toxic for women, especially on issues related to sexuality and reproduction, and they decide not to engage further with Christianity's images, symbols, and doctrines. My scholarship continues to wrestle with the ambiguities of the tradition, finding resources there that could be meaningful for believers who still make Christianity their spiritual home.

Some scholars object to using the terms pro-life and pro-choice in relation to abortion. Kathy Rudy has noted that these binary terms can obstruct attempts within and among Christian communities to "transcend the chasm" of that binary and find solutions to the abortion dilemma.[8] I appreciate this sentiment, in part, because I find most binaries to be largely unhelpful for real-life ethical dilemmas. That said, while some occasional efforts have been made by pro-life and pro-choice Christians to talk across the divide, those opportunities have dwindled as people have retrenched into their opposing camps.[9] I have chosen to continue using the terms pro-choice and pro-life because they offer a helpful shorthand for me to adjudicate the complex theological and ethical debates in this book. Moreover, these terms can be nuanced, as needed, and they are among the least inflammatory from among the many epithets that are used.[10] I do not mean to suggest that all pro-life or all pro-choice proponents think alike. I will discuss important differences within each group, including where my pro-choice position builds on but sometimes differs from the positions of other pro-choice scholars.

8. Rudy, *Beyond Pro-Life and Pro-Choice*, xxii.

9. For one set of meetings in the late 1990s, see Anne Fowler et al., "Talking with the Enemy," *The Boston Globe* (January 28, 2001), https://www.feminist.com/resources/artspeech/genwom/talkingwith.html. For an evaluation of the 2010 "Open Hearts, Open Minds" conference at Princeton University, see Aimée Thorne-Thomson, "My Take on 'Open Hearts, Open Minds,'" *Rewire.News* (October 21, 2010), https://rewire.news/article/2010/10/21/take-open-hearts-open-minds-fairminded-words%E2%80%9D/. See Charles Camosy, "(Final Post) The Princeton Abortion Conference One Year Later: Exchanges with Reproductive Justice Activist Hilary Hammell," *Catholic Moral Theology* (October 9, 2011), https://catholicmoraltheology.com/the-princeton-abortion-conference-one-year-later-guest-post-by-reproductive-justice-activist-hilary-hammell/.

10. At some points, I use the term "anti-abortion" in order to reflect the real distinctions between extreme anti-abortion and moderate pro-life groups. I do not use polemical terms such as "pro-abortion" or "anti-choice," which are negative epithets that groups on each side pin on each other.

I take seriously the objection that the pro-choice/pro-life binary is, in part, a white feminist construct that often silences the wider justice concerns of peoples of color. Andrea Smith records this revealing exchange she had while interviewing a Native woman:

> *Me:* Would you say you are pro-choice or pro-life?
>
> *Respondent 2:* Well, I would say that I am pro-choice, but the most important thing to me is promoting life in Native communities.[11]

Many scholars of color writing on this issue have opted to use the term "reproductive justice" instead of "pro-choice" as an intentional political strategy for broad coalition-building efforts, encompassing a range of interrelated social justice agendas, including forced sterilization, the right to parent, disability rights, and access to abortion services.[12] Scholarship about reproductive rights and motherhood in recent decades has made significant efforts to move beyond liberal, white, secular, feminist abortion rights slogans, in order to probe the racial, economic, religious, and other complexities of a diverse range of women's reproductive lives. For example, womanist scholars insist that pregnancy, reproductive rights, and mothering mean something different for African American women, who are still affected in overt and inchoate ways by the cultural legacy of enslavement, when "Black women's bodies literally were not their own."[13] Scholarly commitments to listen to the diversity of women's voices—on their own terms—have produced illuminating ethnographic accounts, and themes drawn from these ethnographies make a significant contribution to my pro-choice proposals.

In this project the reader will also find arguments that are informed by the work of leading secular feminist philosophers and ethicists writing about abortion, which is part of what makes this project an intentionally feminist one. Contrary to the ways in which many pro-life writers vilify feminism, feminist thinking on reproductive rights has moved significantly beyond the content and tone of pro-choice discourse in the immediate *Roe v. Wade* period, as exemplified in Mary Anne Warren's too-blithe quip from the early 1970s that "if the right to life of a fetus is to be based upon its resemblance to a person, then it cannot be said to have any more right to life than, let us

11. Andrea Smith, "Beyond Pro-Choice versus Pro-Life: Women of Color and Reproductive Justice," *NWSA Journal* 17, no. 1 (2005): 119.

12. See Kimala Price, "What Is Reproductive Justice? How Women of Color Activists Are Redefining the Pro-Choice Paradigm," *Meridians: Feminism, Race, Transnationalism* 10, no. 2 (2010): 42–65.

13. Monica A. Coleman, "Sacrifice, Surrogacy and Salvation: Womanist Reflections on Motherhood and Work," *Black Theology* 12, no. 3 (2014): 202.

say, a newborn guppy."[14] Current feminist ethicists are increasingly critical of the earlier feminist knee-jerk opposition to ever speaking about fetuses as, for example, unborn babies. Efforts to remain attentive to the discourse of women who abort reveal that their words rarely reflect politically correct feminist lingo. Jeannie Ludlow recounts that in her research, while working as an abortion clinic patient advocate, the discourse of women getting an abortion tends to be familiar, not clinical: "Very few patients say 'fetus' or 'embryo.' The majority say 'baby,' as in . . . 'I just can't have this baby at this time.'" Some even write good-bye notes, such as, "All my love, the mom you'll never meet."[15] I take seriously the personal, often maternal terms used by these women—terms that belie both the older pro-choice avoidance of "baby" talk as well as the rampant pro-life caricature of women who abort as selfishly having no maternal regard for the being in their womb.

Some secular feminist philosophers are even willing to speak of a mode of ethical reflection about abortion in terms of "a work of mourning," as seen in the writings of Karen Houle, who revisits her own abortion experience and elucidates how she was able to begin responding ethically to the death of a being who might have been her son or daughter, "the child-who-was not."[16] I see writings like Houle's as marking a larger, significant feminist shift from earlier pro-choice rhetoric, and I affirm looking seriously at abortion as an experience of reproductive loss. This book reinforces all of these secular philosophical trends, with particular attention given to the impact of religious beliefs on Christian women who have an abortion.

Even secular scholars today concede that the religiosity of women who abort deserves to be theorized rather than merely discounted as false consciousness. As Ludlow notes, one clinic worker shared with her, "Sometimes, patients ask me to baptize their fetuses," and she recalls that other patients "asked the deity to which they pray to send back to them the child they are aborting, at a time in the future when they are better able to care for it."[17] Secular scholars recognize that they do not have the theoretical resources to speak more than superficially to issues of religious piety and belief. If a woman using clinic services is a conservative Christian, she may want deeper

14. Mary Anne Warren, "On the Moral and Legal Status of Abortion," *The Monist* 57, no. 1 (1973): 58.

15. Jeannie Ludlow, "Sometimes, It's a Child and a Choice: Toward an Embodied Abortion Praxis," *NWSA Journal* 20, no. 1 (2008): 43, 44. Ludlow is also a board member of "Abortion Conversation Projects," a national organization that works to reduce abortion stigma and enhance respectful public conversation about abortion. See http://www.abortionconversation project.org/mission-and-vision/.

16. Karen Houle, *Responsibility, Complexity, and Abortion: Toward a New Image of Ethical Thought* (Lanham, MD: Lexington Books, 2014), 220.

17. Ludlow, "Sometimes, It's a Child and a Choice," 27, 43.

spiritual reasons to carry her through, during the abortion and afterward, than a generic affirmation that it is appropriate for her to "honor her life goals"[18] or "exercise 'fidelity to myself and its becomings.'"[19] Believing women especially experience their abortion through the lens of ubiquitous pro-life Christian rhetoric that labels abortion as the sinful destruction of an innocent child who bears God's image. Unbiased, professional pastoral counselors should be tasked with assisting these women with tools for whatever self-reflectiveness they wish to engage in, free from shame and self-recrimination.[20] Religious practitioners from various traditions have developed postabortion rituals to meet the spiritual needs of women who experience loss.[21] In addition, pro-choice theologians and ethicists owe these women doctrinally and biblically based proposals to help them understand their rightful place in the Christian tradition in light of unwanted pregnancy and abortion death. This book endeavors to make a contribution to this difficult but important task.

CRITIQUE AND CONSTRUCTIVE PROPOSALS

Abortion and the Christian Tradition is structured in two parts. The first part delivers a sustained critique of two sets of arguments at the heart of the pro-life position: that the historical church maintained a continuous anti-abortion and pro-natal stance, and that a person exists from the moment of conception. Chapter 1 addresses one of the most repeated claims across popular and scholarly pro-life literature—namely, that opposition to abortion was "an almost absolute value in [Christian] history," and it was motivated by a concern for innocent unborn life.[22] This notion, promulgated by Catholic jurist John Noonan in the early 1970s, still forms the historical basis for almost all Christian pro-life polemics. A number of feminist scholars in past decades have challenged this reading of church history, arguing that most

---

18. Jeannie Ludlow, "The Things We Cannot Say: Witnessing the Trauma-tization of Abortion in the United States," *Women's Studies Quarterly* 36, no. 1 (2008): 40.

19. Houle, *Responsibility, Complexity, and Abortion*, 218.

20. There is sparse unbiased published literature on this topic. See Jane Ranney Rzepka, "Counseling the Abortion Patient: A Pastoral Perspective," *Pastoral Psychology* 28, no. 3 (1980): 168–80; Christie Cozad Neuger, "The Challenge of Abortion," in *Pastoral Care and Social Conflict*, ed. Pamela D. Couture and Rodney J. Hunter (Nashville: Abingdon Press, 1995), 125–40.

21. See June O'Connor, "Ritual Recognition of Abortion: Japanese Buddhist Practices and U.S. Jewish and Christian Proposals," in *Embodiment, Morality, and Medicine*, ed. Lisa S. Cahill and Margaret Farley (Dordrecht: Kluwer Academic Publishers, 1995); Jeff Wilson, *Mourning the Unborn Dead: A Buddhist Ritual Comes to America* (Oxford: Oxford University Press, 2009).

22. See John T. Noonan Jr., "An Almost Absolute Value in History," in *The Morality of Abortion: Legal and Historical Perspectives*, ed. John T. Noonan Jr. (Cambridge, MA: Harvard University Press, 1970).

early church and medieval writings on abortion were not pro-natalist and were, instead, obsessed with controlling nonprocreative sexual practices. In addition, I present recent scholarship that sheds new light on a number of issues challenging this pro-life narrative, including: the apostle Paul's possible Hellenistic Jewish views on abortion, the compassionate aspects of medieval penitential practices recognizing women's struggles with reproductive issues, and some early church fathers' apparent acceptance of physicians' determinations about the necessity of therapeutic abortions to save a woman's life. These glimmers of understanding about women's reproductive challenges faded from church history with the rise of canon law—with pro-life proponents today suggesting good riddance. Recapturing a fuller historical picture of the church's various stances on abortion reveals that a Christian pro-choice position is not necessarily out of line with the theological and pastoral intuitions of some past church authorities.

Chapters 2, 3, and 4 analyze and criticize three types of pro-life arguments for fetal personhood: biblical, doctrinal, and philosophical. In chapter 2, we see how scholarly and popular pro-life writers try to make the biblical case that each embryo, as human, must be asserted as bearing the image of God, who predestines it to be born. I demonstrate the inability of pro-life scholars to surmount the hermeneutical hurdles of explaining how the Genesis 1 and 2 creation stories about the first human beings created in God's image plausibly apply to fetuses at all, or explaining what the few biblical references to being called by God from the womb really mean. Pro-life scholars fail to provide a convincing biblical basis for fetal personhood from conception, and, in addition, their claims lack the support of the New Testament, which focuses on exhorting believers to be conformed to Christ's image. I strongly question the theological legitimacy of deriving from biblical uterine call stories the claim that God elects all in-utero life to be born. No proper understanding of a doctrine of providence or predestination would definitively link God's will to the biological event of conception.

A growing group of pro-life theologians is turning to the creeds of the early church in order to argue for the doctrinal necessity of accepting personhood from conception. These theologians claim that because an orthodox (Chalcedonian) view of the incarnation teaches that the Word assumed ensouled embryonic flesh in Mary's womb, the believer must accept that all human embryos are ensouled persons from conception. Chapter 3 refutes this theological claim by exposing how these pro-life scholars give a narrow reading of a few patristic sources and remain rigidly locked in a body-soul paradigm for defining the human person. Some pro-life scholars even draw the unwarranted, almost mythological, conclusion that because of Christ's incarnation as an embryo, all embryos should be seen as sacred. This chapter presents an alternative, and still arguably Chalcedonian, interpretation of the incarnation that reflects a more modern evolutionary and historical understanding of human nature. It is not doctrinally necessary nor even widely credible anymore to say that the union of Christ's divine and human natures was fully accomplished in the blink of an eye in Mary's womb. I argue that seeing the incarnation as an emergent and historical process of deification occurring throughout Jesus' life adheres to Chalcedonian principles and provides a compelling alternative to the pro-life approach that tries (unconvincingly, in my view) to posit belief in personhood at conception as a requirement of doctrinally correct Christian faith.

Christian pro-life philosophers offer various arguments to ground the metaphysical and moral claim that a person exists at conception. Some argue for a substantialist view of personhood, claiming that the individual, self-directing human substance that comes into existence at syngamy is the same substance that exists continuously in the born person until death. If the (genetic) essence is the same, the rights should be the same. Roman Catholic moral philosophy makes a different sort of argument, appealing to the notion of probabilism—namely, even the probability that a fetus is a person at conception means that one must attribute to the fetus full personhood rights and dignity. Chapter 4 critically assesses both of these pro-life philosophical arguments. The most that substantialist philosophers succeed in showing is the abstract idea of a fetal person, but that idea bears little resemblance to any actual fetuses living in women's bodies. Probabilism, which is a mode of moral argumentation that in some situations is meant to justify the withdrawing of rights, is used in a backward way to grant fetuses more rights than they are due, given the Catholic magisterium's recognition that the personhood of the fetus cannot be definitively proved. In addition, some of these Christian philosophers see themselves as not simply offering philosophical proposals but also trying to prevent murder (to their way of thinking), which gives an ominous political undertone to their objectives about protecting fetal life, no matter what the circumstances of how that fetus came to be in whatever woman's or girl's body.

The chapters in part 1 of this book thus demonstrate that attempts to secure fetal personhood fail on the merits of each type of argument—historical, biblical, theological, and philosophical. Moreover, these pro-life arguments fail to meet any plausible burden of proof that warrants overruling a woman's right to make reproductive decisions about her body and the dependent fetus she bears. Pro-life proponents seem to assume that, based on their understanding of Christian sources, the default moral position on abortion is that it is immoral and should be banned—until pro-choice proponents prove otherwise. I argue the reverse. Given my reading of Christian sources, and given the legal consensus in most all of the modern world about women having at least some reproductive rights, the burden of proof falls on pro-life proponents to give credible reasons why all abortions are immoral and should be banned. Part 1 of this book determines that, even on a Christian basis alone, pro-life proponents fall far short of meeting that burden of proof.

On one point, however, I am in agreement with pro-life proponents, and that is the intuition that a living fetus has value. However, that value will have to be delineated apart from spurious claims that the Bible, Christian doctrine, or philosophy can prove personhood from conception. Moreover, I insist that the concept of fetal value should not be used as a moral leash, so to speak, to restrain the actions of pregnant women, on the cynical and misogynous assumption that these women somehow do not understand what they are gestating and are incapable of exercising moral judgment and making reasonable practical choices for their lives and those in their care.

In part 2, I offer constructive ethical and theological proposals on themes I believe are central for a comprehensive pro-choice position. The chapters in this part of the book address three sets of topics: the pregnant woman's authority to make reproductive decisions and the nature of fetal value; the parameters of obligations, rights, and fairness pertinent to Samaritan acts of gestational hospitality; and the theological reasons for why abortion should not be categorized as sin ipso facto. Chapter 5 addresses the first set of issues, which I see as reciprocal: a pregnant woman's authority to abort and the nature of fetal value. The guiding question is this: How should we think of the pregnant woman—her identity, obligations, and bodily rights—such that she would be morally authorized to end the life of a fetus, whose value is not negligible? Some pro-choice feminists appeal to a woman's pre- or non-mothering consciousness early in pregnancy to justify abortion of a very unformed fetus. I argue, instead, that the decision-making authority a pregnant woman exercises in abortion is precisely a maternal one—a decision that no child should come into the world for whom she would have some kind of mothering obligations. The argument I make philosophically actually reflects the maternal tone in the words of ordinary women, many of whom speak of their abortion in terms of not feeling able to have the baby and not being ready to mother it. From this perspective, an argument for fetal value follows. Value inheres for an embryo and then a fetus because it is a genetically individual human being, existing contingently and contiguously to its gestating mother, and progressing toward being a born person. The fetus is best understood in terms of a tensive, dual claim: the fetus is not a nonperson without value, but neither is the fetus a person with the status of an already born child.

No comprehensive pro-choice position can ignore that, along with securing women's rights, one must address whether there is any moral claim incumbent on the pregnant woman to offer her fetus gestational welcome. This issue is pertinent for Christian women, especially, given the teaching about love of neighbor found in the parable of the good Samaritan. Chapter 6 addresses the issue of the moral obligations and justifiable limits of Samaritan hospitality—of a woman to her fetus and of the church and society to the woman with an unwanted pregnancy. I strongly criticize the ways in which pro-life Christian writers have mobilized Samaritanism to suggest that the church is warranted to compel, or even try to persuade, a reluctant pregnant woman or girl to gestate an unwanted pregnancy. I propose instead a paradigm of gestational hospitality—based on ethical principles of caring, fairness, and justice. This paradigm is attentive to the profound message of Samaritan self-giving but also wisely insists that women in caretaking roles involving bodily self-giving need to make decisions and allocate their resources so that they will be able to emulate the Samaritan in the parable, who "finished his journey."[23] Without moral limits and legal protections regarding pregnancy—the burdens and risks of which are not inconsequential—pro-life proponents will continue to allegorize the parable as a tale of a vulnerable fetus needing care, and women will continue to be relegated to the role of the beast of burden, carrying the wounded traveler to safety, with no say in the matter.

Beyond the need to set ethical parameters for gestational hospitality, a pro-choice position must theologically address the problem of the stigma borne by Christian women who have had an abortion or even considered a pregnancy to be unwanted. Chapter 7 offers specifically theological reasons for validating a pregnant woman's decision making, her right to give consent, and the validity of choosing to pursue callings other than motherhood. This chapter addresses the widespread pro-life theme, based on the theology and spirituality surrounding the Virgin Mary, that gestating an unplanned pregnancy is a Christian woman's spiritual calling and that even deeming one's pregnancy unwanted is a kind of religious anathema. I offer two readings—of the birth narratives in Luke's Gospel and the spiritual autobiography of medieval mystic (and mother of fourteen) Margery Kempe—in order to make the case that Marian spirituality supports the notion that not wanting to gestate and not wanting to mother are also acceptable spiritual callings for believing women. For women who do abort, however, there looms the pervasive and debilitating pro-life message that abortion is a grievous sin, indeed, murder. I argue for why abortion should not be labeled as ipso facto sin (and certainly not murder), and why Jesus' definitive sacrifice on the cross

---

23. Jeanne Stevenson-Moessner, "From Samaritan to Samaritan: Journey Mercies," in *Through the Eyes of Women: Insights for Pastoral Care*, ed. Jeanne Stevenson Moessner (Minneapolis: Fortress Press, 1996), 323.

should be seen as freeing women from offering their bodies for compulsory gestation. Finally, I address women's reproductive loss, including abortion loss, which many women experience as death within their womb. I interpret the crucifixion event through the lens of a mothering God in order to propose a theology of death that enables one to imagine how all reproductive losses, including abortion deaths, are taken up and healed within the womb of the Trinitarian God.

A PERSONAL NOTE

This book is unavoidably marked by my own perspectives and context. My theological proclivities are Protestant, feminist, and what has come to be informally called the postliberal "Yale school."[24] My philosophical and ethical commitments emphasize embodied relationality, attentiveness to contextual lived realities, and concern for issues of marginality as well as for ideals of the common good. I have a reproductive history. This book is not about my story, but I think it is important to say a few relevant things. I am a white, cisgender woman who, for many years in my young adult life, did not want to get pregnant and who, at a later point in my life, has mourned miscarriage, who has experienced the throes of reproductive challenges, but who has been able to birth two children, now teenagers, whom I am mothering with fear and trembling and great joy. Mentioning these aspects of my own reproductive experiences is not meant to establish my credentials to speak about abortion. Nevertheless, I deem it important that someone arguing for the justifiability of a pregnant woman ending the uterine life within her should be able to speak with some experiential authority about gestation, reproductive loss, birthing, and motherhood. That said, my subjective experience is only my own: thinking of my wanted pregnancies, from the earliest embryonic moment, in terms of "my babies" can never be imposed on how another woman thinks of her pregnancy. Moreover, when I subject my own reproductive experiences to rigorous analysis, I cannot but conclude that what makes one call an embryo or fetus a "baby" is deeply contextual and discursively constructed.

 This book aims to analyze critically the fallacies and weaknesses in Christian pro-life discourse. I offer as a counterargument my feminist pro-choice theological ethic regarding pregnancy, fetal value, and the choice to abort. I

24. My reference here is meant to indicate that this so-called school shaped me to appreciate the theological, ethical, and political possibilities of continuing to engage closely with the Christian tradition, while critically "following at a distance," to adapt Gene Outka's felicitous phrase: "Following at a Distance: Ethics and the Identity of Jesus," in *Scriptural Authority and Narrative Interpretation*, ed. Garrett Green (Philadelphia: Fortress Press, 1987).

do not presume to tell women with unwanted pregnancies what to think or do in this most difficult of decisions and life experiences, and I certainly will not pontificate on what God's mysterious will is. I hope this book provides theological, moral, and spiritual resources for Christian women, and perhaps women in other religious traditions as well, who have had an abortion or who may face an abortion choice (and those who support them). As I interpret church history, Scripture, philosophical ethics, and Christian doctrine, I see support for a number of principles that this book promotes: the importance of consent to pregnancy, an insistence that gestational hospitality be deemed a virtue and not a duty, and a commitment to fostering women's moral authority and spiritual agency—principles that do not negate the value of fetal life but remind us that there is no fetal existence without the embodied labor of a moral agent: the fetus's gestating mother. Most important is the persistent reminder from the biblical text that "just as you do not know how the breath comes to the bones in the mother's womb, so you do not know the work of God, who makes everything" (Eccl. 11:5). This verse about the inscrutability of God inclines me to listen all the more carefully to the needs and hopes of the person most intimately engaged with that breath and those bones—the mother who must decide her fetus's fate and her own.

PART 1

Critique of Pro-life Arguments

1

The History of Abortion: Neither Univocal nor Absolute

Current pro-life literature paints a history of the church's supposedly unyielding condemnation of abortion and univocal view of the sanctity of fetal life. John Noonan's famous phrase from the early 1970s about abortion being "an almost absolute value" in the church's history is still cited by scholars today.[1] Professor of New Testament Michael Gorman's *Abortion and the Early Church*, which has wide influence in pro-life circles, also presents the early church as consolidating an overwhelmingly anti-abortion stance.[2] Roman Catholic bioethicist David Jones, in his *The Soul of the Embryo*, concludes that despite ongoing debates on some theological and philosophical issues, "the Christian understanding remained unchanged in its essentials from the time of Christ to the mid twentieth century"—namely, "an enduring desire to protect the human embryo."[3] These scholars trace a litany of anti-abortion statements beginning as early as the end of the first century CE, in documents like the *Didache*: "You shall not slay the child by abortions."[4] Noonan lists a thread of

---

1. John T. Noonan Jr., "An Almost Absolute Value in History," in *The Morality of Abortion: Legal and Historical Perspectives*, ed. John T. Noonan Jr. (Cambridge, MA: Harvard University Press, 1970).

2. Michael J. Gorman, *Abortion and the Early Church: Christian, Jewish and Pagan Attitudes in the Greco-Roman World* (Eugene, OR: Wipf & Stock, 1998).

3. David Albert Jones, *The Soul of the Embryo: An Enquiry into the Status of the Human Embryo in the Christian Tradition* (London: Continuum, 2003), 245, 246. Jones's views have had a significant influence in the U.K. Church of Scotland bioethicist Calum MacKellar echoes Jones in stating that "Christianity has always recognized a sacred value to the human embryo and foetus." MacKellar, *The Image of God, Personhood and the Embryo* (London: SCM Press, 2017), 93.

4. *Didache* 2:2, quoted in John T. Noonan Jr., "Abortion in the Catholic Church: A Summary History," *Natural Law Forum* 12 (1967): 91; see Gorman, *Abortion and the Early Church*, 49; D. Jones, *Soul of the Embryo*, 57.

similar anti-abortion pronouncements that continue in subsequent centuries, concluding that these condemnations were "so uniformly expressed" that they "took the form of legislation."[5] The habit of including a list of anti-abortion statements from historical church leaders, such as the ones Noonan, Gorman, and D. Jones quote, is now so ubiquitous in popular pro-life writings that historical names like Tertullian and Basil of Caesarea, hitherto unknown to ordinary Christians, are now regularly discussed.[6]

These scholars' erudition notwithstanding, their accounts oversimplify the historical record. They obscure the complex, varied, and contested ways the church historically tried to address not only the idea of abortion but also actual instances of women with unwanted pregnancies attempting an abortion. Current historical scholarship, more attentive to cultural, political, and theological complexities of the historical source material, paints a different picture, which is neither univocal nor absolute—especially when one can get a glimpse of the real lives of Christian women from the distant past and why they turned to abortion. No one disputes that the church pronounced early and long that abortion is a moral evil and that the women who attempted or succeeded with an abortion are sinners; however, these pronouncements are just the tip of the iceberg. The historical particularities of the church's abortion discourses and the diverse range of theological viewpoints on abortion and fetal life can only be seen by an approach that eschews a predetermined ecclesial standpoint and is open to see that the church bequeathed some fragments of compassionate pastoral guidance amid its problematic perspectives on women and sexuality.

This chapter provides a glimpse into a counternarrative about abortion views in church history, based on historical source material that indicates not univocal condemnation but a range of opinions on issues surrounding abortion among early and medieval church authorities. What should be the penance for a poor woman who aborts? If a father commits incest and then impels his daughter to take an abortive potion, who is guilty and of what crime? If a monk causes a miscarriage by violence, how should he be punished? Is aborting an unformed fetus a homicide? The church did not have one answer to these and many other dilemmas regarding fetal demise. My objective is not only to complicate today's pro-life claims about the church's

---

5. Noonan, "An Almost Absolute Value," 14.

6. Stephen Tu, *Pro-Life Pulpit: Preaching and the Challenge of Abortion* (Eugene, OR: Wipf & Stock, 2011), 32–35. T. L. Frazier, "The Early Church on Abortion," *OrthodoxyToday.org*, http://www.orthodoxytoday.org/articles/EarlyChurchAbortion.php; Jared Dobbs, "What Did the Early Christians Think about Abortion?" *Alliance Defending Freedom* (January 17, 2018), https://www.adflegal.org/detailspages/blog-details/allianceedge/2018/01/17/what-did-the-early -christians-think-about-abortion.

anti-abortion stance but, more importantly, to show how the pro-life push to embed a myth of historical unanimity actually masks the little one can glean about how moral deliberation in the church transpired, when magisterial pronouncements came uneasily face-to-face with the real reproductive struggles of women and families. The fits and starts of how the church tried to address reproductive realities is, I argue, the crucial history lesson to learn as a basis for understanding the extent to which those ancient and medieval pronouncements should—or should not—be authoritative for Christians today.[7] Moreover, the glimpses one can find of compassion toward women's reproductive challenges bolster the claim that a pro-choice stance is not cut off from the historical Christian tradition.

Initial critiques of Noonan came in the early 1980s from feminist ethicist Beverly Harrison, who insisted that all historical condemnations of abortion need to be contextualized in light of the church's arguably deeply rooted androcentrism, sexism, and antisexuality bias, which are still timely critiques. In addition, pro-life historical claims can be challenged by newer scholarship in two areas: studies comparing attitudes toward abortion in medieval penitential manuals and medieval legal canons, which call into question the pro-life preference of the latter over the former; and research into how Greco-Roman medical knowledge influenced the early church fathers, which belies pro-life claims that Christianity repudiated all so-called pagan attitudes toward therapeutic abortion.

EARLY FEMINIST CRITIQUES OF SEXISM AND ANTISEXUALITY

Pro-choice feminist scholars in religion writing in the 1980s insisted that historical church documents, laws, and theological texts cannot be taken at face value; rather, pronouncements about abortion and fetal life must be contextualized in light of the church's overall sexism and its antisexuality bias. Harrison emphasizes the importance of not only including social history with doctrinal

---

7. The church's position in the modern era brings up different historical debates. David Jones summarizes 19th- and 20th-century anti-abortion efforts in Britain and the U.S. as reflecting a pro-natalist "common Christian morality" shared by legislators, physicians, and church leaders. D. Jones, *Soul of the Embryo*, 202. One finds a different viewpoint in Leslie J. Reagan, *When Abortion Was a Crime: Women, Medicine, and Law in the United States, 1867–1973* (Berkeley: University of California Press, 1997), 6–8, 62–63. A middle-ground interpretation is given in Marvin Olasky, *Abortion Rites: A Social History of Abortion in America* (Wheaton, IL: Crossway Books, 1992), esp. chap. 13. See also Mark G. Toulouse, "Perspectives on Abortion in the Christian Community from the 1950s to the Early 1990s," *Encounter* 62, no. 4 (2001): 327–403.

history but also including a feminist liberation theological perspective that exposes how "Christianity has functioned structurally or institutionally as part of the social system of male supremacy."[8] Once these contextualizing and ideological analyses are done, one can see that the supposedly almost absolute anti-abortion stance in the church was more a factor of condemning contraception, nonprocreative sex, and women's sexual sins and only distantly a factor of "a clarified moral evaluation of fetal life."[9] Many of these arguments have been exhaustively made by feminist Christian writers.[10] I summarize them here briefly.

Harrison charges that Noonan uses a questionable historical methodology whereby he converts the church's anti-abortion statements into a pronatalist position. That is, he takes the church's condemnation of abortion and assumes that the theological and moral motivation was to protect innocent unborn human life. Harrison contests this approach to the historical sources, arguing, "I find no evidence until the modern period that compassion for the presumed 'child' in the womb was a generating source of Christian moral opposition to abortion."[11] Harrison's claim that concern for innocent fetuses was not the church's central concern is supported by a number of historical points: the church could not come to consensus on the issue of when fetal ensoulment happened;[12] the assumption that infants were born with original sin (and hence were not inherently innocent) became widespread especially under the influence of Reformation teachings;[13] when church leaders had the authority and the means to enforce civil penalties for abortion, they did not seem inclined to do so (as in Calvin's Geneva).[14] Harrison's point is not to identify when, in history, a modern notion of children as innocent or sacred beings emerged; rather, her focus is to expose the myopia that causes pro-life historians to mistake past anti-abortion invectives for "a positive valuation

8. Beverly Wildung Harrison, *Our Right to Choose: Toward a New Ethic of Abortion* (Boston: Beacon Press, 1983), 154.

9. Harrison, *Our Right to Choose*, 142.

10. In addition to Harrison, see Susan T. Nicholson, *Abortion and the Roman Catholic Church* (Knoxville, TN: Religious Ethics, 1978); Jane Hurst, *The History of Abortion in the Catholic Church: The Untold Story* (Washington, DC: Catholics for a Free Choice, 1983).

11. Harrison, *Our Right to Choose*, 131. Harrison applies this critique to the work of Catholic ethicist Germain Grisez as well, whose work she finds to be "more adamantly an ideological over-reading" of the historical material than even Noonan's (290 n. 17).

12. See Harrison, *Our Right to Choose*, 134–35, 142, 145.

13. See Harrison, *Our Right to Choose*, 145–46.

14. See Harrison, *Our Right to Choose*, 147. On how the issue of abortion was addressed in Calvin's Geneva, see John Witte and Robert M. Kingdon, *Sex, Marriage, and Family in John Calvin's Geneva: Courtship, Engagement, and Marriage* (Grand Rapids: Wm. B. Eerdmans Publishing Co., 2005), esp. 257–58.

of fetal life."[15] In addition to the historical evidence that points away from pro-natalism, two issues rise prominently to the surface in Christian history, which delegitimize many of the church's anti-abortion pronouncements: sexism and an antisexuality bias.

Sexism

That the early church morphed from pockets of relatively egalitarian, Spirit-inspired, missionary-oriented communities into more gender-stratified and hierarchical structures of a state religion has been well argued by a number of feminist historians and biblical scholars.[16] Whether or not those claims hold up under scrutiny, few would deny the impact and pervasiveness of patriarchy in the historical church. As Rosemary Ruether has so crisply stated the issue, "Roman Catholic Christianity has a problem with women. This problem is deeply rooted in its history, in its assumptions about gender and sexuality."[17] There is a stream of rigorist and sexist Christian preaching in the early church that pronounced women to be the "Devil's gateway."[18] Some church leaders demanded that women not consecrated to virginity accept procreativity and that even contraceptive acts were, in essence, a kind of homicide. As Bishop Caesarius of Arles pronounced, *"As often as she could have conceived or given birth, of that many homicides she will be held guilty,* . . . damned by eternal death in hell."[19] The Reformation may have brought a change in views on the spiritual primacy of the celibate vocation, but the Reformers did not dislodge male privilege or views that linked sexuality with sin and women with sexual temptation.[20] Thus, church condemnations of women who abort must be seen against the backdrop of patriarchy, sexism, gender dualism, and even misogyny. Despite the apocalyptic, gnostic, or pro-celibacy viewpoints in the early church, which offered women avenues for a spiritual vocation outside of marriage, marriage was institutionally solidified into a patriarchal form where women's reproductive life was supposed to come under the authority of her husband, as ordained by Scripture.

15. Harrison, *Our Right to Choose*, 127.
16. This theme permeates the work of Elisabeth Schüssler Fiorenza, beginning with *In Memory of Her: A Feminist Theological Reconstruction of Christian Origins* (New York: Crossroad, 1983, 1994); see also Elizabeth Ann Clark, "Introduction," in *Women in the Early Church* (Collegeville, MN: Liturgical Press, 1990).
17. Rosemary Radford Ruether, "Women, Reproductive Rights and the Catholic Church," *Feminist Theology* 16, no. 2 (2008): 184.
18. E. Clark, *Women in the Early Church*, 39.
19. Quoted in Harrison, *Our Right to Choose*, 293 n. 41, italics by Harrison.
20. See Rosemary Radford Ruether, *Women and Redemption: A Theological History* (Minneapolis: Fortress Press, 2011), 96–103.

Feminist historiography claims to have unearthed a persistent thread of gynocentric culture related to women's reproductive lives so that "even when men controlled the treatment of illnesses, women oversaw fertility control, pregnancy, prenatal care, and the birth process, and the transmission of pro-creative wisdom . . . integral to women's culture."[21] This wisdom included knowledge of pregnancy prevention and herbal or other abortifacient methods to terminate an unwanted pregnancy. That these methods were probably largely ineffective or even dangerous makes the advent of modern safe methods of contraception and abortion an all the more welcome "breakthrough."[22] I tend to be skeptical of claims about "a 'golden age' in which women practiced medicine and shared knowledge about their bodies freely with each other."[23] Whatever the case may be, the notion that, somewhere, women might be helping other women with reproductive matters apart from male supervision elicited anxieties and suspicions among male church authorities, especially because of suspicions of sorcery (as we will see below).

Antisexuality

Most historians agree that early church writings at best exhibit a high degree of ambivalence about sexuality, and at worst show outright pleasure-phobic attitudes directed especially toward women's sexuality. As Harrison argues, "Nearly all extant early Christian objections to abortion . . . either directly condemn wanton women . . . or denounce the triad of adulterous, pleasure-oriented sex, contraception, and abortion."[24] While pro-life historians today would like to construe the church's historical anti-abortion statements as pro-natalist and pro-family, the church from its origins actually manifested a deep suspicion of sexual activity even in marriage and attempted to restrict it to an exclusively procreative function. Harrison attributes the intensity of the condemnation of abortion to the church's obsession with "sexual sin,"[25] and she argues that one cannot conclude that the church's outrage over abortion is primarily because of fetal demise. For example, the fourth-century Council of Elvira directed its invectives equally against the "crime" of adultery as against that of the abortion meant to hide the illicit pregnancy that resulted from adultery.[26] Even attempting to prevent conception was considered to be a use

21. Harrison, *Our Right to Choose*, 165.
22. Harrison, *Our Right to Choose*, 169.
23. Monica H. Green, "Gendering the History of Women's Healthcare," *Gender & History* 20, no. 3 (2008): 489.
24. Harrison, *Our Right to Choose*, 130.
25. Harrison, *Our Right to Choose*, 140.
26. Council of Elvira, canon 63, quoted in Harrison, *Our Right to Choose*, 294 n. 49.

of sexuality as evil as killing the product of conception. Some church leaders even implied that contraceptive acts are more evil than abortion killing—which is an antisexuality and not a pro-natalist viewpoint. Harrison notes how Noonan misses this point in a passage he quotes from late fourth-century archbishop John Chrysostom, who apparently condemned some kind of contraceptive act in saying, "Indeed, it is something worse than murder and I do not know what to call it: for she does not kill what is formed but prevents its formation."[27] While some church leaders undoubtedly had a concern for fetal life, the church's stance overall on matters related to sexuality manifested a deep anxiety about any use of sexuality without a procreative intent. For Harrison, the thread that ties together centuries of anti-abortion statements from church leaders is predominantly an antisexuality message, not a pro-fetal-life message. The antisexuality subtext "explains why the condemnation of abortion did not falter during those periods when Church fathers rejected the notion that a human being was present from conception onward."[28] That is, even when an embryo was not seen to be an ensouled person, aborting it was considered a grievous sin because the embryo's existence was linked with illicit sexuality.

Here we have a situation of competing ideological interpretations of history. That historians would disagree on the meaning of historical records is itself not unusual. Nor is it surprising that scholars with a pro-life ideology would find in history what appears to them to be a laudable concern for fetal life; whereas, pro-choice feminist historians find each historical anti-abortion church pronouncement to be tainted with sexism, misogyny, and deep suspicion of sexual pleasure. I agree with many of Harrison's critiques of Noonan (critiques that neither D. Jones nor Gorman seems to have taken into consideration).[29] I wish to go further, however, in order to display more complexity in the history of abortion and to identify a counternarrative with historical lessons that Christians can retrieve as relevant to the situation of abortion today.

---

27. John Chrysostom, *Homily 24 on the Epistle to the Romans*, quoted in Harrison, *Our Right to Choose*, 291 n. 19.

28. Harrison, *Our Right to Choose*, 128.

29. What Harrison criticizes as an antisexuality theme has been named more recently as the "perversity position" because it "rests *simpliciter* on the view that abortion is a perversion of the true function of sex and marriage." See Daniel A. Dombrowski and Robert J. Deltete, *A Brief, Liberal, Catholic Defense of Abortion* (Urbana: University of Illinois Press, 2000), 2, 19. The sexual perversity is twofold: the perversity of engaging in acts of fornication, such as adultery, for which abortion would be needed to dispose of the products of those guilty acts; and the perversity, especially by married couples, of any act meant to prevent conception—whether that means contraception or abortion.

A COUNTERNARRATIVE
ABOUT ABORTION IN CHURCH HISTORY

Significant new historical research has emerged since Noonan's influential writings in the late 1960s and early 1970s and even since Harrison's rebuttal in 1983. The four areas of research include the following: (1) The apostle Paul's Jewish background in relation to his possible views on fetuses and abortion; (2) penitential literature, which specifies a range of atoning practices for those who confess to involvement with abortion; (3) the criminalization of abortion with the development of canon law; and (4) the influence of ancient and medieval medical knowledge on the early church's abortion discourse. When these four new areas of historical scholarship are included in a social and theological history of the church on abortion, the preponderance of evidence points away from pro-life claims of a consistent pro-fetal condemnation of abortion. Pro-fetalism does not seem to be a factor in the teachings of the apostle Paul. Early church theologians and pastors who cared to be informed about reproductive issues discovered that procreation was, in real life, more complicated than what the Bible, conciliar or papal pronouncements, penitential practice, or legal rulings could adequately capture. The historical evidence also indicates that instead of deepening its theological and pastoral understanding of procreative complexity, the church moved in a direction of increasingly legalized definitions of abortion as willful homicide, regardless of the realities of actual women struggling with unplanned and unwanted pregnancies.

The Apostle Paul and Abortion

Pro-life writers all concede that the New Testament does not address abortion; however, they find ways to attribute a pro-child, anti-abortion stance to the New Testament writers. The evidence is thin. Noonan suggests that Paul's instructions to the church at Galatia to avoid "*pharmakeia*," translated "sorcery" in Galatians 5:20 (NRSV), would have included "drugs with occult properties for . . . contraception or abortion."[30] To infer from this word alone that Paul might have been condemning abortion practices in Galatia is arguably a stretch and shows the lengths to which pro-life proponents will go to find evidence of an unbroken anti-abortion message from the church's beginnings. Paul notably does not take a personal moral stance on abortion, as he does on other moral issues such as divorce (see 1 Cor. 7:12). Some

---

30. John T. Noonan Jr., "Abortion and the Catholic Church: A Summary History," *Natural Law Forum* 12 (1967): 90. Gorman repeats this same point in *Abortion and the Early Church*, 48.

pro-life authors take Paul's silence to indicate what is obvious to them: Paul did not condemn abortion because it was a practice he "clearly and universally regarded as immoral."[31] However, as we will see, first- and second-century Jewish and Christian views on abortion are more complicated than what pro-life proponents wish to admit. Among the historiographical errors pro-life proponents make is to assume that abortion in ancient times (a risky practice that endangered the lives of women) can be equated with the relatively safe medical procedure today. Nor should we conclude that because abortion and infanticide are often mentioned together in condemnations from Jews and Christians in ancient times, they understood abortion to be the murder of (what pro-life proponents today often call) a preborn baby.[32] Paul's silence on abortion practices in his day cannot be taken to mean what pro-life proponents assume—namely, tacit condemnation of abortion understood, as pro-life proponents do today, to be the killing of an unborn child created in the image of God.[33]

Neither is it historiographically justifiable to conclude, as some liberal pro-choice scholars do, that Paul's silence on abortion can be taken as a marker of his revolutionary theology of grace that freed Christians from "the harsh dictates of unbending rules and laws," presumably the kinds of anti-abortion dictates that eventually found their way into documents like the *Didache*.[34] Rather than try to link Paul to or distance him from the anti-abortion rhetoric of the *Didache*, I suggest a more circumscribed historical project of trying to discover the meaning of the little Paul does say about the unborn and creation in God's image—and what connection, if any, he saw between the two.

Paul neither condemns nor allows abortion; yet there is a cryptic New Testament reference to abortion in 1 Corinthians 15, a chapter where we also find *imago* discourse. In the context of discussing his apostolic authority, Paul depicts himself as the least among the apostles because he is the last to whom the resurrected Jesus appeared: "Then he appeared to James, then to all the apostles. Last of all, as to *one untimely born*, he appeared also to me" (vv. 7–8, emphasis added). The phrase "one untimely born" is an uninspired translation of the Greek ἔκτρωμα (*ektrōma*), a term found nowhere else in the New Testament, which most scholars agree should be translated as "an abortion"— meaning the procedure or the bodily remnants of the procedure, whether

---

31. Michael J. Gorman, "Scripture, History, and Authority in a Christian View of Abortion: A Response to Paul Simmons," *Christian Bioethics* 2, no. 1 (1996): 91.

32. See Gorman, *Abortion and the Early Church*, 49, 58, 60.

33. This discussion of Paul anticipates my critique of pro-life views on personhood and the *imago Dei* in the next chapter.

34. Paul D. Simmons, "Biblical Authority and the Not-So Strange Silence of Scripture about Abortion," *Christian Bioethics* 2, no. 1 (1996): 75.

intentional or accidental.[35] The definitive meaning of this verse has eluded New Testament scholars, but if we look at the context of the first-century world, we can get a glimmer of Paul's possible views on the status of the fetus. While Paul cannot be said to be pro-choice (an anachronism, to be sure), my investigation concludes that Paul likely held typically Hellenistic Jewish views of embryonic development and of creation in God's image as well.[36]

What were first-century Jewish notions of the *imago Dei* and of abortion that may have functioned as a backdrop for Paul's reference to himself as "an abortion"? The notion of humans as the *zelem* (Hebrew, "image") of God is rare in the Hebrew Bible, but in rabbinic literature the emphasis is consistently on the importance of human embodiment.[37] The rabbis took the Genesis 1 text to mean "that God created humans in his image, which is the ability to generate new life and to guard the creation."[38] Life was thought to hold immense value, so much so that the rabbis established the halakic rule that Jewish men are required to try to have children. A man who refuses to have children "diminishes the image [of God]."[39] The *imago Dei* in Jewish thought pertains almost always to an adult "corporeal and procreating human body and person" because it has to do with duties only an adult person would be asked to fulfill.[40] Unlike more philosophically oriented Jewish thinkers like Philo, who associated the *imago Dei* with rational faculties,[41] traditional rabbinic writings depicted the *imago* as pertaining to the whole person, so that even neglecting personal hygiene or the physical needs of the sick, or leaving a dead body unburied was an affront to the image of God.[42] Overall, the *imago*

35. Harm W. Hollander and Gijsbert E. van der Hout, "The Apostle Paul Calling Himself an Abortion: 1 Cor. 15:8 Within the Context of 1 Cor. 15:8–10," *Novum Testamentum* 38, no. 3 (1996). One scholar flatly states that the NRSV translation ("one untimely born") "is simply not what Paul says." Matthew W. Mitchell, "Reexamining the 'Aborted Apostle': An Exploration of Paul's Self-Description in 1 Corinthians 15.8," *Journal for the Study of the New Testament* 25, no. 4 (2003): 475.

36. For more on Paul's Jewishness and convergences in his thought with rabbinic positions of his times, see Peter J. Tomson, *Paul and the Jewish Law: Halakha in the Letters of the Apostle to the Gentiles* (Assen, Netherlands: Van Gorcum, 1990).

37. Alon Goshen Gottstein, "The Body as Image of God in Rabbinic Literature," *Harvard Theological Review* 87, no. 2 (1994): 174–75.

38. Y. Michael Barilan, "Abortion in Jewish Religious Law: Neighborly Love, *Imago Dei*, and a Hypothesis on the Medieval Blood Libel," *Review of Rabbinic Judaism* 8, no. 1 (2005): 11.

39. Barilan, "Abortion in Jewish Religious Law," 14. The requirement to bring children into the world is not incumbent on Jewish women.

40. Barilan, "Abortion in Jewish Religious Law," 16.

41. See Gottstein, "The Body as Image of God," 176.

42. Y. Michael Barilan, "From *Imago Dei* in the Jewish-Christian Traditions to Human Dignity in Contemporary Jewish Law," *Kennedy Institute of Ethics Journal* 19, no. 3 (2009): 233–34, 237–38. Interestingly, the rabbis' insistence "on the duty to bury the bodies of aborted fetuses as human beings endowed with *imago Dei*" exists concurrently with the understanding that abortion is sometimes a necessity (247).

Dei was not a central category in early rabbinic Jewish thought and "cannot be seen as a paramount feature of rabbinic anthropology or moral teaching."[43]

Jewish views on the fetus were largely determined by two factors: Greco-Roman philosophy and medicine and the passage in Exodus 21:22–25 on penalties for causing a miscarriage.[44] I will say more about Greco-Roman medicine below, but suffice it to say that the consensus opinion, from the time of Hippocrates in the fifth century BCE, was that unformed embryonic matter developed into an increasingly formed fetal person. This unformed/formed viewpoint is reflected in the Hellenistic Jewish writings of Josephus and Philo.[45] Philo, commenting on the Exodus 21 passage, uses this conceptuality: "But if anyone has a contest with a woman who is pregnant, and strike her a blow on her belly, and she miscarry, if the child which was conceived within her is still unfashioned and unformed, he shall be punished by a fine."[46] We see articulated here the notion that the loss of an unformed fetus would only incur a fine rather than a penalty of homicide. Moreover, in the early third-century CE Jewish legal text, the Mishnah, even the killing of a formed fetus can be justified to save the mother's life: "If a woman is having difficulty giving birth, one may dismember the infant in the womb and remove it limb by limb, because her life comes before the fetus's life."[47] While it is incontrovertible that the rabbis extolled the biblical call to be fruitful and multiply, that halakic mandate did not play out either in claims about the sacredness of fetal life nor in the rejection of therapeutic abortion to save a birthing mother's life.[48]

Against this backdrop of Jewish views of the image of God and of the unformed/formed fetus, we have a fuller perspective on Paul's reference to himself as an "abortion" (*ektrōma*) in 1 Corinthians 15:8. As some scholars

---

43. Gottstein, "The Body as Image of God," 195.

44. "When people who are fighting injure a pregnant woman so that there is a miscarriage, and yet no further harm follows, the one responsible shall be fined what the woman's husband demands, paying as much as the judges determine. If any harm follows, then you shall give life for life, eye for eye" (Exod. 21:22–24; all Bible quotations are from the NRSV unless otherwise noted).

45. See Daniel R. Bechtel, "Women, Choice, and Abortion: Another Look at Biblical Traditions," *Prism* 8, no. 1 (1993): 76–77; Nina L. Collins, "Notes on the Text of Exodus XXI 22," *Vetus Testamentum* 43, no. 3 (1993): 291–92.

46. Philo, *Special Laws* 3.108, http://www.earlychristianwritings.com/yonge/book29.html.

47. Mishnah *Ohalot* 7:6, quoted in Alan Jotkowitz, "Abortion and Maternal Need: A Response to Ronit Irshai," *Nashim: A Journal of Jewish Women's Studies & Gender Issues* 21, no. 1 (2011): 99.

48. I find thoroughly unconvincing Michael Gorman's claim that in first-century Judaism there was an "anti-abortion consensus" and only later did "some rabbis" allow for the exception for the mother's life (Michael J. Gorman, "Why Is the New Testament Silent about Abortion?," *Christianity Today* 37, no. 1 [1993]: 28). Presumably Gorman is referring to the Mishnah (see Gorman, "Scripture, History, and Authority," 86). Gorman's apparent trivializing of a Jewish legal position that has been foundational for all subsequent rabbinic Judaism is troubling.

have explained, even though the term *ektrōma* was rare in Hellenistic writings, one can find closely related terms in medical writings known at that time (such as those of Hippocrates), referring to a therapeutic abortion that is medically necessary to save the mother's life in an obstructed birth.[49] Because Hellenistic Jewish philosophy and rabbinic writings associate miscarriage with danger—principally to the life of the gestating mother—scholars infer that Paul, in calling himself an abortion, was figuratively implying that he presented a danger to the church, insofar as he had "persecuted the Church of God and thereby sowed death."[50] The term is also found in Numbers 12:12 in the Septuagint (the third-century BCE Greek translation of Hebrew Bible), where it is used figuratively, as Paul did, to refer to those "whose lives are miserable and worthless."[51] In this Numbers passage, Aaron pleads with Moses on behalf of Miriam, who has been afflicted by God with leprosy: "Do not let her be like one stillborn (. . . ἔκτρωμα), whose flesh is half consumed when it comes out of its mother's womb."[52] The early church's understanding of this term combined literal and figurative senses to produce "a metaphor for something or someone not yet wholly formed," in the spiritual sense of "not yet 'formed' or redeemed by the Saviour (Christ)."[53] In none of the literature, including Paul's use of the term, is the *ektrōma* associated with the idea of an unborn child bearing God's image who should be protected from assault. Quite the reverse: the unformed *ektrōma* was considered a dangerous entity.

While we cannot know what Paul thought about the Exodus 21 or Numbers 12 passages, it is reasonable to conclude that Paul, an educated Hellenistic Jew, would have been familiar with the commonplace viewpoints of Jews and Gentiles in his day regarding the distinction between an unformed and formed fetus. It is also possible that he was familiar with the views of emerging rabbinic authorities who allowed intervening in an obstructed birth in order to save the mother's life.[54] As we will see below, this type of therapeutic abortion was extensively discussed by Hellenistic medical practitioners. Thus Paul's reference to himself as "an abortion" plausibly suggests that he might have viewed fetuses, as did most people of his day—from Jewish rabbis to Greek physicians—as having less legal consequence when in an unformed

---

49. See Hollander and van der Hout, "The Apostle Paul Calling Himself an Abortion," 227.

50. Andrzej Gieniusz, "'As a Miscarriage': The Meaning and Function of the Metaphor in 1 Cor 15:1–11 in Light of Num 12:12 (LXX)," *Biblical Annals* 3 (2013): 106.

51. Hollander and van der Hout, "The Apostle Paul Calling Himself an Abortion," 230.

52. Hollander and van der Hout, "The Apostle Paul Calling Himself an Abortion," 229.

53. Hollander and van der Hout, "The Apostle Paul Calling Himself an Abortion," 233; see Mitchell, "Reexamining the 'Aborted Apostle,'" 477.

54. Paul predates the Mishnah, but many rabbinic viewpoints that were codified in that text circulated in Paul's day. Peter Tomson argues that "halakha was pervasive in Paul's thought" (*Paul and the Jewish Law*, 264).

state than in a formed state and, even when ready to be born, not to be valued over the life of the mother when she is in peril.

Scholars have noted that in addition to the abortion metaphor, Paul makes one other prenatal reference to himself in Galatians 1:15, where he seems to borrow the trope of the prophetic call from the womb: "God . . . had set me apart before I was born." Some pro-life scholars read this passage as they would similar passages in Hebrew Bible—namely, as proof that God calls forth and cares for all fetuses as persons. One scholar interprets the Galatians passage as Paul's attestation that a "'person' is already present in core. . . . With this, Paul very much mirrors Jewish notions about a fetus," which reflects a typical Christian pro-life claim about Jewish views of fetal life.[55] As we will see in the following chapter, there is lack of consensus even among pro-life scholars about how much weight to put on biblical verses about life in the womb, given exegetical uncertainty about their meaning.[56] Therefore, while one can find prenatal prophetic callings in Scripture, thinking of an unformed fetus as a person was not an accepted Jewish notion in Paul's day—whether from a Hellenistic perspective or a halakic one—contrary to what pro-life writers claim. It would have been odd for Paul on his own to have developed the notion of prenatal personhood so alien to the prevalent Jewish assumptions of which he was undoubtedly aware. Paul's reference to himself as an *ektrōma* is enigmatic and obscure, but scholars give plausible reasons for seeing the influence of a Hellenistic Jewish unformed/formed view of fetal development. Recent scholarly studies of this term in Paul and related writings of his day militate against pro-life scholars' attempts to claim that Paul was an early contributor to a univocal anti-abortion and pro-natalist message for the nascent Christian church. If anything, the evidence points to an inverse hypothesis—namely, that Paul would not have seen an unformed fetus as having legal status and certainly not as a bearer of God's image.

Penitential Manuals

The church voiced its opposition to abortion in various ways and with various degrees of severity in penitential guides, which were instructions for confessors that had become established in Ireland by the seventh century and in

---

55. Reidar Aasgaard, "Paul as a Child: Children and Childhood in the Letters of the Apostle," *Journal of Biblical Literature* 126, no. 1 (2007): 141. Like Gorman (see n. 48), Aasgaard assumes an anti-abortion, pro-natalist view among Greco-Roman Jews; not surprisingly, he is confused by Paul's reference to himself as an *ektrōma* (see Aasgaard, "Paul as a Child, 141–42).

56. For example, "Before I formed you in the womb I knew you, and before you were born I consecrated you" (Jer. 1:5).

Britain and Europe by the ninth century.[57] Scholars have long noted relatively
lenient ecclesial stances in the penitential material regarding the sin of abortion.[58] Recently, historians are paying more attention to how the penitential
materials can function as a source not only for official positions on abortion
but also for "real-life practices" of the reproductive lives of parishioners.[59]
While abortion continued to be associated with fornication and labeled as
murderous in some church writings, the designated penance for abortion fell
significantly lower than that for murder. Some penitential manuals graded
the penance according to whether the abortion was procured in the first forty
days after conception (reflecting a delayed ensoulment viewpoint). A penance
of fasting might be as brief as one year if the woman procured an early abortion of an unformed fetus, but after animation (of a formed fetus), "she ought
to do penance as a murderer,"[60] in which case the penance in some rigorist
canons could entail up to twenty-five years of some kind of fasting and other
acts of repentance.[61]

Even more significant than the influence of an unformed/formed conceptuality is the mention in some penitential writings that the penance should
be linked to the condition of the mother. In other words, socioeconomic and
other mitigating circumstances were taken into account: "But it makes a great
difference whether a poor woman (*paupercula*) does this [abortion] because
of the difficulty of rearing," for which the penalty was less, "or a fornicating
woman for the sake of hiding her crime," for which the penalty was more
severe, reflecting a sexual perversity viewpoint.[62] Similarly, medical conditions might lessen the penance, as in the case of a pregnant woman who uses
an abortifacient potion because of her fear of "death or the narrowness [of the
birth canal] in childbirth."[63] Historians find that rape was seen as an extenuating circumstance in some penitential texts, which "explicitly state that a
woman is 'not guilty,'" if she commits abortion after being raped: *illa non est
culpanda.*"[64] Penance was still required, but it was much reduced. While the
penitentials hinted at the possibility that some women might be forced into
having an abortion, they tended to see women as the primary agent and her

57. See Zubin Mistry, *Abortion in the Early Middle Ages, c. 500–900* (Woodbridge, Suffolk: York
Medieval, 2015), 126–31.
58. See Hurst, *History of Abortion in the Catholic Church*, 10–11.
59. Mistry, *Abortion in the Early Middle Ages*, 130. Mistry acknowledges here the "grey area" of
determining actual practices filtered through the ideals of penitential writings.
60. Mistry, *Abortion in the Early Middle Ages*, 148.
61. See Marianne J. Elsakkers, "Reading between the Lines: Old Germanic and Early Christian
Views on Abortion," PhD diss., University of Amsterdam (2010), 468, https://pure.uva.nl/ws
/files/1578588/76065_00_a_officiele_titelpagina.pdf.
62. Mistry, *Abortion in the Early Middle Ages*, 160.
63. Mistry, *Abortion in the Early Middle Ages*, 187.
64. Elsakkers, "Reading between the Lines," 450.

accomplices as primarily other women, since the method would probably have involved an herbal potion that women were thought to know how to concoct. The penitential authors were highly suspicious of magic or sorcery, which elevated the evil of the abortive act.[65] Thus abortion was not seen as just one thing—an act of killing an unborn child—but was viewed and judged variously in relation to fetal development and the woman's motivations, methods, and circumstances.

The medieval penitentials reflected received ecclesial norms (on issues of sexual sin and murder) yet also at times displayed a more contextual pastoral approach. David Jones, for that reason, characterizes the penitentials negatively because they were marked by the theme of "leniency toward the woman" regarding abortion and the lack of "firm legal or ecclesiastical authority." Jones approvingly notes that penitential manuals were condemned at the Third Council of Toledo (589) and that they were eventually supplanted by the development of formalized canon law after the eleventh century.[66] Was Toledo's condemnation a positive step for the church? Historian Zubin Mistry gives some contextual background for the Council of Toledo that leaves this an open question. First, Mistry notes that the council's severe anti-abortion statements highlighted not adultery or prostitution but attempts of married couples to restrict family size with contraceptive sexual practices. About these parents the council gave a harsh directive: "If it is burdensome for them to have a greater number of children, they should first scold themselves from fornication," meaning refrain from all nonprocreative sex. Second, the motivating issue at Toledo may not have been primarily morality but something more political. The fact that the Spanish bishops at the council extol the newly converted "glorious" Visigoth king for apparently initiating criminal investigations of "this dreadful outrage" (of couples resorting to contraceptive sex or abortion) indicates a thinly veiled support for the authority of the king in exchange for his nod to the authority of the church in his domain.[67]

That the penitential form of pastoral oversight was suppressed as the church entered into a period of solidification of canon law is historically accurate, but simply stating that fact ignores the question of whether the move to a top-down, uniform code of law was a change for the good. Some scholars of the medieval period point out that what was lost in the move to codify rules governing procreation was the pastoral connection to parishioners and the opportunity for compassion. For example, some penitential manuals included an interrogatory method of listing sins, which the penitent might

65. See Elsakkers, "Reading between the Lines," 457; Mistry, *Abortion in the Early Middle Ages*, 76.
66. D. Jones, *Soul of the Embryo*, 68.
67. Mistry, *Abortion in the Early Middle Ages*, 106.

then admit to having done: "Have you drunk any . . . herbs or other things, so that you were not able to have infants, or given [potions] to someone else, or wanted to kill someone by a potion?"[68] Because the penitential script could not exhaustively list all possible configurations of sins, it did not function as a legal document but took the form of a dialogue meant to initiate the sinner's self-reflection and verbal confession.

Based on an abundance of primary source material, medievalist Marianne Elsakkers claims, "We can safely conclude that early medieval women committed (or tried to commit) abortion." Historians also conclude that the penitentials demonstrated compassion "for poor women, the *pauperculae*. This compassion also shows us that the sins they describe reflect real-life situations, and that the penitentials must have been part of practical Christianity."[69] The penitential literature leaves us with three lasting impressions: (1) abortion was practiced or at least attempted by women in medieval times; (2) the church was not of one mind about how abortion could be curtailed but understood that condemnation did little to address the real-life issues that made women turn to abortion (and contraception); (3) even while condemning abortion, confessors recognized that sometimes women did seem to have understandable reasons and extenuating circumstances that mitigated their guilt.

Canon Law and the Criminalization of Abortion

The penitential handbooks were slowly supplanted by church legal writings in the Middle Ages—a move praised by pro-life scholars but which marked a turn away from a pastoral approach to morality and toward a rigorist, legalist approach. One of the first major codifications was accomplished by the twelfth-century ecclesiastical jurist Gratian in his *Decretum*. Prior to the advent of this classical period of canon law development, one could find any number of canons promulgated by particular councils that may or may not have tried to maintain rigorous coherence with or invoke the precedent of prior canons.[70] The culminating code was published by Pope Gregory XIII in the sixteenth century as the *Corpus iuris canonici*, which solidified the notion of "the independent law of the Roman Catholic church" and consolidated Rome's authority on issues of morality and church practice.[71]

---

68. Mistry, *Abortion in the Early Middle Ages*, 194.
69. Elsakkers, "Reading between the Lines," 458.
70. See Peter D. Clarke, "Canon Law," in *The Routledge History of Medieval Christianity 1050–1500*, ed. R. N. Swanson (London: Routledge, 2015), 77–78.
71. Keith Pennington, "*Corpus iuris canonici*," in *The Oxford Dictionary of the Middle Ages*, ed. Robert E. Bjork (Oxford University Press, online, 2010), http://www.oxfordreference.com/view/10.1093/acref/9780198662624.001.0001/acref-9780198662624-e-1567.

David Jones speaks of how canon law formalized "contraception and abortion as homicide" and created the basis, from that point onward, for concluding that even if one assumed a formed/unformed view of the fetus, the law made any abortion (and contraceptive act) the ethical "equivalent of homicide" and opened the door to any attempt to prevent birth being "treated as homicide for some legal purposes."[72] Jones concludes that the canon law specification of abortion as homicide was an achievement of moral clarity. While morality may have been a motivating factor with some medieval canon lawyers, there were other less lofty influences at work in the church. Harrison has exposed the "sex-negativity" of the decretalists especially.[73] Other historians point out that a key reason for the push toward legal codification in the Middle Ages was, in part, to assert "papal primacy over the Church and papal decretals as sources of law."[74] Addressing sins contextually threatened the authority of Rome. The decretals supplied that authority though the medium of law, and this included abortion. As historian Wolfgang Müller explains, "In the twelfth and thirteenth centuries, the Latin West embarked on a path that was to distinguish it from all other civilizations by associating abortion with the new concept of criminal behavior."[75] In so doing, ecclesial oversight regarding abortion changed locations from the confessional to the courtroom.

Müller's scholarship on abortion and medieval law is extensive, so I will simply summarize a few salient points. First, canon law signaled a change from late antique "post-Roman [Empire] concepts of liability."[76] Especially in early medieval Northern Europe and the British Isles, liability was the operative secular legal concept, where wrong was not determined based on "universally binding principles" established by some centralized authoritative legal entity; rather, liability was a factor of adjudicating local disputes between clans or powerful families.[77] In the absence of an independent judicial body, liability was assessed in terms of negotiated "damage payments," including for homicide.[78] Within clans or family groups, payment for a homicide might be adjudicated based on one's family allegiance, or social status, or the degree to which the homicide was seen as "'honorable' violence" for the benefit of

72. D. Jones, *Soul of the Embryo*, 69, 70. Jones mentions the 12th-century canonist Rufinus with no citation; his point seems to follow John Connery's extended discussion that is roundly criticized by Harrison (*Our Right to Choose*, 142, 295 n. 56).

73. Harrison, *Our Right to Choose*, 142.

74. Clarke, "Canon Law," 79.

75. Wolfgang Müller, *The Criminalization of Abortion in the West: Its Origins in Medieval Law* (Ithaca: Cornell University Press, 2012), 6.

76. Müller, *Criminalization of Abortion in the West*, 38.

77. Müller, *Criminalization of Abortion in the West*, 43.

78. Müller, *Criminalization of Abortion in the West*, 37.

the family group or tribe.[79] A forced miscarriage within a family group or within marriage (initiated by the woman herself or instigated by a husband or father) was usually not considered a liability issue requiring damage payments. Canon law stood diametrically opposed to these types of contextual juridical arrangements.

Second, church canonists solidified the familiar unformed/formed distinction for a fetus, but now with a new legal consideration. Abortion of an unformed fetus could be dealt with penitentially (mostly privately in the confessional);[80] whereas abortion of a formed fetus, post-Gratian's *Decretum*, was subject to (mostly public) punitive judicial measures for homicide.[81] Legal scholar that he was, Noonan showed great interest in the development of canon law but struggled with how to account for the overwhelming consensus in Roman Catholic canon law that abortion of an unformed fetus was not considered homicide. Noonan claimed that Pope Gregory IX overcame this distinction in his thirteenth-century code of law, ruling that if there is any attempt to intervene so that "no offspring be born," then "let it be as homicide." Noonan claims that one can derive from this turn of phrase ("as homicide") a firm legal principle that any act meant to prevent a birth at whatever stage (even at conception and while the fetus is unformed) should be "on par with the killing of a man."[82] While this principle was promoted by some canon lawyers, the preponderance of medieval legal rulings operated on the basis of the settled legal opinion "that bodily formation separates homicidal abortions from nonhomicidal ones."[83] Hence, pro-life scholars today approve of the medieval instituting of top-down authority of canon law, but they do not approve of the actual unformed/formed legal principle that ruled church law until the modern period.

Third, punishment for abortion went public. The penitentials considered abortion at any stage to be a sin, but the confession and the punishment was religious, relatively private, and often with a pastoral intent that recognized extenuating circumstances. With the criminalization of abortion under canon law, the death of a formed fetus was considered a homicide. The punishment was more severe than mere liability payments or penance, and it was made public in a court of law. The punitive measures (handed down by ecclesiastical or secular courts) might have included fines, flogging, incarceration, loss

79. Müller, *Criminalization of Abortion in the West*, 39.
80. Müller, *Criminalization of Abortion in the West*, 43.
81. See Müller, *Criminalization of Abortion in the West*, 62–63, 71–72.
82. Decretal of Pope Gregory IX, quoted in Noonan, "Abortion and the Catholic Church," 99–100.
83. Müller, *Criminalization of Abortion in the West*, 25.

of property, exile, or even burning at the stake.[84] The guilty parties might have included a monk who caused the woman bearing his child to miscarry; a cuckold husband who beat his wife and caused her to miscarry; or a daughter pregnant by incest who was forced to abort by the father who impregnated her.[85] Extenuating circumstances were irrelevant in the courtroom under canon law. The only factor that had to be contextually determined was whether the aborted fetus had achieved a formed state or not.

There were occasional rulings or proclamations that specified any intentional fetal death as homicide, no matter at what stage. Noonan sees these rulings as "bursts of . . . prudence" and cites the infamous bull *Effraenatam* by Sixtus V in the late sixteenth century, which eliminated the distinction between a formed and unformed fetus for purposes of criminalization and excommunication.[86] Müller gives a sobering assessment of this rigorist papal bull, which specifies that "convicted parties and their accomplices were to be held liable for murder" and that suspected cases should be treated in the same inquisitorial fashion as those charged with "heretical depravity."[87] Popes and jurists after Sixtus V fortunately pulled back from his extreme views, but one could say that the cat was out of the bag. Attempts to label abortion as criminal murder at any stage of pregnancy gradually chipped away at the fragile distinction between an unformed/formed fetus. The issue of abortion remained unsettled in canon law until 1869, when Pope Pius IX ruled to apply the penalty of "excommunication to all cases of abortion, not just for those where the fetus was older than forty days. The tightening continued with the new Code of Canon Law in 1917."[88] In medieval Europe, canon law and civil law were often linked, unlike today, where there is a separation of church and state in most Catholic-majority countries; nevertheless, canon law still exerts

---

84. See Müller, *Criminalization of Abortion in the West*, 202–7.

85. Müller collected archival court materials on these and other cases (see his *Criminalization of Abortion in the West*, 54, 56, 190–91). The reader will note that the wife-beating was ignored and incest did not provide grounds for clemency for the young woman, who was still seen as voluntarily and thus culpably drinking the abortifacient potion.

86. Noonan, "Abortion and the Catholic Church," 109. David Jones finds nothing untoward with *Effraenatam*, except that requiring papal absolution for abortion was "unworkable" (D. Jones, *Soul of the Embryo*, 71). Keith Cassidy notes that the bull was "severe" but makes no criticism of it. Cassidy, "A Convenient Untruth: The Pro-Choice Invention of an Era of Abortion Freedom," in *Catholicism and Historical Narrative: A Catholic Engagement with Historical Scholarship*, ed. Kevin Schmiesing (Lanham, MD: Rowman & Littlefield, 2014), 83.

87. Müller, *Criminalization of Abortion in the West*, 83, 84 n. 10. Courts dealing with heresy dispensed with regular modes of interrogation, procedural rules, and requirements of evidence, which opened the door to "forcible questioning" or even "torture for verification" (187). We do not know if these procedures regarding abortion were used in the short reign of Sixtus V.

88. Cassidy, "A Convenient Untruth," 92.

a strong influence in a few countries where any abortion is illegal and is prosecuted in often draconian ways.[89]

In discourse about abortion, much hinges on the nature of fetal bodies. Theologians, confessors, and canon lawyers often found themselves turning to medicine and science in an effort to clarify when an embryo became animated and, therefore, became a person. The quest to determine fetal personhood continues today with fervor, as pro-life authors find in genomics the evidence they think supports their theological claim that a complete, ensouled human being exists at conception. Modern science, David Jones believes, vindicates pro-life appeals to historical anti-abortion pronouncements such as Tertullian's statement that *"the soul also begins from conception,"*[90] because embryologists and geneticists are clear that "human beings begin as human embryos . . . generated by fertilization."[91] I raise a strong note of caution about correlating theological statements of the church fathers about ensoulment with modern scientific descriptions of the genetics and biological processes in embryos and fetuses. Not only is this questionable historiography and a questionable application of scientific evidence, but this method also obscures the kind of intellectual interactions some church leaders pursued with the science of their day, especially obstetric medicine.

Medical Science, the Early Church, and Saving Women's Lives

Abortion today is not abortion of the Hellenistic or early medieval period. This seems to be self-evident, but it needs to be stated because pro-life scholars refer to the early church's condemnations of abortion as if ancient abortion procedures can be equated with legal abortion in today's world. Reliable contraception was nonexistent, and most abortions in the ancient world were a dangerous, often lethal business for the woman. Hence it is not surprising that the Hippocratic Oath contains the promise to "not give a woman a pessary to cause abortion," because it was seen as a risk to the woman's health. This oath has been much touted in pro-life literature as an indication that even the ancient Greeks frowned on "nontherapeutic abortions."[92] Even so,

---

89. According to a 2015 Pew Research Center study, five Catholic-majority countries do not allow abortion even to save the mother's life, and they prosecute women who have had or try to have an abortion. See "Worldwide Abortion Policies," *Pew Research Center* (October 5, 2015), http://www.pewresearch.org/interactives/global-abortion/.

90. Tertullian, *Treatise on the Soul*, chap. 27, quoted in D. Jones, *Soul of the Embryo*, 247, italics by Jones.

91. D. Jones, *Soul of the Embryo*, 240.

92. Gorman, *Abortion and the Early Church*, 20.

pro-life scholars do not hold the Greco-Roman medical establishment in high regard because, they claim, "abortion flourished" in the ancient world. Gorman seems to attribute this situation to the development of gynecology as a science and the activity of "women physicians . . . [who] wrote handbooks on abortion."[93] The narrative Gorman and others promote about Greco-Roman culture is that of loose morals and pagan women getting abortions on demand from accommodating gynecologists—a situation opposed by Judaism[94] and definitively reversed by the advent of Christianity, which properly put the moral focus back on the fetus.[95] It is precisely this type of generalized, biased, and historically inaccurate claim that needs to be examined lest we only see an anti-abortion antagonism between Greco-Roman physicians and the early church fathers. Once we free ourselves from this bias, we discover that the historical record indicates an occasionally more positive interaction between the church fathers and physicians of their day, including (perhaps grudging) respect for those physicians' attempts to save a woman's life in a difficult birth.

What did ancient physicians of the first century know about pregnancy and fetal life? Though primitive by today's standards, obstetrical medicine in the Hellenistic and early medieval world was not completely without merit, and vigorous debate among physicians did advance medical knowledge. By the third century CE, two somewhat opposing streams of scientific opinion about how conception happens and how gestation occurs were known and discussed among learned men, and perhaps women, of the day. Those two streams could be traced back to Aristotle (late fourth century BCE), on the one side, and Hippocrates (late fifth to early fourth century BCE) and Galen of Pergamum (second century CE), on the other.[96] Galen's influential stature in Greco-Roman medicine is well known, and most scholars would agree that "Galenism was the dominant medical philosophy of the Greek-speaking

93. Gorman, *Abortion and the Early Church*, 27. Gorman cites Will Durant's *Caesar and Christ* (New York: Simon and Schuster, 1944), which makes this assertion with no evidence given to support it. I am not aware of women authoring medical manuals that possibly include instructions for abortion until the 12th-century Trota of Salerno. See Monica H. Green, "Gendering the History of Women's Healthcare," *Gender & History* 20, no. 3 (2008): 439, 495, 500–501.

94. See Gorman, *Abortion and the Early Church*, 54, 66, 72. I question Gorman's portrayal that the Jewish moral sense of the "sanctity of life" (34) stood in contrast with Judaism's "legal" allowance of therapeutic abortion to save a mother during difficult birth (43). Gorman concludes that Jewish morality, not Jewish law, "formed a natural foundation" for Christianity (45), which seems to denigrate halakic Judaism. D. Jones makes similar claims in *Soul of the Embryo*, 56. I will discuss Jewish views on abortion in chap. 2.

95. Other scholars contest the narrative of Christianity's novel, superior morality over Rome. See Mistry, *Abortion in the Early Middle Ages*, 53–54.

96. See Owsei Temkin, *Hippocrates in a World of Pagans and Christians* (Baltimore: Johns Hopkins University Press, 1991), 5–7; see Ann Hanson, "Roman Medicine," in *A Companion to the Roman Empire*, ed. David S. Potter (Malden, MA: Blackwell, 2006).

Roman Empire."[97] Educated in centers around the Mediterranean, including Alexandria, active in Rome in the late second century, he cemented many aspects of Hippocratic theories of medicine.[98] Regarding reproductive issues, Aristotle promoted the notion that the woman "provides only the passive material (menstrual blood) which the male semen . . . forms into the fetus." Hippocrates and, later, Galen advocated the notion of male and female contributions of procreative seed. Galen based his views not only on the fact that children resemble both parents but also on the "discovery . . . of the ovaries[,] which he called 'female testicles.'"[99] Hellenistic philosophers and physicians, whether they espoused a one- or two-seed theory of conception, agreed that fetal development was gradual and that personhood meant having a rational soul. They linked their medical knowledge of fetal development with their views of ensoulment and theorized that rational ensoulment was not immediate but delayed until the fetus was more formed.

Many church fathers interacted with the medical science and philosophy of their day, and that knowledge seems to have influenced their views on fetal personhood, which in most cases mirrored the common opinion that ensoulment was delayed. This delayed ensoulment viewpoint cohered with their reading of Exodus 21, with its gradations of fines in the case of a fetal death versus maternal injury from assault. These early church attitudes diverge from today's pro-life narrative of a univocal anti-abortion, pro-natalist history of the church, and pro-life writers try to suppress this fact. The most eminent Christian thinker in the West by the early fifth century, Augustine of Hippo, affirmed an unformed/formed understanding of fetal development, concluding that an early forced miscarriage "is not counted as homicide," a viewpoint David Jones finds as "less than satisfying."[100] Like other church leaders of his day, Augustine condemned abortion, linking it with illicit sexuality; however, his condemnation of abortion did not seem to affect his theological and pastoral reflections on fetal ensoulment. Augustine is known to have agonized over the question of when God infuses a fetus with its soul—an issue that arose for Augustine in his theological attempt to determine whether fetuses, given the ambiguous nature of their bodily form, would be included in the final resurrection. Augustine seems to throw up his hands, saying, a "question may be

97. Paul A. Anthony, "Sex, Sin and the Soul: How Galen's Philosophical Speculation Became Augustine's Theological Assumptions," *Conversations: A Graduate Student Journal of the Humanities, Social Sciences, and Theology* 1, no. 1 (2013): 5.
98. See Vivian Nutton, "The Fatal Embrace: Galen and the History of Ancient Medicine," *Science in Context* 18, no. 1 (2005): 114–15.
99. Basim Musallam, "The Human Embryo in Arabic Scientific and Religious Thought," in *The Human Embryo, Aristotle and the Arabic and European Traditions*, ed. G. R. Dunstan (Exeter, UK: University of Exeter Press, 1990), 32, 33.
100. D. Jones, *Soul of the Embryo*, 119.

most carefully discussed by the most learned men, and still I do not know that any man can answer it, namely: When does a human being begin to live in the womb?"[101] Since he could not find biblical evidence that proved the divine infusing of a soul at conception, all he could do was speculate with hope that there might be "there some form of hidden life" in an unformed fetus that could pass into eternal life.[102]

Augustine, without question, opposed abortion for all the reasons historians note, but he would not pronounce definitively on the issue of fetal personhood, unlike pro-life proponents today. Thus, at his most reflective, he remained agnostic, and they seem dogmatically sure.[103] Augustine's agnosticism about the question of fetal ensoulment is widely known. Pro-choice scholars, like Daniel Dombrowski and Robert Deltete, have roundly criticized the way pro-life scholars contort Augustine into saying precisely that which he would not, claiming (as Gorman does) that "Augustine chose to emphasize the value of all [human] life, whether actual or potential."[104] Dombrowski and Deltete have thoroughly exposed this misinterpretation of Augustine and have convincingly argued that Augustine adhered to a delayed ensoulment view that would have prevented him from considering an early abortion to be homicide (even if he might have attacked the sinful lust that may have precipitated the need to end an unwanted pregnancy).[105] Another and even more difficult figure to interpret is late second-century theologian Tertullian, who also does not fit easily into the pro-life narrative. Tertullian baffles pro-life scholars, who do not understand how a theologian who did affirm ensoulment at conception might also condone therapeutic abortion.

In an effort to mobilize Tertullian's anti-abortion statements, pro-life theologians find themselves confronted with two sets of issues that thwart their efforts: Tertullian's traducianism and his view of fetal development. Tertullian held a traducian view of the soul—meaning, he believed that the soul was

---

101. From the *Enchiridion* in Augustine, *Confessions and Enchiridion*, trans. Albert C. Outler (Philadelphia: Westminster Press, 1955), 23.86, https://www.ccel.org/ccel/augustine/enchiridion .chapter23.html.

102. Augustine, *Confessions and Enchiridion* 23.86. For a discussion of historical views on the fate of unbaptized infants, see Francis A. Sullivan, "The Development of Doctrine about Infants Who Die Unbaptized," *Theological Studies* 72, no. 1 (2011): 3–14.

103. Scholars note that this early self-reflective Augustine makes a more definitive statement in his later *City of God*, where he affirmed that an ensouled fetus will attain eternal life, but he leaves the issue of the unformed fetus unaddressed. See Danuta Shanzer, "Voices and Bodies: The Afterlife of the Unborn," *Numen* 56, nos. 2–3 (2009): 348–49. On 350–51 Shanzer offers some intriguing theories about how Augustine's personal life as a father may have influenced his early ambiguity on fetal ensoulment.

104. Gorman, *Abortion in the Early Church*, 70–72, quoted in Daniel A. Dombrowski and Robert J. Deltete, *A Brief, Liberal, Catholic Defense of Abortion* (Urbana: University of Illinois Press, 2000), 20.

105. See Dombrowski and Deltete, *Liberal, Catholic Defense of Abortion*, chap. 1.

a material substance transferred to the embryo through intercourse;[106] on the other hand, most pro-life scholars today hold a creationist view of the soul as infused directly by God (which reflects Augustine's belief). Ensoulment at creation for today's pro-life writers means a child is created at conception—a viewpoint that Tertullian would have found odd, given his medically informed views of the unformed/formed fetus, as we will discuss below. Tertullian's notions about ensouled yet unformed fetuses do not cohere well with today's anti-abortion polemics, so pro-life writers resort to a misleadingly selective citing of Tertullian's statements on abortion. I object to the attempt to funnel this complicated thinker into their narrow and univocal anti-abortion and pro-natalist narrative, when the source material suggests that Tertullian is an example of an early church theologian who actually seemed to struggle with the abortion issue, informed in part by medical science of his day. His apparent struggle is the morally significant historical lesson for current debates about abortion.

Tertullian lived in North Africa, which coincidentally was also the locale of a vibrant scientific and medical community, including some Christian physicians.[107] Tertullian knew of Hippocrates[108] and his own contemporary Soranus of Ephesus, whom Tertullian lauded as "a most accomplished authority in medical science."[109] Soranus was the notable author of several medical texts included the widely respected *Gynecology*, which gives detailed instructions for becoming pregnant, obstetrical care, birth, gynecological diseases, and newborn care.[110] Scholars find "remarkable parallels" to Soranus's views in the way Tertullian spoke graphically of the symptoms of pregnancy, the birthing process, and lactation.[111] Regarding the issue of ensoulment, Tertullian agreed with the views of "the medical profession," including Soranus, who

---

106. See Lindsey Disney and Larry Poston, "The Breath of Life: Christian Perspectives on Conception and Ensoulment," *Anglican Theological Review* 92, no. 2 (2010): 275–77.

107. See Louise Cilliers, "Roman North Africa in the 4th Century AD: Its Role in the Preservation and Transmission of Medical Knowledge," *Acta Classica: Proceedings of the Classical Association of South Africa*, Supplement 2 (2008): 49, 58–59.

108. See Temkin, *Hippocrates in a World of Pagans and Christians*, 247.

109. Tertullian, *A Treatise on the Soul*, trans. D. D. Holmes, in *Ante-Nicene Fathers*, vol. 3, ed. Alexander Roberts and James Donaldson (New York: Scribner's, 1899), chap. 6, http://www .tertullian.org/anf/anf03/anf03-22.htm#P2621_863011. Augustine was also aware of medical science in North Africa. See Shelley Annette Reid, "'The First Dispensation of Christ Is Medicinal': Augustine and Roman Medical Culture," PhD diss., University of British Columbia (2008), 103–111, 129–30.

110. See Petr Kitzler, "Tertullian and Ancient Embryology in *De carne Christi* 4, 1 and 19, 3–4," *Zeitschrift für Antikes Christentum / Journal of Ancient Christianity* 18, no. 2 (2014): 204. Tertullian seems to get his embryological knowledge from Soranus, who did not support the two-seed theory but regarded the women's contribution as passive. See Kitzler, "Tertullian and Ancient Embryology," 209.

111. Thomas F. Heyne, "Tertullian and Obstetrics," *Studia Patristica* 53 (2013): 427.

thought of the soul as a corporeal substance. Tertullian may have been influenced as well by Galen in believing that the soul was passed on to offspring at conception through the father's semen as the embryo's "vital principle."[112] In any case, Tertullian adamantly rejected any creationist idea of the soul "originating elsewhere and externally to the womb."[113] David Jones recognizes that Tertullian believed the soul "begins from conception,"[114] a statement that can only be fully understood in light of Tertullian's traducianism. Pro-life thinkers attempt to downplay or ignore his traducianism (which is hard to do and still be referring to Tertullian),[115] in order to associate him with today's pro-life understanding that any destruction of life from conception onward is the "murder" of a being with "body and soul."[116] Not only is Tertullian's view of the soul different from pro-life thinkers today, but his biological understanding of the fetal body is also different—a difference that had an impact on his ethics of the maternal body.

The issue of an unformed/formed fetus surfaced for Tertullian (as for Augustine) in his interpretation of the miscarriage passage in Exodus 21. Tertullian accounted for the difference in penalty due to the woman miscarrying only "the rudiment of a human being," as Tertullian referred to it. Jones is aware that Tertullian sometimes suggested an unformed/formed embryology, for example, when he wrote, "The embryo therefore becomes a human being in the womb from the moment that its *form is completed*."[117] Nevertheless, Jones cannot make sense of why Tertullian was apparently "untroubled" by the fetal demise discussed in the Exodus passage, since Tertullian emphatically emphasized ensouled human life beginning at conception.[118] Gorman also seems perplexed by Tertullian's discussion of Exodus 21, which Gorman cannot reconcile with Tertullian's statement "We may not destroy even the foetus in the womb."[119] To Jones and Gorman, Tertullian seems ambivalent or confused because he does not strongly condemn the forced miscarriage as the murder of a human being. Indeed, not only does Tertullian not call it a homicide but emphasizes, instead, that the in-utero fetus, by virtue of "living still in the mother . . . for the most part shares its own state with the

---

112. Tertullian, *Treatise on the Soul*, chap. 25. Tertullian's view of the vivifying force of sperm seems to match Galen's opinion that "the female blood is a matter out of which the embryo arises, and the semen is the force which brings it into motion without, nevertheless, contributing materially to the formation of the embryo." Kitzler, "Tertullian and Ancient Embryology," 207.
113. Tertullian, *Treatise on the Soul*, chap. 25.
114. Tertullian, *Treatise on the Soul*, chap. 27, quoted in D. Jones, *Soul of the Embryo*, 114.
115. See D. Jones, *Soul of the Embryo*, 113; Gorman, *Abortion and the Early Church*, 55.
116. D. Jones, *Soul of the Embryo*, 113.
117. Tertullian, *On the Soul*, chap. 37, quoted in D. Jones, *Soul of the Embryo*, 114, emphasis by Jones.
118. D. Jones, *Soul of the Embryo*, 114.
119. Gorman, *Abortion and Early Church*, 55.

mother."[120] For Tertullian, the status of the fetus cannot be determined apart from this biological fact.

One scholar suggests that Tertullian's varying statements may be a result of having "moderated" his position on the issue of abortion.[121] While this is possible, I suggest that situating Tertullian in the context of the medical science of his day gives us an additional piece of the puzzle. Seeing Tertullian as a medically informed theologian provides an effective way to understand how he could be strongly opposed to abortion but still be able not only to differentiate between unformed and formed fetal life but also to consider the fetal-maternal connection that might endanger a mother's life. Here I turn to one of the most controversial passages in Tertullian's *A Treatise on the Soul*, which discusses the specific medical practice of embryotomy in an obstructed birth (a procedure that is today misleadingly labeled "partial birth abortion").[122] Jones is aware of both Soranus's description of this procedure and Tertullian's discussion of it, but Jones, apparently, does not know what to make of Tertullian's comments.[123] In this passage from Tertullian's treatise, I see an indication of respect, even if reluctant, for Soranus's obstetrical recommendations in this dire birthing situation.

Soranus's *Gynecology* devotes a chapter to treating a difficult labor. While Soranus saw delivering a healthy infant as the goal, he recognized that it was not always possible in an obstructed birth. In these cases, Soranus believed the physician has an obligation to try to save the mother. Soranus gave a detailed description of the embryotomy procedure and when it might be required: "If the fetus does not respond to manual traction, because of its size, or death, or impaction in any manner whatsoever, one must proceed to the more forceful methods, those of extraction by hooks and embryotomy. . . . Even if one loses the infant, it is still necessary to take care of the mother; . . . one should not withhold assistance."[124] Soranus's textbook gives extensive details, including: how to position the patient for the procedure; how carefully to access the uterus; which blade, hook, or forceps to use in a head-first, breech, or

120. Tertullian, *A Treatise on the Soul*, chap. 37.
121. Julian Barr, *Tertullian and the Unborn Child: Christian and Pagan Attitudes in Historical Perspective* (London: Routledge, 2017), 125, where Barr also notes that Tertullian's earlier writings speak of abortion as homicide but his later *Treatise on the Soul* (written in approximately 207 CE) seems influenced by Soranus's "cautious approach to abortion."
122. The American College of Obstetricians and Gynecologists rejects this term, which "is not a medical term and is vaguely defined in the law." American College of Obstetricians and Gynecologists, "Increasing Access to Abortion: Committee Opinion No. 613," *Obstetrics & Gynecology* 124, no. 5 (2014): 613.
123. See D. Jones, *Soul of the Embryo*, 37–38.
124. Owsei Temkin, trans., *Soranus' Gynecology* (Baltimore: Johns Hopkins University Press, 1991), 189–90. Hippocrates also referenced this procedure. See Temkin, *Hippocrates in a World of Pagans and Christians*, 247.

transverse presentation; how to deflate the skull "if the fetus suffers from hydrocephalus"; how to dismember an impacted dead fetus; and how safely to deliver the placenta, given inflammation of the cervix from the embryotomy.[125] Tertullian seems to have knowledge of Soranus's text, directly or indirectly, because in the midst of a theological discussion about fetal ensoulment in his *Treatise on the Soul*, Tertullian describes specific elements of an embryotomy procedure:

> Sometimes by a cruel necessity, whilst yet in the womb, an infant is put to death, when lying awry in the orifice of the womb he impedes parturition, and kills his mother, if he is not to die himself. Accordingly, among surgeons' tools there is a certain instrument, which is formed with a nicely-adjusted flexible frame for opening the *uterus* first of all, and keeping it open; it is further furnished with an annular blade, by means of which the limbs within the womb are dissected with anxious but unfaltering care; its last appendage being a blunted or covered hook, wherewith the entire *foetus* is extracted by a violent delivery.[126]

Tertullian was not advocating for abortion here. The fact that Tertullian condemned abortion does not mean that he was not also persuaded by Soranus's medical opinion about when abortion was necessary and how to perform it carefully. Tertullian agreed with Soranus that pregnancy means "a living being had been conceived," but, in this passage, he seemed to credit Soranus (among other physicians) with having developed effective medical tools and a careful surgical procedure to accomplish safely this "harsh treatment," the medical "necessity" of which Soranus had "no doubt." Tertullian did not deny the value of fetal life, given his traducian belief that a fetus was endowed with a corporeal soul from conception. Nor did Tertullian deny the danger and even gruesome nature of the procedure, but he seemed to see that when the procedure is done quickly and professionally, the "luckless infant" will "escape being tortured alive" by dying along with its mother in a protracted, futile labor.[127] There is plausible reason to conclude that this passage indicates Tertullian's "recognition that embryotomy could be necessary in cases where the foetus would impede parturition" and endanger the mother's life.[128]

---

125. Temkin, *Soranus' Gynecology*, 192. Heyne gives a physician's analysis of Soranus's procedure and confirms that an "embryotome," a hook-like knife similar to what Soranus described, is still used today "for rare embryotomies." Heyne, "Tertullian and Obstetrics," 432.

126. Tertullian, *Treatise on the Soul*, chap. 25.

127. Tertullian, *Treatise on the Soul*, chap. 25. Augustine also referenced this procedure in the *Enchiridion* 23.86, seeming to conclude as well that the procedure was a necessity "lest the mothers die."

128. Barr, *Tertullian and the Unborn Child*, 125.

Noonan categorically rejects interpreting this passage as an acceptance of therapeutic abortion. From the translation Noonan himself makes of the Latin original, he paints a graphically different picture—one of Tertullian recoiling at the criminal slaughter of an infant. Noonan acknowledges that Tertullian is aware of physicians' opinions of "the necessity" that the infant must "be killed lest a live woman be rent apart";[129] however, Noonan reads Tertullian as sarcastically standing in opposition to those doctors: "What the physicians find necessary Tertullian finds a crime."[130] However, as classics scholar Julian Barr concludes, after careful study of Tertullian's polemical approach, "it is difficult to see Tertullian as a particularly zealous defender of the unborn child."[131] While sarcasm can be found in Tertullian's writing, I do not think the evidence supports reading sarcasm in this passage. Quite the contrary. Given Tertullian's glowing approbation elsewhere of Soranus, his own dependence on Soranus's medical knowledge, and his awareness of the life-and-death situation of an obstructed birth—all this evidence points to Tertullian's agreement (albeit reluctant) with Soranus's medical opinion on embryotomy. I find Noonan's suggestion disturbing that it would be acceptable for any church leader, then or now, to approve of doctors standing idly by while a woman is "rent apart" in an obstructed birth. We do not know if Tertullian himself had children, but we do know he had a wife,[132] and I prefer to imagine that he would not have held back the physician's hand if his wife had been in extremis during birthing.

In part, here we are again confronting an issue of differing historical interpretations. Noonan, Gorman, and Jones describe Greco-Roman views on abortion as one of more or less acceptance, with Jewish and Christian attitudes standing in "sharp contrast to those of their pagan contemporaries."[133]

129. Tertullian, *Treatise on the Soul*, chap. 25 quoted by Noonan, "An Almost Absolute Value," 13. I include here more of the translation that Noonan uses on page 13: "But still in the womb an infant by necessary cruelty is killed when lying twisted at the womb's mouth he prevents birth and is a matricide unless he dies. . . . There is among the arms of physicians an instrument by which . . . the interior members are slaughtered . . . so that the whole criminal deed is extracted with a violent delivery."
130. Noonan, "An Almost Absolute Value," 13. Cassidy agrees with Noonan, in part, because he sees in Tertullian "ignorance of biological processes." Cassidy, "A Convenient Untruth," 78. I see the opposite. Tertullian possessed medical awareness, which sometimes sat uneasily with his religious convictions but, nevertheless, he gave credence to medical opinion, commensurate with his respect for the knowledge of physicians like Soranus.
131. Barr, *Tertullian and the Unborn Child*, 174.
132. See Heyne, "Tertullian and Obstetrics," 425, 433. Barr also suggests that some passages describing pregnancy from a woman's point of view in Tertullian's *Treatise on the Soul* indicate that Tertullian could have been influenced by the views of women leaders in the Montanist sect, with whom he no doubt had some contact after joining the group. See Barr, *Tertullian and the Unborn Child*, 49.
133. D. Jones, *Soul of the Embryo*, 42.

Noonan describes Roman culture as having an "indifference to fetal and early life."[134] Gorman is dismissive of any Roman attempts to regulate abortion because Roman lawgivers did not reflect the pro-life morality Gorman believes was prevalent in the early church—namely, "concern for the unborn."[135] If one looks at the ancient world in terms of this kind of binary, Judeo-Christian versus pagan, then Tertullian's words will be probably taken as sarcastically attempting to separate himself from immoral pagan physicians. If, however, one sees Tertullian as a Christian thinker who not only was informed by Greco-Roman medical views but who also esteemed trained physicians, like Soranus, then it is possible to read him as contextually putting medical wisdom over a principle of protecting fetal life at all costs. Pro-life proponents have focused so myopically on isolated anti-abortion and anti-infanticide statements from early church leaders that they have overlooked the strong possibility that early church condemnations of abortion may have stood concurrent with an acknowledgment of the medical necessity of therapeutic abortion, as in the case of Tertullian's discussion of embryotomy.

Pro-life scholars continue to defend the claim of the church's historical defense of unborn life, arguing that it merely took an advance of embryological knowledge in the modern period to dismantle definitively the conceptuality of the unformed/formed fetus, which had afforded women some protection from prosecution or excommunication for early abortions. The modern scientific discoveries of sperm and ova did help foster an anti-abortion movement in many sectors of American society (though the reasons for the American Medical Association's anti-abortion platform in the nineteenth century have been hotly debated).[136] Science is depicted by pro-life writers as inspiring the church to make a break with outmoded embryology and an unformed/formed conceptuality of personhood. Once this break was made, the church definitively called all abortions murder. I contend that even when early church leaders—without the benefit of modern science—asserted that a valued life begins at conception, they were still able to concede, concurrently, that some abortions may be necessary. It is too simplistic to say that faulty embryology was holding the church back from seeing what its moral position

134. Noonan, "An Almost Absolute Value," 7.
135. Gorman, *Abortion and the Early Church*, 32.
136. Pro-life voices claim a victory for pro-natalist science from the likes of physician Horatio Storer. See Charles I. Lugosi, "When Abortion Was a Crime: A Historical Perspective," *University of Detroit Mercy Law Review* 83, no. 51 (2006): 64–65; Mark Y. Herring, *The Pro-life / Choice Debate* (Westport, CT: Greenwood, 2003), 42–45. Other scholars level charges against Storer and other 19th-century white physicians of eugenics, nativism, and patriarchy. See Olasky, *Abortion Rites*, 114–18; Reagan, *When Abortion Was a Crime*, 11–13; Rebecca Todd Peters, *Trust Women: A Progressive Christian Argument for Reproductive Justice* (Boston: Beacon Press, 2018), 106–8.

should be. Even a moral rigorist like Tertullian, who believed that a type of ensouled life began at conception, nevertheless understood that early fetal life was rudimentary, pregnancy impinged on women's bodies, and a physician had a duty to try to save a pregnant woman in an obstructed birth. How far we have come, sadly, from Tertullian's moral reasoning when pro-life writers today try to convince fellow Christians that "a man ought rather to let the mother perish than that he himself . . . [commit] the crime of homicide in killing the foetus"![137]

These brief comments about history have hopefully provided a wider perspective and an alternative narrative than that given by pro-life scholars. Church history is marked by complexities and inconsistencies regarding how unwanted pregnancy and abortion were addressed, and despite church condemnations, abortion happened. Noonan and other pro-life scholars account for this fact historically by blaming the loose morals of pagans, the rise of forbidden gynecological knowledge, and the moral laxity of confessors, who made pastoral allowances for extenuating circumstances voiced by women who had abortions. Pro-life scholars read the sweep of church history as a positive move to suppress what seems to them to be the permissiveness of the medieval penitential manuals. They also see as positive the modern undoing of the unformed/formed conceptuality, which had exempted early abortions from the charge of criminal homicide.

I have indicated a counternarrative and a different set of lessons that we can take away from church history. First, there never was a univocal sanctity-of-fetal-life message in Christianity. It is my hope that those who are attracted to this simplistic narrative will be willing to see the much more complicated picture based on recent historical scholarship, which supplements earlier feminist critiques. Confessionals and penance, for all their moralizing and inconsistencies, actually allowed medieval women to speak about their unwanted pregnancies and what brought them to the extreme and dangerous act of abortion. While the penitential and legal texts do not always give us women's voices firsthand, one can hear traces and discern parts of their stories—confessions of lust and sinfulness but also complaints of economic hardship, domestic violence, incest, illness, and so on. These voices are part of the lay church's *sensus fidelium*, linked to how actual believers attempted to live their faith. Christian pro-choice proponents can take heart that the historical church was not devoid of moral intuitions marked by compassion toward

---

137. John Haldane and Patrick Lee, "Aquinas on Human Ensoulment, Abortion and the Value of Life," *Philosophy* 78, no. 2 (2003): 278. I will say more in chap. 4 about Haldane and Lee's view of fetal personhood that grounds this, to my mind, abhorrent theological claim.

women's reproductive struggles. The church's criminalizing of all behaviors that impeded or fell outside of marital procreativity was a top-down imposition of morality that was more concerned with sex outside of marriage (and even sexual pleasure within marriage) than protecting fetal life or promoting the raising of healthy children.

A second historical lesson we learn is that church leaders, marked as they were by sexism and even misogyny, were at their best when attending seriously to the real ambiguities of life, especially related to pregnancy and birth. To the extent that one can draw a straight moral line from church history to the pro-life movement today, it would not be from the likes of Tertullian. For all his anti-abortion invectives and his belief in human ensoulment from conception, Tertullian was apparently able see that killing a fetus during an obstructed birth, in order to avoid the gruesome death of both the mother and child, was a tragic but morally justifiable medical action. Pro-choice Christians can affirm this endorsement of the value of a woman's life. Today's pro-life movement has its origins arguably in the politicized rise of the late medieval criminalization of abortion in canon law, including the justification of intrusive and coercive inquisitional procedures to determine which miscarriages were actual intentional abortions and who was involved. One can arguably draw a strong line from those authoritarian medieval legal developments to the dogmatic anti-abortion stances and activities today, including militant anti-abortion violence. While one cannot hold moderate pro-life proponents responsible for the extremist anti-abortion tactics they do not condone, both moderate and militant wings of the anti-abortion movement are grounded in the same claim: that direct abortion is the murder of an innocent child, which justifies intervening to save that child from death. Christian history, carefully read, does not support such an extreme, dogmatic stance. Moreover, as I will argue in the chapters that follow, pro-life writers today fail to make a convincing case—biblically, doctrinally, or philosophically—that fetuses are persons from conception, whose sacredness and innocence justifies overriding the reproductive choices of all women.

2

Biblical Arguments for Personhood

Pro-life proponents, no matter what their Christian affiliation, understand that a key plank of their platform is to secure adequate evidence that the Bible supports their claims for personhood from conception. They face many hermeneutical and theological challenges in this endeavor, given that the biblical text does not define human personhood and only rarely speaks of conception or life in the womb. Hence, pro-life writers must rely on related general ideas that they believe undergird a biblical pro-life worldview—principally, creation in God's image and God's providential plan for all people. As we will see, they have a large hermeneutical obstacle to surmount in order to link those general ideas to their specific pro-life claim that abortion is "clearly incompatible" with a biblical worldview.[1]

The concept of humans created in the image of God is rooted in a few decisive verses from the book of Genesis: "Then God said, 'Let us make humankind in our image. . . .' So God created humankind in his image, in the image of God he created them" (1:26–27). Appealing to the *imago Dei* has a long and venerable history in Christian theology, to which pro-life proponents see themselves connected. These verses are used ubiquitously in scholarly and popular pro-life arguments for embryonic and fetal personhood. This chapter demonstrates that these writers not only fail to connect the notion of creation in God's image with prenatal beings but also the ways in which they define the *imago Dei* diverge widely, and their interpretations even conflict with each other. Taken singly or as a group, these arguments for personhood

---

1. John Jefferson Davis, *Abortion and the Christian: What Every Believer Should Know* (Phillipsburg, NJ: Presbyterian & Reformed, 1984), 37.

from conception based on the notion of creation in God's image fail to provide a convincing biblical basis for fetal personhood. Moreover, their claims lack the support of the New Testament, which presents the image of God in terms of Christian discipleship, not ontology.

In an equally problematic use of the biblical text, many pro-life proponents argue for personhood from conception based on mostly poetic verses about life in the womb, generally, and the prenatal call of prophets or other chosen figures in the Bible, specifically. They argue that passages such as "Before I formed you in the womb I knew you, and before you were born I consecrated you" (Jer. 1:5) indicate God's providential hand in prenatal life and, therefore by extension, whenever any conception occurs, one should assume that God elects or predestines that person to be born. This attempt to prove biblically that an embryo is a predestined person is based on a dubious exegetical approach that extrapolates a universal theological claim from a handful of mostly poetic verses in the Hebrew Bible. Moreover, applying notions of predestination, election, or providence to human reproductive matters is, I argue, a biologically deterministic way of doing theology that most serious theologians should agree is a mistaken way of speaking of God's involvement in human lives.

ARE FETUSES CREATED IN THE IMAGE OF GOD?

The creation story in Genesis 1 has been widely read and interpreted in expansive and diverse ways throughout Christian history to describe God as creator and humans as God's valued creatures.[2] Into the modern period, theologians continued to propose paradigms for understanding how humanity images God. Some Christian writers promote a functional understanding of the image of God—that is, the *imago Dei* is not what we are but what we do, as exemplified by Wesleyan teachings about sanctification or the views of social reform-minded writers, such as nineteenth-century Christian abolitionists.[3] Other modern Christian writers espouse various relational understandings of the *imago Dei*, as seen in a diverse range of writings, including those of

2. See J. Richard Middleton, *The Liberating Image: The* Imago Dei *in Genesis 1* (Grand Rapids: Brazos Press, 2005); Michelle A. Gonzalez, *Created in God's Image: An Introduction to Feminist Theological Anthropology* (Maryknoll, NY: Orbis Books, 2014). My discussion of Jewish views of the *imago Dei* is found in the previous chapter.
3. See Kenneth H. Carter Jr., "Recovering Human Nature through Christian Practice," *Quarterly Review* 23, no. 1 (2003): 45–47; Dan McKanan, *Identifying the Image of God: Radical Christians and Nonviolent Power in the Antebellum United States* (Oxford: Oxford University Press, 2002), esp. chap. 5.

Karl Barth,[4] a variety of white feminist and Latina feminist theologians,[5] womanist scholars,[6] and theologians using concepts from disabilities studies.[7] Some theologians propose an eschatological *imago*;[8] others question the exclusive association of the *imago Dei* with Homo sapiens.[9] Thus, appealing to creation in God's image is a common trope in the historical stream of Christian thought and, especially in the modern period, a common method for theologically grounding human, animal, or environmental rights. Pro-life proponents see themselves in a similar social-justice light—in this case, advocating for the rights of vulnerable preborn persons. However, the peculiarity of the pro-life application of the *imago Dei* to the unborn puts their appeal to fetuses created in God's image on the margins of this historical stream of social-justice-oriented theology.

This section raises exegetical and theological concerns about how pro-life writers appeal to the creation stories in Genesis 1 and 2 generally, and Genesis 1:26–27 in particular, in order to claim that embryos and fetuses, created in God's image, should be accorded the value and right to life of a born person. My critical assessment of a representative range of pro-life appeals to the *imago Dei* demonstrates not only the insuperable problems these writers have in hermeneutically connecting the Genesis 1 text with prenatal beings but also the ways in which their biblical interpretations diverge and even conflict. Finally, the New Testament provides little to no support for the pro-life understanding of the *imago Dei* in relation to unborn beings or even for ontological claims about humanity's created nature; instead, New Testament writers appeal to God's image as a means of exhorting believers to follow Christ.

4. See Karl Barth, *Church Dogmatics*, vol. III/1, *The Doctrine of Creation*, trans. G. W. Bromiley (London: T&T Clark, 2010), esp. paragraph 41.

5. See Anne Clifford, "When Being Human Becomes Truly Earthly: An Ecofeminist Proposal for Solidarity," and Mary Catherine Hilkert, "Cry Beloved Image: Rethinking the Image of God," in *In the Embrace of God: Feminist Approaches to Theological Anthropology*, ed. Ann O. Graff (Maryknoll, NY: Orbis Books, 1995), 173–89, 190–205; Gonzalez, *Created in God's Image*, 124–39.

6. See Kelly Brown Douglas, "To Reflect the Image of God: A Womanist Perspective on Right Relationship," in *Living the Intersection: Womanism and Afrocentrism in Theology*, ed. Cheryl Sanders (Minneapolis: Fortress Press, 1995), 76–77.

7. See Amos Yong, *Theology and Down Syndrome: Reimagining Disability in Late Modernity* (Waco: Baylor University Press, 2007), 169–174; Thomas E. Reynolds, *Vulnerable Communion: A Theology of Disability and Hospitality* (Grand Rapids: Brazos Press, 2008), 175–88.

8. See F. LeRon Shults, *Reforming Theological Anthropology: After the Philosophical Turn to Relationality* (Grand Rapids: Wm. B. Eerdmans Publishing Co., 2003), 236–38.

9. See Wentzel Van Huyssteen, "Fallen Angels or Rising Beasts? Theological Perspectives on Human Uniqueness," *Theology and Science* 1, no. 2 (2003): 170–73; Anna Case Winters, "Rethinking the Image of God," *Zygon* 39, no. 4 (2004): 813–26.

Hermeneutical Leaps in Pro-life Appeals to the *Imago Dei*

It is a commonly accepted position among exegetes and theologians that the Hebrew Bible does not emphasize the theme of creation in the image of God. David Fergusson comments that "the lack of interest in the *imago Dei* after the opening chapters of Genesis indicates that it is not the core concept of a developed anthropology" in the Hebrew Bible.[10] Even some pro-life writers agree, saying, "It would not be appropriate to use 'image of God' passages to determine whether or not the fetus is a person."[11] Nevertheless, scholarly and popular pro-life appeals to the *imago Dei* are numerous and widespread. I will examine three representative examples from the numerous scholarly pro-life discussions, as well as a sampling of popular online writings. While unified in a pro-life commitment, these pro-life appeals display very different and even conflicting ways of linking the *imago Dei* with the preborn. All the expositions begin with a fairly standard affirmation of men and women created in God's image based on the Genesis 1 verses, but they diverge, in some cases significantly, when it comes to the difficult issue of how to make the biblical case that those verses should apply to fetuses and even embryos. In my estimation, none is able to defend that claim convincingly, and the overall picture is one of confusion and lack of coherence about how the *imago Dei* applies to unborn beings at all.

Ethicist David Gushee states upfront that in his approach to "creation theology" in the Bible, the terms "'human being' and 'persons'" are for him synonymous,[12] so that his argument for fetal personhood is simply an argument that fetuses are valued humans. To be a valued human, for Gushee, does not mean having any particular inherent capacity that most born human persons have to some degree and that a fetus could develop, which would classify it as at least a "potential person."[13] Instead, Gushee asserts that a truly "incalculable" value is "*conferred*" on humankind by God, who created them in his image; this is "an ascribed status willed by God."[14] Gushee gives an eloquent declaration about the ethical implications of this God-given value: "God has consecrated each and every human being—without exception and in all circumstances—as a unique incalculably precious being of elevated

---

10. David Fergusson, "Humans Created according to the *Imago Dei*: An Alternative Proposal," *Zygon* 48, no. 2 (2013): 446.

11. Donal O'Mathuna, "The Bible and Abortion: What of the 'Image of God'?," in *Bioethics and the Future of Medicine*, ed. John Frederic Kilner, David L. Schiedermayer, and Nigel M. De S. Cameron (Grand Rapids: Wm. B. Eerdmans Publishing Co., 1995), 205.

12. David P. Gushee, *The Sacredness of Human Life: Why an Ancient Biblical Vision Is Key to the World's Future* (Grand Rapids: Wm. B. Eerdmans Publishing Co., 2013), 40, 44.

13. Gushee, *Sacredness of Human Life*, 45.

14. Gushee, *Sacredness of Human Life*, 400, 46; italics in original.

status and dignity, . . . and [God] will hold us accountable for responding appropriately."[15] In other words, Gushee devises a kind of syllogistic moral argument: God ascribes value to humans by declaring that they are created in God's image; fetuses are human; therefore fetuses are created in God's image. What seems simple and straightforward is actually a weak argument that depends on slippage between the terms "person" (which he does not use but implies) and "human" (which he uses to mask the controversy about personhood in abortion debates).

No reader of the Bible disputes that Genesis 1 and 2 are creation stories about the first people created directly by God to bear God's image. No one disputes that a fetus is human. However, simply declaring that the Genesis texts apply to human uterine life is not an argument at all. Gushee is aware that some scholars try to make a philosophical case for fetal personhood, but he discounts these arguments as "purely speculative" and subjective. Gushee implies that by staying grounded in biblical revelation and not using the term "person," he avoids problematic arguments that "hinge on somebody's definition of what makes a human being a person" and might be "skewed" by various preconceptions or ideologies.[16] As a reputable scholar, Gushee accepts that any biblical exposition also risks being skewed, I assume, so that avoiding philosophy and appealing directly to the Bible is not a solution to the issue of fetal personhood but the beginning of a set of hermeneutical challenges.[17]

For example, while some pro-life scholars try to build a case that the Bible asserts fetal personhood based on various passages mentioning life in the womb, Gushee makes only passing reference to these verses, admitting that "not everyone finds the biblical evidence open-and-shut," apparently himself included.[18] Instead, Gushee's biblical argument that the meaning of the Genesis creation stories can be applied to fetuses amounts to a series of inferences. He claims that, based on the reference to male and female beings created in God's image (Gen. 1:26–27) and the Adam and Eve story in Genesis 2, one

15. Gushee, *Sacredness of Human Life*, 411.

16. Gushee, *Sacredness of Human Life*, 45.

17. Gushee is a Baptist professor of ethics who publishes widely in scholarly circles and popular media outlets. He has long been active in evangelical circles, but in a recent autobiography, Gushee speaks of his break from evangelicalism, in particular because of LGBTQ issues. However, he still seems to embrace what he calls his "compassionate, 'soft' pro-life position." David P. Gushee, *Still Christian: Following Jesus out of American Evangelicalism* (Louisville, KY: Westminster John Knox Press, 2017), 125.

18. Gushee, *Sacredness of Human Life*, 357. Other pro-life authors agree. According to John Jefferson Davis, *Abortion and the Christian*, 43, even though passages like Ps. 139:13–16 seem to imply prenatal personhood, the "language is merely poetic and therefore precludes strict conclusions concerning the personhood of the unborn." Ron Sider will only say that these types of Scriptures give "signs which point in [the] direction" of indicating fetal personhood. Sider, *Completely Pro-Life* (Downers Grove, IL: InterVarsity Press, 1987), 45.

can infer that God's image is inclusive of all humans, who together constitute "one race—the human race. . . . All are children of Eve, all are part of our one human family."[19] The one-family metaphor is unproblematic and widely used in moral discourse to argue for universal human rights. However, Gushee then makes the additional inference that fetuses, as human, should be considered as part of the human family and, hence, bearers of rights along with everyone else. Again, the truism that fetuses are human has never been in question, even by pro-choice proponents. The problem for Gushee is traversing the gap between that truism and his very speculative claim that the value and rights that the creation stories ascribe to the first humans (portrayed as adult persons) should be applied to human beings in the womb. It is a massive hermeneutical leap, and I suspect that Gushee is aware of the tenuousness of his biblical inference from Adam and Eve to fetuses; hence he turns to other types of evidence.

Gushee makes a brief reference to "amazing" fetal development, and he finds in prenatal sonography especially what strikes him as self-evident: "It should be hard to avoid the commonsense conclusion that the prenatal human being is indeed human from the beginning"[20]—meaning, for Gushee, a fetus is a person, although Gushee avoids the term "person" in an attempt to bypass its controversy. Despite his theological insistence that human value is not intrinsic but conferred, Gushee seems to concede that being a valued human (person) created in God's image is simply synonymous with and intrinsic to being a biologically conceived human organism. I see nothing wrong with claiming that biologically conceived human organisms progressing toward personhood have value (I will say more about this in part 2 of this book). However, it stretches one's powers of inference to then say that such a being is what the biblical writers had in mind, when speaking of the first human persons created in God's image and given important tasks to accomplish in God's creation. Gushee's approach, to be convincing, requires that the reader accept the large inference that the Genesis 1 and 2 texts apply to human fetuses and that, somehow, modern prenatal ultrasounds bolster the validity of making that inference.

Taking a very different tack, evangelical writer Andrew White, who is also a practicing obstetrician, promotes the idea of a corporeal *imago Dei*, with an

---

19. Gushee, *Sacredness of Human Life*, 40.

20. Gushee, *Sacredness of Human Life*, 358. Other pro-life authors put more stock in the argument of genetics than in ultrasounds. See John Rankin, "The Corporeal Reality of *Nepeš* and the Status of the Unborn," *Journal of the Evangelical Theological Society* 31, no. 2 (1988): 157. Sider admits that genetics "tells us nothing about whether the *imago Dei* is present," but one should nevertheless "act on the assumption that from conception the developing fetus is truly a human being made in the image of the Creator." Sider, *Completely Pro-Life*, 49.

emphasis on procreation. By this approach White hopes to avoid the philosophical personhood dilemma, because "while some have denied the 'personhood' of the fetus, no rational medical experts have denied its corporeality."[21] For White, the fact that the *imago* passage in Genesis is followed by the command to be fruitful and multiply demonstrates "the significance of the association between procreation and the image of God in Gen. 1:27, 28." The call to rule over the earth is also how humans enact God's image, but dominion is subordinate to and "dependent on procreation of divine likenesses."[22] That is, people have to be born before they can act as God's representative rulers on earth, and therefore Christians are called to reproduce in order to "extend the kingdom of God."[23]

What about those who are unable to fulfill the Genesis command to reproduce and rule? White assures "infertile couples, . . . unable to procreate," that they are created in God's image too—ontologically even if not functionally—because they are living, corporeal beings. Similarly, a "fetus cannot constructively rule over lower creation or procreate" yet, but it can also be said to bear God's image ontologically because it too is living and has "corporeality."[24] Like Gushee, White attempts to avoid making an argument for fetal personhood by substituting an alternative term, in White's case, corporeality, with the result that the notion of a person bearing God's image is made synonymous with acquiring body mass as a result of being biologically conceived.

Needless to say, White's categories of corporeality and procreation are undeveloped, with troubling implications.[25] White's view of the *imago Dei* seems to codify compulsory reproductive sexuality in a way that goes beyond what even many conservative Christians would promote for missional purposes. He seems to imply that killing a fetus is abhorrent not only because it destroys a being carrying God's image but also because, in doing so, "we reject our procreative function as the image of God."[26] The functional aspect of a procreative *imago Dei* injects a troublesome utilitarian aspect to fetal

---

21. Andrew A. White, "The Corporeal Aspect and Procreative Function of the *Imago Dei* and Abortion," *Journal of Biblical Ethics in Medicine* 6, no. 1 (1992): 19.

22. White, "Corporeal Aspect and Procreative Function," 18. This journal is no longer published and is not self-identified as a peer-review publication (see their Web site: http://bmei .org/).

23. White, "Corporeal Aspect and Procreative Function," 19. White's far-right views are in evidence in other writings where he condemns homosexuality and declares AIDS to be God's judgment. Andrew A. White, "AIDS as Divine Judgment, Part II," *Journal of Biblical Ethics in Medicine* 2, no. 4 (n.d.): 17–21.

24. White, "Corporeal Aspect and Procreative Function," 19.

25. White implies that some type of corporeality applies to God, supported by scriptural references to God appearing in "visible form." White, "Corporeal Aspect and Procreative Function," 16.

26. White, "Corporeal Aspect and Procreative Function," 19.

value, implying that a fetus should be allowed to live because of what it could potentially contribute to increasing the population of God's kingdom. Even more troubling is White's interpretation of Genesis 9:6 as support for capital punishment for murder:[27] "By destroying and devaluing the image of God, . . . the murderer forfeits his right to life." White does not name abortion doctors or women who abort as murderers but, by including the murder discussion in his essay, he implies a connection. It should come as no surprise that the extreme fundamentalist Web site "Jesus-Is-Savior" cites White's writings in its virulent anti-abortion materials.[28] White's approach, to be convincing, requires the reader to believe that the principal message of Genesis 1 is a command to reflect God's image by procreating and that participating in abortion makes one potentially liable for a capital crime.

A third very different approach to creation in the image of God can be found in the writings of professor of Old Testament Bruce Waltke, who presents a conservative Reformed theological interpretation of the story of creation. For Waltke, humanity was created "in God's image as a spiritual, rational, moral being," but since the time of Adam, all humanity has acquired a sinful nature inherited from the original parents God created (a story he takes literally as "written by Moses").[29] In order to prove biblically that a fetus is a person who bears the image of God, Waltke must identify passages in the Bible demonstrating that a fetus, like any human person, has a moral nature marked by "inherited sin."[30]

First, beyond making a typical pro-life appeal to verses mentioning God as fashioning life in the womb (e.g., Job 10:8–12; Ps. 139:13–16),[31] Waltke argues further that a fetus shares sinful human nature from the moment of conception, which he claims is revealed in Psalm 58:3: "David lamented, 'The wicked are estranged from the womb.'" Second, quoting an obscure passage in Genesis 5, Waltke claims that Adam bequeathed to his offspring

27. "Whoever sheds the blood of a human, by a human shall that person's blood be shed; for in his own image God made humankind" (Gen. 9:6).
28. See Andrew White, MD, "Abortion and the Ancient Practice of Child Sacrifice," posted on the "Jesus-Is-Savior" Web site: http://www.jesus-is-savior.com/Evils%20in%20America/Abortion%20is%20Murder/sacrifice.htm (warning: there are graphic pictures on this Web site that some may find disturbing).
29. Bruce K. Waltke, "Reflections from the Old Testament on Abortion," *Journal of the Evangelical Theological Society* 19, no. 1 (1976): 10, 9. Waltke was a longtime and respected professor at Reformed Theological Seminary until he was forced to resign in 2010 over his controversial, because positive, statements about evolution and a scientific worldview. See Scott Jaschik, "The Video That Ended a Career," *Inside Higher Ed* (April 9, 2010), https://gussf.wordpress.com/2010/04/10/the-video-that-ended-a-career/.
30. See Waltke, "Reflections from the Old Testament on Abortion," 12. Inherited sin is what theologians often call original sin.
31. See Waltke, "Reflections from the Old Testament on Abortion," 10.

his own sinful nature, which was passed on "seminally" through reproduction.[32] In other words, Waltke affirms a traducian viewpoint, accepted in some parts of Reformed Christianity, that a person's soul, marked by original sin, is transferred from the parents to the offspring through procreation.[33] Finally, Waltke finds biblical evidence that an actual "spiritual, moral faculty is already present in the fetus."[34] This last point takes some exegetical gymnastics regarding a passage in Psalm 51 where the psalmist speaks of his own formation in his mother's womb: "Behold, thou desirest truth in the inward parts: and in the hidden *part* thou shalt make me to know wisdom."[35] Waltke takes "hidden part" to mean the womb, and he takes "make me to know wisdom" to mean that the fetal David was already learning from God. This passage leads Waltke to the "inescapable" conclusion that David, as a fetus in his mother's womb, already had a functioning moral consciousness and, therefore, by extrapolation, "the image of God is already present in [every] fetus."[36]

Neither Gushee nor White thinks that an embryo or fetus has the capacity functionally to enact the *imago Dei*. For Gushee, the image of God is not a capacity at all but the value that God confers on the fetus. For White, the *imago* is the ability to procreate, which is lodged corporeally in the fetus but is only potential. Waltke says the opposite: a fetus, and presumably even an embryo, has a functioning *imago Dei*, understood as a working moral consciousness embedded in its inherited fallen human nature. Waltke avoids the term "person," instead substituting an alternative concept—a being who has inherited sin at conception—with the effect that his argument for the fetus as a person bearing God's image amounts to no more than the claim that biologically conceived humans inherit original sin. Waltke's position, to be convincing, requires from the reader a belief in a doctrine of inherited sin, a literalist approach to Scripture, and a suspension of any scientific or even commonsensical notions about the cognitive capacities of an embryo or a fetus.

Apart from these widely divergent scholarly interpretations of the *imago Dei* published in recognized journals (at least for Gushee and Waltke), appeals to creation in God's image are ubiquitous on popular pro-life Web sites. The

32. Waltke, "Reflections from the Old Testament on Abortion," 12. Waltke derives this meaning from Gen. 5:3: "Adam fathered . . . a son in his own likeness and according to his image" (12; cf. CSB).

33. Waltke's traducian position is discussed in Lindsey Disney and Larry Poston, "The Breath of Life: Christian Perspectives on Conception and Ensoulment," *Anglican Theological Review* 92, no. 2 (2010): 276.

34. Waltke, "Reflections from the Old Testament on Abortion," 12.

35. Waltke, "Reflections from the Old Testament on Abortion," 13, quoting Ps. 51:6 KJV; emphasis by Waltke.

36. Waltke, "Reflections from the Old Testament on Abortion," 13. John Davis agrees that Ps. 51 supports the view that "even in his prenatal state David was being taught the moral law of God." Davis, *Abortion and the Christian*, 42.

popular construals do not differ materially from the scholarly viewpoints except perhaps in tone and rhetoric. One pro-life Web site emphasizes the clarity of the biblical stance on fetal life: "In Genesis 1:26–27, God tells us that people are created in the image of God. This is the source of human rights. The Bible is also very clear that life begins in the womb, calling John the Baptizer a 'baby' when he was still in the womb (Luke 1:44), and saying that God knits a person together in their mother's womb (Ps. 139:13)."[37]

Another Web site appeals to similar biblical passages about life in the womb to prove that fetuses are human. In addition, this Web site promotes creationism and suggests that evolutionary theories of how the human species originated contribute to the devaluation of all human life, including preborn life because "even if the unborn baby is human, such humans are dispensable if we are just mammals."[38] Other arguments link the *imago Dei* and a doctrine of original sin in a way similar to Waltke's writings. Namely, the Bible says we are "sinful from the time we are conceived," and since only a person can be sinful, an embryo must be a person beginning at conception. This Web site also holds extremist theological views that "abortion can also take eternal life away from an aborted child who has unbelieving parents."[39] Some writers focus on the theme of murder, saying that the killing of babies by abortion as well as the killing of abortionists are both violations of the *imago Dei*.[40]

As the above scholarly and popular pro-life discussions of the *imago Dei* show, writers attempting to defend fetal personhood based on the notion of creation in God's image consistently face a hermeneutically insurmountable wall between the Genesis text and the claim that a fetus is a person created in God's image. Many try to overcome it, but such attempts, as we have seen, require deferring to ancillary biblical texts about life in the womb, the visuals of fetal sonograms, or disputed doctrinal views such as traducianism or anti-evolutionary creationism. Pro-life proponents will continue to insist that the *imago Dei* applies to the fetus and will quote Scriptures they believe prove or imply fetal personhood. However, continuing to recycle these arguments will not make them more coherent or convincing, especially because not only are these various pro-life definitions of the *imago Dei* different, they are also at some points exegetically or theologically in conflict. I doubt that Gushee

---

37. Brian Sauvé, "*Imago Dei*: Bringing the Gospel into Conflict with a Culture of Death," *Deeply Rooted* (January 22, 2015), http://www.deeplyrootedmag.com/blogs/blog/16812780-imago-dei -bringing-the-gospel-into-conflict-with-a-culture-of-death.

38. Paul F. Taylor, "Abortion: Is It Really a Matter of Life and Death?," *Answers in Genesis* (May 2, 2014), https://answersingenesis.org/sanctity-of-life/abortion/is-it-really-a-matter-of-life -and-death/.

39. Ron Borkey, "Abortion," *Abide with Christ*, http://www.abidewithchrist.org/h1.htm.

40. Jason Foster, "George Tiller, Abortion, and the Imago Dei" (June 1, 2009), http://jasonf foster.blogspot.com/2009/06/.

would accept anti-evolutionary pro-life arguments. White would not accept Waltke's claim that all fetuses have a functioning moral capacity that reflects God's image. Even though Waltke believes that a conceptus is marked by sin, I doubt that he would accept extreme fundamentalist views that aborted fetuses of unbelieving parents are sent to hell. Pro-life Genesis-based arguments for fetal personhood—whether scholarly or popular—are conflicted, confused, and at cross-purposes within the pro-life Christian community. They fail to achieve more than asserting the uncontroversial point that fetuses are human; none makes a plausible biblical case that fetuses are persons to which the Genesis 1 text applies.

Imago Dei in the New Testament—Discipleship, Not Ontology

Crafting a pro-life biblical understanding of fetal personhood is difficult based on the few verses in Hebrew Scripture about the *imago Dei* or life in the womb. Pro-life arguments become even more tenuous when one tries to find New Testament support for fetuses created in God's image. White, not surprisingly, finds in the New Testament an affirmation of his favorite theme: procreation. He makes a weak attempt to argue that Jesus' genealogy or the fact that Christ is spoken of as "firstborn" and "Son" lends supposedly "strong support" for his claim that pro-life Christians should spread the *imago Dei* through reproduction.[41] In the New Testament Waltke finds an affirmation of his traducian and literalist reading of the Adam-and-Eve story.[42] Gushee is more circumspect and concedes that *imago* discourse in the New Testament differs from that of the Genesis text. New Testament discussions of the image of God address both "ascribed sacredness" (because of redemption that Christ accomplished on behalf of sinners) as well as "imperative calls for followers of Christ to cooperate with a Christ-shaped transformative process," or what might be called sanctification.[43] Gushee concurs with what most exegetes and theologians affirm, that the New Testament references to the *imago Dei* are largely christological and focused on the Christian life. There is nothing in the New Testament that indicates or even implies that one should think

41. White, "Corporeal Aspect and Procreative Function," 18. White does not discuss the nativity account of the encounter between the two pregnant women, Mary and her cousin Elizabeth, which other pro-life writers take as literal biblical revelation that personhood begins at conception. For example, Graham Scott insists that the "six month old fetus to be named John responded to the arrival of a zygote [Jesus] not even implanted in the wall of the womb." Scott, "Abortion and the Incarnation," *Journal of the Evangelical Theological Society* 17, no. 1 (1974): 37.
42. Waltke sees in Paul's statement that "'God has made from one all nations of men . . .' (Acts 17:26)" (trans. Waltke) an affirmation of a traducian interpretation of the Adam-and-Eve story about the human race descending from "the original life breathed into Adam and passed on seminally." Waltke, "Reflections from the Old Testament on Abortion," 11.
43. Gushee, *Sacredness of Human Life*, 109.

of fetuses as created in the image of God. Indeed, while Gushee believes that the New Testament supports a general ethic of "the sacred worth of human beings," he can offer no New Testament arguments to justify applying that ethic to uterine life.[44] For Christian theology, in my perspective, the meaning of the *imago Dei* referred to in Genesis should be normed by how that concept is formulated in the New Testament. Even a brief look at *imago* discourse in the New Testament leads us to conclude that it is exegetically and theologically mistaken to claim New Testament support for pro-life claims about the sacredness of fetuses bearing God's image.

In the preceding chapter I have already argued that Paul's Hellenistic Jewish background would not have led him to consider a fetus as a person created in God's image. When we look at Paul's and other New Testament references to the image of God, the evidence mounts that New Testament *imago* discourse speaks only obliquely to the issue of human created nature and, instead, is marked by a different set of emphases. The image of God is referenced predominantly in the genre of pastoral exhortations about discipleship. These exhortations imply an embodied believer and do not seem suitably applicable to a fetus existing in utero.

While the New Testament writers grounded their use of *imago* language in their understanding of Hebrew Scriptures and were no doubt familiar with the Genesis creation stories, the New Testament reflects attempts to carve out new theological directions for followers of Christ. As Claudia Welz notes, "The New Testament presupposes something that is not reported in the Hebrew Bible, namely that the human self needs to be renewed in the image of its creator (Colossians 3:10), and that it is first and foremost Christ who is the image of the invisible God (2 Corinthians 4:4; Colossians 1:15)."[45] Similarly, David Kelsey argues that "the principal anthropological significance of the notion of the *imago Dei* emerges, not from its role in Genesis 1:26–27, but from its role in christological contexts in the New Testament"—that is, Christ as the image of God.[46] The texts with the most direct allusion to Genesis 1:27 are in James 3:9 and 1 Corinthians 11:7–9; however, the purpose of these texts is not to explicate the nature of humans as the image of God. The author of James addresses the rude speech of those who curse their fellow humans "made in the likeness of God" (Jas. 3:9). The Corinthians text offers

44. Gushee, *Sacredness of Human Life*, 114. Gushee debates with Richard Hays on this point. I will discuss Hays's New Testament ethic of abortion in chap. 6.

45. Claudia Welz, "*Imago Dei*: References to the Invisible," *Studia Theologica—Nordic Journal of Theology* 65, no. 1 (2011): 79–80.

46. David H. Kelsey, *Eccentric Existence: A Theological Anthropology*, vol. 2 (Louisville, KY: Westminster John Knox Press, 2009), 938. To the extent that creation themes are alluded to in New Testament texts, Kelsey argues, they draw more from the wisdom tradition than from the Genesis creation accounts and are not intended to explicate human nature ontologically.

an "obscurely argued" polemic about women's head coverings, implying that veiling practices follow from the claim that men image God "but woman is the reflection of man (1 Cor 11:7)"—a claim that contradicts the Genesis affirmation that men and women are created in God's image.[47] As F. LeRon Shults explains, "Paul and the other New Testament authors are not looking backward at Adam and Eve, but forward to what lies ahead"—namely, the kingdom that Christ has inaugurated.[48] In short, there is scant biblical basis for deriving a cohesive, general ontology of human nature from the New Testament.

In terms of genre, New Testament *imago* discourse can be mostly categorized as "pastoral exhortation" to the faithful,[49] as seen, for example, in Paul's statement that God has called believers to be "conformed to the image of his Son" (Rom. 8:29). The agential or participatory aspects of the *imago Christi* predominate: believers are exhorted to be transformed by the work of the Holy Spirit so that they may "bear the image of the man of heaven" (1 Cor. 15:49) and be "conformed to the body of his glory" (Phil. 3:21).[50] This call for the believer to be conformed to the image of Christ properly applies to agents capable of some response to this call. Even if the transformation of the sinner is acknowledged to be a graced process, it is never completely without the assent, will, or agency of the believer. Colossians 3 speaks of believers having "clothed [them]selves with the new self, which is being renewed in knowledge according to the image of its creator" (v. 10), which emphasizes participation or *theōsis* in Christ.[51] Ephesians similarly exhorts believers: "Clothe yourselves with the new self, created according to the likeness of God in true righteousness and holiness" (4:24). This transformation may be understood in a Roman Catholic mode of grace perfecting nature, or a Protestant mode of *sola gratia* and *sola fide*, or an Eastern Orthodox mode of deification—nevertheless, the actual participation of the individually embodied believer is indispensable. The image of Christ rests on all creatures insofar as all things "on earth or in heaven" were created in and through Christ (Col. 1:20);[52] however, even

47. Kelsey, *Eccentric Existence*, 2:939.
48. F. LeRon Shults, *Reforming Theological Anthropology: After the Philosophical Turn to Relationality* (Grand Rapids: Wm. B. Eerdmans Publishing Co., 2003), 239–40.
49. Kelsey, *Eccentric Existence*, 2:1003.
50. For a discussion of this "strong" participatory aspect, see Kathryn Tanner, *Christ the Key* (Cambridge: Cambridge University Press, 2010), 37, 58. The strength of the image derives in part from the fact that the believer is participating in and through Christ, who is himself a perfect image of God. See K. Tanner, *Christ the Key*, 13–14.
51. See Benjamin C. Blackwell, "You Are Filled in Him: *Theosis* and Colossians 2–3," *Journal of Theological Interpretation* 8, no. 1 (2014): 117–18.
52. This is similar to what Tanner calls a "weak" level of participation in the image of God; K. Tanner, *Christ the Key*, 23. By weak, Tanner does not mean insignificant, since this level of participation is synonymous with creaturely existence itself. See K. Tanner, *Christ the Key*, 8.

in this ancient christological hymn, the writer's intention is not to explicate humanity's original created nature but to exhort believers to "continue . . . steadfast in the faith" and to "toil and struggle" (Col. 1:23, 29). It goes without saying that the existence of a fetus in the womb does not cohere theologically with the idea of being called to toil and struggle in the faith.

A second important aspect of the New Testament's *imago* statements is that only a creature who is an embodied, "living being" (1 Cor. 15:45) can bear Christ's image. As New Testament scholar Max Turner explains, when believers are called to be "sons/children" of God (John 1:12), this relationship is spiritual but also "establishes the importance of 'bodily' existence for authentic human personhood."[53] For Turner, in the New Testament's view of renewal, the believer is called, instructed, and exhorted to be clothed with "the new self, created according to the likeness of God" revealed in Christ (Eph. 4:24). The person to whom this call is directed is best defined as "an individual who is publicly identifiable as a distinct, continuous and integrated social location, . . . whence communication may originate and to which it may be directed."[54] This view of individual embodiment informs the distinction Turner makes between a zygote (a genetically "individuated" human but not yet a living body) and a "stereotypical" born person who "is publicly identifiable as . . . distinct, continuous and integrated [and] who has the capacity for autonomous engagement." A zygote is far from having functional autonomy; whereas a child able to be born is welcomed by a community, such as a believing family or a congregation that can begin directing the child toward a "theocentric relationship in the image of Christ."[55] The call to be clothed with a new self in Christ should be seen as directed to persons who have begun their bodily, independent life journey.

Even this brief discussion of *imago* passages in the New Testament indicates the persistent emphasis on the believer's call to participate in the process of conforming their minds and bodies to the image of God as found in Christ. From this perspective, the *imago Dei* cannot be said to apply to a fetus, much less an embryo—not because God's Spirit might not rest on one or even all embryos and fetuses, but because the New Testament does not address a being existing in its mother's womb as a disciple. The idea that God's Spirit does rest in a special way on some beings in the womb is, however, a theme

53. Max Turner, "Approaching 'Personhood' in the New Testament, with Special Reference to Ephesians," *Evangelical Quarterly* 77, no. 3 (July 2005): 218, 221. Max Turner is Professor Emeritus of New Testament at London School of Theology.
54. Turner, "Approaching 'Personhood' in the New Testament," 230.
55. Turner, "Approaching 'Personhood' in the New Testament," 230; on 231 Turner briefly engages the fetal personhood debate and takes a liberal developmental approach to fetal personhood, which is similar to many feminist pro-choice theologians and ethicists. My critical assessment of this viewpoint is given in chap. 5.

in some passages of Hebrew Bible and a few New Testament verses. These verses are enthusiastically quoted by pro-life writers, not as proof that all fetuses are persons created in God's image but as proof—to my mind, dubious—that all fetuses are persons predestined to be born.

ARE FETUSES PREDESTINED TO BE BORN?

Many pro-life writers argue for personhood from conception onward based on the prenatal call of prophets or other chosen figures in the Bible. A number of well-known and poetic verses express this idea. The psalmist praises God, saying, "You knit me together in my mother's womb. . . . Your eyes beheld my unformed substance" (Ps. 139:13, 16), and the prophet Isaiah proclaims, "The LORD called me before I was born, while I was my mother's womb he named me" (Isa. 49:1). Pro-life writers see this same theme of God at work in the womb presented in the Gospel stories of the birth of John the Baptist and Jesus. They extrapolate from these and other similar verses mentioning prenatal life in order to make claims about God's providential protection and plan for all embryos and fetuses: "Since he provides for their protection, it is clear that he wills that they be born."[56] In other words, if a conception occurs, one should assume that God elects or predestines a person to be born.

I raise two objections to this theology of predestined unborn persons: first, this approach extrapolates a universal theological claim from a few, mostly poetic, verses in the Hebrew Bible or Luke's nativity stories;[57] second, applying notions of predestination, election, or providence to human reproductive matters is a biologically deterministic way of doing theology. Pro-life authors claim to have found a providential pattern of "how the unborn are regarded by God";[58] however, readers who do not come to the text with a predetermined idea of fetal personhood will see these pro-life efforts as a crude form of eisegesis: finding in the Bible the idea that one brings to it. Moreover, there is a lack of coherence among pro-life scholars about how to determine which pregnancies display God's providential will that a fetal person be born.

A few examples will suffice to display the problematic ways in which pregnancy and prenatal life are construed providentially in some pro-life writings. As we have seen, pro-life appeals to creation in God's image are hermeneutically convoluted and conflict with each other theologically. The same problem

---

56. O'Mathuna, "The Bible and Abortion," 207.
57. An early critique of this pro-life view can be found in Robert N. Wennberg, *Life in the Balance: Exploring the Abortion Controversy* (Grand Rapids: Wm. B. Eerdmans Publishing Co., 1985), 60–63.
58. O'Mathuna, "The Bible and Abortion," 206.

occurs in pro-life views about ordained birth. According to the Jesuit biblical scholar William Kurz, the Bible presents humans as the actors, yet God is in control not just of the fetal life but of the entire procreative process. Referencing Job 10:10, Kurz explains that the phrase "'Didst thou not pour me out like milk' . . . refers to God's agency [in] the pouring out of the seminal fluid into the female organism." The message conveyed by the Bible, according to Kurz, is that the depositing of semen in order to fertilize an ovum is under God's providential control, and "humans have no choice or decision in being so formed."[59] The reproductive process is a completely God-directed matter because God has a "purpose and destiny" for every zygote.[60] For Kurz, God is directly involved in every conception, and a successful conception implies God's will for a child to be born. To give biblical support for this claim, Kurz references a fairly standard set of passages used in pro-life literature such as "The LORD called me from the womb, from the body of my mother He named my name" (Isa. 49:1 ESV).[61] Reading these passages together "clearly shows God's role in the creation of human life and His plans for human lives even before and certainly from their conception."[62] Despite Kurz's claim about what these verses "clearly" show, the most he (or other pro-life authors) can succeed in proving is a pattern of biblical "type scenes" about prenatal commissioning of particular important individuals.[63] However, to extrapolate from this biblical literary motif a claim about God's universal call to all uterine life is an unwarranted hermeneutical leap that would strike many readers as a thinly disguised eisegetical attempt to claim biblical evidence for the idea

59. William S. Kurz, "Genesis and Abortion: An Exegetical Test of a Biblical Warrant in Ethics," *Theological Studies* 47, no. 4 (1986): 675, 676. Kurz relies on Waltke for his interpretation of Job 10:10.

60. Kurz, "Genesis and Abortion," 673. One sees a similar argument about God's control over the processes of procreation in Calum MacKellar's description of procreation as the "creation of another person by God through the human couple." MacKellar, *The Image of God, Personhood and the Embryo* (London: SCM Press, 2017), 87.

61. Kurz also mentions Pss. 51:5–6; 139:13–17; Isa. 49:1–5; Jer. 1:5; Luke 1:15; Gal. 1:15. See Kurz, "Genesis and Abortion," 675–78.

62. Kurz, "Genesis and Abortion," 673 n. 17. Francis Beckwith further argues that drawing a distinction between a person and a developing but not fully human person would have been a modern "foreign frame of reference" unknown to the biblical authors. Francis Beckwith, "Brave New Bible: A Reply to the Moderate Evangelical Position on Abortion," *Journal of the Evangelical Theological Society* 33, no. 4 (1990): 493. On the contrary. It is highly likely, based on Exod. 21:22–25, that the ancient biblical authors, familiar as they must have been with miscarriage, understood the distinction between a formed and unformed human being. See my discussion of this passage in chap. 1.

63. On type scenes in the Bible, generally, see Robert Alter, *The Art of Biblical Narrative*, revised and updated (New York: Basic Book, 2011), 57–60; on biblical uterine commissioning scenes and their parallels in other ancient Near Eastern texts, see Yosefa Raz, "Jeremiah 'Before the Womb': On Fathers, Sons, and the Telos of Redaction in Jeremiah 1," in *Prophecy and Power: Jeremiah in Feminist and Postcolonial Perspective*, ed. Christl M. Maier and Carolyn J. Sharp (London: Bloomsbury, 2014), 94–98.

one brought to one's reading of the text. When Kurz concludes that "if God has a plan for humans from the womb, . . . this is relevant evidence against the right of other humans to abort God's plan by killing the fetus God has chosen," his argument does not rest on any solid biblical basis other than a few literary type scenes.[64]

Like Kurz, other pro-life writers affirm that God predestines in-utero life to be born but, unlike Kurz, some also find ways to argue for some exceptions. South African Reformed theologian Nico Vorster cites Psalm 139 and Job 10 as scriptural proof that "abortion is clearly wrong since every person is created by God according to a fore-ordained [*sic*] plan, and each one receives its calling even before its birth." From his conservative Calvinist perspective, the sin of abortion is not just the killing of a single fetal life but also the attempt to thwart God's providential plan. Besides being weakened by the same eisegetical move found in Kurz's exposition, Vorster's argument has internal inconsistencies. On the one hand, Vorster states that the biblical text indicates that "it is immoral to deliberately interrupt the natural process" of life in the womb.[65] On the other hand, Vorster argues that not every pregnancy can be automatically declared as ordained by God, since pregnancy from rape is a sign "that such life is not part of God's foreordained plan."[66] This claim is asserted and not biblically argued, so one can only assume that Vorster is relying on some principle of compassion or a sensitivity to the moral implications of forced pregnancy which overrule his previously stated biblical principle that uterine life, in and of itself, is a sign of God's will.

Gordon-Conwell Theological Seminary professor John Davis approaches the predestination issue in terms of Paul's discussion of Jacob and Esau being elected by God in their mother's womb in Romans 9.[67] Davis draws the conclusion that God had a plan for these two fetuses; even though they may not have yet developed "marks of 'personhood,'" their lives were part of God's "sovereign initiative in election."[68] Davis takes care not to draw a definitive theological conclusion that all fetuses are thereby elected by God to be born, and he suggests that some references to life in the womb might be "metaphorical."[69] However, one should not conclude that because Davis, in

---

64. Kurz, "Genesis and Abortion," 677.
65. Nico Vorster, "The Value of Human Life," *The Ecumenical Review* 59, no. 2–3 (2007): 381.
66. Vorster, "The Value of Human Life." Some pro-life writers urge women to carry their pregnancies resulting from rape. See Francis J. Beckwith, "Answering the Arguments for Abortion Rights (Part Two): Arguments from Pity, Tolerance, and Ad Hominem," *Christian Research Journal* 13, no. 3 (1991): 11–12. I will say more about the issue of abortion and rape in chap. 4.
67. Rom. 9:11–12: "Even before they had been born or had done anything good or bad (so that God's purpose of election might continue, not by works but by his call) she was told, 'The elder shall serve the younger.'"
68. Davis, *Abortion and the Christian*, 47.
69. Davis, *Abortion and the Christian*, 49.

the role of biblical interpreter, allows for some indeterminacy of meaning in the biblical passages referencing life in the womb, his position translates into a moderate or compassionate pro-life stance. Just the opposite. Davis holds a firm anti-abortion position. He opposes abortion even in the case of rape, arguing that the Bible supports the claim that "newly conceived life is an *actual* human being," which would mean continuing the pregnancy "would take precedence over the possible hardship and inconvenience to the woman" who had been raped.[70] He does not merely assert this as a moral point of view to which the Christian woman should adhere; he also vigorously supports the so-called human life amendment to the U.S. Constitution, which would define all abortion as homicide.[71] Thus, even though Davis concedes that the Bible does not definitively say that God elects every fetus to be born, he feels justified in advocating politically for a complete abortion ban so that all women, including those who are raped, would be prevented from obtaining an abortion.

The idea of the unborn predestined by God is rampant in popular pro-life literature, which reflects an approach to the biblical text that is more literalist than those of the scholars discussed above, but the conclusions about predestined fetuses are similar. One pro-life Web site asserts that the "Bible most definitely condemns abortion," as exemplified in the fact that David and Jeremiah and others "were predestined by God" in the womb.[72] Another Web site describes various passages referring to life in the womb as a "biblical fetology" indicating that "all the days which God decreed for the fashioning of a fetus . . . were written and set" in God's "book."[73] Another pro-life writer situates these biblical verses about life in the womb within a "cosmology" that reveals "God's very being and nature [to be] defined by *begetting*" and that God's "providential and salvific work" is focused on preserving the life of each unborn child.[74]

70. Davis, *Abortion and the Christian*, 64. Davis also bases his opinion on specious medical evidence that pregnancy from rape is rare because "psychological trauma tends to inhibit normal ovulation, and men who commit this crime are frequently infertile because of other aberrant sexual behavior." Davis, *Abortion and the Christian*, 64. Some research even indicates that per-incident rates of conception may be higher for forced as compared to consensual intercourse. See Jonathan A. Gottschall and Tiffani A. Gottschall, "Are Per-Incident Rape-Pregnancy Rates Higher than Per-Incident Consensual Pregnancy Rates?," *Human Nature* 14, no. 1 (2003): 1–20.
71. See Davis, *Abortion and the Christian*, 93, 94.
72. David Factor, "The Bible and Abortion: Pro-choice or Pro-life?," http://www.eaglesnest home.com/bible.htm.
73. "What Does the Bible Say about Abortion?," *American Right to Life*, http://americanrtl.org /what-does-the-bible-say-about-abortion.
74. Joe Boot, "The Cosmology of Killing, Part III," *Ezra Institute for Contemporary Christianity* (December 27, 2014), https://www.ezrainstitute.ca/resource-library/blog-entries/the-cosmology -of-killing-part-iii/.

Whether by scholarly or popular writers, pro-life interpretations of biblical verses about God's involvement in prenatal life bring predetermined assumptions about fetal rights to the biblical text and find there a confirmation. I do not refute the validity of seeing themes of God's providence in Jeremiah 1:5 or Psalm 139 or some other such text. My critique is that even if God decided to call a specific being developing in the womb to an important prophetic or kingly task, one can only logically conclude that God has called that particular being. The apostle Paul applied this prophetic-call trope to himself (Gal. 1:15); however, I see nothing in Paul's writings indicating that he thought all fetuses were called by God merely because he believed he had been.[75] Nevertheless, pro-life proponents conclude that because the Bible speaks of God calling from the womb the prophet Jeremiah or John the Baptist or the apostle Paul to serve God's divine plan, the Christian should consider every embryo, by the sheer fact of having been fertilized, to be an unborn child predestined by God to be born.

Besides the dubious exegetical moves that these pro-life scholars engage in to support the idea of the predestination of all embryos, there are also troublesome theological implications. When pro-life writers appeal to Jeremiah 1:5 ("Before I formed you in the womb I knew you"), they are faced with the problem of implying the predestination of a being not yet conceived, which could also imply a disembodied soul. Unless one wishes to espouse a theological anthropology of preexistent souls—most notably associated with the early third-century theologian Origen and denounced as heretical by the early church[76]—one has to be more circumspect about claiming biblical support for the idea that God ordains even not-yet-conceived beings to be born.[77] Pro-life theologians would do well to attend more carefully to authorities like Thomas Aquinas, who rejected the idea that any biblical prophet's special calling from the womb should be automatically applied to others.[78]

Another troubling aspect of applying notions of predestination, election, or providence in matters of human reproduction is that it is a biologically deterministic way of speaking about God's acts. Most theologians working with a doctrine of providence today caution against using the notion of God's rule to

75. For my discussion of Paul's views on fetal life, see chap. 1.
76. See Ted Nelson, "Traducianism? Creationism? What Has an Ancient Debate to Do with the Modern Debate over Abortion?" *Denison Journal of Religion* 13, no. 1 (2014): 3.
77. Another problematic implication is that the notion of God predestining disembodied souls would preclude the use of contraception or even natural family planning, since one might inadvertently thwart a predestined preexistent soul from being conceived.
78. "Nor are we to believe that any others, not mentioned by Scripture, were sanctified in the womb." Thomas Aquinas, *Summa Theologica*, trans. Father of the Eastern Dominican Province (New York: Benzinger, 1947), III Q.27, a.6, resp., https://dhspriory.org/thomas/summa/TP/TP027.html#TPQ27A6THEP1.

find divine cause and effect in world events or personal histories. David Fergusson explains that "particular events may . . . be received gratefully in this [providential] light—birth, marriage, and sometimes even death—but their reception as such must always be provisional and tentative [because] . . . our vision is partial at best, and our confession at this juncture remains a modest one."[79] If one accepts (which any theologian who is circumspect about claims of immediate revelation must) that all knowledge about God's will is partial, then one cannot make a sweeping claim that either a particular fetus is destined to be born or that all fetuses are destined to be born.

I think it is safe to say that no Christian woman who aborts does so because she claims prophetically to know that her fetus was *not* predestined by God and, therefore, the abortion is carrying out God's will. All the woman can do is to determine, to the best of her ability, whether or not she herself is called to pregnancy and motherhood as part of her Christian identity and vocation. To suggest that the biological reality of a woman becoming pregnant always and necessarily entails the religious requirement that she bring that fetus to life eviscerates the agential aspect of following Christ. One Christian woman might experience becoming pregnant with a sense of assurance that it is God's will that she become a mother, but few serious theologians speak of bearing a child as something for which a woman is predestined—with the exception of Mary in some Catholic theologies.[80] I urge pro-life theologians to reconsider espousing theologically and biblically questionable views about the predestination of fetuses that could result in enforced pregnancy. The pro-life argument for predestined fetuses implies that there is a biblical basis for urging or even compelling a woman to gestate every pregnancy. I argue that the biblical basis is weak and entails highly questionable notions that God's will is coterminous with the biological event of the fertilization of an ovum. Based on my assessment, pro-life proponents have not come close to making a convincing case for predestined fetal personhood that would justify overruling a woman's exercise of moral discernment in deciding what she will do regarding an unwanted pregnancy.

Within the diversity of women's experiences of and thinking about abortion, we can affirm that the demise of a fetus, whether by miscarriage or abortion, is a loss not just because any and all parts of God's creation have value but also because it was the ending of a being that lived intimately connected to a woman's body. Most women who have had an abortion know that the abortion was not nothing. Christian women have the religious responsibility

---

79. David Fergusson, "The Theology of Providence," *Theology Today* 67, no. 3 (2010): 276.
80. See Juniper B. Carol, "The Absolute Predestination of the Blessed Virgin Mary," *Marian Studies* 31, no. 1 (1979): 188–90; Edward T. Oakes, "Predestination and Mary's Immaculate Conception: An Evangelically Catholic Interpretation," *Pro Ecclesia* 21, no. 3 (2012): 290–92, 296.

to make this decision *coram Deo* (in the presence of God), but it must be their decision, not a foregone conclusion based on a dubious application of a doctrine of election or a doctrine of providence to uterine life.

One objective of this chapter was to expose the muddle of Christian pro-life biblical claims about fetal personhood. Despite the fact that the notion of the *imago Dei* has never had a singular definition in Christian history and is diversely interpreted even in recent theological writings, pro-life proponents claim that the Bible clearly reveals how the *imago Dei* speaks directly to the abortion issue. However, they struggle in their attempts to make a coherent biblical case that the notion of God's image in Genesis 1:26–27 even applies to embryos and fetuses. I have indicated a lack of coherence as well in pro-life claims that Scripture establishes that conception in and of itself is an indication of God's providence. Trained theologians should see that this kind of biological determinism threatens to undercut the mystery of God's providential will. Finally, morally and spiritually, to compel a pregnant woman, based on an appeal to ambiguous verses in the Bible, that her Christian duty is to do only one thing—gestate—diminishes her humanity as a creature bearing God's image and diminishes her agency as a follower of Christ.

3

Fetal Personhood
and Christ's Incarnation

A number of contemporary theologians have argued that abortion is not consistent with orthodox faith, based on how the incarnation is articulated in the creed of Chalcedon (451 CE) and subsequently developed in certain streams of patristic Christology. Chalcedon declared that the second person of the Trinity assumed a human "rational soul and body" in the womb of the Virgin Mary.[1] According to pro-life theologians, this declaration indicates that human personhood generally must be defined as having a body-soul unity immediately at conception. These theologians do not just offer this pro-life interpretation as one option for the Christian, but they also insist that if one wishes to adhere to orthodox belief about the incarnation, then the immediate ensoulment of all humans at conception must also be conceded. This chapter brings a critical analysis to bear on this doctrinal type of pro-life argument, as found in the writings of three scholars: David Jones (whose views on church history were discussed in chapter 1), John Saward (formerly an Anglican priest and now ordained in the Catholic Church), and Oliver Crisp (a professor in the Reformed tradition).[2]

---

1. "Chalcedon," trans. Robert Butterworth, in *Decrees of the Ecumenical Councils*, vol. 1, *Nicaea I to Lateran V*, ed. Norman Tanner, SJ (Washington, DC: Georgetown University Press, 1990), 86. All other quotes from the creed of Chalcedon are from this translation.
2. See biographical details for David Jones at https://www.bioethics.org.uk/detail/about _us/staff_and_fellows/david-jones; John Saward at http://www.christendom-awake.org/pages /jsaward/saward.html; and Oliver Crisp at https://www.fuller.edu/posts/oliver-crisp-accepts -new-position-at-st-andrews/.

Saward asserts that "apart from the novelty of its virginal manner, the conception of Christ is in all respects like ours,"[3] meaning the *when* of what theologians call the hypostatic union and the *when* of any person's beginning is the same: the moment of conception. Crisp concurs: "Christ is the template for what occurs in normal human conceptions. . . . Like Christ, other human beings are conceived with a complete human nature"—namely, a "body-soul composite" at conception.[4] This interpretation of the incarnation, he asserts, is the only "orthodox" one, as far as he is concerned,[5] and constitutes the theological basis for the conclusion that abortion at any stage is murder.[6] Given the centrality of the doctrine of the incarnation to Christian faith, it is vital to rebut what I deem to be these scholars' overly narrow and uncritical reading of their patristic sources, which at times seems to twist the words of the early church fathers to fit their current pro-life perspectives.

I will state from the start that I concur with one principle these theologians use—namely, that "whatever must be said of . . . the human embryo must be said of the embryonic Jesus, and vice versa."[7] Nevertheless, I argue that defining a person philosophically as a body-soul entity is not a Chalcedonian requirement of faith. The body-soul paradigm used by the early church was a Hellenistic one, and scholars now recognize it as encumbered by a number of problems, including negative views of the body and sexuality. There are other interpretations of the incarnation (more intelligible to modern Christians) that arguably adhere to the formal principles of Chalcedon without depending on a problematic definition of personhood as a body-soul composite beginning at conception. I present one promising alternative interpretation of the incarnation, based on the writings of Kathryn Tanner and Henry Novello, who combine patristic teachings on divinization with modern historical and evolutionary views of the world, in order to develop what I call a processive and emergent understanding of Christ's incarnation. This interpretation of the incarnation is arguably Chalcedonian and allows one to affirm that Christ's human development from conception coheres with any ordinary human embryonic and fetal development—namely, an incremental process toward full personhood. This approach challenges the pro-life claim that Chalcedonian faith requires belief in personhood from conception. Deflating this personhood claim in turn delegitimizes pro-life charges that abortion at any point in a pregnancy is murder of a person. The ways in which

3. John Saward, *Redeemer in the Womb: Jesus Living in Mary* (San Francisco: Ignatius Press, 1993), 12. See David Albert Jones, *The Soul of the Embryo* (London: Continuum, 2003), 129.

4. Oliver D. Crisp, *God Incarnate: Explorations in Christology* (London: T&T Clark, 2009), 109, 79.

5. Crisp, *God Incarnate*, 111

6. See Crisp, *God Incarnate*, 121 n. 26.

7. D. Jones, *Soul of the Embryo*, 138.

a processive, emergent view of the incarnation can also positively support pro-choice theological efforts—especially in order to combat the stigma of abortion as sin—will be taken up in the second part of this book.

A CRITIQUE OF PRO-LIFE USES OF CHALCEDON

The problems in contemporary pro-life appeals to Chalcedonian theology are multiple; I will present three. First, pro-life theologians narrowly focus on select passages from a few early church fathers, which seem to determine the timing of the incarnation but actually are more concerned with other issues. This selectiveness leaves the reader with an uncomfortable sense of cherry-picked proof texts from the ancient sources. Second, these pro-life theologians uncritically adopt the Hellenistic body-soul anthropology of their patristic sources, seemingly unconcerned by problematic entailments (i.e., a soul-body hierarchy and denigration of sexuality). Third, they either endorse or remain uncritically silent on patristic formulations about the inviolate womb of Mary, with debilitating consequences for believing women who live real sexual and reproductive lives. All three of these problems amount to an uncritical use or a misuse of the source material that significantly weakens pro-life arguments for a Chalcedonian basis for personhood at conception.

Chalcedon—A History Reality Check

The controversies—political and theological—that swirled around the convening and the decisions of Chalcedon have been documented and studied by historians, so I merely summarize some relevant points for my purposes of providing a reality check.[8] Chalcedon is authoritative (but not revelatory) for Christianity, and not everything the church fathers said about it should be taken at face value. Many of the bishops who gathered at Chalcedon at the request of the emperor did not even want to formulate a new creed, contending that the Council of Nicaea (325) stated what was sufficient for the faith. The Chalcedon participants eventually drafted a new statement but did so "under heavy pressure from both imperial authorities and papal representatives."[9] The creed affirmed Christ to be

8. See Henry Chadwick, *The Early Church*, rev. ed. (London: Penguin Books, 1993), 200–205; Richard A. Norris Jr., ed. and trans., *The Christological Controversy* (Philadelphia: Fortress Press, 1980), 123–59; Michael Slusser, "The Issues in the Definition of the Council of Chalcedon," *Toronto Journal of Theology* 6, no. 1 (1990): 63–69.

9. See Richard Price and Michael Gaddis, ed. and trans., with Introduction, *The Acts of the Council of Chalcedon*, vol. 1 (Liverpool: Liverpool University Press, 2005), 37 n. 137.

the same perfect in divinity and perfect in humanity; the same truly
God and truly man, of a rational soul and a body; consubstantial with
the Father as regards his divinity, and the same consubstantial with us
as regards his humanity; . . . begotten before the ages from the Father
as regards his divinity, and in the last days, the same for us and for our
salvation, from Mary, the virgin God-bearer, as regards his humanity;
. . . one and the same Christ, Son, Lord, only-begotten, acknowledged
in two natures which undergo no confusion, no change, no division,
no separation; . . . the property of both natures is preserved and comes
together into a single person and a single subsistent being.[10]

The overriding issue that Chalcedon tried to address was how to speak of the
combined divine and human natures in Christ—what theologians of the day
referred to as the hypostatic union.

Part of the background for Chalcedon, which comes into play for its pro-
life defenders today, was the attempt to fend off two heresies of opposite
kinds: Apollinarianism and Nestorianism. From the time of the Council of
Nicaea (325), two "schools" of theology developed, associated with different urban centers of learning: Alexandrine theology, tending to focus on
the unity of divine and human; and Antiochene theology, tending to focus
on how they were separate. The fourth-century theologian Apollinaris of
Laodicea represented what F. LeRon Shults calls an anti-Arian "Alexandrian
enthusiasm."[11] Apollinaris emphasized how Christ's divinity held the divine
and human natures together by means of "the Logos as the mind of Christ,
empowering the human body of Jesus in place of the usual rational human
soul."[12] Chalcedon condemned this position as heretical because it implied
that the nature assumed by the Logos was not fully human, because it lacked
a human soul. Apollinarianism was believed to threaten soteriology, based on
the widely known rule of faith expressed by Cappadocian theologian Gregory
of Nazianzus that what is not assumed is not healed. If the Logos did not
assume a human soul along with Jesus' body, then Christ could not heal a
complete person, body and soul.

Some early church thinkers, who tried to steer clear of Apollinarianism,
were tempted to doctrinal enthusiasms in the opposite direction. Antiochene-
influenced thinkers were appalled at how expressions of popular piety lost
sight of the distinction of natures in Christ. Nestorius, the fifth-century bishop
of Constantinople, recoiled at hymns that spoke about "God in swaddling

10. "Chalcedon," in N. Tanner, *Decrees of the Ecumenical Councils*, 1:86.
11. F. LeRon Shults, *Christology and Science* (Hampshire, UK: Ashgate, 2008), 26, 27.
12. Mark Harris, "When Jesus Lost His Soul: Fourth-Century Christology and Modern Neuroscience," *Scottish Journal of Theology* 70, no. 1 (2017): 2.

bands,"[13] and he attempted to suppress such talk.[14] His attack on hymns might have been allowed to pass, but his challenge to the title of Mary as *Theotokos* (God bearer) was beyond the pale for many church and imperial authorities, and Nestorianism was condemned at the Council of Ephesus (431),[15] which affirmed that "the Word took flesh and became man and from his very conception united to himself the temple he took from her [Mary]," and "from the very womb of his mother he was so united."[16] As we will see below, pro-life theologians read into these statements a creedal affirmation not just about the nature of the hypostatic union but its definitive in-utero timing. This problematic historical and theological approach creates a weak basis for their pro-life claims.

Pro-life Misuses of the Patristic Sources

We see an example of the first problem mentioned above (proof-texting from patristic sources about the timing of the hypostatic union) in Jones's discussion of the "Formula of Reunion," a document penned amid feuding factions by Bishop Cyril of Alexandria almost two decades before Chalcedon.[17] A dominant issue was the *Theotokos* controversy, about which Cyril wrote: "We confess the holy virgin to be the mother of God because God the [W]ord took flesh and became man, and *from his very conception* united to himself the temple he took from her"[18] (the italics are added by Jones to emphasize his point about the timing). However, the Formula's intent was not to establish that the hypostatic union happened in the blink of an eye; rather, the point was that it happened with human flesh from Mary, hence the christological basis for her title *Theotokos*. In addition, even though the church leaders who drafted Chalcedon drew from the "Formula of Reunion," they chose not to include the turn of phrase "from his very conception" in the creed itself.[19] However, it is precisely short phrases like this one that pro-life theologians selectively emphasize as a basis for their claim that all personhood begins at conception. Jones seems to read into this phrase from the Formula his own

---

13. "Nestorius of Constantinople," *Westminster Handbook of Patristic Theology*, ed. John Anthony McGuckin (Louisville, KY: Westminster John Knox Press, 2004), 238.

14. Shults, *Christology and Science*, 33.

15. For a fascinating history of anti-Nestorian factions preceding Chalcedon, see Price and Gaddis, *Acts of the Council of Chalcedon*, 17–33.

16. "Ephesus," trans. Anthony Meredith, in N. Tanner, *Decrees of the Ecumenical Councils*, 1:42, 70.

17. See Price and Gaddis, *Acts of the Council of Chalcedon*, 62–64.

18. D. Jones, *Soul of the Embryo*, 129.

19. Richard A. Norris Jr., "Chalcedon Revisited: A Historical and Theological Reflection," in *New Perspectives in Historical Theology: Essays in Memory of John Meyendorff*, ed. Bradley Nassif (Grand Rapids: Wm. B. Eerdmans Publishing Co., 1996), 142.

pro-life beliefs when, in fact, the early church fathers were preoccupied with different theological concerns.

Similarly, John Saward quotes a passage from a 634 CE synod letter by Sophronius, patriarch of Jerusalem, that Christ "was made man in truth at the very instant of his conception in the all-holy Virgin."[20] Saward places this letter in an unbroken line from Chalcedon and implies that Sophronius's intention was to confirm the *when* issue of the incarnation, which Saward, like Jones, believes was a key accomplishment of Chalcedon. In fact, Sophronius was caught up in a very different and contentious debate—less about the timing of the incarnation (which he addressed obliquely primarily to refute any lingering Nestorianism) and more about whether it was proper to speak of Christ as having one or two wills.[21] Saward presents Sophronius's letter as if it represents a settled post-Chalcedonian theological consensus, because of the letter's acceptance at the third ecumenical council of Constantinople (680).[22] David Jones follows Saward's lead, concluding that Sophronius gave the authoritative "working-out of the definition of Chalcedon" on the issue of the timing of the hypostatic union, such that one can conclude that to be "fully human" means possessing "a human soul from conception."[23] However, scholars of the patristic era emphasize the ongoing unsettled nature of the theological language used to describe Christ's divine and human natures, and Sophronius's letter is no exception.[24] Thus, even a cursory look at the Chalcedonian period shows that trying to read patristic statements as pronouncing on the timing of the hypostatic union, in order to draw pro-life conclusions for today, distorts the complexity of the doctrinal issues and how they were debated in the patristic era.

This problem of trying to draw definitive pro-life principles from patristic writings is acute when it comes to how these pro-life theologians rely on the early seventh-century Byzantine monk Maximus the Confessor, whose interpretation of Chalcedon they invest with a theological authority that cannot be justified. Saward and Jones find in Maximus a confirmation of their understanding that Christ "possessed the complete nature and existence" of a human person from the moment of his conception and that this christological point reveals the true nature of every in-utero human ensoulment.[25]

20. Saward, *Redeemer in the Womb*, 5. In *Soul of the Embryo*, 131, D. Jones borrows this Sophronius quote directly from Saward's book.

21. Price and Gaddis, *Acts of the Council of Chalcedon*, 55.

22. Saward, *Redeemer in the Womb*, 4.

23. D. Jones, *Soul of the Embryo*, 131.

24. See Pauline Allen, "Sophronius and His *Synodical Letter*," in *Sophronius of Jerusalem and Seventh-Century Heresy: The Synodical Letter and Other Documents*, ed. and trans. Pauline Allen (Oxford: Oxford University Press, 2009), 29–33.

25. Saward, *Redeemer in the Womb*, 9, 10, 11; see D. Jones, *Soul of the Embryo*, 136.

The path from Maximus's interpretation of the hypostatic union to pro-life ethics today is syllogistically clear: "If Jesus acquired a rational soul at the moment of conception, and Jesus shares the same human nature as all other human beings, then everyone acquires a rational soul at conception."[26] Pro-life theologians elevate Maximus to the status of the "author of the crowning synthesis of Greek patristic theology," pick select quotes from his writings that seem to prove their pro-life points, and pretend not to notice that Maximus's synthesis comes at a price—namely, a dubious soul-body hierarchy and an antisexuality bias even within marriage.[27] The latter aspects of Maximus's patristic thought would not be acceptable for modern Christians, including, I presume, even these pro-life theologians; however, they do not assess Maximus critically in this regard.

Scholars agree that, for Maximus, the soul, which "is immortal, invisible, and incorporeal," is superior to the body, which "is mortal, visible, and corporeal."[28] The body is particularly inferior because it comes into being by the process of sexual intercourse and, hence, the passions and sin. For Maximus, cultivation of the spiritual faculties of the soul remained paramount, and he privileged the celibate, ascetic life and expressed a strong aversion to sexuality. Although procreation is allowed within marriage, Maximus believed it "amounts to the 'bestializing' of human nature so that in this act man resembles the irrational . . . animals."[29] Consequently, "the more human nature strives to perpetuate its existence through birth, the more it binds itself to the law of sin."[30] The remedy that the incarnation supplies in this regard is the breaking of the cycle of sinful procreation by means of Christ's unique incarnation. Not only is Christ conceived in a virginal womb, but "no sexual pleasure precedes the Lord's conception."[31] Christ became human in the absence of sexual passion from Mary, so that humanity could henceforth become divine by following the ascetic path as a foretaste of passionless resurrected existence.[32] For Maximus, Christ, who was seedlessly as well as passionlessly conceived,

---

26. D. Jones, *Soul of the Embryo*, 132. For Crisp's agreement with Saward on Maximus, see Oliver D. Crisp, *Divinity and Humanity: The Incarnation Reconsidered* (Cambridge: Cambridge University Press, 2007), 71.

27. Saward, *Redeemer in the Womb*, 8.

28. Adam G. Cooper, *The Body in St Maximus the Confessor: Holy Flesh, Wholly Deified* (Oxford: Oxford University Press, 2005), 106.

29. Cooper, *Body in St Maximus*, 215; see 80: Maximus believed sexual intercourse was introduced after the fall, and it was not possible to engage in sex without a sinful loss of rationality.

30. Maximus as quoted in Cooper, *Body in St Maximus*, 213.

31. Cooper, *Body in St Maximus*, 220.

32. "[Christ] purified nature from the law of sin (Rom. 7:23, 25; 8:2) in not having permitted pleasure to precede his incarnation on our behalf." Maximus as quoted in Paul M. Blowers and Robert L. Wilken, trans., *On the Cosmic Mystery of Jesus Christ: Selected Writings of St Maximus the Confessor* (Crestwood, NY: St. Vladimir's Seminary, 2003), 243.

is the "firstfruits" of other sex-abstinent persons who strive to approximate the mode of his "rationally animated holy flesh."[33] Even in the womb and after birth, Mary remained a virgin, "unharmed," because God "tightened the bonds of virginity in her, though she was a mother." Mary's inviolate state was necessary not only to preserve Christ free from "corruption"[34] but also to foreshadow the life of the Christian whose virginal soul will give birth to virtuous acts—preferably free from all sexual taint.[35]

To be fair, this antisexuality viewpoint was not atypical for patristic authors. However, it is problematic that Saward and Jones endorse Maximus's anthropology of ensoulment at conception, with no critical distance from his soul-body hierarchy and his denigration of sexuality that influence his interpretation of the incarnation.[36] It is almost as if, for Maximus, Mary's lack of passion in conceiving Jesus (about which Chalcedon says nothing) is as soteriologically important as her virginity. One cannot help but wonder if the immediacy Maximus posits of Jesus' conception might not, in part, be influenced by his assumption that it was an event untouched by any hint of sexual desire and, hence, should be thought of as quickly completed.

Needless to say, the insistence by these pro-life scholars that Chalcedon is correctly interpreted along the lines of what Maximus asserts renders heterodox some significant theologians in history, notably Thomas Aquinas. Following Aristotelian embryology, Aquinas believed ensoulment of a human being happened in stages, as one type of soul supplanted another, the last being the rational soul infused by God when the fetus was sufficiently formed. For the hypostatic union, however, Aquinas argued that Christ's ensoulment was unique because immediate at conception, a theological viewpoint that distinguishes him from Maximus.[37] Aquinas stated, "It was unbecoming that He should take to Himself a body as yet unformed. . . . Therefore, in the first instant in which the various parts of the matter were united together in the place of generation, Christ's body was both perfectly formed and assumed."[38]

---

33. Cooper, *Body in St Maximus*, 112.

34. Maximus, quoted in Cooper, *Body in St Maximus*, 220.

35. See Cooper, *Body in St Maximus*, 224.

36. Moreover, this uncritically positive estimation of Maximus continues to recycle among pro-life scholars. See Calum MacKellar, *The Image of God, Personhood and the Embryo* (London: SCM Press, 2017), 135.

37. See Robert Pasnau, *Thomas Aquinas on Human Nature: A Philosophical Study of* Summa Theologiae, *1a 75–89* (Cambridge: Cambridge University Press, 2002), 114; Pamela M. Huby, "Soul, Life, Sense, Intellect: Some Thirteenth-Century Problems," in *The Human Embryo: Aristotle and the Arabic and European Traditions*, ed. G. R. Dunstan (Exeter, Devon, UK: University of Exeter Press, 1990), 119.

38. Thomas Aquinas, *Summa Theologica*, trans. Fathers of the Eastern Dominican Province (New York: Benzinger, 1947), III Q.33 a.1, resp. (hereafter *ST*), http://dhspriory.org/thomas /summa/TP/TP033.html#TPQ33A1THEP1. Regarding Christ's gestation, Aquinas says little, except to posit that Mary gave birth to Jesus without pain and did not need to be attended by

Aquinas insisted that belief in the miraculously formed fetal Christ at conception should not govern one's views about how all humans are ensouled. Jones, Crisp, and Saward thus agree with Aquinas that the hypostatic union was instantaneous but reject Aquinas's claim that immediate ensoulment at conception was unique to Christ.[39] I do not endorse thinking about persons hylomorphically (as a body-soul unity);[40] however, if one is going to adopt this kind of viewpoint, it makes sense to affirm the scientific intuition behind Aquinas's medieval anthropology—namely, an ordinary human embryo could not possibly be formed enough to accept the infusion of its rational soul. In other words, even if Aquinas's embryology was deficient, he knew enough to affirm that human uterine life develops incrementally toward personhood. My proposal below argues that a doctrine of incarnation should not completely flout what science tells us about normal human embryonic development.[41]

Crisp seems to see the hermeneutical challenge of appropriating patristic-era vocabulary about conception; however, his solution is no less problematic than what Jones and Saward do. Crisp tries to translate obscure patristic terms (such as "flesh" and "seed") into modern scientific concepts in order to explain the details of the hypostatic union for a contemporary audience. Crisp redescribes the incarnation as "the miraculous asexual action of the Holy Spirit in generating the human nature of Christ in the womb of the Virgin Mary, using an ovum from the womb of the Virgin and supplying the missing genetic material (specifically the Y chromosomes) necessary for the production of the human male."[42] This kind of gynecological and embryological literalism is precisely what the early church seemingly wanted to avoid, for any number of reasons. The patristic theologians had a sense of how maternal blood, as they referred to it, developed into an embryo in relation to male seed,[43] but they declined to comment on the details of Christ's conception other than to assert that it was virginal. Crisp himself worries about the "docetic implications" of Jesus with only a partial set of humanly derived DNA; however, he speculates that Docetism is avoided if one can posit that a sufficient "threshold amount" of human nature was achieved through the genetic contribution of Mary's

---

midwives to help her. See Thomas Aquinas, *ST* III Q.35 a.6, ad 3, http://dhspriory.org/thomas/summa/TP/TP035.html#TPQ35A6THEP1.

39. See D. Jones, *Soul of the Embryo*, 140; Crisp, *God Incarnate*, 88; Saward, *Redeemer in the Womb*, 15–16. See also MacKellar, *Image of God*, 122–23.

40. Aquinas's type of hylomorphism mediated between an Aristotelian view of the soul as the form of the body and a Christian affirmation that the soul is an "incorporeal substance" able "to exist and to operate independently of the body." Pasnau, *Thomas Aquinas on Human Nature*, 72.

41. Most pro-life proponents believe that current embryology supports their claims of ensoulment at conception. My critique of these claims is given in the next chapter.

42. Crisp, *God Incarnate*, 79–80.

43. For a more ancient embryology, see my discussion in chap. 1. See also D. Jones, *Soul of the Embryo*, chap. 2.

ovum, so that one can affirm that Jesus was truly human not just apparently so.[44] I take Crisp's discussions about the Holy Spirit and DNA to be a kind of analytical theological thought experiment, and not a statement about doctrinal orthodoxy. Nevertheless, his attempt to articulate how one might reasonably assent to the notion of an immediate hypostatic union, in light of modern science, exposes the extraordinary lengths to which one must resort in order to delineate the *when* and *how* of the hypostatic union and then draw pro-life conclusions for today's believers.

Mary's Womb and Gestational Realism

The final criticism I raise about pro-life views of the incarnation is the lack of critical assessment of increasingly fantastical beliefs that arose during the patristic and early medieval period about Mary's inviolate womb. On this issue pro-life authors take two different stands, both equally problematic. Saward endorses the sacralizing of Mary's womb as part of his pro-life argument for seeing all embryos as sacred; Crisp considers the state of Mary's womb as theologically irrelevant to his pro-life claim about Christ's incarnation at conception, in effect reducing Mary's role to that of the human biological conduit for Christ's arrival on earth. Neither view is a requirement for Chalcedonian faith, and both views create damaging images for ordinary pregnant women today.

Mary's perpetual virginity is not just a quaint belief that flourished in patristic or medieval times or a belief circulating only in Roman Catholic or Eastern Orthodox circles today. The virginal conception of Christ is an evangelical article of faith, and the doctrine of the ever-virgin Mary was affirmed by the Protestant Reformers.[45] Most evangelicals and many other Protestants today reject the idea of Mary's perpetual virginity and will debate it vigorously with their Catholic counterparts, which indicates that it is not a dead topic in Christian circles.[46] What precisely should Christians take Chalcedon to mean by its declaration of "Mary, the virgin God-bearer," and does this creedal phrase require a pro-life stance? I argue that one can hold orthodox Christian beliefs without either sacralizing Mary's womb or rendering her gestational labors irrelevant to the incarnation.

---

44. Crisp, *God Incarnate*, 84.
45. See Timothy George, "The Blessed Virgin Mary in Evangelical Perspective," in *Mary, Mother of God*, ed. Carl E. Braaten and Robert W. Jenson (Grand Rapids: Wm. B. Eerdmans Publishing Co., 2004), 109.
46. See Dwight Longenecker and David Gustafson, *Mary: A Catholic-Evangelical Debate* (Grand Rapids: Brazos Press, 2003), chap. 4.

Ironically, the early church fathers may have condemned abortion, but they were viscerally ill-disposed to see fetuses, conceived and nourished by women's blood, as sacred images of God. It is not surprising that Marcionite and docetic theologians recoiled at the notion that God would ever deign to be enfleshed, much less from and in a woman's body. It took a concerted effort from theologians like Tertullian to fight against such views.[47] In reaction, Tertullian extolled how God stooped to associate with the supposed uncleanliness of the fluids and other matter in pregnancy, such as "the filth of the generative seeds within the womb, of the bodily fluid and the blood; the loathsome, curdled lump of flesh which has to be fed for nine months off this same muck."[48] Similarly the late fourth-century Latin theologian Jerome seemed to relish the theological significance of Christ's "humiliation" during gestation and birth: "the womb growing larger for nine months, the nausea, the birth, the blood."[49] Early church theologians believed that affirming Christ's humanity meant affirming that he took part in all these supposedly repulsive realities. In addition, Tertullian was adamant that Christ's birth obeyed the natural "law of the opened body," and thus Mary's womb was not inviolate during or after parturition.[50] Tertullian perhaps comes the closest of all the early church theologians to christological and Mariological thinking that attempted to remain scientifically intelligible according to the gynecological knowledge of the Greco-Roman period, which was clear about how a baby developed gestationally and was born.[51]

By the time of Chalcedon, theologians were not primarily fighting the Marcionites and Docetists, who undermined the reality of Christ's humanity; rather, they were striving to explicate, according to the metaphysics of their day, the relationship—specifically, the unity without confusion—of the divine and human natures of Christ. Patristic construals of the incarnation became entangled with fanciful gynecological beliefs about Mary's pure and undisturbed virginal womb. Theological and liturgical language morphed away from gestational realism, and early church writers increasingly portrayed the purity of Mary's womb and the serenity of all aspects of Christ's conception and birth. The fourth-century Cappadocian theologian Gregory

---

47. See Geoffrey D. Dunn, "Mary's Virginity *in Partu* and Tertullian's Anti-Docetism in *De Carne Christi* Reconsidered," *Journal of Theological Studies* 58, no. 2 (2007): 471–80.

48. Tertullian, *On the Flesh of Christ* 4, as quoted in Norris, *Christological Controversy*, 67.

49. Jerome, *The Perpetual Virginity of the Blessed Mary* 20, as quoted in Luigi Gambero, *Mary and the Fathers of the Church: The Blessed Virgin Mary in Patristic Thought*, trans. Thomas Buffer (San Francisco: Ignatius Press, 1999), 208.

50. Tertullian, *On the Flesh of Christ* 23, as quoted in Willemien Otten, "Christ's Birth of a Virgin Who Became a Wife: Flesh and Speech in Tertullian's *De carne Christi*," *Vigiliae Christianae* 51, no. 3 (1997): 247.

51. For more on Tertullian's views of gestation and birth, see chap. 1 above.

of Nyssa wrote that "as the Virgin did not know how the body that received divinity was formed in her own body, so neither did she notice the birth."[52] At the visitation of the angel, one fifth-century bishop said, Mary's "blood was quiet, flesh was still, her members slept, and the virgin's womb was entirely unmoved in that heavenly visit."[53] In addition, the church fathers emphasized the painlessness of parturition, because the lack of Mary's labor pangs was the physical signal that Jesus' conception was situated outside of the punishment for original sin that fell on Eve and her descendants. Even an authority like Basil, bishop of Caesarea (the brother of Gregory of Nyssa), who conceded that Mary's perpetual virginity was not an article of faith, noted that faithful believers "do not allow themselves to hear that the Mother of God (*Theotokos*) ceased at a given moment to be a virgin."[54] Mary's title, which was solidified as part of fourth- and fifth-century controversies about the meaning of the hypostatic union, became inextricably linked with widespread belief in her painless birth experience and postpartum virginity, despite the fact that such assertions flew in the face of what many early church leaders knew directly or indirectly about human birth.[55]

Pro-life authors take two different, both equally problematic, stands on this issue. Saward gives a straightforward endorsement of the doctrine of the ever-virgin Mary, asserting that, in gestation and through the birth process, "God the Word treats Mary's womb with infinite courtesy and gentleness, leaving, as he enters, without breaking its maidenly seal."[56] Even apart from the disturbing implications of this statement for understanding any other normal gestation and birth, there is the theological problem that the humanity of the embryonic Christ is suppressed in a docetic way. Claiming that an infant, conceived and gestated in Mary's womb, was born (as the creeds affirm, without any mention of a miracle at parturition), all the while leaving Mary's uterus, cervix, and vagina completely undisturbed, seems to deny the real humanity of Jesus. That said, Saward's concern is not to take on christological disputes

---

52. Gregory of Nyssa, *On the Song of Songs* 13, as quoted in Gambero, *Mary and the Fathers of the Church*, 158.

53. Peter Chrysologus, "*Sermon* 117," in *The Faith of the Early Fathers: Pre-Nicene and Nicene Era; A Source-Book of Theological and Historical Passages*, ed. and trans. William A. Jurgens, vol. 3 (Collegeville, MN: Liturgical Press, 1970), 267.

54. Basil of Caesarea, *On the Holy Generation of Christ* 5, as quoted in Gambero, *Mary and the Fathers of the Church*, 146.

55. For more on how these views developed in the medieval period, see Jacqueline Tasioulas, "'Heaven and Earth in Little Space': The Foetal Existence of Christ in Medieval Literature and Thought," *Medium Aevum* 76, no. 1 (2007): 24–48.

56. See Saward, *Redeemer in the Womb*, 58; on page 160 Saward also endorses the Catholic notion of Mary's sinlessness when he writes that in Mary's womb, Jesus "takes in all that she has to give, flesh from her bodily substance, love from her immaculate heart, . . . with immaculate generosity she gives it."

but to make a Mariological point with a pro-life message. He suggests that the preservation of Mary inviolate is a miraculous sign of the fetal Christ being divinely protected with his mother's undisturbed womb, so that if the Virgin's "womb has for nine months been found worthy of the presence of God, then the attack on the unborn is an act of sacrilege."[57] Just as the unborn Christ was protected and Mary's womb revered, so should all fetuses be protected and all wombs be seen as sanctified places of nurture.

Neither Crisp nor Jones addresses Mary's perpetual virginity—either to affirm or deny it. However, Crisp does suggest that it is possible to refrain from attributing to Mary any special gestational status generally. He argues that the condition of Mary's womb and hymen is theologically irrelevant to safeguarding what he considers to be two christological necessities—namely, that the hypostatic union happened at conception and that Christ remained sinless throughout his life. On both points, "the preservation of the Christ foetus from conception to birth (and thereafter) in a sinless state is a matter of the hypostatic union, not the Virgin Birth."[58] Furthermore, what has a bearing on abortion is the instantaneous aspect of the hypostatic union for the embryonic Christ, not Mary's virginity or the condition of her womb during or after the birth.

Crisp's lack of enthusiasm about ascribing to Mary's womb any theological significance can, in part, be attributed to his Protestant sensibilities. Crisp concludes that even belief in Mary's virginity is technically not a theological necessity but is, nevertheless, a traditional and "fitting" element of Christian faith. This viewpoint allows for a much more reduced claim about Mary: she was a virgin at the Annunciation, as indicated in the Bible, and then "became pregnant, gestated, and gave birth [to] . . . the sole and solitary person of the Son of God."[59] However, I perceive that there is more than Protestant reticence in Crisp's silence about Mary's sacred womb. There is what one might call an almost Alexandrine "enthusiasm" (to use Shults's term mentioned above) about how Christ's divine nature ensures what Crisp takes as christological requirements. The human components of his incarnation (such as embedding in Mary's womb, gestating, and being birthed) are theologically ancillary. Thus, Saward emphasizes the intimate gestational interaction of Mary and the divinely protected fetal Christ, which he believes secures the sanctity of Mary's womb—and all other wombs with unborn children. Crisp denies the theological necessity of positing Mary's inviolate womb and, instead, emphasizes the moment when the Word acquires the ensouled

57. Saward, *Redeemer in the Womb*, 165.
58. Crisp, *God Incarnate*, 98.
59. Crisp, *God Incarnate*, 101. "Fitting" is an important category for Crisp's argument; chap. 4 of his book is a sustained argument about "The 'Fittingness' of the Virgin Birth."

human embryo that will become Jesus—a christological emphasis he finds decisive for pro-life purposes as well.

For all their advocacy of protecting unborn life, these pro-life authors say almost nothing about ordinary gestation and birth. Saward's image of Mary's holy, unchanged womb distances her gestational experience from all other women's. Crisp gives an almost perfunctory nod to Mary for having birthed Jesus, and one is left with the impression that the birth happened, not because her water broke and she went into labor, but because it was theologically necessary for Christ to be born. Yet, it is precisely the gestational realities of embryonic and fetal development as well as women's experience of nausea, swollenness, heaviness, and the urge to push in labor that should not be ignored when speaking of the incarnation, since pregnancy and birthing are all of those bodily things. Pregnancy, including Mary's, should be seen in a realistic gynecological light; otherwise theologians will not be able to speak relevantly about the meaning of the incarnation in relation to women's experience of pregnancy, birth, reproductive loss, and abortion.

The above discussion has demonstrated that pro-life arguments about the incarnation privilege one stream of Chalcedonian thought and, in addition, focus in a distorting way on select passages that seem to pronounce on the timing of the incarnation. Moreover, the pro-life affinity for a particular patristic version of the hypostatic union (i.e., Maximus's) is marked by a lack of critical distance from that version's debilitating soul-body hierarchy and antisexuality bias. While pro-life theologians differ regarding what to say about Mary's womb, they promote either her impossibly inviolate womb or the decisive moment of Christ's conception in order to find theological grounds, which I deem tenuous, for a pro-life message.

A PROCESSIVE, EMERGENT VIEW
OF THE INCARNATION

The model to which I am drawn as a particularly fruitful place for rethinking the hypostatic union is a version of what is referred to in many theological circles as deification theology. This originally patristic approach to God-human relations, in terms of the perfecting or sanctifying of human nature, has a long history in Eastern Orthodoxy and has gained traction in contemporary theologies more associated with Christian traditions on the West.[60] The theological writings of Kathryn Tanner and Henry Novello are examples of this

---

60. See Roger E. Olson, "Deification in Contemporary Theology," *Theology Today* 64, no. 2 (2007): 188.

trend and, when read together, paint a picture of the incarnation as Christ's processive and emergent divinization. I argue that this interpretation of the incarnation is arguably Chalcedonian, reflects modern scientific views of fetal development and pregnancy, and challenges the very basis of pro-life claims about the nature of embryonic personhood.

Jesus' Deified Humanity: An Emergent, Historical Process

Tanner's christological writings are extensive, so I will restrict myself to her proposal about deification, which builds on the thought of primarily patristic theologians, who interpreted the incarnation as a process by which Jesus increased in wisdom and perfection toward full divinization.[61] Tanner elaborates on this motif in light of a more contemporary understanding of the "essentially historical character of human life," so that Jesus' deification is not seen as "happen[ing] all at once, but over the course of Jesus' life and death."[62] The Logos assuming Jesus' human nature was not an immediate union of substances but an interactive movement of the divine and human over a lifetime: "Each aspect of Jesus' life and death . . . is purified, healed and elevated over the course of time, in a process that involves conflict and struggle with sinful conditions of its existence."[63] In order to bring salvation, Jesus shared in and was affected by humanly felt temptation, the fear of loss, physical frailty, and even the universal human experience of death. That Jesus faced a real death is decisive for the redemptive aim of his deification, which is not fully achieved until his death is overcome in the "final glorification of Jesus' humanity" in the resurrection.[64] Because God assumed in Christ a human nature in its embodied historicity, believers in their embodied historicity are drawn into Jesus' "process of purification and elevation" and enabled by grace to grow in perfection in the course of their lives.[65]

Similar to Tanner, Novello sees the incarnation in terms of a process of divinization. Novello, himself a trained scientist, brings an evolutionary perspective to his theology and attempts to shift the philosophical paradigm from classical "substance thinking" to relational "event thinking." Things in the world—animate and inanimate—are not seen as static substances; rather, it is more scientifically correct to say that the world is made up of "unfolding and

61. See Kathryn Tanner, *Christ the Key* (Cambridge: Cambridge University Press, 2010), 170. K. Tanner, who affiliates with the Episcopal tradition, currently teaches at Yale University Divinity School.

62. Kathryn Tanner, *Jesus, Humanity and the Trinity: A Brief Systematic Theology* (Minneapolis: Fortress Press, 2001), 27.

63. K. Tanner, *Jesus, Humanity and the Trinity*, 27.

64. K. Tanner, *Jesus, Humanity and the Trinity*, 52.

65. K. Tanner, *Jesus, Humanity and the Trinity*, 32.

emerging" events.[66] Novello engages closely with Chalcedon and its inter-preters but argues that Christology today "should be reflected upon with the contemporary evolutionary perspective of the world as dynamic, processive and therefore 'emergent.'"[67] Emergentism is a significant modern alternative to the traditional and long-standing body-soul paradigm of personhood. This theory postulates both the evolutionary emergence of the human species and the developmental emergence of each human individual as "a particular psychosomatic unity, a complex organism in which mental phenomena 'supervene' upon physical processes," allowing for self-consciousness.[68] When the doctrine of the incarnation is approached from an emergent perspective, "it is simply not plausible or credible to conceive of the Incarnation as complete at the moment of Jesus' conception,"[69] and Novello contests the intelligibility of the notion of the hypostatic union as an instantaneous "act fully consummated . . . in the womb of Mary."[70] Novello emphasizes the historical embeddedness of the incarnation as narrated in the Gospel accounts, and he contrasts this "history-like" understanding with a "non-historical" one that would claim that "Christ possessed everything from the time of his conception."[71] He references Thomas Aquinas on this point, but his critique of Aquinas's notion of an instantaneous incarnation would apply to the pro-life scholars I have discussed above.

Part of what informs this processive and emergent approach to the incarnation has to do with Tanner's and Novello's particular views of human nature and the human condition. Christ's incarnation must be processive because humans are mutable, interactive, historical creatures, not static, essential natures.[72] The hypostatic union inaugurates an ontological change whereby a new God-human relationship is constituted, so that mutable, finite, sinful persons now have the possibility, through grace, to grow in perfection, as God's Spirit begins to "knit [itself] into the fabric . . . of our humanity." In this process of sanctification, the believer, who is still finitely human, does not become divine but gains "a sort of natural connection to the

66. Henry L. Novello, *Death as Transformation: A Contemporary Theology of Death* (Farnham, Surrey, UK: Ashgate, 2013), 9, 10. Novello currently teaches at Flinders University and is active in the Roman Catholic archdiocese in Adelaide, South Australia.
67. Novello, *Death as Transformation*, 7.
68. Novello, *Death as Transformation*, 40. See also Henry L. Novello, "Integral Salvation in the Risen Christ: The New 'Emergent Whole,'" *Pacifica* 17, no. 1 (2004): 34–54. Novello is aware of the work of Charles Hartshorne and Alfred North Whitehead, but he does not use their process theism. See Novello, *Death as Transformation*, 150 n. 117.
69. Novello, *Death as Transformation*, 168.
70. Novello, *Death as Transformation*, 26; see 85, 93, 167.
71. Novello, *Death as Transformation*, 167 n. 9. The term "history-like" is drawn from Hans Frei; see Novello, *Death as Transformation*, 20.
72. See K. Tanner, *Christ the Key*, 37–46.

divine."[73] This salvific connection to the divine does not mean that the material conditions of human existence are miraculously alleviated. The world continues to be such that believer and nonbeliever alike may endure lives that are often "short and brutish" and that may end in a "premature, painful and community-rending" death.[74] Tanner paints a sober picture of the "hiddenness of the Spirit in and under the human," which means that believers may not see clearly how to navigate "the messy course of human history" and may not see clearly how "God's Spirit is making its way in and through" to lead them.[75] This realism about the ambiguity of the human condition within the process of divinization is an important point to make for women facing difficult reproductive choices.

Novello also emphasizes the dynamism of human nature, but his focus, one might say, is more diachronic—that is, concerning macro changes over time—in part, because of his evolutionary and emergent emphases. Evolutionarily, the human species has progressed to a higher mode of self-reflectiveness but is still mired in the "present situation of corruptibility, incompleteness and perishability."[76] Salvation comes to human creatures in Christ, the "new emergent whole,"[77] who renews creation by drawing it upward "into the life of the Trinity as its final destiny."[78] When humans die, they "do not die into nothingness but into the mystery of the triune God."[79] Novello affirms, quoting Jürgen Moltmann, that despite death, "nothing will be lost" to God.[80] The way Novello shifts the soteriological emphasis from the idea of saving an immortal soul[81] to God's act of recuperating all that is destroyed or lost in the world carries an important message for reproductive loss.

This glimpse of a processive, emergent approach indicates a new path for thinking about the incarnation that is more credible to modern ears attuned to relational, historical, and scientific ways of seeing the world. Pro-life theologians claim that Chalcedonian orthodoxy requires belief in an immediate hypostatic union in Mary's womb and that this belief, by extension, repudiates abortion. The next section argues that a theology of the processive, emergent incarnation is regulatively Chalcedonian and offers a credible alternative to belief in the immediacy of the incarnation in Mary's womb. The credibility

---

73. K. Tanner, *Christ the Key*, 72–73.
74. K. Tanner, *Jesus, Humanity and the Trinity*, 115–16.
75. K. Tanner, *Christ the Key*, 298, 299.
76. Novello, *Death as Transformation*, 41; page 8 shows that Novello is influenced by Karl Rahner's notion of human evolutionary "active self-transcendence."
77. Novello, *Death as Transformation*, 10 and passim.
78. Novello, *Death as Transformation*, 210.
79. Novello, *Death as Transformation*, 203.
80. Novello, *Death as Transformation*, 155.
81. See Novello, *Death as Transformation*, 157.

of this alternative deflates assertions about Christ's embryonic life for pro-life purposes.

Chalcedonian Faith without Pro-life Entailments

Contemporary pro-life supporters emphasize a particular approach to Chalcedon that sees adopting the creed's Hellenistic philosophical anthropology (e.g., the notion of a soul-body composite) as part and parcel of orthodox belief. Here I argue for an alternative methodology that shows how present-day Christians can still adhere to Chalcedonian faith without having to adopt outmoded anthropologies and without falling into a narrow literalism about the inscrutable *when, where,* and *how* of the hypostatic union. This method is informed by George Lindbeck's regulative approach to doctrine and Sarah Coakley's proposal about the apophatic nature of the creeds.[82] This approach encourages identifying which elements of a doctrine should be taken as formally normative rules for belief and which elements are of an apophatic nature where literal or propositional explanation would be inappropriate. This argument will hopefully cause theologically trained pro-life proponents to pause before asserting that orthodox faith entails the belief that an embryo is an ensouled person from the moment of syngamy.

Lindbeck's theories have been much discussed, so I will summarize very briefly two components that are relevant to the issues of this chapter. He suggests that there are three broadly understood approaches to the creeds of the church: propositionalist, experiential-expressive, and regulative. The pro-life interpreters I have discussed represent a version of propositionalism, so I will focus on that approach in order to make my case for the greater usefulness of a regulative approach.[83] Propositionalists take the creeds as statements of truth whose authoritativeness is based on some combination of their revelatory origin, their referentiality to objective truth, and the unchanging meaning of the words. In this approach, there is supposed to be a true interpretation of doctrine that is "not only normative but permanent," a "self-identical core

---

82. George A. Lindbeck, *The Nature of Doctrine: Religion and Theology in a Postliberal Age* (Philadelphia: Westminster Press, 1984). After a monumental career at Yale University, Lindbeck passed away in 2018. Sarah Coakley, "What Does Chalcedon Solve and What Does It Not? Some Reflections on the Status and Meaning of the Chalcedonian 'Definition,'" in *The Incarnation: An Interdisciplinary Symposium on the Incarnation of the Son of God,* ed. Stephen T. Davis, Daniel Kendall, and Gerald O'Collins (New York: Oxford University Press, 2002), 143–63.

83. Crisp acknowledges that this rubric fits his approach. See Oliver D. Crisp, "Is Ransom Enough?," *Journal of Analytic Theology* 3 (May 2015): 3 n. 1. However, Crisp seems to move toward a more regulative approach when he speaks of Chalcedon's "minimal claims" and axioms. Oliver D. Crisp, *The Word Enfleshed: Exploring the Person and Work of Christ* (Grand Rapids: Baker Academic, 2016), 94.

[that] persists down through the centuries" as a deposit of faith.[84] In a propositionalist approach, much emphasis is put on determining who has given an authoritative interpretation of this permanent doctrinal truth and who has given a heterodox interpretation. The pro-life theologians discussed in this chapter have determined, for example, that Maximus the Confessor has a clearer grasp on the meaning of the hypostatic union than, for example, Thomas Aquinas. Not surprisingly, Maximus's views seem to lend support to their pro-life beliefs.

A regulative approach, on the other hand, is meant to try to find doctrinal continuity in light of change and difference across ecclesial or cultural contexts by focusing on formal, stable guiding principles rather than on particular, changing material instantiations. In a regulative approach to interpreting the meaning of the ancient creeds for today's church, "the terminology and concepts of 'one substance and three persons' or 'two natures' may be absent," but one might still be following the normative rules or principles for Nicene or Chalcedonian faith.[85] This theory of doctrine expects that theologians will make important judgment calls about what is a material instantiation that need not be "slavishly repeated" and what is a formal rule of faith that is a "permanent authoritative paradigm."[86] Thus a regulative approach impels the theologian to bring a critical eye—a hermeneutics of suspicion, if you will—to the creeds and their interpreters to engage in those kinds of judgments. I do not see these pro-life scholars engaging in that type of critical work; on the contrary, I see them picking particular patristic formulations convenient for their pro-life polemics and baptizing them as propositional doctrinal truths.

From Coakley I draw the methodological lesson that the creeds often refrain from providing crucial explanatory information; for example, Chalcedon "does not tell us how *hypostasis* and *physeis* are related" so that the believer would know how those terms refer to reality. To insist that Chalcedon leaves some things unsaid does not mean, Coakley insists, that the creed should be characterized as mere rule or metaphor, lacking any referentiality or ontological content that has normative meaning for faith and practice. The believer can and should act on a belief in the creed's referential truth, while still acknowledging that the full meaning of that truth is cloaked in mystery. In other words, the theologian interpreting Chalcedon should not "expect of it something more metaphysically and substantially precise than it can yield";[87] instead, one's disposition toward the creeds should at some points

---

84. Lindbeck, *Nature of Doctrine*, 73.
85. Lindbeck, *Nature of Doctrine*, 95; see page 94 for Lindbeck's sketch of some of these rules.
86. Lindbeck, *Nature of Doctrine*, 96.
87. Coakley, "What Does Chalcedon Solve and What Does It Not?," 162.

be apophatic. If ever there was a moment to invoke apophaticism, it would be regarding the embryonic life of Christ.

Lindbeck and Coakley provide a refreshing antidote to the way Crisp, Jones, and Saward approach the Chalcedonian Definition propositionally in order to derive from that creed a particular material formulation of the hypostatic union such that the truth of all embryos as persons is believed to be a settled matter. A regulative approach to Chalcedon, on the other hand, would refrain from such literalism and, instead, look for the regulative principles of Chalcedonian faith. One example of Chalcedon, viewed regulatively, would be the principle: at every point of Jesus' existence, ascribe a divine nature and a human nature without confusion or separation. One can adhere to this formal principle when speaking of the identity of Jesus without having to endorse a body-soul approach to the hypostatic union and without claiming that Chalcedon implies that all embryos are sacred persons.

With these methodological guidelines in mind, it is possible to make the case that a processive, emergent way of interpreting the incarnation adheres to Chalcedon regulatively understood, avoids heresies such as Apollinarianism and Nestorianism, and coheres with modern understandings of gradual fetal development. It is beyond the scope of this book to give a complete Chalcedonian defense of this interpretation of the incarnation, so I will focus on the regulative principle I have outlined above: at every point of Jesus' existence, ascribe a divine nature and a human nature without confusion or separation. Not only does a processive, emergent approach adhere to this principle, but it does so without recourse to a problematic body-soul anthropology and associated claims about an immediate hypostatic union. In showing that there are viable and compelling alternatives to those problematic viewpoints, the theological basis for a pro-life position crumbles.

Specifying Christ's two natures at every point in his existence means addressing not just Jesus' born existence but his fetal development as well. Neither Tanner nor Novello says much about Christ in utero,[88] but one can extrapolate that a processive, emergent view of the hypostatic union would assert that Jesus' life in the womb followed normal embryonic development and that the hypostatic union occurred as a process concurrent with the emerging fetal Jesus. How does this view of the emergent embryonic and fetal Christ adhere to my proposed Chalcedonian regulative principle?

---

88. K. Tanner, in *Christ the Key*, 144, merely says that the humanity of Christ is "united with the Word . . . from the start." She briefly notes how Christ's birth was accomplished "without 'intercourse and conception and time and travail,'" quoting the 4th-century bishop Hilary of Poitiers. K. Tanner, *Christ the Key*, 215. Novello specifies that God "shape[d] a body for his Son in the womb of the Virgin." Novello, *Death as Transformation*, 85.

First, the *divine nature*, which one must affirm as being present at every point, must be thought of not as imparted immediately but, rather, *processively*. Jesus' human nature was divinized continually, incrementally, and progressively, as the Logos assumed each new emergent event of Jesus' human existence—from conception, blastocyst, to birth, and then throughout his life in daily interactions with the joys, sufferings, and temptations of the world, culminating in his death and resurrection. The Chalcedonian affirmation of "perfect in divinity and perfect in humanity"[89] can, thus, be understood as referring to "the process of purifying and elevating . . . *each* aspect of Jesus' life"—the completion of which happens at Christ's resurrection.[90] One need not posit an immediate hypostatic union at conception; indeed, it makes little sense to do so from a processive, emergent perspective on the world.

Second, the *human nature*, which one must affirm as being present at every point in Jesus' existence, must be thought of not as a static substance but, rather, an emergent *event*. An emergent perspective asserts that "the human being is not merely the product of its genetic endowment and its environment; . . . human nature cannot be thought of as a closed system . . . but rather [refers] to an unfolding and emergent reality."[91] Jesus' emergent human nature is divinized in "a process of purification and elevation," beginning at conception and continuing over the course of his lifetime, seen as an embodied, dynamic, relational event.[92] Adhering to the Chalcedonian principle about the divine and human without confusion or separation does not require asserting that a substantial entity, the God-Man, was constituted at conception; indeed, any such assertion would fly in the face of what science tells us about the emergent event of human life from beginning to death.

We can further see how a processive, emergent view of the incarnation is Chalcedonian by explicating how it avoids the specific heresies of Apollinarianism and Nestorianism. The Appollinarians overemphasized the unity of the two natures of Christ under the governance of the divine Logos. The rule for avoiding the heresy of Apollinarianism is that one may not assert that the Logos supplied a divine soul or divine mind for Jesus' flesh (as the patristic theologians would have worded it). This heresy is a special concern for Crisp, who suggests that to deny immediate ensoulment of every human embryo would amount to a crypto-Apollinarian stance, because it would imply that the Logos controlled the flesh of a not fully human fetal body until Jesus was infused with a human soul. In this scenario, Crisp concludes, "for the period between conception and [human] ensoulment, Apollinarianism obtains!" Even

---

89. N. Tanner, *Decrees of the Ecumenical Councils*, 1:86.
90. K. Tanner, *Jesus, Humanity and the Trinity*, 30.
91. Novello, *Death as Transformation*, 10.
92. K. Tanner, *Jesus, Humanity and the Trinity*, 32.

if positing delayed ensoulment implies only a "temporary Apollinarianism,"[93] Crisp believes it would still be a heterodox view of the hypostatic union. For Crisp, who defines a person as a body-soul composite, the *when* of the hypostatic union must be asserted as happening at conception in order to avoid falling into an Apollinarian heresy.

Does denying that embryos have souls at conception make one an Apollinarian heretic? I would say that is a rigged question because it can only be answered within a body-soul anthropological paradigm, which was assumed by the early church fathers and is endorsed by pro-life theologians but is in no way a requirement of faith for Christians today. While fighting Apollinarianism obsessed many early church leaders, it is less of a theological threat today than people like Crisp think. If one's anthropology is not dependent on a body-soul conceptuality, one actually avoids the kind of Apollinarianism the church fathers had in mind, which turns on positing such a thing as pre-ensouled human flesh. Crisp claims that he knows "of no orthodox classical theologian that claims human beings are without souls"[94] and that a body without a soul would be "rather like a zombie."[95] Today while many theologians continue to find soul language useful, others dispense with the notion, in part, because of the hierarchy of soul over body that seems almost unavoidably to follow.[96] Using a body-soul theological anthropology seems to lead to a particular lack of critical attentiveness to such hierarchies (and other problems like an antisexuality bias) in historical theology, as shown in pro-life uses of Maximus's theology. An emergent, processive view of the incarnation asserts that the Word assumed Jesus' human nature continually and incrementally as it emerged developmentally in utero and during his life, without employing a body-soul "idiom."[97] The Apollinarian idea of the Word taking over Jesus' body (Crisp's worry) makes no evolutionary or scientific sense

93. Crisp, *God Incarnate*, 87. Some might say that Crisp, in his efforts to avoid Apollinarianism, falls into a kind of Nestorianism. See Brian Leftow, "A Timeless God Incarnate," in *The Incarnation: An Interdisciplinary Symposium on the Incarnation of the Son of God*, ed. Stephen T. Davis, Daniel Kendall, and Gerald O'Collins (Oxford: Oxford University Press, 2002), 280.

94. Crisp, *God Incarnate*, 80.

95. Crisp, *God Incarnate*, 112 n. 16.

96. For critiques of the notion of an immaterial soul: See F. LeRon Shults, *Reforming Theological Anthropology: After the Philosophical Turn to Relationality* (Grand Rapids: Wm. B. Eerdmans Publishing Co., 2003), 179–81 and 186–87; Rosemary Ruether, *Gaia and God: An Ecofeminist Theology of Earth Healing* (San Francisco: HarperSanFrancisco, 1993), 28–31; Lisa Isherwood and Elizabeth Stuart, *Introducing Body Theology* (Sheffield: Sheffield Academic Press, 1998), 62–68; Kelly Brown Douglas, *What's Faith Got to Do with It? Black Bodies / Christian Souls* (Maryknoll, NY: Orbis Press, 2005), 22–23, 36–38; Nancey Murphy, "Nonreductive Physicalism," in *In Search of the Soul: Perspectives on the Mind-Body Problem*, ed. Joel B. Green (Downers Grove, IL: InterVarsity Press, 2005), 115–52.

97. K. Tanner and Novello both wish to move away from a body-soul formulation to a more "contemporary idiom." K. Tanner, *Christ the Key*, 50. See Novello, *Death as Transformation*, 86.

within a paradigm of emergent, processive divinization, which sees Christ's divine and human natures emerging together concurrently. In a processive divinization paradigm not only is Apollinarianism avoided, but the pro-life insistence that all embryos are ensouled at conception is significantly deflated.

The rule for avoiding the heresy of Nestorianism is that one may not assert that the incarnation was a joining of two subjects—one divine and one human—into some composite third thing. Nestorians stressed the distinctions between the two natures, so much so that they appeared to overemphasize the separation and lose the unity of what Chalcedon called "a single subsistent being." Some anti-Nestorian theologians fended off this problem by emphasizing that the hypostatic union was completed in Mary's womb, with the implication that one could affirm Mary as the God-bearer. However, it is possible to avoid the Nestorian heresy without positing an immediate completion of the hypostatic union at conception. In an emergent, processive approach, there is only ever Christ as a single emergent subject with his divine and human natures—from conception through death. One could even make a processive, emergent theological argument for the title of *Theotokos* for Mary, if one is willing to imagine her as gestating and birthing normally the fetal Christ whose human and divine natures are one, co-emerging subject. In a processive divinization paradigm not only is Nestorianism avoided, but again the pro-life appeal to the necessity of ensoulment at conception is significantly undercut.

This Chalcedonian, processive, emergent view of the incarnation stands in stark contrast to the type of Chalcedonian belief proposed by pro-life theologians and challenges the way in which they apply the concept of divinization to all embryos. As Novello explains, "The divinization of the human does not mean that the human becomes God" or that any person somehow ceases "to be a finite existent different from God."[98] Tanner also clarifies that divinization is "the process of purifying and elevating the human" but is in no way an alteration of human nature to make it sacred.[99] By contrast, Saward claims that "by becoming man at his conception, the Son of God has . . . made all womb-life not simply sacred but divine."[100] Jones concurs that "Jesus in the womb sanctifies the earliest phase of human life," and other pro-life theologians make similar claims.[101] From the theological claim that "unborn life has been assumed and therefore divinized," Saward then draws the pro-life moral

---

98. Novello, *Death as Transformation*, 60 n. 102. Novello is quoting Karl Rahner.
99. K. Tanner, *Jesus, Humanity and the Trinity*, 30.
100. Saward, *Redeemer in the Womb*, 159.
101. D. Jones, *Soul of the Embryo*, 139. MacKellar writes in *Image of God*, 136: "Christ's incarnation as a human conceptus . . . thus bestows a sacred status on all human embryonic life for all time."

and political conclusion that any embryo has "the right to be protected from attack."[102] I raise two critiques of this pro-life theological overreach about divinization.

Appeals to fetuses as sacred are common in pro-life writings and usually indicate an effort to express, in the strongest terms one can muster, the belief that the unborn are valuable and loved by God, have dignity and rights, should be treasured and protected, and so on. It is understandable for ordinary Christians to speak this way, as many a pregnant mother has done, in order to express that her unborn child is sacred to her. Even theologians sometimes speak nontechnically of their children as sacred; however, claiming or implying that the hypostatic union effected an ontological change such that all unborn life is divinized is theologically mistaken.[103] The concept of divinization is not a Christianized version of the Midas myth where everything Christ touches turns to gold. To claim, by virtue of the Word assuming human flesh in Mary's womb, that all embryos are thereby rendered sacred is mythological thinking and has nothing to do with the doctrine of the incarnation or the process of the believer's divinization.

Second, if one affirms (as a processive, emergent approach does) that Jesus lived a real human life from conception onward, and if one refuses to abstract the fetus from its real existence—a gestational process intimately interconnected to its mother's body—then one should speak of deification in a way that reflects these realities. The divinizing process of Jesus' unborn life was not separate from or in conflict with the divinizing process the Spirit nurtured in Mary's life. This whole physically intertwined, relational pregnancy event was assumed by the Word in his incarnation—not just the embryonic Jesus alone, not just Mary's womb alone, but the whole emergent process of gestation and pregnancy that produced the Christ child. To claim that a fetus has its own special kind of sacral life, walled off from its gestating mother, misunderstands the dynamic biological reality of fetal-maternal interconnectedness and harkens back to premodern images of the tiny "homunculus Christ" descending fully formed into the womb of Mary.[104]

---

102. Saward, *Redeemer in the Womb*, 164.

103. See David P. Gushee, *The Sacredness of Human Life: Why an Ancient Biblical Vision Is Key to the World's Future* (Grand Rapids: Wm. B. Eerdmans Publishing Co., 2013), 3. Gushee seems to avoid making an ontological claim about fetal sacredness and the incarnation, implying, instead, that Christ becoming divine "elevates the worth of every human being." Gushee, *Sacredness of Human Life*, 95. This is a moral claim and falls short of asserting that all fetuses are actually sacred.

104. See Tasioulas, "Heaven and Earth in Little Space," 26; Daniel A. Dombrowski and Robert J. Deltete, *A Brief, Liberal, Catholic Defense of Abortion* (Urbana: University of Illinois Press, 2000), 35–36.

This view of embryos as rendered sacred at conception is also linked, as least for Saward, to the very speculative claim that "even before his birth the Child Jesus is at his saving sanctifying work" and even experiencing "the beatific vision of God."[105] I find the notion of a salvific, God-conscious fetal Jesus theologically troubling on many levels (Saward himself notes the difficulties of claims about Jesus' "pre-natal perfections"),[106] not the least of which is that it seems only tangentially linked to the little we know about the birth and infancy of Jesus based on the Gospel accounts. What happened in Mary's womb is shrouded in apophatic obscurity, as Coakley might say. One cannot know how far along the pregnancy was when Mary went to visit Elizabeth, but it was early enough so that Elizabeth felt the fetal John move in a way she perceived to be a joyful recognition of Jesus' presence (Luke 1:44), but Mary felt no corresponding quickening or consciousness from the fetal Jesus. Likewise, Matthew's Gospel recounts miraculous signs that led the magi to the abode where Mary and Jesus were staying, but there is no mention of the newborn Jesus performing any signs and wonders for the magi or for anyone the holy family met on the road to Egypt when they were fleeing Herod (Matt. 2:11–15, 19–21). The infant Jesus is not portrayed as showing an awareness of the impending slaughter of Jewish male infants, nor did he intervene in power to prevent the mass killing (Matt. 2:13–18). In short, the biblical narratives seem to support an understanding of Jesus in utero and in infancy as developmentally emergent in terms of his humanity and his divinity. As an embryo, he had only embryonic humanity; as an infant, he acted as an infant. Saward's claim that the embryonic Jesus experienced knowledge of God is not credible and has no Chalcedonian basis that I can detect. Pro-life fervor seems to push Saward to make the claim that, like Jesus, "every child from conception is capable of relationship with God," which is marginally orthodox at best and incredible from a scientific or even commonsensical perspective.[107]

One pro-life theologian has commented that "it is very difficult to rationally consider the incarnation as a progressive process taking place over time."[108] While this idea may be difficult for those locked into a body-soul paradigm of personhood, it seems to have increasing support among theologians and philosophers of religion. Since the modern church has mostly reconciled itself to the notion of God's indirect providential involvement in evolutionary processes, it makes sense for theologians to speak of Christ's incarnation

105. Saward, *Redeemer in the Womb*, 27, 70.
106. Saward, *Redeemer in the Womb*, 71.
107. Saward, *Redeemer in the Womb*, 76.
108. MacKellar, *Image of God*, 130.

in terms of processive and emergent dynamics, which are more intelligible to today's scientifically informed Christians.[109] It is not doctrinally necessary nor even widely credible anymore to say that the hypostatic union was fully accomplished at Jesus' conception in the blink of an eye. One can affirm the principle "at every point in Jesus' existence, ascribe a divine and human nature without confusion or separation," while also seeing the incarnation as an emergent and historical process of deification occurring throughout Jesus' life. This approach has the added advantage of steering theologians away from the hyperbolic pro-life claims, which have no foundation in Chalcedon, that Jesus experienced the beatific vision prenatally and that all embryos are sacred beings with the capacity to enjoy a relationship with God.

The regulative approach to Chalcedon employed in this chapter provides a pathway to a modern interpretation of the incarnation that effectively challenges the pro-life claim that Chalcedonian faith requires belief in personhood from conception. Not only do pro-life theologians provide a weak patristic foundation for their claims about an instantaneous hypostatic union, but they also fail to make a convincing case that it is the only orthodox way of understanding how the divine and human are united without confusion in the incarnation. This chapter challenged the legitimacy of pro-life interpretations of the incarnation, which in turn, challenged the basis of pro-life theological claims that a person must be understood as a body-soul composite that comes into existence at conception. While a processive, emergent paradigm may not be the only anthropology that theologians decide to use, it provides a compelling conceptuality for adhering to Chalcedonian faith, free of questionable pro-life claims that abortion at any point in a pregnancy is the heinous murder of a sacred and fully human person.

109. K. Tanner also sees her proposal for Jesus' deification as guided by the principle she calls "non-competitiveness" between the creaturely and the divine spheres. K. Tanner, *Jesus, Humanity and the Trinity*, 2–5.

4

Christian Philosophy and Fetal Personhood

While some pro-life Christian thinkers make their case about abortion and the nature of fetal personhood based on appeals to Scripture and tradition, many turn instead to philosophical literature on these issues. This chapter offers a critical assessment of two prominent approaches in Christian philosophical ethics in order to demonstrate how these arguments not only falter significantly in their attempts to prove fetal personhood but also imply troubling and even callous views of the personhood of pregnant women. Exposing these problems supports my claim that trying to solve the complexity of the abortion debate with an appeal to the elusive category of "person" is logically and morally flawed. The two types of pro-life personhood arguments to be discussed are widely known as substantialist and Roman Catholic probabilist approaches. While these philosophical writings may be geared to a scholarly, specialized audience, some of the ideas have been uncritically absorbed into and further disseminated by popular pro-life writings and have been used to lend credence to anti-abortion campaigns globally. It is therefore important to critically address their arguments and assumptions.

Weaknesses in the substantialist pro-life philosophical approach include an overdependence on the evidence of genetics as a way of bolstering ontological claims and an unargued appeal to the innocence of fetal life. The main weakness in probabilist arguments is claiming to secure more rights at conception than is logically warranted given the presence of doubts about the personhood of an embryo. Both pro-life approaches suffer from giving inadequate attention to actual fetal life in a woman's body, which results in these thinkers presenting a picture of the fetus that is so materially decontextualized as to be hardly recognizable as a real in-utero being at all. Furthermore, the gestating mother is assigned to a more or less utilitarian role, based on these philosophers' assumption that one can resolve the question of the status of the fetus completely abstracted from its necessary embeddedness in a woman's womb. This assumption contributes to a final and, to my mind, disturbing flaw in pro-life arguments for fetal personhood. Even if these philosophers could prove the plausibility of some fetal rights, they still do not secure the personhood of the fetus to any extent that would justify suppressing the mother's reproductive rights. I will show that these scholars presuppose (rather than attempt to prove) that a pregnant woman (or girl) is always morally obligated to offer her body to the fetal person she is carries in her womb—no matter how that fetus was conceived and no matter what the danger the pregnancy poses to her well-being.

To the extent that philosophical discourse can tend toward abstraction, the problem of speaking of fetuses in the abstract is not surprising. Nevertheless, the Christian philosophers engaged in these debates purport to be concerned with actual fetal lives (and some even purport to be concerned about women) in order to influence philosophical and ethical discourse. Some of these philosophers, moreover, are politically involved in anti-abortion legal and legislative causes. In short, they are not simply proposing theoretical thought experiments but trying to prevent murder (to their way of thinking); for that reason, they should be held accountable for what they do and do not say about the material reality of fetuses and the obligations of real women and girls who are gestating them. The critiques in this chapter set the stage for my proposals in part 2 of this book for how to recognize the moral value of real fetuses apart from the contested term "person," while also recognizing the moral authority of real women, who daily must make decisions for their lives and the lives of all those in their care.

PRO-LIFE SUBSTANTIALISM: FETAL PERSONHOOD IN ABSTRACTION

The majority of pro-life arguments for fetal personhood fall under the rubric of what can be called substantialist arguments, which assert that a person is an individual, self-directing human substance that begins to exist upon fertilization. We will see how substantialist philosophical arguments employ a definition of the person that might possibly apply to the idea of a genetically individual being but is ill-suited to apply to any actual being living and developing in a woman's womb. My analysis of substantialism draws from a number of Christian philosophers who, while they do not speak with one voice, share a similar definition of personhood as it applies to the embryo or fetus.

I find flaws in at least three areas in their arguments: (1) they depend on an amorphous metaphysical category of substance and an amorphous moral category of fetal innocence; (2) they make misleading or overinflated claims about genetics and embryonic or fetal self-directedness; and (3) there is an almost complete lack of attention to or distortion of the contribution of the gestating woman, whose role they speak of in utilitarian if not demeaning ways. In other words, pro-life philosophers may secure the personhood of an idea of innocent embryos or fetuses but not the personhood of actual human beings developing in real women's wombs. Hence their claim that their arguments for fetal personhood are successful enough to justify making abortion illegal is specious.

Substantialist approaches all share a similar definition of a person as an individual, unified, self-directing substantial being. Pro-life substantialist philosophers claim that the essential substance of a person comes into existence at the moment of conception. Patrick Lee states: "When a human being comes to be, then a substantial entity that is identical with the entity that will later reason, make free choices, and so on, begins to exist."[1] This substantial entity, to be a person, need not have even a rudimentary brain but merely a capacity to "maintain identity through change." Francis Beckwith describes substantial personhood as the ontological identity that is "prior to" that organism's abiding and subsisting "parts." If any of the parts turn out to be human, one can reasonably conclude that the ontological identity of those parts is human from the beginning. One does not even need to see evidence of the development of the parts and their functions to make this claim: a kitten, before it can purr, has the ontological identity of feline nature.[2] In an analogous way, an embryo, before it can think, possesses "the self-same substantial entity that persists" until it becomes an actual born thinking person.[3] J. P. Moreland and Scott Rae concur that there is an essential identity between the "preconscious fetus" and the born person throughout all their various life states leading to final death.[4] Or, to say it another way, the person I am now and my "fetal self are the same substance" merely at different stages of my unified existence.[5] For Lee, a human organism simply is the "persisting subject of rational and free acts"—that is, a "person"—from the moment it comes into

1. Patrick Lee, "A Christian Philosopher's View of Recent Directions in the Abortion Debate," *Christian Bioethics* 10, no. 1 (2004): 16. Lee is a professor of Roman Catholic bioethics.
2. Francis J. Beckwith, "The Explanatory Power of the Substance View of Persons," *Christian Bioethics* 10, no. 1 (2004): 35. Beckwith, a Roman Catholic, teaches philosophy at Baylor University.
3. Patrick Lee, "The Pro-Life Argument from Substantial Identity: A Defence," *Bioethics* 18, no. 3 (2004): 257.
4. J. P. Moreland and Scott B. Rae, *Body & Soul: Human Nature & the Crisis in Ethics* (Downers Grove, IL: InterVarsity Press, 2000), 379. Both authors teach at Talbot School of Theology.
5. Beckwith, "Explanatory Power of the Substance View of Persons," 36.

existence until it dies.[6] Substantialist philosophers like Lee are confident in asserting that the embryo that I was and the person I am now "clearly have a physical *identity*, not just a continuity," as Lee puts it.[7] Lee's claim about what is "clearly" the case is an indication of the status of his argument—that is, he can offer no proof for this ontological state of affairs, only an appeal to what appears, according to his worldview, to be so.

Substantialist philosophers are not just making a metaphysical claim but a moral one as well. They claim that one should not differentiate between the value put on a born person and an embryo because "between the embryonic human being and that same human being at any stage of her maturation, there is only a difference in degree." At any point, a human being has "value as a subject of rights."[8] Thus, even at its earliest moment of existence, "the human embryo is an entity with the same substantial nature as, and so equal in dignity with, you or me."[9] In this line of argument, everything depends on this category of "substance" and the work these philosophers want it to do—namely, to create an unbroken ontological and moral line between the conceptus that was me and myself now. The weak link in this approach is that even if one could provide a convincing argument for an unbroken ontological and moral line between the prenatal me and me now (which these philosophers do not do, in my estimation), all one will have achieved is the idea that my fetal self should have the same right to life I enjoy now. However, this argument (even if it did succeed) does not explain why my fetal human rights should be favored over those of my mother.

The only basis these scholars give for according rights to a fetus that trump the mother's rights is a claim to fetal innocence. The latter point is asserted and not argued philosophically—in part because it is not a philosophical point. Lee quotes a Catholic encyclical prohibiting "the direct taking of the life of an innocent human being."[10] Beckwith references fetal innocence, with no justification: "Abortion is an act in which an innocent human being is intentionally killed."[11] Pro-life philosophers sometimes appeal to innocence

6. P. Lee, "The Pro-Life Argument from Substantial Identity," 256. Lee goes even further to claim the embryo already "is a developing substantial entity with the basic, natural capacities to reason and make free choices" (262). The fact that an embryo cannot reason yet is brushed aside by Lee with the analogy to someone in a coma (see 263); however, the analogy between a comatose patient and an embryo strikes me as inappropriate because it compares a born person who has lost abilities with an unborn being whose basic neurological and other bodily systems have not even developed.

7. P. Lee, "The Pro-Life Argument from Substantial Identity," 257, italics in original.

8. P. Lee, "The Pro-Life Argument from Substantial Identity," 254.

9. P. Lee, "The Pro-Life Argument from Substantial Identity," 262.

10. *Evangelium vitae*, quoted in P. Lee, "A Christian Philosopher's View," 8.

11. Francis J. Beckwith, "Answering the Arguments for Abortion Rights (Part One): The Appeal to Pity," *Christian Research Journal* 13, no. 2 (1990): 2.

to secure fetal personhood rights as more worthy than the rights of a pregnant woman considering an abortion (who, needless to say, is not spoken of as innocent). Ironically, as we saw in some biblical arguments for personhood in chapter 2 above, it is not fetal innocence but fetal sinfulness (that is, the inheritance of original sin) that is the marker of personhood from conception. In the end, the appeal to innocence is a rhetorical flourish, not a philosophical argument at all, since a substantialist approach is only intended to display the persistence of an essential human entity from conception until old age—not the innocence of that entity in its prenatal state.

Not only is the claim for innocence on shaky ground, but also the persuasiveness of the substantialist approach overall: because it depends on the appeal to an amorphous ontological category, it would almost take an act of faith to assent to it. Apparently, substantialist philosophers recognize this, and they attempt to get more empirical by rallying scientific evidence in support of their fetal personhood claims. Not surprisingly, many of these philosophers point to a genetic basis for a personhood substance, arguing that "the 'blueprint' for the entire human body is defined within the first few hours of life," as John Meyer remarks.[12] Beyond invoking the DNA blueprint metaphor, substantialists attempt to bolster their claims of personhood from conception by pointing to biological evidence of the embryo's own self-initiating activity. That is, with the joining of sperm and ovum, a new entity, the fertilized egg, itself initiates its ongoing development. "If there is no extrinsic agent responsible for the regular, complex development, then the obvious conclusion," for John Haldane and Patrick Lee, "is that the cause of the process is within, that it is the embryo itself."[13] Mark Johnson argues that the zygote contains its own "central organizer" that "coordinates its parts and their activities" and makes it, while not completely self-sufficient in its cellular division, still an active initiator of its own biological activity.[14] This activity is taken as rudimentary substantial personhood. The choice, for Johnson, is clear: "Either the preembryo is an organism, or it is a heap."[15] If it is self-organizing, it also can be said to have functioning "cognition and intellective appetite," hence

<hr />

12. John R. Meyer, "Embryonic Personhood, Human Nature, and Rational Ensoulment," *Heythrop Journal* 47, no. 2 (2006): 213. Meyer is a priest of the conservative Opus Dei Prelature.

13. John Haldane and Patrick Lee, "Aquinas on Human Ensoulment, Abortion and the Value of Life," *Philosophy* 78, no. 2 (2003): 271. Haldane is a Roman Catholic professor of philosophy at the University of St. Andrews in Scotland.

14. Mark Johnson, "Delayed Hominization: Reflections on Some Recent Catholic Claims for Delayed Hominization," *Theological Studies* 56, no. 4 (1995): 757. Johnson teaches Roman Catholic thought and philosophy at Marquette University. He is quoted as calling abortion "the single most important civil-rights abuse that this country has ever been involved in" (Brian Fraga, "Tim Kaine: 'A Joe Biden Catholic,'" *National Catholic Register* (September 23, 2016), http://www.ncregister.com/daily-news/tim-kaine-a-joe-biden-catholic.

15. M. Johnson, "Delayed Hominization," 761.

rationality—not potentially but actually, even if extremely limited in scope.[16] With a zygote we have "the active self-development of a whole, though immature organism which is already a member of the [human] species."[17] These philosophers do not deny the science of the maternal contribution in embryology, but they interpret that contribution as a sign that the embryo is, from the start, an individual interacting with something other than itself: "The zygote or early embryo is a living organism—a substance—with certain powers and properties, including the capacity to be acted upon by maternal molecules."[18] In other words, the fact that the maternal organism, which is contributing something materially to the embryo's and fetus's development, is an adult moral agent is irrelevant to their argument that the in-utero being is a genetic individual to be accorded the full recognition of human dignity. These pro-life scholars see in the embryological data the picture of a fetus they already presuppose: a self-directing individual.

In addition to the overarching problem of trying to claim a scientific basis for metaphysical claims, there are challenges to the way these philosophers interpret the embryological data itself. A substantialist viewpoint depends, first and foremost, on the notion of a substantial human being coming into existence at the moment of conception, since it would make no philosophical sense to claim that an essential substance was added to the embryonic or fetal tissue at a later point in time (that claim would be analogous to the classic theological argument for delayed animation, which these philosophers reject). Scientifically, however, as biologists point out, "there is no 'moment of fertilization,' but rather a lengthy process that can take days to complete."[19] Up until about fourteen days after fertilization, the blastocyst can spontaneously divide so that two separate embryos develop into twins. Indeed, the zygote

16. M. Johnson, "Delayed Hominization," 763 n. 37. In this claim for actuality, substantialist arguments diverge from potentialist ones. The latter are less numerous among Christian philosophers. For two examples see Francis C. Wade, "Potentiality in the Abortion Discussion," *Review of Metaphysics* 29, no. 2 (1975): 239–55; and Michael Robinson, "Divine Image, Human Dignity and Human Potentiality," *Perspectives in Religious Studies* 41, no. 2 (2014): 65–77. For a general critique of philosophical potentiality arguments, see Lynn M. Morgan, "The Potentiality Principle from Aristotle to Abortion," *Current Anthropology* 54, no. S7 (2013): S15–S25.

17. Haldane and P. Lee, "Aquinas on Human Ensoulment," 269.

18. Beckwith, "Explanatory Power of the Substance View of Persons," 50. T. F. Torrance even suggests that the genetically driven movement of the developing fetus is related to its soul: "It is through the soul that in an ineffable way information bears upon the genetic structure of the foetus, informing it from its conception . . . [so that] body and soul develop together within the womb of the mother." T. F. Torrance, *The Soul and Person of the Unborn Child* (Edinburgh: Handsel Press, 1999), 7.

19. Scott F. Gilbert, "When 'Personhood' Begins in the Embryo: Avoiding a Syllabus of Errors," *Birth Defects Research* 84, no. 2 (2008): 168. Gilbert, the Howard A. Schneiderman Professor of Biology (emeritus) at Swarthmore College, is author of the widely used textbook, now in its 11th edition, with a new coauthor, Scott F. Gilbert and Michael J. F. Barresi, *Developmental Biology* (Sunderland, MA: Sinauer, 2016).

is "totipotent," meaning that any of its cells alone "can become a complete, separate organism" by virtue of "its possession of the complete genome," which is what happens in twinning, as Mark Johnson himself admits.[20] Totipotency and the biological possibility of twinning call into question these philosophers' claim that a single human being begins its individual, unified substantial existence directly upon fertilization of an ovum. Substantialists like Johnson try to offset the totipotency problem by arguing, unconvincingly to my mind, that the zygote quickly develops so that the cells "communicate with, and regulate, one another" and that twinning is a rare and, hence, "accidental" occurrence and should not be interpreted as the zygote's radical indeterminacy.[21] Lee also acknowledges but discounts the ontological significance of the possibility of twinning and asserts that the embryo overall acts "regularly and predictably."[22] In other words, biological data that undercut the substantialist philosopher's argument about personhood from conception are simply shunted aside.

Enthusiasm about genetic individuality has caused pro-life proponents to overplay the genetic blueprint metaphor and claims about the self-initiating activity of the conceptus. Pro-life substantialists assume that maternal contributions do not impinge on or significantly contribute to the embryo's or fetus's self-directing biological dynamism, which they take as a defining mark of its personhood. Meyer claims that "the embryo has the active potentiality to *develop* into a mature human being on its own," with the mother providing only "nutritive assistance"—a claim that echoes a metaphor from ancient times of the female womb as a mere field in which the male seed grows.[23] Stephen Heaney comments that the mother supplies "for a while" some "instrumental" material that "*enable[s]* the zygote to do its own work."[24] This

---

20. M. Johnson, "Delayed Hominization," 747.

21. M. Johnson, "Delayed Hominization," 759. Jean Porter has a companion essay and critical response to Johnson where she challenges him on, among other things, the twinning issue ("Individuality, Personal Identity, and the Moral Status of the Preembryo: A Response to Mark Johnson," *Theological Studies* 56, no. 4 [1995]: 767–68). Spontaneous, monozygotic (identical) twinning is not that rare and occurs at a fairly constant rate worldwide. See Judith G. Hall, "Twinning," *The Lancet* 362, no. 9385 (2003): 735–43.

22. P. Lee, "The Pro-Life Argument from Substantial Identity," 258. John Meyer also tries to downplay twinning by speculating (rather wildly) that at the point of twinning, an ensouled individual loses some of its (totipotent) matter, which then becomes another immediately ensouled individual, without threatening the "substantial unity" of the original embryo. See John R. Meyer, "The Ontological Status of Pre-implantation Embryos," in *Contemporary Controversies in Catholic Bioethics*, ed. Jason T. Eberl (Cham, Switzerland: Springer, 2017), 21, 28.

23. Meyer, "Embryonic Personhood," 212.

24. Stephen Heaney, "Aquinas and the Presence of the Human Rational Soul in the Early Embryo," *Thomist* 56, no. 1 (1992): 47. A Catholic philosopher and bioethicist, Heaney is active in pro-life politics. See "Stephen Heaney," *Argument of the Month: Men's Forum on Catholic Apologetics*, http://www.aotmclub.com/index.asp?PageID=10&SID=21.

downplaying of the maternal contribution to developments in the zygote is open to challenge by the biological evidence that an embryo is significantly dependent on maternal cytoplasm to help initiate and fuel cell division, which would not be able to proceed even with the presence of the embryo's own genetic material. An intact genome is but one vital contributor to a complicated and not fully understood developmental process of fetal-maternal chemical and biological interactions. As biologist Althea Alton has explained, given what we know from the mapping of the human genome, the DNA-as-blueprint metaphor is misleading: "In fact DNA does not provide blueprints for human traits or characteristics but rather the information encoded on the linear sequence of the DNA controls the processes of development that always occur in an environment."[25] That environment includes most significantly a "maternal 'cytoplasmic' inheritance" of "maternal RNAs, maternal DNA (in mitochondria), maternal organelles, proteins, substrates, and nutrients" on which the embryo depends to proceed with cell division.[26] Every born child was a particular embryo with the same DNA code; however, it is biologically misleading to say that the zygote I was genetically coded to become already became, at conception, the substantial person that I am now. Even new techniques of pre-implantation genetic screening cannot read the DNA of an embryo and say if or how it will develop as a fetus.[27]

A final weakness of the substantialist position, alluded to above, has to do with how these philosophers interpret the mother's role in gestation. While pro-life substantialists cannot but acknowledge that a fetus develops within and connected to the female womb, they do not find that biological reality in any way determinative for fetal status. One reason for this viewpoint is that they have already secured, to their satisfaction, that a genetically autonomous, self-directing human individual exists even in the pre-implanted embryo. However, it is scientifically misleading to ignore the influence of the gestating

25. Althea K. Alton, "Staying within an 'Understanding Distance': One Feminist's Scientific and Theological Reflections on Pregnancy and Abortion," in *Interdisciplinary Views on Abortion: Essays from Philosophical, Sociological, Anthropological, Political, Health and Other Perspectives*, ed. Susan A. Martinelli-Fernandez, Lori Baker-Sperry, and Heather McIlvaine-Newsad (Jefferson, NC: McFarland, 2009), 122, 132. Alton was an associate professor of biology at Western Illinois University and has her MDiv from Garrett Theological Seminary. See her autobiographical statement: http://www.stmatthewshillsborough.org/dfc/newsdetail_2/3181712.

26. Evan Charney, "Cytoplasmic Inheritance Redux," *Advances in Child Development and Behavior* 44 (2013): 226; doi.org/10.1016/B978-0-12-397947-6.00008-8.

27. In Great Britain, some experimental research has begun on genetic manipulation of embryos in order to explore the possibility of gene repair. While this research is experimental and the law prevents these embryos from being implanted into a woman's uterus, one can image that one day this might happen, which would challenge substantialist philosophers' claims that a stable genetic identity exists at syngamy that persists in the life of the born person. Ewan Callaway, "UK Scientists Gain Licence to Edit Genes in Human Embryos," *Nature* 530, no. 18 (February 4, 2016): 18, doi:10.1038/nature.2016.19270.

woman's body, which is "the environmental context for the genetically influenced developmental processes required for embryonic/fetal development."[28] Developmental biologist Scott Gilbert remarks that scientists are focusing on "new concepts in developmental biology," such as how "the environment plays crucial roles in regulating gene expression during development" in the uterus. Especially concerning to neonatologists are the effects on fetal development of a pregnant woman being exposed to pollutants containing "fetotoxic compounds." Gilbert finds the pro-life view that the presence of a complete genome denotes personhood as a kind of "genetic determinism" to be scientifically "erroneous."[29] Indeed, environment can be more determinative than genetics in some developmental outcomes.[30] Gilbert concludes: "New concepts in modern embryology have made scientists revise their views concerning the autonomy of the embryo."[31] While I am no embryologist, these scientific views do seem significantly to deflate substantialist philosophers' attempts to prove personhood at conception by claiming scientific evidence for a self-regulating conceptus and the continuity of fetal identity based on DNA. Even this cursory, nonspecialist's look at embryological science exposes the degree to which pro-life philosophers misunderstand or manipulate embryological data in order to ground ontological claims.

These scholarly arguments that the essence of a fetus's personhood is separate from its gestating mother are echoed in popular pro-life writings. One anti-abortion Web site states: "Embryos and fetuses live inside the womb, and newborn babies live outside the womb, . . . an inconsequential difference. *Where* someone lives has nothing to do with the essence of *who* that someone is. Moving from the bedroom to the kitchen, or from indoors to outdoors, . . . doesn't affect your personhood in the least."[32] This author is more picturesque in his analogy, but the argument is the same as that of the substantialist philosophers. Both sets of pro-life writers argue that personhood is secured by the fact that the embryo is a living, genetically individual, small human person, with the gestating mother reduced to mere nutritive, ancillary, temporary housing.

Establishing embryonic demarcation from the mother is key to the attempts of these pro-life philosophers to bolster the picture of an embryo's self-initiating personhood. Indeed, autonomy is part of Beckwith's definition of personhood as having "the aptitude to exist *in itself* and not as a part of any

28. Alton, "Staying within an 'Understanding Distance,'" 132.
29. Gilbert, "When 'Personhood' Begins in the Embryo," 167, 165.
30. Gilbert, "When 'Personhood' Begins in the Embryo," 166.
31. Gilbert, "When 'Personhood' Begins in the Embryo," 164.
32. "Inconsequential Differences," *Abort73.com*, http://abort73.com/abortion/inconsequential _differences/.

other being."[33] However, to apply Beckwith's definition to a fetus, one would have to discount the material fact of the fetal-maternal biological connection. A pregnant woman can go on existing as who she is if she is separated at any point from her fetus; an embryo or developing fetus, on the other hand, cannot continue to exist apart from its gestating mother. Gestation is not just temporary nutritive dependency analogous to a hospital patient on a feeding tube or connected to a ventilator. The fetus is a developing human being uniquely interconnected with its mother, within her body. Beckwith ignores the significance of this reality by suggesting that "maternal molecules" passed to a fetus can be likened to the antibiotics I might take to kill a serious bacterial infection—that is, they are important to my health but not determinative of my existence.[34] Beckwith's example implies that we should think of the fetus as analogous to a person sitting on the examining table at the doctor's office and getting a penicillin shot, which is an analogical stretch to say the least. Beckwith's analogy confirms to me that the substantialist's argument secures only the idea of fetal personhood, not the personhood of any actual embryo or fetus, which must develop toward natal personhood in an intimate dependence on and interaction with its mother's body.

Embryonic and fetal development is patterned but not determined—certainly not in the embryo's totipotent stage and not even later, when environmental factors can affect gene expression, how the fetus develops, and if it even develops successfully toward birth or not. Neither is a fetus just living its self-directed existence in a uterus analogous to how a born premature neonate lives in an incubator or connected to intravenous nutrition in the neonatal intensive care unit of the maternity ward. The intimate interactions between a mother's body and that of the fetus are of such a scale that few embryologists, neonatologists, or pregnant women themselves would describe pregnancy as merely feeding or housing a baby. Moreover, the enormous physical efforts required by the woman in the gestation and birthing processes testify to how uniquely enmeshed a real fetus is with its gestating mother's body.

Finally, the embryo or fetus is not just in any person's body but in that of its gestating mother. Not only do substantialist arguments present embryonic or fetal personhood in abstraction, but they actually downgrade the mother's status to that of a merely utilitarian, obligatory role. Women's needs and rights, or any extenuating circumstances of how the pregnancy came about (stranger rape, marital rape, rape as a tool of war, incest, contraceptive failure, and so on), are completely irrelevant to the ways in which these pro-life philosophers prosecute their anti-abortion arguments. Beckwith explicitly

33. Beckwith, "Explanatory Power of the Substance View of Persons," 34, italics original.
34. Beckwith, "Explanatory Power of the Substance View of Persons," 52.

asserts that because (he believes) a fetus is a person, "abortion cannot be justified in the cases of rape and incest" and should be illegal even in these hor-
rendous cases. Beckwith denies that his stance "forces a woman to carry her
baby against her will"; he tries to slough off the responsibility and to appear
politically innocent, claiming that "it is the rapist who has already forced this
woman to carry a child, not the pro-lifer" (such as himself).[35]

One might hope that this is a single harsh voice among pro-life substantialists, but one would be wrong. Other reputable scholars hold similar views. Lee
questions women's motives for wanting an abortion after rape, implying that
women might be trying to take out their "displaced emotions of revenge or
hatred" on the fetus; moreover, he claims, the suffering of a raped woman—
even a raped "girl"—being forced to gestate is not greater than the "burden" placed on the aborted fetus.[36] I understand that Lee is trying to argue
the point that post-rape physiological injury or psychological anguish cannot compare with loss of life. However, to claim that a nonsentient aborted
fetus feels anguish more than a living girl who has been raped and forced to
give birth and will live with that trauma for the rest of her life is beyond my
comprehension. Even in the situation where the mother's life is in danger,
John Haldane and Patrick Lee have no compunctions about arguing that "a
man ought rather to let the mother perish than that he himself . . . [commit]
the crime of homicide in killing the foetus."[37] Such statements render one
speechless with the misogyny that is not even thinly veiled. Even if substantialist philosophers' personhood arguments did rise to the level of plausibility
(which they do not, as I have argued), there is no moral basis for claiming that
the supposed personhood of the fetus should take precedence over a woman's
very survival. I find this viewpoint abhorrent, and its disdain for the value of
women's lives infects all other aspects of pro-life personhood arguments.

Needless to say, such equally crude viewpoints are widely disseminated
in popular writings. One anti-abortion pamphlet claims that abortion after
rape or incest invades a woman's body as a kind of "medical rape"; letting the

---

35. Francis J. Beckwith, "Answering the Arguments for Abortion Rights (Part Two): Arguments from Pity, Tolerance, and Ad Hominem," *Christian Research Journal* 13, no. 3 (1991):
12. Beckwith's claim that pregnant women are not being forced by "pro-lifers" rings hollow
when one notes that Beckwith publicly supports anti-abortion civil disobedience at abortion clinics: "I maintain that pro-lifers have a *right* to violate anti-trespassing laws in order to rescue
unborn children." In other words, Beckwith does not just think laws should restrain women from
abortion; he also advocates that pro-life vigilantes should intervene as well. Francis J. Beckwith
and Paul Feinberg, "Operation Rescue: Debating the Ethics of Civil Disobedience," *Christian
Research Institute* (April 17, 2009), https://www.equip.org/article/operation-rescue-debating-the
-ethics-of-civil-disobedience/.
36. Patrick Lee, *Abortion and Unborn Human Life*, 2nd ed. (Washington, DC: Catholic University of America Press, 2010), 130–31.
37. Haldane and P. Lee, "Aquinas on Human Ensoulment," 278.

pregnancy continue after rape is a good "way to expose the criminal who is abusing her"; and rape or incest is wrong, but it is even worse to punish an "innocent human being" by aborting it.[38] In other words, this anti-abortion pamphlet suggests the rape or incest survivor who aborts would impede a crime investigation and all but asserts that she is more evil than the man who victimized her. Another anti-abortion Web site directly equates rape and the abortion: "They are both acts of violent assault against an innocent victim. Aborting a child conceived through rape simply extends this pattern of violence and victimhood. It does not 'unrape' the woman."[39] Pro-life scholars do not disabuse their readers of these types of hyperbolic claims in popular anti-abortion writings; indeed, in many cases, they share the same viewpoints.

While a born person may appropriately be defined as an organism that "may lose and gain parts, and yet remain the same thing over time," this substantialist definition of personhood does not cohere with fetal reality.[40] The philosopher who wants to argue that the fetus's uterine existence is one stage in an ontologically unified life of the same substantial entity, merely happening in a different location, will need to make that argument without the support of current embryological science. Even if the genome stays the same from syngamy to birth, the embryo and then the fetus must interact with its uterine environment and change significantly, substantively, and irrevocably in order to become a birthed person. It is the born child who would, then, be appropriately defined as a substantial individual who "may lose and gain parts, and yet remain the same thing over time," if one wishes to use Beckwith's definition of personhood.[41] Moreover, the womb is not just temporary and expendable housing but the body of a living woman, who is not morally expendable, contrary to what some pro-life writers imply or even state explicitly. That she has every right to be able to give her consent to pregnancy and to decide the disposition of her body and the fate of her fetus, without the accusation of being a murderer, are arguments I will make in part 2 of this book.

PROBABILISM IN CATHOLIC MORAL REASONING

Another set of pro-life writings supports a probabilist approach, as found in Roman Catholic encyclicals and other magisterial documents, which asserts

---

38. See the pamphlet, "Abortion for the Victims of Rape and Incest?," https://prolifeaction.org /wp-content/uploads/docs/RapeAbortion.pdf.
39. "Common Abortion Fallacies," *Abort73.com*, http://abort73.com/abortion/common _objections/.
40. Beckwith, "Explanatory Power of the Substance View of Persons," 36.
41. Beckwith, "Explanatory Power of the Substance View of Persons," 36.

that an embryo should be accorded the full rights and dignity that any human person has, based on the probability that the embryo already is an ensouled human person. "Probabilism" is a technical term referring to a mode of Catholic moral reasoning where an ethical stance is defended based on a probable state of affairs. This word "probabilism" took on more importance in Vatican pro-life arguments once the "distinction between the ensouled and the unensouled fetus was removed from canon law" by Pope Pius IX in 1869.[42] From this point onward, the theological pressure was on, so to speak, to find ways to argue assertively for personhood from conception rather than remaining agnostic about the status of an unformed human being.

The notion of a probable state of affairs is used in official Catholic literature, such as the encyclicals *Evangelium vitae* and *Dignitas personae* and other Vatican documents that pronounce on the status of the embryo and fetus. While probabilist arguments for personhood are mostly directed to a Catholic audience, it is a massive global audience, and the viewpoint carries significant political weight even outside Catholic circles; therefore, these arguments merit critical comment here. We will see that contrary to how most pro-life Catholics speak of the Vatican's unequivocal defense of fetal life, the actual wording on fetal personhood in these documents is philosophically nuanced, such that they stop short of asserting that a person begins at conception. Nevertheless, as Catholic bioethicist Carol Tauer argues, there are fallacies in the way these documents assign certainty to the notion of fetal personhood, which calls into question the validity of the personhood claims in these magisterial teachings. In addition, the other Catholic teachings that are enlisted to support this pro-life viewpoint entail troubling stereotypes of women's maternal nature and moral obligations—namely, in the event of any sexual intercourse (consensual or not), she must always to be open to maternity.

As we have seen above, pro-life substantialist arguments state unequivocally that the fetus—indeed the conceptus—is, in its essence, the same human person it will be all its life and, hence, deserves all the rights accorded to a born person. The Vatican's encyclicals do not promote a substantialist view of personhood from conception when discussing embryos and fetuses. Indeed, despite popular pro-life Catholic assertions about human personhood beginning at conception,[43] papal documents exercise some terminological

42. Carol A. Tauer, "The Tradition of Probabilism and the Moral Status of the Early Embryo," *Theological Studies* 45, no. 1 (1984): 9. These doctrinal changes by Pius IX set in motion the decision to make immediate excommunication the punishment for abortion in the 1917 Code of Canon Law. For the historical setting for this development, see chap. 1.
43. See "Bishop Vasa Says: A Human Embryo Is a Human Person," *Catholic Action for Faith and Family*, https://www.catholicaction.org/bishop_vasa_says_a_human_embryo_is_a_human_person.

reserve regarding when a human person actually comes into existence. *Dignitas personae* (2008) affirms that dignity should be afforded to all human life "from conception to natural death" (§1).[44] Ample theological arguments are offered for this position, including themes studied in previous chapters of this book, such as appealing to humans beings created in the image of God and to the incarnation in which God affirmed humanity's "meaning and value" (§7). Quoting Pope Benedict XVI, the encyclical states, "God's love does not differentiate between the newly conceived infant still in his or her mother's womb and the child or young person, or the adult and the elderly person" (§16). While these are strong theological and moral statements, they still fall short of pronouncing definitively that an embryo is a person. *Dignitas personae* arguably leaves some sliver of wiggle room regarding personhood philosophically understood. The encyclical describes the biological reality of the fetus as a "human body [that] develops progressively according to a well-defined program with its proper finality, as is apparent in the birth of every baby" (§4). In addition, the document states that the zygote should "be *treated* as a person from the moment of conception" (§4, emphasis added) but not that it *is* a person from the moment of conception.[45] Instead of acting "as if the human embryo were simply a mass of cells" (*Dignitas personae* §14), one is enjoined to act as if there is an actual person. There is no ex cathedra or even magisterial and decisive pronouncement on fetal personhood here.[46]

Similarly, *Donum vitae* (1987) distinguishes between the absolute moral rejection of all abortion and the limited nature of what can be asserted biologically or philosophically about fetal personhood:[47]

> Certainly no experimental datum can be in itself sufficient to bring us to the recognition of a spiritual soul; nevertheless, the conclusions

---

44. Congregation for the Doctrine of the Faith, "Instruction *Dignitas personae* on Certain Bioethical Questions" (September 8, 2008), http://www.vatican.va/roman_curia/congregations /cfaith/documents/rc_con_cfaith_doc_20081208_dignitas-personae_en.html.

45. Some pro-life Catholics feel so strongly about the personhood issue that they are willing to attribute to the Vatican certain positions it does not state: "Though the Church has not stated *infallibly* [that] the newly fertilized ovum 'is a human person,' the Church has stated it must be 'respected and treated as a person.' . . . Not only is the necessary conclusion to all of this that the human being that comes into being at the moment of conception is a human person, but this is the teaching of the Church." Tim Staples, "A Person from the Moment of Conception," *Catholic Answers* (January 17, 2015), https://www.catholic.com/magazine/online-edition/a-person-from -the-moment-of-conception.

46. Francis A. Sullivan discusses the various ways to interpret the magisterial authority of encyclicals like *Evangelium vitae*; see "The Doctrinal Weight of *Evangelium Vitae*," *Theological Studies* 56, no. 3 (1995): 560–65.

47. Congregation for the Doctrine of the Faith, "*Donum Vitae:* Instruction on Respect for Human Life in Its Origin and on the Dignity of Procreation" (February 22, 1987), http://www .vatican.va/roman_curia/congregations/cfaith/documents/rc_con_cfaith_doc_19870222_respect -for-human-life_en.html.

of science regarding the human embryo provide a valuable indication for discerning by the use of reason a personal presence at the moment of this first appearance of a human life: how could a human individual not be a human person? The Magisterium has not expressly committed itself to an affirmation of a philosophical nature, but it constantly reaffirms the moral condemnation of any kind of procured abortion. (§I.1)

The interrogative "How could a human individual not be a human person?" is striking here. Instead of a definitive statement that an individual human embryo is an ensouled person, the Vatican only poses a rhetorical question, recognizing the philosophical difficulties of defining personhood and applying that definition to an embryo.

The Vatican also concedes that scientific opinion varies regarding when a human person can be said to exist and that "doubts" exist regarding the personhood of the embryo; nevertheless, *Dignitas personae* takes the moral position that until those "doubts have been clarified" (§30), abortion must be rejected. To make this point, the document appeals to what is probable by quoting the passage in *Evangelium vitae* (1995) where the probability issue is explicitly presented: "From the standpoint of moral obligation, the mere probability that a human person is involved would suffice to justify an absolutely clear prohibition of any intervention aimed at killing a human embryo" (*Evangelium vitae* §60).[48] The "Declaration on Procured Abortion," issued by the Congregation for the Doctrine of the Faith in 1974, similarly states: "It suffices that this presence of the soul be probable (and one can never prove the contrary)" for one to refrain from "the risk of killing a man."[49] In short, morally, the conceptus should be accorded the rights and dignity of a human person, because there is a chance that it is a person. Several Vatican documents then draw legal and political conclusions that killing a fetus, like killing a born child, are "abominable crimes" (*Donum vitae* §I.1) that constitute "kinship" murder (*Evangelium vitae* §8), and governmental authorities are remiss not to ensure that every abortion is "severely punished."[50]

Carol Tauer has written a definitive essay analyzing the logical problems in these appeals to probability, arguing that the magisterium is mishandling the issue of doubt in relation to its probabilism argument about fetal life. As Tauer explains, there are many ways the term "probable" has been used

---

48. Pope John Paul II, *Evangelium vitae* (March 25, 1995), http://w2.vatican.va/content/john -paul-ii/en/encyclicals/documents/hf_jp-ii_enc_25031995_evangelium-vitae.html.

49. Congregation for the Doctrine of the Faith, "Declaration on Procured Abortion" (November 19, 1974), §19, http://www.vatican.va/roman_curia/congregations/cfaith/documents/rc_con _cfaith_doc_19741118_declaration-abortion-en.html.

50. Congregation for the Doctrine of the Faith, "Declaration on Procured Abortion" §20.

in traditions of Catholic teaching, and certain rules of moral reasoning are standard. If by "probable" one means, for example, a probable opinion about a fact relevant to the loss of someone's life, then caution is morally required and lack of caution is a serious matter. An analogy might be that of a pharmacist who should refrain from dispensing a prescription if he thinks the bottle may contain a poisonous substance. The rule of moral reasoning is that "one *must* at times choose the safer alternative . . . [when] a doubt of fact exists and human life is at risk."[51] The Vatican's documents seem to be applying this rule in a straightforward manner to call for protecting at-risk fetal life. However, while the pharmacist could with effort come to a factual determination about the solution being poisonous or not, neither biologists nor theologians can make a factual determination about when personhood begins. A moral stance regarding embryonic life, in other words, is not a "doubt of fact" situation and should not follow the example of the cautious pharmacist since no factual determination regarding embryonic personhood is possible.[52]

Another aspect of probabilistic moral reasoning has to do with protecting or removing rights in the presence of uncertainty. According to an expert in probabilism, "rights of an uncertain subject . . . are automatically uncertain rights."[53] Consider the example of a missing person. If a person has been missing for years and there is doubt about whether that person is still living, forfeiting that person's rights could be justified. However, the current Roman Catholic arguments for fetal personhood rights do the opposite: they argue for more rights in the presence of doubt. The Declaration on Procured Abortion (1974) states: "Even if a doubt existed concerning whether the fruit of conception is already a human person, it is objectively a grave sin to dare to risk murder" (§13); *Dignitas personae* asserts that from conception, the embryo's "rights as a person must be recognized" (§4). Given that an embryo is, by the Declaration's own admission, a subject whose status is open to uncertainty, its rights should be acknowledged as uncertain and not equal to those of a born person. In probabilism, doubt is not supposed to translate into more rights.

One might say that this is an issue of probabilistic overreach—that is, more certainty is being attributed to a situation where one lacks the ability to make a factual determination (namely, that an embryo is or is not a person). As Tauer explains, the Vatican "appears to be saying that if there is the slightest chance that some type of being falls under the law, then we may not kill

---

51. Tauer, "Tradition of Probabilism," 18.
52. Tauer, "Tradition of Probabilism," 18.
53. Tauer, "Tradition of Probabilism," 28.

it."[54] However, if one were to correctly follow the standard rules of Catholic probabilistic moral reasoning, the rights of an embryo should be less certain than what the magisterium asserts. Invoking probabilism should place the burden of proof on those who want to accord more rights and protections to the embryo, given doubts and ambiguity. The Declaration on Procured Abortion tries to reverse the burden-of-proof requirement, arguing that those who do not want to accord personhood rights should prove that the embryo is not a person.[55] Whether there is a strong probability that early embryos are ensouled persons is open to more debate than some Vatican officials admit,[56] although at least the magisterial documents concede that a situation of doubt—and not factual certainty or revealed truth—obtains regarding fetal personhood.

Tauer points out the technical misuses of probabilism in Vatican statements on fetal rights (her own views on fetal personhood will be discussed in the next chapter). In addition, I criticize the abstract nature of the Vatican's discussions of fetuses—discussions that are largely silent on the role of the uterine environment for this probable human person. The developmental aspects of the fetus are sometimes mentioned, but the maternal body is irrelevant to the Vatican's arguments on personhood, other than implying that the pregnant woman is morally required to offer her body. This portrayal is not surprising since, in other documents, Rome's pronouncements on women's roles—and motherhood, in particular—are notoriously sexist and gender-biased and trade on a stereotype of women's natural maternal receptivity, as Catholic feminist scholars have noted for decades.[57]

A full treatment of the Vatican's views on women and motherhood is beyond the scope of this chapter, but some points are relevant for understanding Roman Catholic personhood arguments. In his 1988 apostolic letter *Mulieris dignitatem*, Pope John Paul II wrote: "Motherhood *in the bio-physical*

---

54. Tauer, "Tradition of Probabilism," 32.
55. No other Vatican document of which I am aware demands that one prove the embryo is not a person.
56. Indeed, Tauer believes that embryological science should cause us to conclude "that it is actually highly improbable that the zygote [is] ensouled." Tauer, "Tradition of Probabilism," 29–30.
57. See Christine E. Gudorf, "Encountering the Other: The Modern Papacy on Women," *Social Compass* 36, no. 3 (1989): 298–300; Cristina L. H. Traina, "Papal Ideals, Marital Realities: One View from the Ground," *Sexual Diversity and Catholicism: Toward the Development of Moral Theology* (Collegeville, MN: Liturgical Press, 2001), 275–88; Rosemary Radford Ruether, "Women, Reproductive Rights and the Catholic Church," *Feminist Theology* 16, no. 2 (2008): 184–93; Susan A. Ross, "Joys and Hopes, Griefs and Anxieties: Catholic Women since Vatican II," *New Theology Review* 25, no. 2 (2013): 35–37; Sheila Briggs, "Separate and Unequal," *Conscience* 2 (August 15, 2017), http://consciencemag.org/2017/08/15/separate-and-unequal/.

sense appears to be passive: the formation process of a new life 'takes place' in her, in her body, which is nevertheless profoundly involved in that process" (§19).[58] *Mulieris dignitatem* accords women dignity but links it to their willingness to adhere to their "essential" femininity, resist "masculinization" (§10), and choose one of two options of "women's vocation"—motherhood or virginity (§17). A pregnant woman who does not accept her fetus is, according to this theology, contravening her essential self: "Motherhood implies from the beginning a special openness to the new person: and *this is precisely the woman's 'part.'* In this openness, in conceiving and giving birth to a child, the woman 'discovers herself through a sincere gift of self'" (§18, emphasis added). There is choice here: to give birth (in the context of marriage, preferably) or remain sexually continent and express her maternal nature spiritually. A woman who does anything other than these two, according to this theology, contradicts her created womanhood.

Among all its other patriarchal and antisexuality problems, this perspective also obscures the pregnant woman in her active, laboring, and decisive role in sustaining the life of her fetus and her born child. Motherhood risks being degraded into the worst sort of embodied exploitation when women's maternal labor is not given recognition and when the exercise of her own conscience is overruled. As Beverly Harrison has warned, "Any definition of 'a human life' or 'person' that neglects the moral reality required to nurture and sustain life after birth is very dangerous to our self-understanding" as a society.[59] Tina Beattie also makes a pointed critique of this theology, arguing that it binds the majority of Catholic women to "the imperative to produce children . . . in such a way that the woman who seeks to explore the meaning of her own life through some channel other than motherhood is denying the very purpose of her body's existence."[60] This theology of motherhood tries to hold together opposite claims: the passivity and activity of motherhood. In marriage, a woman's self is marked by an essential passiveness, meaning that she should always be open to receive her husband's love, respect, and life-generating sperm; on the other hand, she should actively give all she has to sustain the new life whose "formation process . . . 'takes place'" in her (§18). This description of gestation has the appearance of activity but, even here, the woman is the container for a process; she has no right to impinge upon

---

58. Pope John Paul II, *Mulieris dignitatem* (August 15, 1988), §19, http://w2.vatican.va/content /john-paul-ii/en/apost_letters/1988/documents/hf_jp-ii_apl_19880815_mulieris-dignitatem .html.

59. Beverly W. Harrison, *Our Right to Choose: Toward a New Ethic of Abortion* (Boston: Beacon Press, 1983), 224.

60. Tina Beattie, *God's Mother, Eve's Advocate* (New York: Continuum, 2002), 77.

it—whether to prevent its beginning through contraception or to terminate the biological process once it has begun.

Again, we see a troubling attitude toward women's obligation to sustain fetal life no matter how a conception occurs. The Roman Catholic Church does not consider being impregnated through rape or incest or at a young age as a circumstance where women or girls should be allowed to exercise their moral conscience regarding abortion.[61] This absolute rejection of abortion is not just magisterial teaching or a stance among conservative Roman Catholic philosophers. Various arms of the Roman Catholic Church vigorously and publicly promote the notion of human rights from conception[62] and engage in active outreach that attempts to persuade women to accept maternity as their natural and moral vocation, once a pregnancy occurs, however it occurs, including rape.[63] The Catholic church has a long-standing political presence in Latin America, in particular, where it attempts to influence those countries to ban abortion completely (with no exceptions for rape, incest, or even the life of the mother), which they succeeded in doing in 2006 in Nicaragua. Organizations such as Amnesty International have documented the devastating effects of Nicaragua's total abortion ban in the lives of women and especially girls victimized by rape and incest.[64] Pro-life philosophers are not detached from political anti-abortion efforts and often lend their academic credibility to them. Two prominent Catholic philosophers were signatories of a document drafted in Costa Rica in 2011, subsequently presented at the European Parliament, meant to support more restrictive abortion laws globally. The document argues that there is "no autonomous right to abortion . . . either based on 'private life' or on the 'right to life' or to health," and that "states have the obligation to protect human life, from conception to

---

61. See Ruether, "Women, Reproductive Rights and the Catholic Church," 191.
62. For example, U.S. Catholic bishops have a well-developed plan that includes religious, social, public policy, and legislative activities. "Pastoral Plan for Pro-Life Activities," *U.S. Conference of Catholic Bishops* (2001), http://www.usccb.org/about/pro-life-activities/respect-life-program/pastoral-plan-for-prolife-activities-materials.cfm.
63. See Sandra Mahkorn, "Life Matters: Pregnancy from Rape," *U.S. Conference of Catholic Bishops* (2013), http://www.usccb.org/about/pro-life-activities/respect-life-program/2013/upload/2013-Life-Matters-Pregnancy-From-Rape-secured.pdf.
64. Pregnancy is dangerous for girls, and Nicaragua has the highest teenage pregnancy rate in Latin America; in one report, the highest rate of pregnancy from rape or incest was in the age range of 10 to 14. See Amnesty International, *The Total Abortion Ban in Nicaragua* (London: Amnesty International Publications, 2009): 16, 22, https://www.amnestyusa.org/pdfs/amr430012009en.pdf. See also Anastasia Moloney, "Abortion Ban Leads to More Maternal Deaths in Nicaragua," *The Lancet* 374, no. 9691 (2009): 677, https://www.thelancet.com/journals/lancet/article/PIIS0140-6736(09)61545-2/fulltext.

the natural death."[65] In my opinion, to have participated, even if just as a signatory, in a document of this kind, drafted literally next door to Nicaragua, where pregnant women and girls were and are being injured and dying because of the total abortion ban, is deeply concerning.[66]

Roman Catholic probabilism arguments about the moral value and ontological status of the fetus derive from two assumptions: an independent fetal organism and a morally obligated woman. While the magisterium has invoked the language of probability, it has not adhered to the requirement of probability arguments—namely, restraint about attributing rights to a fetus, given doubts about its personhood. One can only conclude that contrary to its best philosophy, the Vatican does not really think that fetal personhood is open to much doubt at all. Many observers suggest that the church is losing the moral battle to persuade Catholic women to abandon contraception and forgo abortion under any circumstances; if so, it may be that the Catholic church is reacting by intensifying it efforts toward anti-abortion lobbying for legislation that would compel not only Catholic women but all women always to gestate fetal life.[67]

Pro-life philosophers work with the notion of "person" defined as a genetically individual and self-directing organism, and they find that this definition fits even a pre-embryo. I conclude that these philosophers fall far short of achieving a convincing argument that personhood begins at conception, in part, because, outside of an appeal to genetics, the embryo or fetus they describe as meeting this definition of personhood is so abstract as to hardly resemble a real in-utero being at all. At best, these philosophers secure the personhood of their idea of an embryo or fetus, not any actual embryo or fetus that might develop in a woman's womb. Roman Catholic magisterial teachings on abortion appeal to probabilism and even admit that fetal personhood is open to scientific and philosophical debate; however, they do not

---

65. "ECLJ Takes Part in the Launch of the San José Articles at the European Parliament: 'Life, as Well as the Right to Life, Starts at Conception,'" *European Center for Law and Justice* (October 26, 2011), https://eclj.org/eclj-takes-part-in-the-launch-of-the-san-jose-articles-at-the-european-parliament-life-as-well-as-the-right-to-life-starts-at-conception. John Haldane (discussed above) and conservative Catholic law professor John Finnis participated. See Austin Ruse, "Major Pro-life Document, San Jose Articles, Launched at UN," *LifeNews.com* (October 6, 2011), http://www.lifenews.com/2011/10/06/major-pro-life-document-san-jose-articles-launched-at-un/.

66. A total ban on abortion exists in other countries in the region as well. See "Abortion in Latin America and the Caribbean," *Guttmacher Institute* (2017), https://www.guttmacher.org/sites/default/files/factsheet/ib_aww-latin-america.pdf.

67. See Kathryn M. Ott, "From Politics to Theology: Responding to Roman Catholic Ecclesial Control of Reproductive Ethics," *Journal of Feminist Studies in Religion* 30, no. 1 (2014): 138–47.

adhere to the logic of their own principle of probabilism and, instead, accord full personhood rights to an embryo whose personhood is actually in doubt. Both pro-life substantialists and Roman Catholic philosophers and church authorities fail miserably in the way they address women and pregnancy. Both groups disregard women's biological contribution to and labor on behalf of embryonic and fetal development and relegate women to a role of passive fetal incubator. That her well-being and very personhood might be threatened by nonconsensual sex, failed contraception, and state-imposed gestation is a disturbing nonfactor for these pro-life philosophers. These philosophers and magisterial authorities show a callous disregard for the societal implications of their unargued claims of fetal innocence and their offhand remarks that banning abortion does not oppress raped women.

It is time to abandon the spurious objective of securing fetal personhood in ways that denigrate women's moral consciousness and threaten their self-determination and, sometimes, their very lives. If one must speak of personhood at all, one can only say that a fetal being develops toward becoming a person by means of complex interactions of genetics, maternal contributions, and the fetus's own biological processes. Emphasizing the incremental aspects of gestation does not mean that no value adheres to a fetus. On the contrary. In the chapter that follows, I take a different approach to understanding fetal value and women's gestational obligations and authority. I make the case that one can and should attribute value to the fetus—no matter at what stage of development. Doing so emphasizes the moral seriousness of any abortion decision without undercutting a pregnant woman's maternal authority to determine her reproductive life and the fate of her fetus.

PART 2

Constructive Pro-choice Proposals

5

Maternal Authority and Fetal Value

Two moral questions are posed by this chapter: How should we speak of a pregnant woman's identity, such that she is recognizable as capable of and uniquely authorized to make gestational choices, including to end fetal life? How should we speak of fetal value, given the instability of the notion of fetal personhood? While conceptualizing the authority, responsibilities, and identity of the woman who becomes pregnant—and does not wish to be—is logically and experientially prior to and distinct from the status of the fetus she carries, the pregnant woman's identity is unavoidably and experientially connected to the status of her fetus, and vice versa. Addressing both issues is crucial for building a comprehensive pro-choice moral position.

The first section of this chapter discusses three paradigms that have figured prominently in the defense of abortion rights for how to understand pregnant women's subjectivity. The first paradigm is found mostly in the writings of pro-choice legal scholars, who argue that an unwanted pregnancy amounts to adversarial danger or injury (to use the legal term) from which the woman, designated as victim, has some rights—including even constitutional ones—to be protected. Proponents of a second paradigm present the pregnant woman who has not yet developed a mothering subjectivity as having a pre-mothering identity, which frees her from gestational obligations to her fetus. In critical conversation with both of these positions, I advocate for a third, and what I deem to be stronger, pro-choice philosophical paradigm, which sees pregnancy not as a precursor to motherhood but as a state that automatically places serious mothering responsibilities on a woman. Ending a life in utero is a serious decision that a gestating mother should be seen as having the moral authority to make. If pregnancy termination is not seen as itself a mothering decision, then women who have abortions forever carry the stigma of being women who selfishly or callously rejected motherhood responsibilities. In addition, and even more dangerously, the door will be opened for imposing on women's bodies the requirements of supposedly good mothering, including but not limited to state-imposed forced gestation and imposed forms of birthing.

Some defense of fetal value is a given in pro-choice ethics today. The second section of this chapter examines pro-choice arguments for fetal value, which, somewhat ironically, adhere to a similar personhood paradigm used in pro-life discourse—with one difference being that pro-life writers try to secure personhood from conception and pro-choice writers see personhood as pertaining to a later stage in fetal development. Part 1 of this book made the case that pro-life writers fail to provide convincing arguments (biblical, theological, philosophical) for fetal personhood. In this chapter, I assess the limitations of pro-choice arguments and offer, in the final section of this chapter, what I believe is a stronger alternative for understanding fetal value because it remains attentive to the discourse of many pregnant women of their "baby" and to the material realities of pregnancy. I propose that the status of a fetus is best understood in terms of a tensive, dual claim: a fetus is not a nonperson without value, but neither is a fetus a person whom a woman is morally obligated always to gestate. The being in her womb, even though recognized as having value, does not overrule her maternal authority to decide its gestational fate and her own.

THE PREGNANT WOMAN'S SUBJECTIVITY AND MATERNAL AUTHORITY

This section proposes how best to construe a pregnant woman's subjectivity, as part of a defense of her moral authority vis-à-vis abortion, by critically assessing three paradigms for understanding the gestating woman in relation to her fetus. The first paradigm—what I am calling an endangerment view of pregnancy—is suggested in classic Jewish halakah and articulated today in the writings of feminist legal scholars. The second paradigm, which can be called a pre-motherhood pro-choice stance, is represented by a wide range of feminist philosophers. These thinkers argue in various ways that if women's experience of early pregnancy can be seen as separate from a mothering consciousness, then abortions during that period are morally allowable. I argue instead for a third paradigm, which acknowledges abortion as a mothering decision—a stance that provides not only a stronger philosophical basis for safeguarding women's gestational rights but also coheres with the way many women actually speak about their abortion decision.

Pregnancy as Endangerment

The notion that the fetus might sometimes be in an adversarial position that endangers its mother is an ancient religious viewpoint, classically presenting in the Mishnah, a third-century CE rabbinic legal document that forms the basis of halakic Judaism up to the present day. Ruling on how to handle the life-threatening situation of an obstructed birth, the ancient rabbis specified that one may "dismember the infant in the womb and remove it limb by limb" so as to save the mother's life.[1] Commenting on this passage, medieval Jewish philosopher Moses Maimonides introduced the concept of the fetus as "*rodef* [a pursuer]," whose destruction is justified because its birthing is seen as a threat to its mother's life.[2] In this way, Jewish abortion ethics are based in part on the legal notion of the fetus functioning as a life-threatening aggressor, against which the woman is morally allowed to defend herself.[3]

For legal scholar Eileen McDonagh, the unwanted occupation of a woman's body by a fetus amounts to injury, in the legal sense of the term, just as any kind of nonconsensual use of someone's body would amount to injury for which that person should have legal redress and from which that person should have state protection. Consent to pregnancy is, for McDonagh, the heart of the abortion issue because it goes directly to constitutional protections of bodily integrity. "The Court has ruled, for example, that an individual has a constitutional right to refuse to 'consent' to medical treatment" and even "if a surgeon performs a lifesaving operation on a person, but without that person's consent, in the eyes of the law that surgeon has seriously injured the person."[4] While some pro-choice arguments try to claim that the fetus is not an entity recognizable under the law (making its destruction legally permissible), McDonagh does not consider the status of the fetus to be the crux of the issue in abortion rights. For McDonagh, the personhood status of the fetus is irrelevant, since what is at issue is not "what the fetus 'is'" but the

1. Mishnah *Ohalot* 7:6, as quoted in Alan Jotkowitz, "Abortion and Maternal Need: A Response to Ronit Irshai," *Nashim: A Journal of Jewish Women's Studies & Gender Issues* 21, no. 1 (2011): 99.

2. Maimonides, *Mishneh Torah, Hilkhot Rotzeah* 1:9, as quoted in Jotkowitz, "Abortion and Maternal Need," 100.

3. Jewish scholar Daniel Schiff discusses the various rabbinical debates about the *rodef* principle related to abortion. See Schiff, *Abortion in Judaism* (Cambridge: Cambridge University Press, 2002), 49–52.

4. Eileen McDonagh, "Adding Consent to Choice in the Abortion Debate," *Society* 42, no. 5 (2005): 21.

effect of its incursion into the woman's body when that incursion is unwant-ed.[5] "Legally, if a woman does not consent to the massive transformation of her body resulting from the fetus, she is being injured by the fetus. Though it has no conscious intention to do so." When such an imposition does occur, the woman has a legal right "to use deadly force to stop such injury."[6] McDonagh's reason for stressing that nonconsensual gestation is injury is to move away from the *Roe-v.-Wade*-oriented privacy argument (which ends up favoring the due process rights of privileged pregnant women who can afford private, self-pay abortions)[7] and toward a platform based on the Equal Pro-tection Clause of the Constitution.[8] Under the latter constitutional principle, women with unwanted pregnancies could, in theory, appeal to the state for financial assistance against the injury of an unwanted pregnancy.

Thus, according to the endangerment paradigm, the woman with an unwanted pregnancy can claim to have suffered an injury, whether it turns out to be physiological, psychological, legal, economic, and so on.[9] I agree that there are many reasons for speaking of unwanted pregnancy as an injury, chief among these being legal and legislative. Anti-abortion groups continue effec-tively to etch away at women's abortion rights even with *Roe v. Wade* in place, and feminist activists need ways to strengthen existing and open new legal and legislative avenues for securing access to and medical coverage for reproduc-tive services, including abortion. While some legal scholars might doubt that appealing to the Equal Protection Clause for abortion rights will succeed leg-islatively or in the courts,[10] McDonagh insists that without this legal strategy, abortion may eventually revert to a procedure to which only women with eco-nomic means will have limited access. That said, many feminist scholars wish to give additional arguments that speak to the moral justifiability of abortion, above and beyond an appeal to the injury of unwanted pregnancy. The next two paragidms offer two options—abortion as a pre-mothering or as a moth-ering decision, the latter which I deem to be the stronger option.

5. McDonagh, "Adding Consent to Choice," 22.
6. McDonagh, "Adding Consent to Choice," 20, 23.
7. See McDonagh, "Adding Consent to Choice," 19.
8. Section 1 of the Fourteenth Amendment to the Constitution states, "Nor shall any State deprive any person of life, liberty, or property, without due process of law; *nor deny to any person within its jurisdiction the equal protection of the laws*" (italics added). "The Constitution: Amend-ments 11–27," The National Archives, https://www.archives.gov/founding-docs/amendments -11-27#toc-section-1--2.
9. For pro-life arguments against seeing the fetus as an enemy, see Bernadette Waterman Ward, "Abortion as a Sacrament: Mimetic Desire and Sacrifice in Sexual Politics," *Contagion: Journal of Violence, Mimesis, and Culture* 7, no. 1 (2000): 19–24.
10. For an appreciative critical analysis of McDonagh's position, see Robin West, "Liberalism and Abortion," *Georgetown Law Journal* 87 (1999): 2117–47.

Abortion as a Pre-mothering Decision

A number of feminist thinkers attempt to carve out ethical space for justifiable abortion, based on the relational notion of a pre-motherhood state in early pregnancy. For Tina Beattie, early pregnancy can be seen as a pre-mothering subjectivity, because a woman conceives biologically but only later comes to "consciousness of who she is." Because of this disjunction between the biological processes of pregnancy and the self-consciousness of motherhood, "the developmental process allows a period of grace, . . . when the woman's freedom to decide whether or not to accept the responsibility of motherhood takes precedence over any hypothetical conjecture about the moral status of the embryo."[11] Beattie suggests that there is a narrow, approximately eight-week period of time in early pregnancy when abortion should be permissible even by the Roman Catholic Church. During this window, most women come to realize that they are pregnant but have little to no "maternal consciousness" toward the fetus.[12] This viewpoint of women's subjectivity gives women an emotionally easier and ethically acceptable time frame for terminating a pregnancy. A justifiable abortion is one that occurs before the woman either is aware of the pregnancy or consciously accepts herself as being a mother to a developing child.

Frances Gray similarly claims that pregnancy is not coterminous with motherhood. Taking her phenomenological cues from philosopher Maurice Merleau-Ponty, Gray builds a very particular view of the human person made of "flesh," which is the "sensible and sentient" aspect of the embodied self as it interacts with the world,[13] and "subjective-will," meaning a person's more self-reflective aspect of consciousness. A woman's fleshly body-will and her conscious subjective-will "do not always match," and unwanted pregnancy is a case in point. The pregnant flesh may be hospitable to an embryo, but the subjective will of the woman may wish to "override" the flesh.[14] The phenomenological basis for why this move is justified, according to Gray, is that pregnancy is a kind of "primitive hospitality" that a woman's flesh gives on its own accord but does not entail any automatic obligation from her to continue

11. Tina Beattie, "Catholicism, Choice and Consciousness: A Feminist Theological Perspective on Abortion," *International Journal of Public Theology* 4, no. 1 (2010): 70. Beattie is a professor of Catholic studies in the U.K.
12. Beattie, "Catholicism, Choice and Consciousness," 70, 71. Beattie's corresponding views on fetal personhood will be discussed below.
13. Frances Gray, "Original Habitation: Pregnant Flesh as Absolute Hospitality," in Sarah LaChance Adams and Caroline R. Lundquist, eds., *Coming to Life: Philosophies of Pregnancy, Childbirth, and Mothering* (New York: Fordham University Press, 2013), 78. Gray is a philosopher based in Australia.
14. Gray, "Original Habitation," 86.

that hosting.[15] For Gray, "a pregnant woman qua pregnant woman is not yet mother to this specific life in her uterus," and hence she is "bracketed from the responsibility of the maternal" by virtue of her "pre-maternal" state of being.[16] Gray maintains that hospitality to the in-utero being is not obligatory if no maternal subjectivity yet exists in relation to "embryonic guest."[17]

Jane Lymer, in her *Phenomenology of Gravidity*, argues that a pregnant woman is not obligated to give ethical regard to the fetus until sufficient alterity has been established so that the fetus becomes a genuine "Other" to whom she has a moral responsibility. For Lymer, "until there is an experience of alterity, even at an unconscious embodied level, there is no hospitality and therefore no unethical 'act'" in having an abortion.[18] Lymer's argument depends on maintaining a clear demarcation between the enactment of a conscious maternal identity and the phenomenon of what she calls "gravidity," which is the mere "state of a woman who has conceived."[19] Lymer points to the old-fashioned term "quickening, the time when the woman will experience foetal movement herself," as a developmental marker when the fetus emerges as distinct in the woman's experience.[20] For most women, quickening begins a process of bonding between the woman and the fetus, before which "there is no ethical relation and so an early termination can be seen as morally acceptable." In this way, a phenomenology of gravidity posits a kind of "space prior to" the moral obligation of "unconditional" maternal hospitality in pregnancy.[21]

Beattie's discussion of women's lack of mothering self-consciousness in early pregnancy, Gray's description of pre-maternal subjectivity, and Lymer's phenomenology of gravidity cause us to think seriously about the fleshly, relational reality of gestation. Much happens in pregnancy apart from what a

---

15. Gray, "Original Habitation," 84. Gray contrasts this with the Virgin Mary's "unconditional hospitality." Gray, "Original Habitation," 75. I will discuss Mary in chap. 7.

16. Gray, "Original Habitation," 85.

17. Gray, "Original Habitation," 79.

18. Jane M. Lymer, *The Phenomenology of Gravidity: Reframing Pregnancy and the Maternal through Merleau-Ponty, Levinas and Derrida* (London: Rowman & Littlefield, 2016), 65. Lymer teaches philosophy at the University of Wollongong, Australia.

19. Lymer, *The Phenomenology of Gravidity*, 6. Lymer disagrees with using the term "mother" to refer to a woman who has conceived, arguing that "providing a hiatus between gravidity and maternity gives women permission to choose to be maternal." Lymer, *The Phenomenology of Gravidity*, 20. One finds a version of this viewpoint in Rebecca Peters's description of intersubjectivity in pregnancy: "When a woman chooses to keep a pregnancy, the prenate is becoming a human being during gestation even as the pregnant woman is becoming a mother." Rebecca Todd Peters, *Trust Women: A Progressive Christian Argument for Reproductive Justice* (Boston: Beacon Press, 2018), 159.

20. Lymer, *The Phenomenology of Gravidity*, 55.

21. Lymer, *The Phenomenology of Gravidity*, 186.

woman wills. Many women deeply desire to have a baby, but one-half to even three-quarters of early first-trimester pregnancies spontaneously abort.[22] In one sense, a woman is not really consciously in control of her pregnancy. That said, however, I have misgivings about grounding the morality of abortion on the notion of a woman's supposedly pre-maternal, pre-ethical subjectivity in early pregnancy or her "bracketed" state of fleshly hospitality distinct from motherhood. This approach could open the door to seeing the pregnant woman as someone with a limited perspective on her own pregnancy and, hence, having limited authority to make serious life decisions like abortion.[23]

Abortion as a Mothering Decision

I argue that pregnancy should be seen as a unique stage of a mothering relationship—gestational mothering.[24] My argument has two components: first, I argue that terminating a pregnancy should be seen as a mothering, rather than a pre- or non- or anti-mothering decision; and second, I argue that abortion should be seen not only as a decision not to mother gestationally but also a decision that there be no "future child" to whom one would have maternal obligations.[25] Viewing abortion as a mothering decision is necessary in order to establish that the maternal authority that society commonly accords to women after giving birth also applies to women before they give birth. Unless pregnant women are seen as "rational moral agents,"[26] the biology of the womb, rather than women's moral conscience, will be allowed

22. See Thomas A. Shannon and Allan B. Wolter, "Reflections on the Moral Status of the Pre-embryo," *Theological Studies* 51, no. 4 (1990): 618–19. Katrien Devolder and John Harris, "The Ambiguity of the Embryo: Ethical Inconsistency in the Human Embryonic Stem Cell Debate," *Metaphilosophy* 38, nos. 2–3 (2007): 161.

23. This viewpoint could feed into the current growing pro-life legislative push to make ultrasound a requirement before any abortion, based on the unspoken assumption that women need to be informed about their pregnancy. See "State Policies in Brief: Requirements for Ultrasound," *Guttmacher Institute*, March 1, 2016, updated October 1, 2018, https://www.guttmacher.org/sites/default/files/pdfs/spibs/spib_RFU.pdf.

24. I note that phrases like "gestational mothering" might seem to exclude some transgender and gender nonconforming persons who get pregnant and who prefer the gender-neutral term "parent." Studies show that there are a range of parental self-identifiers among transgender persons. See Marie-Pier Petit, Danielle Julien, and Line Chamberland, "Negotiating Parental Designations among Trans Parents' Families: An Ecological Model of Parental Identity," *Psychology of Sexual Orientation and Gender Diversity* 4, no. 3 (2017): 282. The argument I put forth here about abortion as a mothering decision is meant to apply broadly because gestational mothering can mean biological states and actions of either a cisgender woman or any person who can get pregnant.

25. Catriona Mackenzie, "Abortion and Embodiment," *Australasian Journal of Philosophy* 70, no. 2 (1992): 152.

26. Beverly W. Harrison, *Our Right to Choose: Toward a New Ethic of Abortion* (Boston: Beacon Press, 1983), 7.

to determine the outcome of pregnancy. In addition, linking abortion with mothering acknowledges the experiences of many women whose difficult decision to abort is made precisely from a mothering perspective. Sociologists are increasingly paying attention to how women of many backgrounds, races, and socioeconomic classes who choose abortion do so with the self-understanding that it was "the best choice for me and for the baby."[27] Studies show that many women who find themselves pregnant unexpectedly do begin some kind of deliberation and decision-making process in a mothering mode. I argue that because the gestational mother has the obligation thrust upon her to decide whether to continue the pregnancy or not, she therefore has the primary authority to decide.

One feminist thinker who has made this argument forcefully is the late British philosopher Soran Reader. In her essay "Abortion, Killing, and Maternal Moral Authority," Reader presents pregnancy as a time when a woman is fully engaged in ethical maternal decision making—not because pregnancy automatically gives women some essential or privileged ethical insight but because it automatically constitutes her as someone from whom mothering decisions are required. The uncontroversial assumption grounding Reader's essay is that motherhood unavoidably entails responsibilities—whether one wants them or not: "Motherhood is a monumental, complex, life-structuring relationship."[28] Reader applies the maternal responsibility principle to the issue of unwanted pregnancy, not to argue that a pregnant woman has a prima facie obligation to gestate her child, but to argue that the obligation to decide about whether or not to gestate is the pregnant woman's, and it is a maternal obligation. In other words, Reader argues that a woman's decision to end her fetus's life is not an abdication of maternal responsibility but an early ending of that responsibility: "The mother who cannot go on into the next stage of mothering discharges her maternal responsibility for organizing that whole life, by ending it. She does not relinquish responsibility for her fetus's life. Rather, she exercises her maternal moral authority to complete her responsibility early."[29] Once a woman knows that she is pregnant, or thinks she might be pregnant, the responsibility for making mothering decisions is ipso facto thrust upon her.[30] A maternal decision is required of her, whether or not

27. See Rachel K. Jones, Lori F. Frohwirth, and Ann M. Moore, "'I Would Want to Give My Child, Like, Everything in the World': How Issues of Motherhood Influence Women Who Have Abortions," *Journal of Family Issues* 29, no. 1 (2008): 83.
28. Soran Reader, "Abortion, Killing, and Maternal Moral Authority," *Hypatia* 23, no. 1 (2008): 139.
29. Reader, "Abortion, Killing, and Maternal Moral Authority," 143.
30. Regarding women's moral responsibility to make decisions about gestation, see Mackenzie, "Abortion and Embodiment," 139.

she feels consciously or emotionally connected to the fetus, whether or not she acknowledges the fetus's alterity. Will she continue with her mothering obligations, which will only grow in importance, or will she end her mothering obligations early? This is a decision for which she, as the gestating parent, must be acknowledged as having primary responsibility.

Reader's theory is echoed in the actual voices of women who get abortions. Many women, even those who are not already mothers, see their abortion as a mothering decision. Linda Ellison, who has researched the experiences of conservative Christian women who have had abortions, records this comment from one of her study's participants. The woman recounted a conversation with an opinionated abortion clinic counselor: "I kept telling [the counselor at the clinic] that to me, it wasn't just tissue, and she basically told me that I was wrong, that it wasn't more than a mass of tissue. . . . She kept throwing out phrases like 'It's not a child, it's a choice.' Talking to me in bumper stickers. It was so infuriating. Because really, it isn't one or the other. It is a choice about a child. And it's my choice, and my possible child."[31] Perhaps in an effort to allay the woman's possible emotional trauma or feelings of guilt, this particular clinic counselor tried to direct the patient away from maternal thoughts about a child-that-might-be. However, this woman, who did not already have born children, intuitively experienced her abortion as a mother's decision. Even women who are conflicted speak of their abortion as a decision about a baby, as seen in this young woman's statement about why she had an abortion: "A baby needs someone who is, well, who knows who she is. So I decided the only thing I could do was have an abortion. . . . I felt like I was about to do a really bad thing, but like I also said, I just know I can't do a good job of being a mom now. . . . I hope God forgives me."[32] Not every woman will see their abortion as having to do with the fate of a possible child; however, those who do seem to be claiming their maternal authority to make this decision and refusing to have the reality of what they are doing downplayed.

The second aspect of seeing abortion as a mothering decision is to recognize that abortion is, in effect, a decision that there be no child born in the near future of whom one would be the mother and to whom one would have maternal obligations. This statement may seem self-evident, but this aspect of abortion is not always explicitly explained and argued. As Reader

---

31. Linda Ellison, "Abortion and the Politics of God: Patient Narratives and Public Rhetoric in the American Abortion Debate," PhD diss., Harvard Divinity School (2008), 201. "Ashley" is 24 years old and self-identifies as evangelical and unmarried: "Jesus and I are tight. And I don't think he's mad at all about me having an abortion." Ellison, "Abortion and the Politics of God," 66.

32. Ellison, "Abortion and the Politics of God," 69. "Melanie" is 17 years old and self-described as Catholic.

explains starkly, the woman who aborts "fulfils her maternal responsibility for
her fetus's life" by ruling out birthing, raising, or relinquishing it to another
through adoption; instead, "she has consigned it to oblivion, because as its
mother she has judged this the right thing to do."[33] Even if one holds religious views of the afterlife, abortion should not be referred to with euphe-
misms. Reader is clear that she means "abortion-as-killing," and the being
who dies is not "negligible."[34] We see here a pro-choice argument that
assumes fetal value because they "are developing human beings, the children
of particular parents, of and in their mothers' bodies, and they are morally significant for those reasons," which is why the decision for abortion is a morally
important one.[35] If fetal value were negligible, abortion would be a morally
inconsequential decision, and the need to establish women's maternal authority would be moot.

Reader gives a philosophical argument grounding a woman's right not just
to evacuate a fetus from her womb but also to end the life of an in-utero
developing being, so that she will not be maternally obligated to that being
in any way now or in the future.[36] Other feminist ethicists reiterate this relational point. Nel Noddings argues that abortion, even when the woman's
stated intention is just to be free of the pregnancy, is often also motivated by a
deeper desire that there not "be a baby (a responsive being) who will be [her]

33. Reader, "Abortion, Killing, and Maternal Moral Authority," 143. Reader's apparently
negative views of relinquishment and adoption need more elaboration. Adoption can be positive
for some birth mothers, but studies also point to intense and lingering maternal grief subsequent to relinquishment. See Michael De Simone, "Birth Mother Loss: Contributing Factors to
Unresolved Grief," *Clinical Social Work Journal* 24, no. 1 (1996): 65–76; Janette Logan, "Birth
Mothers and Their Mental Health: Uncharted Territory," *The British Journal of Social Work* 26,
no. 5 (1996): 609–25.
34. Reader, "Abortion, Killing, and Maternal Moral Authority," 143, 147.
35. Reader, "Abortion, Killing, and Maternal Moral Authority," 134. I will address the factors
that speak to fetal value specifically below.
36. Reader recognizes that her proposal could provoke the specter of "infanticide." See Reader,
"Abortion, Killing, and Maternal Moral Authority," 145. I think Reader is mistaken in extending her argument to infanticide at all. The argument I am making about maternal authority and
abortion applies only to the gestational context. That said, infanticide is not a straightforward
phenomenon. Reader notes that in extremis, cases of infanticide could occur, and she cites the
literary example of Toni Morrison's *Beloved*. See Reader, "Abortion, Killing, and Maternal Moral
Authority," 146. One literary critic refers to Morrison's narrative of infanticide as "a model of
historical empathy." Heather Love, "Close but Not Deep: Literary Ethics and the Descriptive
Turn," *New Literary History* 41, no. 2 (2010): 375. New historical research is emerging about
the use of abortifacients and infanticide by enslaved black women as a mode of resistance. See
Loucynda Jensen, "Searching the Silence: Finding Black Women's Resistance to Slavery in Antebellum US History," *PSU McNair Scholars Online Journal* 2, no. 1 (2013); Renee K. Harrison,
Enslaved Women and the Art of Resistance in Antebellum America (New York: Palgrave Macmillan,
2009), 172–73.

. . . biological child."[37] Catriona Mackenzie also argues that abortion should be acknowledged as a decision not just to end an unwanted gestation but also to end responsibilities to a future child:

> What the abortion decision involves is a decision that this part of herself should not *become* a being in relation to whom such questions of parental responsibility and emotional attachment arise. In other words abortion is not a matter of wanting to kill *this particular being*, which is, after all, as yet indistinguishable from oneself. It is rather a matter of not wanting there to *be* a future child, so intimately related to oneself, for which one either has to take responsibility or give up to another.[38]

Even if the mother could terminate her gestational obligations—say, by transferring the developing embryo to an artificial womb—that action would not complete the decision-making obligation that is thrust upon the pregnant woman.

Some women do approach an abortion decision as a desire simply not to be pregnant anymore or to have extraneous tissue removed from their uterus, and my intention is not to tell them how to think about their abortion. That said, I believe that poet Gwendolyn Brooks strikes a deep chord in her evocative poem "The Mother," where she writes: "Abortions will not let you forget. / You remember the children you got that you did not get."[39] I keep in mind this visceral feeling in proposing that a philosophically stable and ethically defensible pro-choice position needs to acknowledge honestly that abortion is a decision not just to end a pregnancy but is also a decision not to have a being come into the world to whom one has a mothering obligation. For this reason, abortion must be starkly defined morally as a decision to kill a living being in utero—a momentous decision that only the gestating mother has the authority to make. It would be morally abhorrent for anyone else to make that kind of decision for her.[40] The only drawback I can see in making this point

37. Nel Noddings, *Women and Evil* (Berkeley: University of California Press, 1989), 152. I discuss Noddings's views in chap. 6.
38. Mackenzie, "Abortion and Embodiment," 152, italics in original.
39. Gwendolyn Brooks, *Selected Poems* (New York: Harper & Row, 1963), 4.
40. The practice of coerced and forced abortions associated with China's former one-child policy is well known and has been repudiated by pro-life and pro-choice groups alike. My discussion of gestational authority does not apply to the complex moral and legal arrangement referred to as gestational surrogacy, which is fraught with concerns about the exploitation of poor woman of color serving as surrogates but also concerns about discrimination against gay couples who use surrogacy to build a family. For more on these issues see Heather E. Dillaway, "Mothers for Others: A Race, Class, and Gender Analysis of Surrogacy," *International Journal of Sociology of the Family* 34, no. 2 (2008): 301–26; Khiara M. Bridges, "Windsor, Surrogacy, and Race," *Washington Law Review* 89, no. 4 (2014): 1125–53.

is that pro-life forces would manipulate this discourse in order to continue to instill guilt in women who abort, as they have done in multiple platforms from sermons, to Web sites, to scholarly publications, and more.[41] Their invectives are mostly linked to their claims of fetal personhood and sacredness—claims whose lack of biblical or theological substance I have addressed in part 1 of this book.

Beyond the philosophical and experiential reasons for categorizing abortion as a mothering decision are political ones. If a pregnant woman is not recognized as having maternal moral authority over her fetus, laws could be passed that, while not overturning her constitutional right to abortion, nevertheless eviscerate it with restrictions. There are statutes in some states where pregnant women can be jailed for drug use because of possible fetal harm,[42] and one judge even jailed a pregnant woman to prevent an abortion from taking place.[43] Even with *Roe v. Wade* still the law of the land, one can imagine (even if it seems fantastical) a statute being passed that allows a woman the right to end her pregnancy but only on the condition that she continue to gestate until a minimally viable fetus could be birthed or surgically removed and given over to state custody for adoption.[44] Or one can imagine the state mandating that only certain types of abortion-termination procedures are allowable because they do not inflict pain on the supposedly sentient fetus.[45]

---

41. See the stories of women who have attended retreats at an organization called Rachel's Vineyard, where women and men are encouraged to share their postabortion feelings and receive pastoral support. See http://www.rachelsvineyard.org/emotions/stories.aspx. The chairman of the board is infamous anti-abortion activist Fr. Frank Pavone, the founder of Priests for Life, who came under diocesan investigation for his anti-abortion tactics. See Peter Jesserer Smith, "Father Pavone Faces Diocesan Investigation over Aborted Baby on Altar," *National Catholic Register* (November 14, 2016), http://www.ncregister.com/daily-news/father -pavone-faces-diocesan-investigation-over-aborted-baby-on-altar.

42. Laura Bassett, "Tennessee Enacts Law to Incarcerate Pregnant Women Who Use Drugs," *Huffington Post*, posted April 30, 2014; updated May 1, 2014, http://www.huffingtonpost.com /2014/04/30/tennessee-to-incarcerate-_n_5241770.html.

43. Yuriko Kawaguchi was jailed for a forgery charge that normally receives a penalty of fines and probation. Judge Patricia Cleary of the Common Pleas Court of Cuyahoga County, Ohio, handed down a jail sentence specifically to block the then-pregnant Kawaguchi from getting an abortion. "Judge Intends Prison Time to Block Abortion," *New York Times* (October 11, 1998), http://www.nytimes.com/1998/10/11/us/judge-intends-prison-time-to-block-abortion.html. The judge was later suspended for her actions. "Reproductive Freedom Press Release," *ACLU of Ohio* (June 3, 2002), http://www.acluohio.org/archives/press-releases/final-settlement-in-suit -over-sentencing-to-prevent-abortion.

44. Ruth Colker, who interprets *Roe v. Wade* as the right to terminate a pregnancy, not to kill a fetus, suggests that "an appropriate response to viability would be to require the woman to cooperate with a physician so that the fetus' life could be preserved if the woman terminates the pregnancy." Colker, "Feminism, Theology, and Abortion: Toward Love, Compassion, and Wisdom," *California Law Review* 77, no. 5 (1989): 1056. I cannot imagine any physician ethically agreeing to arrange a premature birth for this reason.

45. This is not fantastical thinking. See Susan J. Lee et al., "Fetal Pain: A Systematic Multidisciplinary Review of the Evidence," *JAMA* 294, no. 8 (2005): 947–54.

Roman Catholic hospitals already have in place instructions for allowable procedures that would maintain the distinction that Roman Catholic moral teaching considers important between "direct" versus "indirect" killing.[46] All of these scenarios, real or imagined, share the implied viewpoint that a pregnant woman somehow does not sufficiently understand her pregnant state or the fetal life within her; hence, the state or some other authoritative institution is allowed to intervene in her pregnancy, as it sees fit.

It should come as no surprise that seeing abortion as a mothering decision would baffle pro-life proponents for whom motherhood is prima facie defined as a vocation of nurturing life. One pro-life scholar claims that Reader considers the fetus to be "a piece of property over which [the woman] has 'maternal authority.'"[47] Reader nowhere states that a fetus is property, and I am not aware of any current feminist making this claim.[48] Even the most liberal pro-choice feminists would reject the putative notion that a mother owns the fetus she is carrying.[49] Reader asserts that the fetus has value; however, it exists in a situation of dependence upon its gestating mother, who should be seen as having authority over it—not as its property owner but as its gestational parent, who must decide its fate. Another pro-life writer commenting on the notion of abortion as a mothering decision called it "monstrous" and "abhorrent," based on the claim he deems self-evident that there is no difference in the value of life between an intrauterine fetus and a one-week-old born child.[50] My discussion of the status and value of uterine life comes later in this chapter, but I will foreshadow that discussion by saying here that I ground fetal value not in beliefs about a fetus's moral equivalence to a born child but

46. See Christopher Kaczor, *The Ethics of Abortion: Women's Rights, Human Life, and the Question of Justice* (New York: Routledge, 2014), 188–91. For a recent controversial case, see Bernard G. Prusak, "Double Effect, All Over Again: The Case of Sister Margaret McBride," *Theoretical Medicine and Bioethics* 32, no. 4 (2011): 271–83. See also n. 95 below.

47. Charles K. Bellinger, *Jesus v. Abortion: They Know Not What They Do* (Eugene, OR: Cascade Books, 2016), 102. See also Michael J. Gorman and Ann Loar Brooks, *Holy Abortion? A Theological Critique of the Religious Coalition for Reproductive Choice: Why Christians and Christian Churches Should Reconsider the Issue of Abortion* (Eugene, OR: Cascade Books, 2003), 49.

48. Property issues are real in other reproductive contexts such as the legal disposition of *ex utero* (e.g., cryo-preserved) embryos, umbilical cord blood, or donated tissues of stillborn, miscarried, or aborted fetuses. See Jessica Berg, "Owning Persons: The Application of Property Theory to Embryos and Fetuses," *Wake Forest Law Review* 40, no. 1 (2005): 159–217; Mary Mahowald, "As If There Were Fetuses without Women: A Remedial Essay," in *Reproduction, Ethics, and the Law: Feminist Perspectives*, ed. Joan C. Callahan, 199–218 (Bloomington: Indiana University Press, 1995).

49. See Mary Anne Warren, "On the Moral and Legal Status of Abortion," *The Monist* 57, no. 1 (1973): 44.

50. Samuel W. Calhoun, "Valuing Intrauterine Life," *Regent University Law Review* 8 (1997): 72. Calhoun is a law professor and a self-avowed pro-life advocate. See Samuel W. Calhoun, "God's Will and Our Own," Life and Learning Conference XVI (2006), http://www.uffl.org/vol16/Calhoun-panel-06.pdf.

on the material reality that a fetus is a developing human being in a unique state of existence intimately connected to its gestating mother.

Gestation is unavoidably developmental. The further along women get in their pregnancies, the more relationality with the developing fetus they usually experience and express. They may begin to talk to their fetus, argue with it, pat it, give it nicknames, feel protective of it. They are called upon to make more and more mothering decisions as the birth approaches: Should I stay in this relationship with the father? When do I tell my boss? Which obstetrician should I go to? Who can watch my kids when I go into the hospital? Motherhood responsibilities build in number and complexity over the course of a pregnancy and, of course, with birth and beyond. To acknowledge the incrementalism in the mother-fetus relationship does not contradict what I have argued above: that a woman who becomes pregnant should be acknowledged as a person from whom mothering decisions are required. Instead of justifying abortion in its early stages because a subjective maternal relationship has not yet sufficiently developed, I argue that a pregnant woman has mothering decision-making obligations, from the start, regarding her fetus. If a pregnant woman is as certain as she can be that she does not have the means she deems important (psychic, medical, economic, and so on) to fulfill her mothering role gestationally and beyond, it verges on irresponsibility for her to let the pregnancy just take its risky course in the hope that her circumstances will miraculously change for the better. If her situation is such that she is unable to foresee at least some way for her to adequately fulfill her mothering responsibilities, gestationally and postpartum, then ethically she cannot avoid facing a serious mothering decision. She may decide to continue mothering gestationally by carrying to full term, while making arrangements to relinquish the baby temporarily or permanently after birth; or she may decide "to complete [her] maternal responsibility early by ending the life of [her] fetus."[51]

Beattie argues for the moral acceptability of early pregnancy termination because the first eight weeks or so of gestation represent a so-called grace period when most women are either unaware that they are pregnant or have not yet come to consciousness of themselves as mothers-to-be. Moreover, she

51. Reader, "Abortion, Killing, and Maternal Moral Authority," 144. While other actors may have some valid medical, ethical, or legal interest in the child's well-being (e.g., the perinatologist, the obstetrician, the father), the legal status of fathers is settled law. While the courts have not ignored the father's interest in his expectant offspring, the "bodily integrity of the pregnant woman" has been repeatedly deemed more important. See Dara Purvis, "Expectant Fathers, Abortion, and Embryos," *Journal of Law, Medicine and Ethics* 43 (2015): 333. Compelled fetal medical interventions and compelled medical treatment for pregnant women are on the rise, particularly for vulnerable populations of women. See Naira Roland Matevosyan, "Court-Visited Obstetrical and Fertility Procedures," *Archives of Gynecology and Obstetrics* 285, no. 5 (2012): 1195–1203.

notes, we live in a "muddled" world marked by sufferings and tragedies of many kinds. Since the church accedes to some justifiable violence in traditionally male domains (war), it should do the same, Beattie argues, for women in relation to the tragic but often unavoidable "violence" of abortion.[52] I appreciate Beattie's attempt to put at least a crack in the edifice of the Roman Catholic magisterium's anti-abortion stance, which has been implemented in draconian ways by governments in some Catholic-majority countries.[53] Sometimes women are caught up in tragic situations that would make the requirement to gestate unjust and cruel. However, the strategy of pleading for some abortion considerations for women victimized by an imperfect and patriarchal world does not speak to the experience of many women with an unwanted pregnancy.

Sometimes, a woman who is not particularly oppressed or downtrodden simply makes the calculation that giving birth to a child is not in her and her family's self-interest. It may not be a trivial decision for her. She may reflect on it for years to come, but this woman's decision may not be made in a fog of lack of self-consciousness of the embryo developing within her or the baby to come. I return to the words of the Christian women in Ellison's study—in this case, a thirty-seven-year-old mother who expressed her abortion decision this way: "All my kids live at home. So, when . . . I found out I was pregnant, I was like 'No, Lord, No!' I love my kids. Every one of them. . . . It's just that there isn't any more room in the house. . . . [I'm] up in the night changing diapers, cleaning up vomit, listening to broken-hearted nine-year-olds. Maybe that doesn't sound like a lot, but it's taxing. I think God must know that, because God has a lot of children too."[54] We see here a woman of faith and a committed mother making the well-informed decision that she deems best in that moment for her (in this case, large) family. It is unrealistic to think that, once she knew she was pregnant, she could ever put herself into a pre-maternal state of mind, where her abortion decision would supposedly be justified. On the contrary, hers was a fully maternal decision.

A more robust argument for undergirding reproductive rights for all women—societally victimized or not—is the argument for gestational maternal authority. The decision in *Roe v. Wade* accorded woman certain reproductive legal rights. In addition to rights, this essay argues, pregnant women have serious, mothering decision-making obligations, which only they have

52. Beattie, "Catholicism, Choice and Consciousness," 74.

53. See Rosemary Radford Ruether, "Women, Reproductive Rights and the Catholic Church," *Feminist Theology* 16, no. 2 (2008): 184–93.

54. Ellison, "Abortion and the Politics of God," 67. "Patty" self-identifies as "Catholic and Hispanic." She still struggles with her abortion decision; see Ellison, "Abortion and the Politics of God," 217.

the authority to make. Although it may seem counterintuitive and even hor-
rendous to think of a mother deciding to cause the death of her in-utero child,
only a mother should have the authority to make such a decision. Indeed, as
noted above, many women who decide to abort do so in a mothering mind-set.

Thus, my position is that pregnant women should be thought of as mothers obligated and authorized to make mothering decisions. A common reason
pro-life proponents would reject this position is the assumption that women
with unwanted pregnancies are not capable of functioning as moral decision
makers.[55] The latter viewpoint assumes that bad decisions (e.g., lack of contraception planning, promiscuity, etc.) got them into this mess; hence, they
will probably continue to make bad decisions. Christian pro-life proponents
who question women's moral competency assume that feminist pro-choice
proponents deny that pregnant women ever make bad decisions because those
feminists supposedly deny or do not take seriously "original sin."[56] I do not
doubt that, in some situations, immaturity or irresponsibility contributes to
an unwanted pregnancy. Frivolous abortions can happen.[57] Even a cursory
look at human behavior supports the biblical description that "all have sinned
and fall short of the glory of God" (Rom. 3:23). I will say more about sin and
redemption in the final chapter of this book, but here I will make two initial
responses to the issue of sin.

First, an appeal to original sin cuts both ways. If pro-life theologians want
to claim that the choice to abort is a sign of original sin, then pro-choice
theologians could argue, conversely, that judging women who abort is a sinful casting of the first stone. Second, even if selfishness, irresponsibility in
matters of sex, or other "sins" are factors in a woman's decision to abort,
there is no logical reason to assume that the woman does not also have good
reasons for terminating her pregnancy. Just because someone is a sinner does
not mean she does not have a functioning moral conscience or common
sense about her mothering capacities. A woman's statement "I don't want
to have a baby," to herself or aloud, is not an unreflective exclamation akin
to "ouch!" This statement presupposes some intuitive, emotional, or cognitive activity on the part of an agent. Moreover, the discourse of conservative
Christian women indicates that they do not need to be told they are sinners;

---

55. I will not address issues of psychological competence in medical decisions. For the purposes of these arguments, I am assuming pregnant young adults or adults with functioning mental capacities.

56. Bellinger, *Jesus v. Abortion*, 235.

57. The practice of so-called abortion-doping comes to mind. See Lisa Jarvis, "Should the
International Olympic Committee Be Policing Motherhood: Constitutional Implications of
Regulating Pregnancy and the Abortion-Doping Scheme under Domestic Law," *Seton Hall Jour-
nal of Sport Law* 13, no. 2 (2003): 297–319.

they already accept that they are. However, they do not believe that their sinful state renders them incapable, or absolves them of the responsibility, of making a decision about their pregnancy. As one woman remarked about her abortion: "You know, I consider myself to be a smart, well-educated woman. I am. . . . But I'm also the sinner choosing to have an abortion. . . . I made a choice for myself. I made a choice and asked God to support me."[58] Women who abort, especially churchgoers, do not partition off their abortion decision from their Christian identity as a sinner before God. Whatever immaturity or irresponsibility may have contributed to an unwanted pregnancy, whatever acceptance or regret follows from deciding to gestate or to abort, it was a mothering decision. The choice of what to do with an unwanted pregnancy is the woman's to make and is one the woman will need to live with in the most intimate way for the rest of her life.

A third point about original sin that a pro-life Christian would have to acknowledge is that it does not only affect women who abort but also women who have babies. Every day, immature, irresponsible, and selfish women give birth, with sometimes tragic outcomes for those babies. Even mothers (or fathers) intent on doing their best with an unplanned pregnancy often are overwhelmed, with negative consequences for their child.[59] Other than promoting the availability of parenting classes through crisis pregnancy centers, pro-life proponents downplay the problem, claiming that most women come around and bond with their baby with no adverse outcomes.[60] Indeed, a woman's decision not to terminate an unwanted pregnancy but to have her baby is encouraged by pro-life proponents; if she decides to gestate, her maternal authority and mothering readiness are assumed. Analogously, I argue, if a woman remains convinced that her pregnancy is unwanted, her moral conscience regarding motherhood should be respected, and she should not be prevented from making the mothering decision for abortion. Ironically, if women were more affirmed as mothers capable of reproductive decision making—rather than assumed to be morally suspect (as laws imposing mandatory waiting periods or ultrasounds do)—then women might very well feel empowered more often to opt to shoulder the difficult and lifelong responsibility of bearing and mothering another human being.

---

58. Ellison, "Abortion and the Politics of God," 180. "Frannie" self-identifies as an African American business woman and a Methodist, who is single and caring for her seriously ill elderly parents (69).

59. See Kai Guterman, "Unintended Pregnancy as a Predictor of Child Maltreatment," *Child Abuse & Neglect* 48 (2015): 160–69.

60. See Thomas Strahan, "Degree of 'Wantedness' Not a Factor in Abuse or Neglect," *Association for Interdisciplinary Research in Values and Social Change* 4, no. 1 (Spring 1991), http://www .lifeissues.net/writers/air/air_vol4no1_1991.html.

PRO-CHOICE APPROACHES TO FETAL VALUE

In the preceding section I strongly argued for an approach that sees abortion as a woman's mothering decision—not just to terminate her pregnancy but also to abort her fetus so that there will be no child to whom she would have any ongoing mothering responsibilities. This position seems to raise an inevitable question: Does such a claim for maternal authority to abort imply that a fetus is of negligible value, that a mother who aborts has deemed her child worthless? I do not think this implication necessarily follows, but the starkness of the question demonstrates that it is important to pursue.

All pro-choice feminists working within the Christian tradition defend fetal value to some extent, and invoking the notion of fetal personhood has been seen as the only way of doing so—in part, because that notion has dominated pro-life discourse. The difference is that pro-life writers appeal to personhood at conception in order to restrict women's maternal agency in pregnancy, and pro-choice writers appeal to a later development of personhood in order to carve out space for at least some abortion rights. This section argues that pro-choice approaches to fetal personhood, while well-intentioned, have limited use for securing women's rights and are hampered by continuing to employ the same problematic personhood paradigm found in pro-life writings. After assessing these pro-choice writings, I propose a way of speaking of fetal value that is attentive to many pregnant women's experiences but does not imply that a fetus is a person whom a woman has a duty always to gestate.

Pro-choice feminists working within the Christian tradition tend to fall into one of two camps to argue for fetal personhood. A relational approach links fetal personhood to the mother's recognition of and commitment to her fetus, a position argued by Marjorie Maguire. Most Christian scholars take a developmentalist approach to fetal personhood. Some, like Beverly Harrison, argue that personhood is achieved very late, which supports liberal abortion policies. Others, like Tina Beattie (discussed above) and Carol Tauer, believe the minimum components of personhood are developed in the first trimester and, therefore, they only support an ethics of early abortion. I differ from all these feminist scholars in that I argue that value inheres for a fetus throughout the pregnancy and that the gestating mother retains the moral authority to decide about abortion, whether early or late in the pregnancy.

Marjorie Maguire, a lay Roman Catholic lawyer and former activist in Catholics for a Free Choice (CFFC), argues that while human life may begin at conception, personhood begins at the point at which the mother commits to a relationship with that life within her. Maguire defines the human person, generally, as a being with transcendent value who is embedded in the human community: our very personhood is a product of our communal relationships.

Maguire describes this relational process as it pertains to a fetus using a verbal neologism: "Personhood is constituted by a free and gracious act of love that establishes a covenant with the new reality that is being *personed*, calling that person into community."[61] A fetus does not have personhood; a fetus is "personed" relationally in love. The love of which Maguire speaks is not the act of sexual intercourse, which may or may not be loving to achieve conception; rather, the loving process of fetal personing begins when "the mother accepts the pregnancy."[62] Maguire rejects pro-life claims that God gives the conceptus a soul and, "in a moment," creates an individual person. For Maguire, what Genesis 1:26–27 "is really saying . . . is that the image of God is found only in community. . . . Thus, while the mother begins the process [of personing the fetus], the father, if possible, and many others too, are needed to make the child a full human person in the image of God."[63] Maguire insists that if the woman does not consent to the pregnancy, "I do not believe she has killed a person who will then point a condemnatory figure at the mother as she enters eternal life."[64] Thus, Maguire takes a relational approach to fetal personhood in order to secure a pro-choice ethics of abortion that also recognizes the value of the in-utero being. Although Maguire does not link personhood to a specific biological developmental marker, her position does set moral limits. She argues that "there is a point in the pregnancy when the biological development of the fetus is such that the consent of the mother to the pregnancy is implicit, and therefore the fetus should be considered a person," even if the woman has not explicitly covenanted with her fetus. While viability is "a shifting area" to designate, it is an important factor for Maguire.[65] Prior to this point, using the "word 'person' muddies the legal discussion" of abortion since "pre-viable 'persons' are unlike any other persons in our experience, because they alone are absolutely dependent upon the body of another human

---

61. Marjorie Reiley Maguire, "Personhood, Covenant, and Abortion," *American Journal of Theology & Philosophy* 6, no. 1 (1985): 37, italics added. Maguire later broke with the CFFC, branding them as too pro-abortion and not Catholic enough. See Patricia Miller, *Good Catholics: The Battle over Abortion in the Catholic Church* (Berkeley: University of California Press, 2014), 191. Miller discusses the name change from CFFC to Catholics for Choice (CFC); see P. Miller, *Good Catholics*, 240.

62. M. Maguire, "Personhood, Covenant, and Abortion," 38.

63. M. Maguire, "Personhood, Covenant, and Abortion," 42–43. This relational view of personhood is also reflected in Rebecca Peters's discussion of "the unique role that birth mothers play in calling their prenates into personhood." Peters, *Trust Women*, 175.

64. M. Maguire, "Personhood, Covenant, and Abortion," 41.

65. M. Maguire, "Personhood, Covenant, and Abortion," 40–41. One can find a similar relational approach to fetal personhood in Lloyd Steffen, *Life/Choice: The Theory of Just Abortion* (Cleveland: Pilgrim Press, 1994). Although Steffen does not reference Maguire's concept of personing, it is similar to Steffen's category of the "promise-keeping" of the mother to her fetus; see Steffen, *Life/Choice*, 106, 115–21.

being."[66] I agree with Maguire regarding personhood language muddying the waters of abortion debates. My claim that a fetus has value at any point in the pregnancy differs from Maguire's approach, which is an attempt to carve out space for the justifiability of primarily early abortions before an explicit personing relationship between the mother and fetus has taken place.

Beverly Harrison, whose critique of pro-life historiography was discussed in chapter 1, takes a developmentalist approach by proposing "developmental criteria for stipulating the degree of similarity to existing human beings required for counting fetal life as *a* human life."[67] She argues that "full human value" should not be accorded to the fetus until certain "functional requisites" of personhood are achieved.[68] For Harrison, full human value would be appropriate to speak of at or near viability, before which time a fetus is not *"an actually alive organism* with human complexity." Harrison pushes back against the pro-life tendency to impute person-like "conscious self-direction" to even the earliest embryo.[69] She adamantly rejects the concession other pro-choice feminists sometimes make (even if for the sake of argument, as in Judith Thomson's famous essay) that a fetus may be spoken of as a person, because such a concession posits a "dubious" analogy between us "autonomous human beings" and fetuses.[70] Harrison focuses on the biological factors of the fetus's degrees of increasing physical independence from its mother. While a fetus is not mere "tissue," since it is "a developing life system,"[71] the term "person" only begins to apply to a fetus that has acquired the capacity for "discrete biological existence," or viability.[72] Harrison does not elaborate, but she seems to link viability to "pulmonary maturation," or the ability to breath outside the womb.[73]

However, Harrison still cautions against asserting that even a viable fetus should be spoken of as a full person because "'person' is a moral category" not a biologically determined fact.[74] Deciding what personhood is can never be determined on biology alone but emerges from society's ethical task of reasoning together about "our obligations to others, our values, and decisions."[75] A society's sense of its obligation to care for newborns is even more important than biological markers for defining personhood. In other words, rather than focusing on when the fetus becomes viable (which is biologically important),

66. M. Maguire, "Personhood, Covenant, and Abortion," 41, 30.
67. Harrison, *Our Right to Choose*, 209.
68. Harrison, *Our Right to Choose*, 193, 194.
69. Harrison, *Our Right to Choose*, 214, 213.
70. Harrison, *Our Right to Choose*, 215. For more on Thomson, see pp. 156–57 below.
71. Harrison, *Our Right to Choose*, 214.
72. Harrison, *Our Right to Choose*, 220.
73. Harrison, *Our Right to Choose*, 217.
74. Harrison, *Our Right to Choose*, 221.
75. Harrison, *Our Right to Choose*, 221.

society should focus even more on its obligations to "create viable conditions of life for all who are born among us."[76] Rather than trying to curtail women's reproductive rights, it is better for all concerned that society concentrate on its moral obligations toward newborns. Correlatively, it is better for pregnant women to think of themselves as active agents who should approach motherhood with thoughtful "moral seriousness" rather than as passive agents having their choices and responsibilities prescribed for them.[77]

I endorse Harrison's call for society to nurture and promote each individual's free exercise of mature moral responsibility—especially that of women considering or facing motherhood. She is also correct that it is unconscionable for society to pass laws that obstruct women's access to legal early abortions, which are safer and less expensive.[78] However, I question the way Harrison implies a scale of value based on developmental criteria. An early abortion is presented as morally negligible because an "early fetal life does *not* yet possess even the minimal organic requirements for participation in the sphere of human rights";[79] whereas, Harrison believes it makes sense "to accord fetuses in late stages of gestation" a greater degree of moral regard, based on the principle that they have developed sufficient capacities to begin the societal participation to which their human rights are connected.[80] I do not concur with this use of developmentalism to determine fetal status. I insist that fetal value is continuous throughout a pregnancy; it is not negligible for an early fetus. Every abortion decision is morally serious but, by the same token, a woman's maternal moral authority regarding her fetus extends throughout the whole pregnancy.

In the next chapter I will discuss viability and gestational hospitality. Here I will note that the appeal to viability, which may at first seem to be a relatively straightforward solution to an ethical quandary, turns out to have its own set of problems. Viability is a medically slippery concept that involves a range of decisions about intensive or even invasive medical interventions. "Viable," medically, means whatever can be made to live after birth, based on the expertise and technology available—and no one would deny that these things are sometimes scarce or unequally available.[81] Viability has a particular

76. Harrison, *Our Right to Choose*, 224.
77. Harrison, *Our Right to Choose*, 255.
78. See Harrison, *Our Right to Choose*, 226–28.
79. Harrison, *Our Right to Choose*, 224, italics in original.
80. Harrison, *Our Right to Choose*, 226.
81. See World Health Organization, "Born Too Soon: The Global Action Report on Preterm Birth," *March of Dimes* (2012), 1–111, https://www.who.int/pmnch/media/news/2012/201204 _borntoosoon-report.pdf. Significant disparities exist based on race and ethnicity in the U.S. See "Premature Birth Report Card," *March of Dimes* (2016), 1–3, https://www.marchofdimes.org /materials/premature-birth-report-card-united-states.pdf.

legal definition, and its function in *Roe v. Wade* is to limit abortion. These medical and legal meanings do not take the place of moral and philosophical reflection about fetal value and maternal authority. In the next section I will argue for a way of speaking of fetal value that supports moral seriousness vis-à-vis abortion, without implying that pregnant women need to have their reproductive decision making monitored and restricted.

That pro-life scholars would reject Harrison's pro-choice manifesto is to be expected.[82] However, even some of her feminist colleagues who share a developmentalist approach might object that she sets the time for imputing personhood to the fetus too late. Carol Tauer and Tina Beattie posit an earlier, narrower window within which abortion can be morally justifiable. Tauer, in her essay "Personhood and Human Embryos and Fetuses," argues that individuality must be in place for there to be a human person, but it must be based on more than a "genotype," which, though biologically important, "lacks moral relevance."[83] She pushes for a definition of personhood associated with the capacity for "brain activity, a psychological life, and a kind of sentience."[84] Although she acknowledges that there is debate about the time frame for functional brain activity (as early as 6.5 weeks and as late as 28 weeks), Tauer still argues for the moral significance of this criterion. She does not set a definitive date, but she seems fairly convinced that "the late first trimester fetus's relationship to tactile stimuli and to its own movements" is evidence of "fetal 'experience'" of subjectivity.[85] Before this point, one may refer to a "potential person"—a full person being defined, traditionally, by a cluster of attributes that might include moral agency, self-consciousness, and rationality.[86] She is reluctant to say that a strong sense of "psychic" personhood can be applied to a first-trimester fetus, but she seems clear that there would be a claim to its "moral standing" based on its "potential for personhood"; moreover, to "remain on the safe side," she is comfortable in speaking about standards of "fetal protection" from the "seventh week of fetal development."[87] From this time onward, the fetus ought to be given full moral status, meaning that abortion would be morally precluded after that point. In other words, by seven

82. See Sidney Callahan, "Abortion and the Sexual Agenda: The Case for Prolife Feminism (1986)," in *The Ethics of Abortion: Pro-life vs. Pro-choice*, edited by Robert M. Baird and Stuart E. Rosenbaum (Buffalo, NY: Prometheus, 2001), 167–78; Terry Schlossberg, "Abortion Matters," *Touchstone* 8, no. 2 (1995): 30–32, http://www.touchstonemag.com/archives/article.php?id=08-02 -030-f.

83. Carol A. Tauer, "Personhood and Human Embryos and Fetuses," *Journal of Medicine and Philosophy* 10, no. 3 (1985): 261.

84. Tauer, "Personhood and Human Embryos and Fetuses," 256.

85. Tauer, "Personhood and Human Embryos and Fetuses," 258–59.

86. Tauer, "Personhood and Human Embryos and Fetuses," 255.

87. Tauer, "Personhood and Human Embryos and Fetuses," 260, 263. Tauer argues that the status of embryos in the lab would not rise to the level of potential persons but only "'possible persons'" (263).

weeks, fetal development toward full personhood has advanced to such a point that full moral status is in order.[88] Tauer insists that "objective" criteria of fetal cognitive experience or "brain birth" provides an ethically credible way of identifying when one can plausibly say that a morally significant human being is in place.[89] Because of Tauer's focus on the fetus's psychic development, she sets the time limit for a justifiable abortion earlier than Harrison.

Beattie argues that the eighth week is decisive—both for the embryo, since "the primitive streak has emerged and there is no longer any possibility of twinning," and for the mother, as noted in the earlier discussion, since most women "will know they have conceived within the first eight weeks." Calling an early embryo a person is counterintuitive for Beattie, given that it is "microscopic" at conception[90] and most fertilized embryos subsequently die naturally and are evacuated in menstruation as "unidentifiable fleshy matter."[91] Beattie considers the emergence of a "recognizably human" fetal form to be ethically decisive. Beattie's focus on the emergence of a visibly human organism seems intended to dismiss pro-life appeals to the *imago Dei* since, Beattie claims, "women most affected by abortion are unlikely to base their decisions on theological appeals to humans made in the image of God (particularly when the being in question has no recognizable image to speak of)."[92] Like Tauer, Beattie finds neurological development to be significant (e.g., "brain waves").[93] Whether the mother has accepted the pregnancy or not, Beattie deems abortion after the eighth week to be ethically "increasingly problematic,"[94] though she would argue for an extension up to twelve weeks to give women more time to recognize that they are pregnant and then decide what to do. Second-trimester abortions should be allowed only under "exceptional circumstances," and third-trimester elective abortion should be illegal.[95] Thus, Beattie argues on developmental grounds for a narrow "period

88. Tauer, "Personhood and Human Embryos and Fetuses," 255.
89. Carol A. Tauer, "Abortion: Embodiment and Prenatal Development," in *Embodiment, Morality and Medicine*, ed. Lisa S. Cahill and Margaret Farley (Dordrecht: Kluwer Academic Publishers, 1995), 83, 84.
90. Beattie, "Catholicism, Choice and Consciousness," 60.
91. Beattie, "Catholicism, Choice and Consciousness," 61.
92. Beattie, "Catholicism, Choice and Consciousness," 61.
93. Beattie, "Catholicism, Choice and Consciousness," 65 n. 34. A developmentalist position is also argued by Dombrowski and Deltete, who believe that the start of cerebral function at the end of the second trimester is a definitive marker of personhood, which is later than Beattie but earlier than Harrison. See Daniel A. Dombrowski and Robert J. Deltete, *A Brief, Liberal, Catholic Defense of Abortion* (Urbana: University of Illinois Press, 2000), 72.
94. Beattie, "Catholicism, Choice and Consciousness," 70. It seems that Beattie is counting gestational age, not LMP (dating from the last menstrual period), which is the method obstetricians use to calculate a due date and which adds two weeks to actual gestational age. Gestational age can only be definitively known in IVF (in vitro fertilization) procedures.
95. Beattie, "Catholicism, Choice and Consciousness," 71. Beattie suggests that emergency procedures to preserve the life of the mother could be dealt with while using the principle of

of grace" to allow for elective abortion "between conception and the emergence of the human form."[96] In other words, abortion is best done when fetal value and maternal consciousness are minimal.

I agree that abortion is best done early, but I dispute linking fetal moral status to some developmental marker, such as implantation or the presence of a rudimentary brain or a human-like form. There is no clear biological marker before which the fetus can be said to be of negligible value and abortion can definitively be pronounced as morally permissible. Indeed, as this brief discussion shows, even pro-choice feminists are not of one mind on what or when that marker would be. Moreover, from an experiential standpoint, even a very early abortion is morally fraught for some women. For other pregnancies, a late-term abortion, while difficult for the woman and her family, may be medically necessary and cannot proceed without her explicit consent. Whether an abortion is early or late, the life of a fetal being developing toward born personhood is ended.

In the section that follows, I argue for an approach that maintains the moral seriousness of abortion, even early in a pregnancy, without having to rely on an unwieldy definition of personhood linked to difficult-to-establish developmental markers. While I see how arguing for the justifiability of abortion in an early pregnancy could be a pragmatic feminist stance to take in order to secure some abortion rights, I do not think it produces a strong pro-choice ethical position because it relies on minimizing fetal value and maternal consciousness in early pregnancy, which could result in lessening a woman's moral authority to manage all stages of her pregnancy.

FETAL VALUE:
NOT A PERSON AND NOT A NONPERSON

Having assessed, in the first part of the book, failed pro-life arguments for fetal personhood and having shown, in this chapter, the limitations of pro-choice relational and developmental arguments for fetal value, I now propose a different approach. Discourse about fetal value, I suggest, should be

---

double effect. I strongly oppose this approach, which could restrict the kind of medical procedures allowed or even delay or deny live-saving procedures to pregnant women. See Thomas A. Cavanaugh, "Double-Effect Reasoning, Craniotomy, and Vital Conflicts: A Case of Contemporary Catholic Casuistry," *The National Catholic Bioethics Quarterly* 11, no. 3 (2011): 456, 462. See also Julia Kaye et al., "Health Care Denied: Patients and Physicians Speak Out about Catholic Hospitals and the Threat to Women's Health and Lives," *American Civil Liberties Union* (May 2016), 5–39, https://www.aclu.org/sites/default/files/field_document/healthcaredenied.pdf. See also n. 46 above.

96. Beattie, "Catholicism, Choice and Consciousness," 70.

attentive both to the maternal discourse of women who have had abortions, as well as to the concrete materiality of the maternal-fetal relationship in gestation. This approach leads me to a position that attempts to hold in tension the dual claims that the fetus is not a person and the fetus is not a nonperson.

Women's Maternal Discourse of Abortion

Feminist pro-choice defenders of the position that moral value or legal personhood begins only at birth (and maybe even a bit afterward) are a dwindling group. The personhood-at-birth position mostly harkens back to the work of scholars such as Mary Ann Warren, Virginia Held, or Susan Sherman from the late 1980s and early 1990s.[97] Ethicist Bertha Manninen has recently noted how "voices within the younger generation of pro-choice advocacy" are reconsidering speaking of the fetus as having inconsequential value, especially given the reality that some women experience abortion as entailing "loss."[98] A simplistic pro-choice feminist assertion that the fetus is not a person and therefore has little to no value until birth or near birth is as phenomenologically and culturally myopic as a pro-life Christian assertion that a conceptus is an unborn baby. In part, the feminist willingness to reengage with the issue of fetal value emerges from the recognition that the more one attends to women's experiences and the materiality of gestation, the harder it is to discount fetal significance. My claim for fetal value—apart from an appeal to personhood—derives from precisely these two factors: women's experience and the materiality of gestation.

As I indicated throughout this chapter, many women who have abortions speak not of their terminated pregnancy but of their baby who has died. Because the ethnographic material I cited was from self-professed evangelical or Catholic women of faith, one could reductively account for this discourse as some kind of religious false consciousness, whereby these women were influenced to think of their abortions in these personal terms. One researcher speculates that a factor influencing how women in her study used phrases like "the baby didn't ask to be here," or expressed the sentiment "that the abortion was a form of injustice to the 'baby,'" might have been the religious anti-abortion protesters outside the clinic.[99] Nevertheless, whatever the source, many women do have deep-seated feelings in relation to their aborted

---

97. See Lynn M. Morgan, "Fetal Relationality in Feminist Philosophy: An Anthropological Critique," *Hypatia* 11, no. 3 (1996): 58–59.

98. Bertha Alvarez Manninen, "The Value of Choice and the Choice to Value: Expanding the Discussion about Fetal Life within Prochoice Advocacy," *Hypatia* 28, no. 3 (2013): 664, 665.

99. Sri Devi Thakkilapati, "Better Mothers, Good Daughters and Blessed Women: Gender Performance in the Context of Abortion," PhD diss., Ohio State University (2009), 5–6.

fetus, usually spoken of in personal terms. Even if they are not religious, some women devise rituals to structure their grieving. One woman recounted to the interviewer how she keeps "a shoebox at home, in the back of her closet, where she keeps the ultrasound pictures from her two previous abortions" so that she will not forget her "children."[100] What these women are sharing are raw emotions, sometimes in a cathartic moment of the postabortion interview context; yet this data is something feminist theorists should not ignore since the themes are found across pro-life and pro-choice research. In other words, even an early fetus is not a nonperson—at least from the perspective of many women who abort. That said, women's experience of their fetus as valuable and "grievable" should not be the only factor in a moral argument for fetal value.[101] Material biological factors should be part of a moral position on the very embodied reality of abortion.

The Materiality of Pregnancy

I am not alone in showing feminist interest in the materiality of the body in general[102] and as part of an approach to understanding fetal value. Catholic ethicist Lisa Cahill argues that the unique "physical relation of the fetus to the mother ought not to be disregarded as a factor" regarding the morality of abortion.[103] I share this viewpoint, but I draw different moral conclusions from Cahill because I differ from her regarding how to interpret the nature of that physical relationship in pregnancy. She sees the maternal-fetal relationship as natural and positive and, as such, deduces that pregnancy entails a duty from the woman to gestate (with a few exceptions). I see pregnancy as something that women hope will feel like a natural event but that is, nevertheless, risky and, as such, a pregnant woman is not morally obligated to gestate but might be virtuous to do.

Let us begin at the gestational beginning. Once the pregnancy starts, there is a new and completely unique reality. The pregnant woman and the gestating fetus become, for approximately nine months, unique interconnected living entities. Beverly Harrison has argued that pregnancy is a "sui generis . . .

100. Thakkilapati, "Better Mothers, Good Daughters," 1, 39.
101. Butler invokes the notion of grievability in the context of how society accords moral regard to those seen as other. Butler does not include fetuses in the category of grievable beings, and I think Butler misses an opportunity to reflect on fetal value in terms of reproductive rights. See Judith Butler, *Frames of War: When Is Life Grievable?* (London: Verso, 2009), 19–22.
102. For more on how attention to material embodiment and the natural world is gaining feminist attention, see Stacy Alaimo and Susan J. Hekman, eds., *Material Feminisms* (Bloomington: Indiana University Press, 2008), especially "Introduction: Emerging Models of Materiality in Feminist Theory," 1–19.
103. Lisa Sowle Cahill, "Abortion and Argument by Analogy," *Horizons* 9, no. 2 (1982): 284.

human experience" that is "at once a biological, cultural, social and historical reality."[104] Most people would concede that pregnancy is a unique situation in the human life cycle, but few have made the connections between pregnancy as a sui generis bodily human experience and the status of the fetus.[105] The pregnant woman, who was a biologically self-contained being, finds herself radically changing as her body is increasingly linked to another being growing within her. Philosophers, poets, and average women have spoken powerfully to the almost ineffable experience of gestating a child. Iris Young describes the contradictory nature of her experience of pregnancy saying, "I experience my insides as the space of another, yet my own body."[106] Poet Genevieve Taggard imagines the complicated entanglement of pregnancy from the perspective of the fetus who "does not heed our ecstasies, it turns, / With secrets of its own. . . . In the dark / Defiant even now, it tugs and moans / To be untangled from these mother's bones."[107] Philosophers and poets search for the words to describe this unique experience.

Lisa Cahill concurs that pregnancy is undeniably "a unique relation at the physical level between two human individuals, one of whom is dependent in a most fundamental and also a most natural sense upon the other."[108] Cahill's attentiveness to the uniqueness of the maternal-fetal dynamics of pregnancy is one reason why she finds pro-life appeals to personhood language flawed because it is not "straightforwardly" self-evident that fetuses and born babies should be seen as having the same status. Indeed, as I argued in part 1 of this book, pro-life biblical and theological arguments are only convincing to those who already share the viewpoint they purport to prove, that a fetus is an unborn child. I agree with Cahill, that if one does not already hold the presupposition that fetuses are unborn babies, then this kind of language is merely "analogical."[109] Having set aside applying personhood language to secure fetal value, Cahill turns to the maternal-fetal relationship on the assumption that the "biological givens" of the "physical relation of the fetus to the mother" should be included as a factor in determining the morality of abortion.[110] If one intends to take seriously the materiality of maternal-fetal relations, much

104. Harrison, *Our Right to Choose*, 43, 102.

105. For discussions of pregnancy as a sui generis relationality, see Jean Porter, *Moral Action and Christian Ethics* (Cambridge: Cambridge University Press, 1999), 120; Gene Outka, "The Ethics of Love and the Problem of Abortion," in *Church, Society, and the Christian Common Good: Essays in Conversation with Philip Turner*, ed. Ephraim Radner (Eugene, OR: Wipf & Stock, 2017), 150–54.

106. Iris M. Young, "Pregnant Embodiment: Subjectivity and Alienation," *Journal of Medicine and Philosophy* 9, no. 1 (1984): 49.

107. Genevieve Taggard, *Collected Poems*, 1918–38 (New York: Harper & Row, 1938), 20.

108. L. Cahill, "Abortion and Argument by Analogy," 284.

109. L. Cahill, "Abortion and Argument by Analogy," 280.

110. L. Cahill, "Abortion and Argument by Analogy," 284.

depends on how one interprets the nature of that relationship, and this is where I diverge from Cahill.

In her essay "Abortion and Argument by Analogy," Lisa Cahill makes the case that pregnancy is poorly understood through the adversarial metaphors and analogies used in many pro-choice writings. Judith Thomson's dying violinist analogy, for example, glosses over what Cahill calls the "*intrinsic goodness*" of nurturing a fetus.[111] In other words, pregnancies that are dangerous for women cannot be taken to represent the maternal-fetal relationship in pregnancy, which is not "unusual, abnormal, or excessive," and that "barring extraordinary circumstances," gestation is not "aberrant" or "pathological."[112] Cahill implies that the situation of a "burdensome pregnancy," which can present a moral challenge, is the exception to the rule. Another material factor of pregnancy is dependency. Human social life in general is predicated on "mutual interdependence and obligations," which means that we have duties to one another. The maternal-fetal relationship is a unique instance where "one individual is totally and exclusively dependent on a particular other" and, hence, it entails a special duty.[113]

Lisa Cahill thus presents pregnancy as the normal fulfilling of a special duty to maintain an intrinsically good situation of sustaining fetal life. Because she does not see pregnancy, in and of itself, as particularly onerous, it does not seem harsh, to her mind, to insist that the woman is obliged to fulfill this duty whether she consents or not. Cahill makes this claim in opposition to Thomson's assertion that we do not have any "special responsibility" to another being "unless we have assumed it, explicitly or implicitly."[114] For Thomson, gestating an unwanted pregnancy is a "supererogatory" act of "compassion for the enemy in need," as summarized by Cahill.[115] Not only does Cahill find this analogy faulty because it casts the fetus into the role of an enemy but, in addition, the analogy does not recognize that contributing to the "common good" means that people have duties to each other whether they consent or not. Given these views of duty and pregnancy, Cahill asserts that "the special, unique, natural, and essential dependence of the fetus on the mother is a sufficient condition of some duty of nurturance."[116] A woman deeming her pregnancy unwanted does not nullify her duty to gestate. Cahill thus argues for the intrinsic goodness of fetal nurturance and cautiously supports abortion rights only in very limited "extremis" situations.[117]

---

111. L. Cahill, "Abortion and Argument by Analogy," 283.
112. L. Cahill, "Abortion and Argument by Analogy," 283.
113. L. Cahill, "Abortion and Argument by Analogy," 286, 287.
114. L. Cahill, "Abortion and Argument by Analogy," 285–86.
115. L. Cahill, "Abortion and Argument by Analogy," 278.
116. L. Cahill, "Abortion and Argument by Analogy," 286–87.
117. L. Cahill, "Abortion and Argument by Analogy," 285.

I diverge from Lisa Cahill on how to characterize pregnancy. While she sees pregnancy as biologically natural—meaning, a regularly occurring and generally not harmful event—I see pregnancy as a hoped-for natural event but in actuality often a burdensome and even risky event. Among current scholarship, there is a significant stream of pro-choice feminist writings where the notion of danger in pregnancy plays a role. Ethicist Margaret Little puts the case bluntly: "Fetuses live in other people's bodies," and this occupation is a highly intimate "*extraordinary* physical enmeshment" that is not without danger.[118] Gestation entails an increasing demand (emotionally and physiologically) upon the woman that can, in some circumstances, be a dangerous, even lethal, occupation. Little speaks anecdotally of her "sister, whose first trimester 'nausea'—actually gut-wrenching dry heaves every 20 minutes and three hospitalizations—was the equal of many an experience of chemotherapy. Or another acquaintance, whose sudden onset of eclampsia during delivery brought her so close to dying that it left us all breathless."[119] Recent statistics about birthing in the U.S. show that, in 2008, "94.1 percent listed some type of pregnancy complication," including infection, hypertension, or postpartum problems.[120] While pregnancy is not a disease, it is rarely free of some kind of pathology or health complication, some of which require hospitalization or are not temporary. Death remains a significant risk in birth. A Centers for Disease Control and Prevention report shows a worrisome increase in pregnancy-related deaths in the U.S. between 1987 and 2011.[121] If pregnancy is natural, then it is, statistically speaking, naturally dangerous for many women globally.

Little's complaint is not against the fetus but with any legal entity that might have the power to enforce gestation against a woman's will, which would amount to mandating "that she remain in a state of potentially dangerous physical intertwinement against her consent."[122] Even if conception is the result of flagrantly irresponsible sex, the extraordinary degree of the resulting bodily enmeshment is a disproportionate harm. (Nor would one ever want

---

118. Margaret Olivia Little, "Abortion, Intimacy, and the Duty to Gestate," *Ethical Theory and Moral Practice* 2, no. 3 (1999): 299.

119. Little, "Abortion, Intimacy, and the Duty to Gestate," 300. James Mumford argues—anemically, I would add—that pregnancy is a phenomenon whose discomforts, such as morning sickness, are not a real illness (like a tumor), and thus pregnancy cannot arguably be viewed as a threat. See Mumford, *Ethics at the Beginning of Life: A Phenomenological Critique* (Oxford: Oxford University Press, 2013), 171–73.

120. Anne Elixhauser and Lauren M. Wier, "Complicating Conditions of Pregnancy and Childbirth, 2008," NCBI Bookshelf, National Institutes of Health (May 2011), http://www.ncbi .nlm.nih.gov/books/NBK56037/?report=printable.

121. "Pregnancy Mortality Surveillance System," *Centers for Disease Control and Prevention*, http://www.cdc.gov/reproductivehealth/maternalinfanthealth/pmss.html.

122. Little, "Abortion, Intimacy, and the Duty to Gestate," 301.

enforced pregnancy to be used by the state as a punishment for irresponsible sex.) Even apart from the legal issue of forcing a woman against her will
to assume the risks of pregnancy, there is the question of whether pregnant
women have a positive moral duty to gestate, which is what Lisa Cahill con-
tends. Little argues that while gestating an unwanted pregnancy may be a
virtue, "women do not have an automatic role-based moral duty to gestate."[123]
Within an ethics of relationship—of which, to repeat, pregnancy is the most
intimate and sometimes risky instance—Little does not see how any "strong
claim" can be made for gestation if the woman does not want motherhood.
While selfishness may be at play for some women who want abortions, Little
makes the point that many women who abort do so out of a deep sense of relational responsibility: "they know if they continue the pregnancy they will not
be able to give up the child" and that it is a relationship they feel they cannot
take on.[124] Enforced gestation will de facto often amount to enforced motherhood once the baby is born. Even if many such women go on to parent well, I
find the idea of imposed mothering to be an untenable moral position to hold.

While every woman who finds herself pregnant hopes for an uneventful
pregnancy and birth, the fact is that most women can expect some complications during pregnancy, birth, or postpartum. I have to disagree with Cahill's
estimation that pregnancy is mostly a not-too-burdensome fulfilling of a
duty to nurture fetal life. I see pregnancy, in part because of the statistical
incidence of complications, as a momentous and even risky endeavor, which
makes gestation a virtuous act for a woman to undertake—even more so if the
pregnancy is unplanned and unwanted. The risks of pregnancy also call into
question Cahill's claim about consent not being required vis-à-vis the duty
of nurturing fetal life. I agree generally that sustaining the common good
depends on all or at least most members of society being willing to fulfill
duties and obey rules, sometimes without giving prior consent. However, I
do not endorse saying that a particular class of people (women of childbearing
age), according to the principle of obligations to the common good, are bound
to assume the burdensome and risky embodied duty of gestation every time
they find themselves pregnant. Indeed, given the burdens and potential harms
of pregnancy, the issue of consent becomes even more crucial.

Even if I were to convince Lisa Cahill to reconsider her view about pregnancy risks, she would still insist, I expect, that the intrinsic goodness of fetal
life is "a sufficient condition of some duty of nurturance."[125] What Cahill
means by intrinsic is not entirely clear since she does not appeal to revelation,

123. Little, "Abortion, Intimacy, and the Duty to Gestate," 309.
124. Little, "Abortion, Intimacy, and the Duty to Gestate," 312.
125. L. Cahill, "Abortion and Argument by Analogy," 287.

the magisterium, natural law, or some a priori principle, such as this: to exist is more excellent than not to exist. Indeed, her term "intrinsic" seems misplaced since she appears to be appealing "simply to a consensus about the value of human life."[126] But it is precisely a consensus regarding how to value fetal life that is so elusive. To what can we appeal to secure fetal value, given the failure of pro-life attempts to do so and the lack of agreement even among pro-choice feminists? What would fetal value mean?

I argue that attributing value to an embryo or fetus follows not only from women's experience but also from the material reality of an in-utero being.[127] A fetus has value because of its sui generis existence in the womb, which Margaret Little calls enmeshment and I speak of as contingency and contiguousness. After implantation, the fetus is not merely in its mother's uterus, like a ship in a bottle; it is connected (placentally mediated) to her uterine wall, with nutrients, hormones, and other matter passing between them. The fetus is a contingently and contiguously developing being, which makes it unlike any other kind of human being we know. I contend that it is, in part, because of the materiality of the maternal-fetal relationship that value necessarily applies to a fetus from the start. This position separates me from developmentalist pro-choice feminists, who argue that fetal value accrues as personhood (literally) comes more into view. My reasons for attributing value to the fetus from the start are based on four interrelated material realities: a fetus is genetically human; it is an organism not just in stasis but also living dynamically; it is intimately connected—contingently and contiguously—to an already existing moral agent who takes on risks in pregnancy; and it has the potential to reach born personhood.

I have already spoken about the limitations of appealing to genetics; contrary to what some pro-life proponents claim, a complete genome does not constitute personhood. Nevertheless, for syngamy to occur successfully and put in place a genetic code for a human being that could become a born child is not insignificant. It is no wonder that people call pregnancy a miracle. The fact that uterine human life has the biological possibility of developing from zygotic simplicity to the independent complexity of a born baby does strike us as miraculous, even in our technologically advanced era. That the genes of a fetus are human goes without saying; that an embryo (once the possibility of

126. L. Cahill, "Abortion and Argument by Analogy," 283.
127. Here I am using the terms "embryo" and "fetus" in a nonscientific way, to refer to a human-originating organism in a woman's body that has the capacity to develop toward birth (which excludes chimeras, hydatidiform moles, ectopic pregnancies, incubating in vitro or frozen embryos, and other such genetically human organisms). I recognize that a morula moving along a woman's fallopian tube is not contiguous or contingent in the same way as a fetus connected by an umbilical cord; however, there is connectivity of some type at every stage of pregnancy.

twinning is past) is genetically and irreducibly individual also is scientifically sound. However, a genetically individual human embryo will not, and cannot, develop unless it embeds in a woman's uterus and grows there, for approximately nine months. The fetus is an unavoidably developmental uterine being who evolves incrementally toward born personhood.

Giving serious thought to fetal development counterbalances the tendency, on the one hand, of pro-life proponents to make fetal genetic individuality the biological basis for moral personhood, as well as the tendency of some pro-choice feminists to downplay the value of a developing fetus in its very early stages. It should come as no surprise that expectant parents dote on the progression of sonogram photos or video clips of their developing fetus. A pro-choice feminist is not immune to this wonder, and the wonderment does not just kick in at some presumed significant developmental point such as fetal brainwaves or viability. In response to some feminist concerns, I would say that the only reason not to recognize value of even early fetal life is out of fear that pro-life forces will use the discourse of fetal value to try to implement laws and social policies of enforced gestation and other coercive invasions in women's reproductive lives. However, the possible bad political use of a claim should not nullify its moral validity.

Value adheres to a fetus not just because it is a genetically human and developing being but because it can only exist connected, contingently and contiguously, to the maternal body. That body is not a mere incubator or temporary housing but herself an independent moral being, who makes sacrifices, faces health and other risks, and must labor to bring her child into the world. Finally, a fetus develops in this sui generis context of gestation, living contingently and contiguously in its gestating mother's womb, where it develops toward born personhood. A fetus is not remotely analogous to born people who find themselves needing to live temporarily or indefinitely in positions of extreme bodily dependence.[128] The fetus is a kind of human being who, if all goes well, develops fully during gestation so that it eventually becomes a noncontingent and noncontiguous being—or natal person, in an Arendtian, political meaning of the word—who will hopefully be joyously welcomed into a family, a community, a nation.[129] Indeed, in order to continue living, a fetus—once it achieves a certain level of development—must physically enter the world as a separate being. Until or close to that point of

128. A fetus is inappropriately analogized to, for example, a severely disabled person who must live in a so-called iron lung. Neither is a fetal person analogous to born conjoined twins, who would die if separated from each other.

129. Elsewhere I reflect on Hannah Arendt's notion of natality in relation to abortion. See Margaret D. Kamitsuka, "Feminist Scholarship and Its Relevance for Political Engagement: The Test Case of Abortion in the U.S.," *Religion and Gender* 1, no. 1 (2011): 40.

natal appearance, we are impelled to say that the fetus is not a person and the fetus is not a nonperson. A fetus is not a person in any commonplace use of the term, meaning a born individual. A fetus is not a nonperson because we have to take seriously the pregnant woman who sings a lullaby to the "baby" in her belly, or the woman who aborts the "baby" she sadly cannot take care of right now.

Let me clarify what my argument about fetal contingency and contiguity is not saying. In the first section of this chapter, "The Pregnant Woman's Subjectivity and Maternal Authority," I argued that a pregnant woman has maternal moral authority regarding her pregnancy, yet the fetus who lives contingently and contiguously to her body is not her property. Nor am I claiming that a fetus is simply a part of a woman's body, like one of her dispensable internal organs. Few if any feminist scholars today promote either of these reductionist views, and neither do I. To end the life of a contingent and contiguous human organism is not like losing one's tonsils. A fetus, at any stage, carries moral weight because it is a living and genetically human being that is developing intimately connected to its mother until birth. Thus I see the claims of maternal authority and fetal value as reciprocal. To claim that a decision to abort is a significant maternal decision means that what is aborted is a being with value—a being the woman might even call her child. To claim that a fetus has value means that the only person authorized to make the momentous decision to abort is its gestating mother.

To anticipate possible objections, someone might claim that I have asserted fetal value in name only, because maternal authority seems to rule unchecked. I claim that a fetus has value, but I support a woman's maternal authority to abort it. There is a grain of truth to this observation; however, this critique misses the meaning and function of asserting fetal value. I am not asserting fetal value to serve as a restraint for maternal authority, which is how pro-life claims for fetal personhood function. The very notion that pregnant women need to be kept in check and prevented from harming their fetuses is based on profoundly cynical, misogynous, and judgmental presuppositions that have no place in a Christian morality of abortion. Even pro-choice ethical appeals to fetal value, which are not based on suspicions about pregnant women's reproductive decision making, could be seen as functioning as a moral restraint—especially at the stage of viability.[130] I do not see viability either as a marker of

---

130. One can detect a message of needing to restrain women's abortion options in Margaret Little's discussion of how "women should not have an unrestrained right to kill their matured fetuses" because "others could sustain this life." Margaret Olivia Little, "Abortion and the Margins of Personhood," *Rutgers Law Journal* 39, no. 2 (2007): 346, 348. This argument sidesteps the issue I have tried to emphasize, which is that abortion should be seen as a decision that there not be a child born to which one would have mothering obligations.

where fetal value begins or as something to be invoked in any way to badger the statistically few pregnant women who actually face late-term abortions. Viability already exists in this and a majority of other countries worldwide as a settled legal constraint for abortion,[131] so moral discourse about it functions on a different plane. Viability is a significant moral issue that should and usually does affect how a woman makes a difficult late-term abortion decision. In the next chapter I will explain how I believe viability should factor into moral discourse, but I will anticipate that discussion here by saying that in a care-based approach to abortion ethics (which I support), viability functions as an indicator of the seemingly natural or at least widespread human impulse to care for an almost-ready-to be-born human being—an impulse that society should nurture, while also caring for and respecting the decisions of pregnant women with real and often dire needs that can arise late in pregnancy.

Thus my assertion of fetal value is not meant to restrain maternal authority but, rather, to recognize and foster reflection about what most women who have abortions feel: something serious has happened because a being—who is not a person and not a nonperson—has died. The question of whether pregnant women (or old women, or men, or children, or ethicists, or theologians) need moral guidance is appropriate and important. Moral guidance, I believe, is best provided by ethical instruction, based on our common wisdom about how to implement the good for human society. The chapter that follows discusses one of the most well-known principles that grounds the common good: hospitality.

131. "The World's Abortion Laws Map 2013 Update," *Center for Reproductive Rights,* https://www.reproductiverights.org/sites/crr.civicactions.net/files/documents/AbortionMap_Factsheet_2013.pdf.

6

Gestational Hospitality and the Parable of the Good Samaritan

Hospitality is recognized across many cultures as pivotal for a functioning moral society, and the notion plays a central role in Christianity, inspired by biblical references to love of neighbor in the parable of the good Samaritan. What has come to be known as Samaritanism is widely accepted across religions, even in nonreligious ethics. Recently the notion has been appropriated in abortion debates, mostly by pro-life proponents to insist that pregnant women should offer Samaritan gestational hospitality to their fetus. A diverse group of pro-life Christian writers—both popular and scholarly—claims that every pregnancy entails a moral obligation for the Christian woman to be a host to her fetal neighbor in need. On the other hand, pro-choice scholars insist that in light of the asymmetrical and even oppressive reproductive and caregiving burdens that women shoulder, gestational hospitality must be discretionary, the value of women's lives must be recognized, and reproductive choice must be legally protected. The latter is a diverse group including pastoral counselors, secular feminist philosophers, Christian bioethicists, and rabbinic scholars. This chapter draws from the viewpoints of this diverse group in order to construct a paradigm for gestational hospitality that encourages virtues of care but also supports a pregnant woman's choice to refuse her fetus the hospitality of her womb. Moreover, I argue that this view of gestational hospitality is not an abdication of Samaritanism but an instantiation of the best principles of neighbor love.

The first section of this chapter critically analyzes the pro-life Christian claim that Samaritanism is incompatible with abortion. Extreme anti-abortion voices accuse pregnant women who abort of being murderers—an accusation with potentially dangerous real-life implications for anyone involved in abortion services. More moderate pro-life scholars appeal to sacramental theology and the Bible to induce women to protect their fetal neighbor and to exhort congregations to help women with crisis pregnancies. This pro-life viewpoint purports to be compassionate but actually trivializes the burdens of unwanted pregnancy and idealizes the help that churches might actually be able to sustain in support of women with unwanted pregnancies. Whether extreme or moderate, these pro-life proponents share the same mind-set that the lesson of the Samaritan parable, when applied to the issue of unwanted pregnancy, is a simple binary: either Christian hospitality for the fetal neighbor or abortion. I offer a contemporary pro-choice Samaritan allegory that challenges this binary and the judgmental nature of these pro-life views. The second part of this chapter develops a morally serious and realistic paradigm of gestational hospitality in relation to unwanted pregnancy, informed by the following: discussions of neighbor love in Christian pastoral theology and Jewish halakah; feminist approaches to care ethics and the moral demand of the fetal Other; and the bioethics of lifesaving, bodily self-gifting, as exemplified in pregnancy and live organ donation. This paradigm takes seriously the self-sacrifice and burdens of pregnancy, aims to foster the best caring impulses in women trying to respond to the needs of those in their care, and wisely insists that the difficult choices women make in adjudicating care decisions, including reproductive decisions, must be free of coercion and legally protected.

PRO-LIFE VIEWS ON SAMARITAN DUTIES
TO THE FETAL NEIGHBOR

One of the most famous arguments for the right to end an unwanted pregnancy is Judith Thomson's famous 1971 essay "A Defense of Abortion." In this essay, Thomson proposes a fantastical analogy that being compelled to gestate a fetus would be like waking up one day to find you have been kidnapped and hooked up to a famous violinist with kidney failure; if the connection is severed, the violinist will die. Thomson's analogy was designed to grant, for the sake of argument, that the fetus is akin to a person, which allowed Thomson to focus on what rights and responsibilities one morally has to another person who has put extraordinary demands on one's body in order to live. She argues that if curing a famous violinist or gestating a baby could be accomplished in an hour, one might possibly have the moral right to refuse, but it would be "indecent" to do so. Nevertheless, pregnancy is not a one-hour proposition; gestating an unwanted pregnancy is a burden. Taking on that burden could be said to make one a "Splendid Samaritan";[1] nevertheless, Thomson argued, just as there is no moral requirement for a kidnapped person to remain hooked up to an ailing violinist, there should be no moral requirement to gestate an unwanted pregnancy. The appropriation of one's body is too great.

Pro-life writers have reacted strongly to Thomson—as much for her defense of abortion as her appropriation of the Samaritan notion. Indeed, in recent years, perhaps in part because of Thomson's essay, pro-life writers have argued—intentionally to a Christian audience—for the duty of Samaritan gestational hospitality. Let us recall the parable:

> Just then a lawyer stood up to test Jesus. "Teacher," he said, "what must I do to inherit eternal life?" He said to him, "What is written in the law? What do you read there?" He answered, "You shall love the Lord your God with all your heart, and with all your soul, and with all your strength, and with all your mind; and your neighbor as yourself." . . . But wanting to justify himself, he asked Jesus, "And who is my neighbor?" Jesus replied, "A man was going down from Jerusalem to Jericho, and fell into the hands of robbers, who stripped him, beat him, and went away, leaving him half dead. Now by chance a priest was going down that road; and when he saw him, he passed by on the other side. So likewise a Levite, when he came to the place and saw him, passed by on the other side. But a Samaritan while traveling came near him; and when he saw him, he was moved with pity. He went to him and bandaged his wounds, having poured oil and wine on them. Then he put him on his own animal, brought him to an inn, and took care of him. The next day he took out two denarii, gave them to the innkeeper, and said, "Take care of him; and when I come back, I will repay you whatever more you spend." Which of these three, do you think, was a neighbor to the man who fell into the hands of the robbers?" He said, "The one who showed him mercy." Jesus said to him, "Go and do likewise." (Luke 10:25–37)

Whether directly or by allusion, Luke's parable is enlisted in order to frame the maternal-fetal relationship in terms of the pregnant woman's Samaritan duty to gestate her fetal neighbor, or if she is not willing, the pro-life activist's Samaritan duty to intervene. Appeals to the parable range from extreme anti-abortion writings to more moderate pro-life publications by established scholars. While the former harshly level the charge of murder against women and abortion providers—charges that could easily enflame extremist reactions from militant anti-abortion groups—the more widely influential writings

1. Judith Jarvis Thomson, "A Defense of Abortion," *Philosophy & Public Affairs* 1, no. 1 (1971): 65.

exemplify moderate pro-life approaches that attempt to induce pregnant women, based on Christian beliefs and values they may already hold, to carry their pregnancies to term. The latter good Samaritan appeals, while seemingly more compassionate to women in crisis, trivialize the burdens of an unwanted pregnancy and idealize the care that church congregations actually can give to women contemplating abortion.

Extreme Anti-abortion Samaritanism

One example of an extreme interpretation of the Samaritan parable is found in the writings of Bill Muehlenberg, who gives the Samaritan parable a modern allegorical twist by situating it in present-day Australia, where he is an anti-abortion activist. He depicts the Samaritan as the pro-life supporter who comes to the assistance of vulnerable fetuses.

> Jesus said: "A man was going down from Sydney to Melbourne, when he passed by an abortion mill. There he saw innocent babies being led to their destruction, leaving them dead. A priest happened to be going down the same road, and when he saw the mill, he passed by on the other side. So too, a Levite. . . . But a Samaritan, as he traveled, came where the babies were; and when he saw them, he took pity on them. He went to them and did all he could to rescue them. Then he put them in his own car, brought him to an inn and took care of them. . . . Which of these three do you think was a neighbor to those who fell into the hands of the abortionists?"[2]

In this odd allegory, the wounded man on the road is transmuted into still living aborted fetuses at an abortion clinic. There are passersby who do not get involved; then a good (pro-life) Samaritan comes by who believes that it is his moral duty to help. The allegory is bizarrely strained, to say the least, because the chance of a fetus from a botched abortion surviving long enough to be transported by car to a hospital (the "inn") is highly unlikely.[3] It is possible that Muehlenberg had something symbolic in mind; perhaps he was

---

2. Bill Muehlenberg, "Abortion and the Good Samaritan," *Culture Watch* (August 6, 2015), https://billmuehlenberg.com/2015/08/06/abortion-and-the-good-samaritan/. Muehlenberg has an MA from Gordon Conwell Seminary. See "The Team," *Australian Christian Values Institute*, http://www.christianvalues.org.au/index.php/who-we-are/the-board.

3. Pro-life groups sensationalize the unlikely event of babies born alive in botched abortions. See Sarah Terzo, "Looking Back: Jill Stanek Exposed Live Birth Abortions at Illinois Hospital," *Live Action* (July 25, 2015), https://www.liveaction.org/news/looking-back-jill-stanek-exposed -live-birth-abortions-illinois-hospital/. For a counterperspective, see Michele Kurs Frishman, "Wisconsin Act 110: When an Infant Survives an Abortion," *Wisconsin Women's Law Journal* 20, no. 101 (2005): 101–36.

thinking of anti-abortion groups who picket outside abortion clinics in the hope of rescuing fetuses in utero by convincing the mother not to enter the clinic.[4] Muehlenberg does not mention any pregnant woman in his allegory; indeed, the notion that a pregnant woman might be a neighbor in need is not even considered. In other writings, Muehlenberg supports prosecuting abortion doctors for homicide and women who abort for a lesser crime.[5]

Catholic philosopher Christopher Kaczor also gives an extreme interpretation of Samaritanism. Kaczor chides Judith Thomson for interpreting the Samaritan as someone who went "above and beyond the call of duty." He concedes that "supererogatory" demands do exist for the believer,[6] but pregnancy is not seen as onerous by Kaczor, who comments (flippantly to my ears, though he is serious): "The burden need only involve nine months of pregnancy; the woman can put the child up for adoption."[7] For Kaczor, intentional abortion is unequivocally murder of a heinous kind, and he endorses the Catholic prohibition of the direct killing of a fetus or even an embryo in cases of, for example, ectopic pregnancy.[8] While Kaczor does not advocate violence against abortion doctors or their clinics, neither does he strongly condemn such violence, and he leaves open, in theory, that "vigilante justice" could be "justified in extreme situations,"[9] though he does not describe what situation would justify violence regarding abortion. Casuistic comments such as these are precisely the kind of open door a radical anti-abortion activist might seize upon. Indeed, Kaczor's understanding of the Samaritan neighbor's absolute love obligation seems to point in the direction not only of

---

4. See Bill Muehlenberg, "The Sin of Remaining Silent and Doing Nothing," *Culture Watch* (August 21, 2013), https://billmuehlenberg.com/2013/08/21/the-sin-of-remaining-silent-and -doing-nothing/.

5. See Bill Muehlenberg, "Abortion, Prosecution, Ethics and the Law," *Culture Watch* (May 19, 2016), https://billmuehlenberg.com/2016/05/19/abortion-prosecution-ethics-law/.

6. Christopher Kaczor, *The Ethics of Abortion: Women's Rights, Human Life, and the Question of Justice* (New York: Routledge, 2014), 151, where Kaczor also puts "selling all one's possessions and giving the money to the poor" in the supererogatory category.

7. Kaczor, *The Ethics of Abortion*, 170. In chap. 5 I have already discussed how adoption should not be seen as an easy solution for unwanted pregnancies.

8. Kaczor lists treatment options that avoid so-called direct killing, such as removing the fallopian tube with the embedded embryo, attempting to transfer the embryo to the uterus, and possibly even administering methotrexate, which can be interpreted as destroying part of the embryo but not directly killing it. See Christopher Kaczor, "The Ethics of Ectopic Pregnancy: A Critical Reconsideration of Salpingostomy and Methotrexate," *The Linacre Quarterly* 76, no. 3 (2009): 265–82. The first option is invasive, the second has no chance of success, and the third contradicts the U.S. bishops' directives on managing an extrauterine pregnancy. See United States Conference of Catholic Bishops, *Ethical and Religious Directives for Catholic Health Care Services*, 5th ed. (2009), 27 (directive 48), http://www.usccb.org/issues-and-action/human-life-and-dignity /health-care/upload/Ethical-Religious-Directives-Catholic-Health-Care-Services-fifth-edition -2009.pdf.

9. Kaczor, *The Ethics of Abortion*, 204.

saving the wounded man (i.e., the fetus about to be aborted) but other forms of intervention, including violence, in order to stop an abortion.[10]

Charles Bellinger also gives an anti-abortion interpretation of the Samaritan parable in his book with the provocative title *Jesus v. Abortion: They Know Not What They Do*. Bellinger levels his strongest critique against those pro-choice advocates who claim to be believers, insisting that a faithful understanding of the Lukan parable militates against a belief that "the inhabitant of the womb is *not a neighbor*."[11] He insists that the call to protect the uterine neighbor follows from the Leviticus command that is the subtext to Jesus' teaching in this parable, which Bellinger translates as, "You shall not stand by idly when your neighbor's life is at stake" (Lev. 19:16).[12] Anything short of defending the life of a fetus is "rebellion" against this biblical teaching. Bellinger's invocation of the Samaritan story is directed almost exclusively to the pregnant woman. She is presented with the choice of "act[ing] toward her child as a violent robber or as a Good Samaritan."[13] There is some critique of abortion doctors and their clinics, but his principal accusation falls on the woman because, according to Bellinger, abortion is the murder of an innocent child, and he holds the mother responsible, apparently even if she is a victim of a botched abortion.[14] Bellinger intimates that the intention of pro-life discourse should not be name-calling but the winning of "hearts and minds" so that pro-choice supporters today can be brought to "ethical maturity";[15] however, his discourse is severe and condemnatory. He suggests that when a woman hands over her fetus to be aborted, the act is akin to what Pilate did when he "hands over the innocent [Jesus] to be killed."[16] To say that Bellinger ratchets up the anti-abortion rhetoric against women in an ominous way is an understatement.

10. Elsewhere Kaczor states that an undercover infiltration by pro-life activists at a Planned Parenthood clinic that involved lying could be seen as justified on the basis that "those who kill unborn human beings do not have a right to the truth." Christopher Kaczor, "In Defense of Live Action," *Public Discourse* (February 11, 2011), http://www.thepublicdiscourse.com/2011/02 /2538/.

11. Charles K. Bellinger, *Jesus v. Abortion: They Know Not What They Do* (Eugene, OR: Cascade Books, 2016), 81, italics in original. Bellinger teaches at Brite Divinity School in Texas.

12. Bellinger, *Jesus v. Abortion*, 83.

13. Bellinger, *Jesus v. Abortion*, 81, 88.

14. See Bellinger, *Jesus v. Abortion*, 191. The appalling case of Kenneth Gosnell is discussed; see Bellinger, *Jesus v. Abortion*, 200–202. Bellinger voices outrage at Gosnell's killing of late-term, live-born fetuses but only mentions in passing Gosnell's patient who died undergoing an abortion and says nothing about another woman who later died and countless others who suffered perforated uteruses, sepsis, hysterectomies, venereal disease, and other adverse effects as a result of Gosnell's malpractice. See William Saletan, "The Back Alley: What Happened to the Women," *Slate* (February 16, 2011), https://slate.com/news-and-politics/2011/02/kermit-gosnell-and-abortion -clinic-regulation-did-pro-choice-politics-protect-him.html.

15. Bellinger, *Jesus v. Abortion*, 311.

16. Bellinger, *Jesus v. Abortion*, 177.

Muehlenberg, Kaczor, and Bellinger give three different but equally dogmatic and harsh anti-abortion interpretations of Samaritanism, which emphasize the heinousness of the act and the moral imperative for Christian Samaritan bystanders to act decisively on behalf of innocent fetuses. These calls to action might make some uneasy in a world where extreme anti-abortion rhetoric can incite violence from some unstable individuals involved in far-right groups.[17] Other Christian scholars with pro-life convictions take a less harsh tone with their interpretation of the Samaritan parable and neighbor love. However, their use of Samaritanism is equally problematic. Although their pro-life appeals are couched in terms of compassion for the unfortunate woman with a crisis pregnancy, these pro-life authors downplay the burdens of an unwanted pregnancy and exaggerate what church congregations could do to help, if they were even willing.

Moderate Pro-life Samaritanism

Eugene Schlesinger, Stanley Hauerwas, Frederick Bauerschmidt, and Richard Hays are part of a growing group of mainstream Christian thinkers who appeal to the notion of neighbor love in order to make a pro-life theological case to a Christian audience. Their stated purpose is not primarily to change laws; rather, they wish to call the church to its responsibilities as a community of compassion toward women with unplanned pregnancies and to encourage women to nurture gestational life as an expression of their Christian faith. Ironically, however, their pro-life message, which seems at first glance more modulated and compassionate than the harsher anti-abortion views discussed above, actually implies compulsory gestation for pregnant Christian women.

Writing from an Anglican perspective, Eugene Schlesinger attempts to reframe the abortion issue by setting it in "the liturgical and sacramental life of the church," intentionally eschewing an approach focused on "mandating a legislative solution."[18] Schlesinger believes it is possible to create the kind of church environment that will inspire not only women to be hospitable to their unwanted fetuses but also the church to offer helpful material aid to these women. He claims that eucharistic participation "fosters dispositions

17. Bellinger distances himself from "anti-abortion zealots" (Bellinger, *Jesus v. Abortion*, 58) yet draws parallels between abortion and the Holocaust, which is a common trope meant to incite anti-abortion fervor (see Bellinger, *Jesus v. Abortion*, 210–14). Muehlenberg condemned the killing of abortion doctor George Tiller, though one of his blog followers called Tiller's murder "the judgment of God," and Muehlenberg has not removed that post (comment by Steve Swartz, on June 2, 2009, at 6:31 a.m.); https://billmuehlenberg.com/2009/06/01/abortion-tiller-and -murder-compounded/#.

18. Eugene R. Schlesinger, "From Rights to Rites: A Eucharistic Reframing of the Abortion Debate," *Anglican Theological Review* 94, no. 1 (2012): 38.

inclining women away from abortion, moving women to compassionately give of their very substance for the helpless fetal neighbor"—a statement that alludes to the Samaritan parable and implies that Christians should treat fetuses with the dignity accorded to born persons.[19] Once a believing woman properly understands the meaning of the Eucharist, she will more willingly make the necessary sacrifices and reject abortion. If she is thus willing to make a sacrifice, "then the church must ensure that unplanned pregnancies do not lead to an oppressive or intolerable burden."[20] Schlesinger assumes that a Christian woman with a proper sacramental understanding of Christ's "living sacrifice" to God will be moved to gestate her unwanted pregnancy without external coercion either by fellow congregants or the state and without oppressive burdens.[21]

Schlesinger's claim that coercion and exploitation can be avoided, however, is superficial and contradictory. He asserts that the Eucharist "precludes the use of coercion to prevent abortion" and that a woman's decision to gestate should be "voluntary." However, he also asserts that true eucharistic faith "precludes abortion," which seems to indicate that any woman who aborts has betrayed the heart of her Christian faith.[22] If abortion is precluded from a eucharistic viewpoint, then it is compulsory for the believer; I do not see how coercion is avoided. Regarding exploitation, Schlesinger acknowledges the social and biological inequity of pregnancy, which requires that women alone give of their body self-sacrificially. He does not explain how this inequity would not devolve into injustice and exploitation, other than to assert sanguinely and idealistically that "women *cannot* be exploited by a eucharistic ethic regarding abortion."[23] Schlesinger gives no concrete example of how the church would "ensure that unplanned pregnancies do not lead to an oppressive or intolerable burden." I will say more below about how this kind of rhetoric of churches "bearing the burdens" of an unplanned pregnancy plays fast and loose with real women's and children's lives.[24]

Stanley Hauerwas is well known for his critiques of liberal individual rights and his promotion of biblically informed Christian communal character. Regarding abortion specifically, Hauerwas invokes the virtue of Christian

19. Schlesinger, "From Rights to Rites," 51. Schlesinger bases his argument on David Kelsey's theological anthropology, which he believes supports a pro-life position on fetal personhood. In a brief discussion of abortion, Kelsey is much more circumspect, suggesting that embryonic or fetal life is more aptly designated as only a "potential human living body." David H. Kelsey, *Eccentric Existence: A Theological Anthropology*, vol. 1 (Louisville, KY: Westminster John Knox Press, 2009), 263.

20. Schlesinger, "From Rights to Rites," 51.

21. Schlesinger, "From Rights to Rites," 48.

22. Schlesinger, "From Rights to Rites," 50.

23. Schlesinger, "From Rights to Rites," 50, italics in original.

24. Schlesinger, "From Rights to Rites," 51.

hospitality to urge that the fetus, however unwanted, be welcomed by the pregnant woman and the faith community supporting her.[25] Hauerwas is ostensibly not concerned about making anti-abortion laws or influencing public policy[26] but, rather, focuses on urging Christians to reflect on what kind of faith community they should be building—one that welcomes the stranger or one that sees unwanted children as someone else's problem. Hauerwas recounts two brief vignettes of pregnant women being welcomed by their church congregation. For one woman, a divorcée, the church paid her doctor's fees, gave her a baby shower, and at the birth, one church member "was her labor coach. When the woman's mother refused to come and help after the baby was born, the church brought food and helped clean her house while she recovered from the birth. Now the woman's little girl is the child of the parish."[27] A second and even briefer vignette is about a black unwed teenager who had a baby and was sent to live with an older couple in the church who "raise[d] the teenage mother along with the baby."[28] Hauerwas implies that these stories about the pregnant divorcée and the pregnant teen function as a template for faithful church responses to crisis pregnancy situations. However, I do not see faithfulness but a thinly veiled and troubling idealism.

First, in both situations there is no mention of the divorced woman or the teenager wanting to have an abortion, so presumably these were crisis pregnancies but not ones heading for abortion. Hauerwas says nothing about how the church community should act toward a woman who requested church support to have an abortion. Studies show that in general, women do not speak about abortion; and in particular, Christian women with unwanted pregnancies remain silent to their congregations. In her study of over 700 self-identified conservative Christian women and their abortion experiences, Linda Ellison notes that almost 80 percent of the women told no one about their abortion.[29] Ellison shares one woman's words about keeping her abortion secret from her church: "That whole congregation gives me strength, but I have to keep things from them too, just like a normal family. . . . The only person I told 'bout my abortion was Jesus. That's it. And Jesus, He understands. He sees my life."[30] In real life, it seems, women do not ordinarily consult their church about their unwanted pregnancies.

25. Stanley Hauerwas, "Abortion Theologically Understood (1991)," in *The Hauerwas Reader*, ed. John Berkman and Michael Cartwright (Durham, NC: Duke University Press, 2001), 603–22.
26. See Hauerwas, "Abortion Theologically Understood," 619.
27. Hauerwas, "Abortion Theologically Understood," 607.
28. Hauerwas, "Abortion Theologically Understood," 606.
29. Linda Ellison, "Abortion and the Politics of God: Patient Narratives and Public Rhetoric in the American Abortion Debate," ThD diss., Harvard Divinity School (2008), 57.
30. Ellison, "Abortion and the Politics of God," 64.

Second, I dispute Hauerwas's claim that what this church did for the pregnant divorcée constitutes "creativity and compassion" that could be practically adapted to address other situations of unwanted pregnancy in church congregations.[31] Many questions can be posed in light of this woman's story (I will say more about the pregnant teen later). What is the chance that another woman with a crisis pregnancy would find her way to a church community with which she felt comfortable enough to even ask for help? What is the chance that the promise of help from the congregants would be speedy and concrete enough to prevent the woman from turning to abortion as a solution? For how long would this congregation continue to offer assistance? Moreover, according to a leading national crisis pregnancy organization, polls show that a significant percentage of women think churches tend to judge single women who get pregnant and to "oversimplify decisions about pregnancy options."[32] Hauerwas's call for churches to step up and just be compassionate is untenable, irresponsible, and cannot serve as a real-life ethic on which Christian women with crisis pregnancies could depend. There may have been more economic and material support offered to the pregnant divorced woman than a baby shower and some casseroles after the baby was born, but Hauerwas does not mention it. The lack of any mention of concrete economic needs regarding having and raising a child is further proof that this abortion ethic lacks sufficient grounding in reality, since financial considerations loom large in many abortion decisions, given the demographics of abortion patients.[33] Very few women would choose to bring an unwanted pregnancy to term if they are facing serious economic stresses, not to mention a potentially judgmental reception from their church.[34]

I do not criticize Hauerwas's stance on abortion because it is too hard on women; abortion decisions are hard either way. Moreover, I agree that abortion is a "morally serious matter." I criticize his stance because it offers a theological caricature of hospitality and pregnancy. As Hauerwas states in a

31. Hauerwas, "Abortion Theologically Understood," 604.
32. Lisa Cannon Green, "New Survey: Women Go Silently from Church to Abortion Clinic," *Care-Net* (November 23, 2015), https://www.care-net.org/churches-blog/new-survey-women -go-silently-from-church-to-abortion-clinic.
33. According to a Guttmacher Institute fact sheet, "75% of abortion patients were poor or low income." "Induced Abortion in the United States," *Guttmacher Institute* (January 2018), https:// www.guttmacher.org/fact-sheet/induced-abortion-united-states.
34. There is little way of knowing how Hauerwas's abortion views have impacted his Methodist denomination. However, a recent session of the North Carolina Annual Conference published a document of resolutions in which one sees nothing of Hauerwas's recommendations for congregations. Responsibility seems to be sloughed off onto crisis pregnancy centers to "help women find feasible alternatives to abortion." North Carolina United Methodist Church, "Resolutions Presented to the 2015 Session of the North Carolina Annual Conference" (updated June 9, 2015), 12, http://nccumc.org/ac2015/files/2015/06/2015-Resolutions-Report.pdf.

very binary way: there is abortion and then there is "its opposite—hospitality to children and the vulnerable."[35] I do not think Hauerwas means to judge harshly, but his uncompromising binary between abortion and Christian hospitality is judgmental. The way in which Hauerwas discusses abortion theologically swings between idealism and judgmentalism. To be morally serious about abortion, one needs a more realistic view about what embodied gestational hospitality entails.

Idealism is also a problem plaguing Frederick Bauerschmidt's "Being Baptized: Bodies and Abortion," in which he argues that the notion of neighborliness should guide a Christian ethics of abortion.[36] Like Schlesinger, Bauerschmidt approaches the abortion issue in terms of sacramental theology—in this case the sacrament of baptism. First, he argues that the candidate for Christian baptism gives up any "body-right" and, once she passes through the baptismal waters, is "entrusted to the entire community, which must constantly ensure that the body is treated with the dignity of a temple of the Spirit."[37] According to Bauerschmidt, baptism and gestation both entail hospitality, the meaning of which he explicates by referencing the New Testament parable of the good Samaritan. His foil is Judith Thomson, who, as noted above, interprets that parable to be about an expectation of minimum decency, not an obligation of extraordinary bodily hospitality. Bauerschmidt gives the parable a different spin: "the moral achievement of the Samaritan was not the decision to help the wounded stranger, but the ability to recognize that he had no choice but to help this wounded and vulnerable one." Bauerschmidt wishes to impress on his Christian readers that "it is in welcoming the valueless, powerless life of the unborn that we most vibrantly replicate God's baptismal welcome of us."[38] This kind of welcoming is the true meaning of being a Christian neighbor to the needy—which is not an "optional virtue" for the baptized.[39] Bauerschmidt acknowledges the demands of pregnancy that only women can bear, but he seems confident that "Christians . . . may be able to take some of that demand upon themselves."[40] This comment is at best well-intentioned but perfunctory; at worst, it smacks of idealism

---

35. Hauerwas, "Abortion Theologically Understood," 611.

36. Frederick Christian Bauerschmidt, "Being Baptized: Bodies and Abortion," in *The Blackwell Companion to Christian Ethics*, ed. Stanley Hauerwas and Samuel Wells (Malden, MA: Blackwell, 2004), 250–62.

37. Bauerschmidt, "Being Baptized," 255.

38. Bauerschmidt, "Being Baptized," 261. Bauerschmidt implies that theologians and other Christians may also have a duty to work legislatively or in other public venues to "enact laws to protect the needy neighbor," but this point is not emphasized. Bauerschmidt, "Being Baptized," 261.

39. Bauerschmidt, "Being Baptized," 260.

40. Bauerschmidt, "Being Baptized," 262.

that dangerously wagers the well-being of pregnant women and their children against the capacity of average Christians effectively to provide material and other aid to women with crisis pregnancies.

An issue hovering at the fringes of these various pro-life appeals to the good Samaritan is that of abortion and the Bible and how this parable, specifically, should hermeneutically factor into a biblical approach to abortion ethics. New Testament scholar Richard Hays, in his *The Moral Vision of the New Testament*, notes the biblical silence on abortion, which means the Christian must extrapolate a model of moral behavior from the biblical text.[41] Hays turns to the Samaritan parable as a paradigm for compassionate Christian morality and applies it to the ethical complexity of abortion. He dispenses with the pro-life fixation on the fetal personhood issue, which he sees as analogous to the "limiting and self-justifying" question of who is and is not a neighbor, which preoccupies the lawyer in the story. For Hays, Samaritan compassion "*creates* a neighbor relation where none existed before,"[42] which makes the fetal-personhood debate moot and allows the biblical reader to focus instead on actions that comport with Christian faithfulness.

Hays, like the other moderate pro-life scholars above, emphasizes the church's moral obligation to help women with crisis pregnancies so that they will not suffer alone.[43] However, Hays diverges from the other scholars by sympathetically addressing some hard-case scenarios. He discusses an older couple, "Bill and Jennifer," and their difficult decision made in "good conscience" to abort their fetus diagnosed with Down syndrome.[44] In addition, Hays is particularly troubled by the notion of "requiring a young woman to bear the burden of a child conceived through an act of violence against her."[45] Nevertheless, despite these few comments regarding extenuating circumstances that might justify an abortion, Hays concludes that the Samaritan parable does commend neighbor love. There is a "general presumption" in the New Testament against abortion, and church communities should do what they can to welcome "all who are born into the world."[46] What practical ethics does Hays have in mind for how the church should implement its Samaritan compassion?

Hays disapproves of passing anti-abortion laws that "compel women to complete . . . a pregnancy" and explicitly condemns abortion clinic violence

---

41. Richard B. Hays, *The Moral Vision of the New Testament: Community, Cross, New Creation; A Contemporary Introduction to New Testament Ethics* (San Francisco: HarperSanFrancisco, 1996), 209.

42. Hays, *Moral Vision of the New Testament*, 451.

43. See Hays, *Moral Vision of the New Testament*, 453.

44. Hays, *Moral Vision of the New Testament*, 457.

45. Hays, *Moral Vision of the New Testament*, 456. Hays does not explain why he seemingly associates pregnancy from rape with young women.

46. Hays, *Moral Vision of the New Testament*, 455.

"as incompatible with the gospel."[47] Other than these specific directives, his comments echo those of Hauerwas, which again raises the same problems of idealism and possibly coerciveness. Hays quotes the same story Hauerwas mentions of the African American pregnant teen—but with more detail, because Hays reveals that she was fourteen when she gave birth. Hays describes this congregation's "assumption of responsibility for a pregnant teenager" as a glowing example of "a life of disciplined service."[48] Whether or not this situation turned out well for this girl and her baby, I find the use of this vignette deeply disturbing, given the lack of comments about details that are morally and legally pertinent. There is no mention of her parents, which raises a red flag regarding what seems to be an informal, and hence legally ambiguous, foster-parenting situation. Furthermore, as a minor, her becoming pregnant was at least statutory rape and, perhaps, even a more serious sexual assault, so at minimum, this pregnancy would qualify for the exception Hays makes about abortion in cases of rape. If this was a rape, did the church discuss with the girl that abortion was an acceptable Christian option? Hays does not comment on any of these issues (neither does Hauerwas). To my mind, this anecdote is a troubling story with unanswered questions about the physical and psychological well-being of a teenager, who not only was impregnated as a minor but also allowed (possibly encouraged or even pressured)[49] by a church congregation to give birth at age fourteen.

All the pro-life writers above appeal to the Samaritan parable in various ways to induce pregnant women (and possibly even girls) to fulfill their Christian call to be hospitable to their fetal neighbor. I concede that seeing pregnancy as a kind of Samaritan hospitality is a powerful image, and believing women who courageously endure difficult pregnancies might appreciate this recognition of their sacrifice. Nevertheless, I object to the way pro-life authors trivialize gestational hospitality by suggesting that the act of Samaritanism in Luke's parable is analogous to gestating and birthing a child. Let us revisit the biblical parable with more attention to details to test whether the analogy is apt.

In the story, the good Samaritan gave two denarii (about a day's wage) to pay for the wounded man's care—a generous gift. He offered to return and pay for the rest—also very generous. The Samaritan does not seem to be

47. Hays, *Moral Vision of the New Testament*, 458.

48. Hays, *Moral Vision of the New Testament*, 459, 460.

49. The fact that Hays cryptically alludes to the girl bearing the "cross" of the "shame and the physical difficulty of pregnancy" seems to point in the disturbing direction of the church pressuring her to fulfill their sense of what her Christian duty should be. Hays, *Moral Vision of the New Testament*, 460. Even if the church did not suggest to her that she should take up her cross and have the baby, Hays himself suggests seeing unwanted pregnancy in this light. I will say more about this theme in the next chapter.

under any duress when he comes upon the wounded man. He is generous but in a monetary and not a corporeal self-gifting way. Already one can see that the analogy to a crisis pregnancy begins to break down. There is almost nothing about the Samaritan that resembles the desperate pregnant divorcée, not to mention the pregnant fourteen-year-old girl discussed by Hauerwas and Hays. The Samaritan did not say that he would stay and take care of all the wounded man's daily bodily needs for the next nine months, breast-feed him for months, or support him the next eighteen years of his life. The Samaritan aided the wounded man but did not thereby become so emotionally attached to him that he could not consider relinquishing him to another's care; in fact, the Samaritan leaves him with the innkeeper and departs. Thus the deep emotional toll of carrying an unwanted pregnancy to term and then giving up the child for adoption (as Kaczor so callously recommends as a mode of good Samaritanism) finds no analogy in the Samaritan parable. Finally, the extreme idea, which Muehlenberg and Bellinger suggest, that a woman who refuses to be a gestational Samaritan is a murderous criminal finds no support in Jesus' parable. The Samaritan voluntarily helps the wounded stranger; he is not required to by law. Nor does the Samaritan criticize the passersby and advocate passing laws requiring a twenty-four-hour waiting period, or the viewing of photos of wounded people on the side of the road, before a passerby is allowed to continue down the road.[50] If one begins with this Samaritan's generous but limited acts of voluntary caring and then tries to analogize to a woman with an unwanted pregnancy, the proportional difference is much too great to sustain the analogy.

The way pro-life authors invoke the Samaritan parable trivializes the embodied generosity of even a planned pregnancy, grossly distorts the burdens of carrying an unwanted pregnancy to term and becoming a parent, and overly inflates the kind of practical assistance a church congregation would ever be able to sustain—even if one only looks at the economics.[51] If one considers the emotional, psychological, and health aspects of gestating, birthing, and parenting—when the woman does not feel able or willing—the costs are incalculable for her as well as for the child born into a fraught familial situation.

50. Bellinger does not mention waiting-period laws that some states have enacted, but he does speak positively about pregnant women being given an ultrasound to convince them not to abort. See Bellinger, *Jesus v. Abortion*, 184–85 n. 8.

51. The average estimated self-pay cost for having a healthy baby in the United States has been estimated as follows: vaginal hospital birth without complications, about $10,000; C-section without complications, almost $18,000. See "Average U.S. Facility Charges for Giving Birth," *Transforming Maternity Care* (March 16, 2011), http://transform.childbirthconnection.org /resources/datacenter/chargeschart/.

Finally, a brief word about adoption is in order. It is beyond the scope of this book to address adoption and fostering, but a few comments are pertinent because Kaczor speaks of adoption as if it is an obvious solution to an unwanted pregnancy, and Hauerwas and Hays hint at some kind of church-sponsored foster parenting for an unplanned pregnancy. The fact is that few women who go through with an unwanted pregnancy can bear to relinquish the baby for adoption, with some studies suggesting an infinitesimal rate of about 1.7 percent of white women and nearly zero percent for African American women.[52] That means that impelling or pressuring a pregnant woman (or a girl) to continue to gestate probably means that she will keep any child she births, even if she does not feel able or ready to mother that child. Practically, we cannot reasonably expect that having unwanted pregnancies "addressed corporately by the local church community" will ever be a widespread or effective model to address this eventuality. Indeed, in the anecdote Hays himself discusses, Bill and Jennifer did not discuss their abortion decision with their church, "believing—perhaps rightly," Hays concedes, "that their local church was not in fact the sort of community that could meaningfully take responsibility for such a matter."[53] Nor, I would venture to guess, would Jennifer have been able to relinquish the child for adoption if she had carried it to term. To continue to advocate for an ethical model that has little chance of actually helping women with unwanted pregnancies is idealism, pure and simple, that potentially puts at risk the well-being of pregnant women and the children they may be compelled to bring to birth.

The above pro-life authors are trying seriously to exhort Christians to think about hospitality and what it means to be a body of believers who welcome strangers as neighbors. However, the message they actually convey to a pregnant woman is that birthing the baby is the only biblically and sacramentally hospitable act for her to do, which coercively implies that abortion would be a betrayal of her Christian faith. These pro-life scholars imply that church congregations will step up to the plate to assist pregnant women; whereas, it is doubtful that any woman with an unwanted pregnancy will find in her church the support needed to go forward and have the baby. It is time for pro-life writers to abandon the overly simplistic binary of abortion-versus-hospitality, as Hauerwas puts it, and realize that caring women sometimes need to choose abortion and that this choice can be a Christian one.

---

52. U.S. Department of Health and Human Services, "Voluntary Relinquishment for Adoption," *Child Welfare Information Gateway* (March 2005), 2, https://www.childwelfare.gov/pub PDFs/s_place.pdf.

53. Hays, *Moral Vision of the New Testament*, 457.

Proving Neighbor to Women with Unwanted Pregnancies

I began this chapter with extreme anti-abortion interpretations of the parable of the good Samaritan that paint the pregnant woman as a threat to her vulnerable, wounded fetus. Moderate pro-life proponents take a somewhat gentler tone in order to exhort the believing pregnant woman to be a good Samaritan. The extreme and the more moderate interpretations of Samaritanism, however, share the same assumption—namely, the wounded man in the parable should be thought of as a fetus in need of hospitality. I challenged the many assumptions that feed this viewpoint (pregnancy as a not-too-burdensome duty, adoption as an easy option, churches as able and willing to help, and so on). In addition, I offer here my alternative retelling of the parable as a way of prompting pro-life Christians to think in a different way about helping their neighbor, who might turn out to be a woman with an unwanted pregnancy.

> A pregnant woman was going down to the Planned Parenthood clinic in Jericho, PA, and fell into the hands of robbers, who stole her purse with her cell phone, her money, and credit cards, leaving her dazed by the side of the road. Now by chance, a priest and a minister were driving down that road together to attend a pro-life interfaith conference. They went to her, put her in their car, and brought her to the nearest facility, which happened to be a crisis pregnancy center. The technician heard a faint heartbeat and said, "Congratulations, you're about 8 weeks," and offered her a pamphlet on parenting and a package of diapers. "I cannot have another baby right now," the woman groaned. The minister started to say, "Well, I know of a nice older couple willing to adopt . . . ," but when he saw her stricken face, he fell silent and left. The woman said she felt abdominal pain, so the priest took her to the hospital where he was the chaplain. The ultrasound confirmed a normal pregnancy. Afterward, she dejectedly joined the priest, who was waiting for her in the chapel. He tried to be upbeat. "As I explained to my students at the seminary just the other day, if a woman has an ectopic pregnancy, a Catholic hospital's ethics committee can approve removing the fallopian tube . . . ," but when he saw her stricken face, he too fell silent and turned away. She left the hospital, intent on walking to Planned Parenthood on her own. Just then a car pulled up beside her; it was the local sheriff's deputy, a deacon in her church. "I heard there was a purse-snatching up the road. Can I help you?" he asked. The woman hesitated at first, then, seeing the kindness in his eyes, poured out the story of her suffering. He was moved with pity. So he offered her a ride to Planned Parenthood in his cruiser. When they arrived, he escorted her past the protesters into the clinic. Once safely inside, he spoke to the receptionist and discreetly handed her $250: "Take care of this lady, whatever she decides; when I come back, I will pay you whatever more is needed."

He started to leave but then turned around and added, "She's a neighbor of mine."

At this point in the original parable there is an exchange between Jesus and the lawyer: "'Which of these three, do you think, proved neighbor to the man who fell among the robbers?' [The lawyer] said, 'The one who showed mercy on him.' And Jesus said to him, 'Go and do likewise'" (Luke 10:36–37 RSV). For my allegory, one can ask an analogous question, "Which of these three, do you think, proved neighbor to the woman seeking an abortion when she fell into the hands of the robbers?" Based on the pro-life viewpoints I have discussed in this chapter, one can imagine a range of responses.

I image that those who hold strong anti-abortion views (like Bellinger and others) would reject the very premise of my parable—namely, that a woman intending to get an abortion should ever be a worthy recipient of Samaritan help that would aid her in accomplishing that act. These anti-abortion proponents only read the wounded man in the road as a symbol for a vulnerable fetus, who needs protection from the murderous intent of its mother. Some pro-life activists might revise the end of the story so that the Samaritan deputy convinces the woman to change her mind and have the baby or, if that fails, finds an excuse to put her in jail overnight in an effort at least to delay her plan. In effect, any of these anti-abortion responses refuses to see the pregnant woman in the role of the needy person on the road. The only role a woman with an unwanted pregnancy can play in an anti-abortion understanding of the parable is that of the beast—that is, she must be made to carry the wounded man (the fetus) to safety at the inn.

I imagine that moderate pro-life proponents (like Hauerwas and others) might accept the premise of my parable (that some women feel justifiably unable to face a crisis pregnancy), but they would reject how my allegory has the Samaritan deputy showing his Christian compassion by complying with the woman's request and helping her to get the abortion. These moderate pro-life writers might want to change my parable so that the deputy offers to let the pregnant woman and her other children stay in his family's guest room until she gives birth, arranges to have the church start a college fund for the baby, and so on. This alternative ending is possible, in theory, but unlikely in reality—less a parable, more a fairy tale. Pro-life churches and Christian crisis pregnancy centers cannot reliably offer the long-term material aid and emotional support necessary to help women with unwanted pregnancies overcome the obstacles they face in pregnancy, birthing, and child-rearing. Moreover, pro-life attempts to induce or pressure a woman to take on the extraordinary burdens of pregnancy and motherhood, when she does not feel able to do so, find no basis in the parable of the kind, but not heroic, Samaritan.

A PRO-CHOICE PARADIGM
FOR GESTATIONAL HOSPITALITY

Having surveyed and criticized problematic aspects of pro-life appeals to Samaritan hospitality in the previous section, now we turn to what a paradigm of gestational hospitality might look like that does not idealize women's self-sacrifice, trivialize pregnancy, or overinflate the capacities of churches to help women with unwanted pregnancies. I propose a pro-choice paradigm for gestational hospitality that brings together the ethical wisdom of pastoral theology, Jewish reproductive ethics, and a range of ideas from current feminist ethics on abortion. I begin with pastoral theological discussions of the caretaking burdens women disproportionately shoulder, where scholars seek to foster more spiritually healthy modes of caregiving. Against this backdrop, I argue for a gestational hospitality paradigm based on women's best impulses to care for others and best intentions to respond to the fetal Other—a paradigm that recognizes the burdens of pregnancy, deems protecting women's well-being as an ethical requirement, and understands the need for legal protections so that a woman's embodied self-giving to her fetus is not exploited or coerced. This paradigm aims to show how reproductive choice can be not only a realistic but also a richly moral endeavor.

Pastoral Theology, Samaritanism, and Finishing the Journey

A number of Christian pastoral theologians have written about the particular burdens of self-sacrifice carried by women generally, and mothers in particular, in reference to Samaritanism. These pastoral theological interpretations are diametrically opposed to the pro-life demands or exhortations for women to be self-sacrificial in pregnancy, as discussed above, and provide a necessary and perhaps even lifesaving message for Christian women today.

Jeanne Stevenson-Moessner is critical of the church preaching self-abnegating and extreme self-sacrifice, which she warns is not only "dangerous to women's psychological, spiritual, and physical health" but also "is contrary to the real aim of Christian love."[54] Referencing Carol Gilligan's views on how mature moral development requires a balance between giving and receiving care, Stevenson-Moessner applies these views to the parable of the good Samaritan. Even though the Samaritan stopped, gave generously, and acted self-sacrificially, the story does not end with the Samaritan sitting huddled

---

54. Jeanne Stevenson-Moessner, "The Road to Perfection: An Interpretation of Suffering in Hebrews," *Interpretation: A Journal of Bible and Theology* 57, no. 3 (2003): 284. Stevenson-Moessner teaches pastoral care at Perkins School of Theology.

and depleted by the wounded man's side. As Stevenson-Moessner notes, "The Samaritan *finished his journey* while meeting the need of a wounded and marginal person. The Samaritan did not give everything away. . . . He did not injure, hurt, or neglect the self."[55] Stevenson-Moessner directs this message of pastoral care to women especially who carry most of the burdens of caregiver tasks, often in isolated settings in the home as mothers of young children and caring for the elderly, to the detriment of their own physical and psychological health.

Chanequa Walker-Barnes cites Stevenson-Moessner's pastoral viewpoint about finishing the journey, calling it a "liberating message for the Strong-BlackWoman," a term she coined meaning the identity thrust upon and internalized by many black women like herself—an identity that pushes them to take on inordinate caretaking responsibilities at the cost of their own health and well-being.[56] Speaking out of her own experience growing up with a single working mother and having to care for her younger brother, Walker-Barnes remembers seeing black women take care of others, and she fell into this role as well. In her community, the idea of overextending oneself to help others "was normative. It was what Black women did. Black women after all were strong."[57] This dangerously self-sacrificial message is one Walker-Barnes hopes to reverse with a more holistic, womanist approach to pastoral care attentive to black women's experience and the historical legacy of racism, sexism, and reproductive exploitation.[58]

Walker-Barnes recuperates the good Samaritan parable as a resource for womanist pastoral theology by clarifying that the needs of the wounded man and the needs of the Samaritan should not be seen in competition. The Samaritan should not suppress her own needs in order to meet those of the wounded person; rather, both the giver and the receiver are meant to represent examples of self-love reflecting God's love. The Samaritan "embodies self-love" because he "finished his journey."[59] Finishing the journey amid tribulations, for Walker-Barnes, is historically and politically inflected, since she reads the

55. Jeanne Stevenson-Moessner, "From Samaritan to Samaritan: Journey Mercies," in *Through the Eyes of Women: Insights for Pastoral Care*, ed. Jeanne Stevenson Moessner (Minneapolis: Fortress Press, 1996), 323, italics added.

56. Chanequa Walker-Barnes, *Too Heavy a Yoke: Black Women and the Burden of Strength* (Eugene, OR: Cascade Books, 2014), 152. Walker-Barnes teaches pastoral care at the Mercer University McAfee School of Theology.

57. Walker-Barnes, *Too Heavy a Yoke*, 2.

58. Walker-Barnes discusses reproductive exploitation as part of slavery (see Walker-Barnes, *Too Heavy a Yoke*, 83–88), and she cites womanist ethicist Delores Williams's writings in which the theme of reproductive surrogacy is discussed extensively (see Walker-Barnes, *Too Heavy a Yoke*, 140–42). See also Monica A. Coleman, "Sacrifice, Surrogacy and Salvation: Womanist Reflections on Motherhood and Work," *Black Theology* 12, no. 3 (2014): 200–212.

59. Stevenson-Moessner, quoted in Walker-Barnes, *Too Heavy a Yoke*, 154.

Samaritan in the parable as himself part of a marginalized group and possibly familiar with "physical and psychic brutalization"; he does not just have pity on the wounded man but also identifies with him.[60] The Samaritan is aware of his own people's pain as he helps the beaten man; his neighbor love is, in a sense, an effect of solidarity rather than an impulse to be self-sacrificial. The Samaritan helps the man not because he suppresses his own needs but because he sees his struggles reflected in the suffering of the wounded man. Walker-Barnes's pastoral approach exemplifies a womanist ethics of care that values making contextual choices that are attentive to conditions of oppression and marginalization and that provide opportunities for solidarity without self-harm.

Neither Stevenson-Moessner nor Walker-Barnes focuses on mothering, but Sally Purvis does connect mother love and the good Samaritan story. Purvis sees ethical value in the deep commitment to others' well-being, which is exemplified in the Samaritan's "extravagant, compassionate, dedicated care" for the wounded man and in most mothers' loving care for their children.[61] This focus on extravagant, maternal self-giving might at first seem to contradict Stevenson-Moessner's and Walker-Barnes's concerns about women being overburdened with Samaritan self-sacrifice. However, Purvis is not calling for unhealthy, self-wounding giving; rather, she is trying to capture the reality of mother-love that is "always embedded in the messy, rich, deeply invested moments" of human relationality.[62] Can that relationality become burdensome, especially for mothers? Yes, because the child's needs dictate, in often unexpected and perhaps even overwhelming ways, the depth and extent of the mother's giving, and those needs can "interfere with some agenda of her own." Purvis warns of the burdens that mothers carry because of unrealistic societal expectations placed on them, and she insists on "the caveat that the mother-love be healthy and unimpeded by social discrimination."[63] That caveat is a large one, and it is hard to imagine a context where mothers are free to love without some type of societal discrimination or the pressure of cultural expectations about ideal mothering. Indeed, Walker-Barnes's work assumes a context of racial and gender discrimination for black women in positions of caretaking. Walker-Barnes does not discuss legal protections for women, but I imagine that she has a realistic sense that for caretaking to

---

60. Walker-Barnes, *Too Heavy a Yoke*, 154. Not all feminists of color find Stevenson-Moessner's interpretation of the parable liberating. See Hellena Moon, "Immigrant Mothers of Color, Pastoral Theology, and the Law," *Pastoral Psychology* 61, no. 3 (2012): 343–58.

61. Sally B. Purvis, "Mothers, Neighbors and Strangers: Another Look at Agape," *Journal of Feminist Studies in Religion* 7, no. 1 (1991): 31. Purvis is a UCC pastor and independent scholar.

62. Purvis, "Mothers, Neighbors and Strangers," 23.

63. Purvis, "Mothers, Neighbors and Strangers," 31–32.

proceed in an equitable way, black women depend on laws being in place that address multiple intersecting discriminations and burdens.[64]

Abortion is not addressed by Purvis, Walker-Barnes, or Stevenson-Moessner. Only Walker-Barnes touches on the issue of reproductive rights in her discussion of black women's forced reproduction under chattel slavery.[65] I do not presume that these scholars share my pro-choice viewpoints. That said, their pastoral care discussions of Samaritanism speak directly to my concerns about the dangers of pro-life exhortations to pregnant women to make sacrifices on behalf of their fetus. These pastoral theologians wisely emphasize that Samaritanism is distorted when used to coerce self-giving from women caregivers especially. My proposed feminist paradigm of gestational hospitality thus takes this pastoral wisdom as its overarching principle: neighbor love is not love in the fullest sense unless it includes making choices so that one can finish the journey.

Pro-choice Care Ethics

Care ethics have factored prominently in feminist thought, promoting notions of relationality, empathy, and contextual decision making. Nel Noddings, who has written on the ethics of care for decades, ranging from parenting, to childhood education, to the terminally ill, applies a care ethic approach to the issue of abortion. At the heart of Noddings's ethics is the principle that we should nurture every person's natural caring inclinations to respond to "any organism in pain . . . by considering its needs and meeting them if possible."[66] Caring is fundamental to human society but fragile and never completely untouched by moral dilemmas.[67] Abortion is a case in point.

A pro-choice ethics of care does not approach abortion decision making in terms of abstract principles or rights (e.g., of fetal personhood or women's bodily integrity) but in terms of relationality and the human impulse to

---

64. Walker-Barnes discusses the impact of black women being disproportionately affected by lower wages than black men or white women. See Walker-Barnes, *Too Heavy a Yoke*, 54.

65. Until recently womanist pastoral theology and ethics only rarely addressed abortion. Even the few passing mentions suggest an issue fraught with layers of suffering, surrogacy, and trauma as well as "resistance." Emilie M. Townes, "Ethics as an Art of Doing the Work Our Souls Must Have," in *Womanist Theological Ethics: A Reader*, ed. Katie Geneva Cannon, Emilie M. Townes, and Angela D. Sims (Louisville, KY: Westminster John Knox Press, 2011), 39. For a strong womanist theological statement on abortion rights, see Jennifer Leath, "(Out of) Places, Please! Demystifying Opposition to Procreative Choice in Afro-Diasporic Communities in the United States," *Journal of Feminist Studies in Religion* 30, no. 1 (2014): 156–65.

66. Nel Noddings, *Starting at Home: Caring and Social Policy* (Berkeley: University of California Press, 2002), 237. Noddings is professor emeritus of childhood education at Stanford University. See her discussion of natural caring in Nel Noddings, *Caring: A Relational Approach to Ethics and Moral Education*, 2nd ed. (Berkeley: University of California Press, 2013).

67. Nel Noddings, *Women and Evil* (Berkeley: University of California Press, 1989), 184.

nurture those who need care. These impulses are not mere emotions to be ignored but have moral significance. Descriptively speaking, the capacity to elicit a response from the pregnant woman is an unavoidable factor contributing to the fetus's "moral standing" with her or others.[68] The responsive relationality that elicits from the woman a desire to care for the more developed fetus may be absent in an early pregnancy. An embryo or an early fetus "lacks the capacity to respond in ways that are both characteristic of its species and valued by us," Noddings observes.[69] This lack of fetal responsiveness can factor into some women's assessment for why it seems right for her to put her own needs above that of an early "preresponsive" fetus.[70] Noddings is not arguing for abortion rights in early pregnancy based on a prematernal subjectivity, as discussed in the previous chapter. Her point is a contextual and relational one, because, in another context, even an early fetus in an unplanned pregnancy can unexpectedly elicit a caring response from the woman. What might have been experienced as a mere "information speck" or "human tissue" is now experienced as much more. The mother may even be moved to say, "It is sacred. . . . I cannot, will not destroy it."[71] Noddings is not suggesting that either experience—the lack of relationality or the burst of recognition—points to an objective ethical principle that all or some fetuses are valueless or all or some fetuses are sacred; rather, she is making a point about the dynamics of relationships and how they unavoidably affect how we impute value and implement caregiving.

Nodding has had her share of feminist critics, most of whom have focused on what they take to be her overemphasis on caring as traditionally female.[72] Pro-life philosopher Celia Wolf-Devine makes the opposite critique. Wolf-Devine claims that Noddings's ethics of abortion are "chilling" and argues that anyone espousing an ethics of care should be pro-life.[73] However, Noddings is pro-choice, in part because she finds it relationally understandable

68. Noddings, *Women and Evil*, 146, 151. Noddings is clear that a threat to the mother's life removes any moral impediment for abortion. See Noddings, *Women and Evil*, 146.

69. Noddings, *Women and Evil*, 150–51.

70. Noddings, *Starting at Home*, 236. The preresponsiveness in a developing fetus would not be the same as the nonresponsiveness of, say, an elderly person with dementia (most likely a parent) for whom a family member might be the primary caretaker. See Noddings, *Women and Evil*, 151.

71. Noddings, *Caring*, 88.

72. See Claudia Card, "Caring and Evil"; Sarah Lucia Hoagland, "Some Concerns about Nel Noddings' Caring"; Barbara Houston, "Caring and Exploitation"—all in *Hypatia* 5, no. 1 (1990): 101–8, 109–14, 115–19, respectively.

73. Celia Wolf-Devine, "Postscript to 'Abortion and the "Feminine Voice"': The Gutting of the Ethics of Care by Carol Gilligan and Nel Noddings," *Life and Learning III: Proceedings of the Faculty for Life Conference* (1993), http://www.celiawolfdevine.com/pdf/Postscript-to-Abortion-and-the-Feminine-Voice-1993.pdf.

that some women do not connect with an early fetus, do not feel compelled to bring it to birth, and there is nothing immoral about that. Noddings also observes that while many pregnant women experience a deep impulse to care for a fetus, their lives are made up of complicated and overlapping circles of caregiving, and "conflicts of caring may arise."[74] A mother might feel pulled between attending to her born children and an unborn one; between the needs of a spouse to whom she feels many obligations and a fetus to whom she feels few; between her elderly parent living in her home and an uninvited being growing in her womb. Abortion decisions are not simply a choice between caring and selfishness, between hospitality and its opposite.

How does one decide when to care for whom, and how is the decision a moral one? Noddings encourages a contextual, relational approach and tells a hypothetical story to illustrate that: "Suppose the informational speck is mine and I am aware of it"; it becomes sacred to me, such that I could never consider destroying it. I give birth to this child and care for her. "But suppose, now that my beloved child has grown up; it is she who is pregnant and considering abortion. . . . I might like to convey sanctity on this informational speck; but I am not God—only mother to this" now grown-up pregnant daughter, whose "suffering" elicits my response.[75] It would be inconceivable, in this story, for the mother to put the needs of a potential grandchild above the needs of her daughter agonizing with an unwanted pregnancy. The mother's understandable desire to ease the pain of her pregnant daughter contemplating abortion causes her intuitively to reject an abstract ethics of the absolute (e.g., an absolute right to life) in favor of an ethics of responsive care in light of the real and present need of someone she loves.

Is it possible that the needs of a pregnant woman, even a daughter one loves, might be trivial—that is, more selfish want than genuine need? Pro-life writers warn that abortion may be done for trivial reasons, for example, a woman may decide to have an abortion so as not to "postpone her trip to Europe, or because she prefers sons to daughters."[76] No doubt some women do abort for trivial reasons, but if a woman has no compunctions about having an abortion because of her vacation schedule, is she really the type of person we would encourage—even mandate—to assume intensive caretaking responsibilities of gestation and motherhood? Pregnancy and motherhood should not be seen as a compulsory internship for ill-prepared, self-centered, or immature women. One would hope that women could be supported to

74. Noddings, *Caring*, 52.
75. Noddings, *Caring*, 52.
76. Celia Wolf-Devine, "Abortion and the 'Feminine Voice,'" *Public Affairs Quarterly* 3, no. 3 (1989): 93.

choose motherhood at the time in their life when they are mature enough and able to take on that monumental caregiving task.

Noddings's example of the mother's desire to care for her pregnant daughter illustrates Noddings's claim that emotions can be an important moral indicator, which we should not ignore. Noddings is not appealing to emotions as a convenient way to promote empathy for women who want to have an abortion. Emotions can and do connect us with fetal life in compelling ways as well. For example, one widespread visceral human feeling is a "deep revulsion at the thought of destroying a viable fetus."[77] Based on the presence of this feeling, aborting a viable fetus can be deemed in some contexts, Noddings asserts, as "questionable morally"—meaning, one would expect the pregnant woman to respond in a caring way to a nearly fully developed fetus who "can respond to [her] in ways that call forth . . . [her] desire to care," at least in theory.[78] One of the reasons why a viable or even near-viable fetus elicits a care response is that one senses that this uterine being, if born now, actually could act like any other "nuzzling, snuggling, sucking . . . human infant" to whom it would be nearly humanly impossible not to respond positively.[79] These kinds of intuitive reactions and feelings (no doubt culturally influenced) are not "capricious and idiosyncratic" but "widely shared" indicators that have moral import, which is why aborting a healthy, viable fetus is morally questionable from a care ethics perspective.[80]

I find Noddings's approach to the viability issue not only ethically compelling but also practically wise because it is directly connected to the project of cultivating caring in real-life contexts—in this case, a woman's caring response to her own viable fetus. This approach stays appropriately focused on the interpersonal aspect of caring and does not encourage the intervention of third parties who might feel entitled to pronounce on the lack of ethicality of a woman's late-term abortion, simply because they have feelings of compassion toward viable fetuses in general. An ethics of care, for example, would not promote appealing to viability as a means of overruling a pregnant woman's need of a late-term abortion. *Roe v. Wade* specifies a woman's right to an abortion until viability and, if her life is at risk, after viability as well.

77. Noddings, *Women and Evil*, 143. The emotion that Noddings describes is not the same as what law scholar Courtney Cahill has termed "abortion disgust," which she attributes to unease about "gender role disruption" and the perception that abortion "perverts . . . maternal love." These feelings are then mobilized for anti-abortion "fear mongering." Courtney Megan Cahill, "Abortion and Disgust," *Harvard Civil Rights-Civil Liberties Law Review* 48, no. 2 (2013): 442, 447, 429.
78. Noddings, *Women and Evil*, 146, 151.
79. Noddings, *Women and Evil*, 150.
80. Noddings, *Women and Evil*, 149.

However, efforts to restrict late-term abortions have been one of the most active legislative areas in the anti-abortion movement, in part because such laws appeal to the notion that a potentially viable fetus, as a person, should not be aborted, even if it has a lethal abnormality.[81] This kind of law is antithetical to fostering caring responses from parents in the traumatic instance of discovering a late-term fetal abnormality.

I think it is safe to say that most women seeking an abortion wish to do it early in their pregnancy. The statistically small number of women who have a late-term abortion are often facing serious medical threats to their health or have received dire genetic or medical diagnoses for the fetus, some of which cannot be detected until late in the pregnancy.[82] Late-term abortions involve a team that might include obstetricians, nurses, social workers, family members, and chaplains. One study shows that women in their third trimester informed of serious fetal anomalies chose a range of options (e.g., full-term labor and delivery, full-term C-section, or abortion). Given the stress and grief these women and their families faced, it seems compassionately ethical for physicians to offer a range of options "based on the principle of respect for the autonomy of the pregnant woman . . . to make a decision about the management of her pregnancy."[83] I find it patronizing when pro-life advocates warn women who are considering late-term abortions that they will inevitably be overcome by so-called postabortion stress syndrome, once they realize they killed their baby.[84] Indeed, recent studies indicate that the reverse may be true: denying a woman the option of a late-term abortion could be mentally injurious to her.[85]

An ethics of care upholds the significance of viability not as a solution to the ethics of abortion and certainly not as an attempt to restrict supposedly

81. Six states have passed laws making abortion in the case of fetal anomaly either difficult or illegal. See *Guttmacher Institute*, "Abortion Bans in Cases of Sex or Race Selection or Genetic Anomaly" (October 1, 2018), https://www.guttmacher.org/state-policy/explore/abortion-bans -cases-sex-or-race-selection-or-genetic-anomaly, updated.

82. Only about 1 percent of abortions occur after 21 weeks. *Guttmacher Institute*, "Later Abortion" (January 20, 2017), https://www.guttmacher.org/print/evidence-you-can-use/later -abortion. See also David A. Grimes, "The Continuing Need for Late Abortions," *JAMA* 280, no. 8 (1998): 749.

83. Frank A. Chervenak and Laurence B. McCullough, "An Ethically Justified, Clinically Comprehensive Management Strategy for Third-Trimester Pregnancies Complicated by Fetal Anomalies," *Obstetrics and Gynecology* 75, no. 3 (1990): 312–13.

84. See my critique of pro-life scholarship on this putative syndrome. Margaret D. Kamitsuka, "Feminist Scholarship and Its Relevance for Political Engagement: The Test Case of Abortion in the U.S.," *Religion and Gender* 1, no. 1 (2011): 26–27.

85. See M. Antonia Biggs et al., "Women's Mental Health and Well-Being 5 Years after Receiving or Being Denied an Abortion: A Prospective, Longitudinal Cohort Study," *JAMA Psychiatry* 74, no. 2 (2017): 169–78.

selfish pregnant women from killing their babies. Supporting ethics protocols regarding abortion at or near viability is sensible and coheres with the widespread, seemingly natural impulse that most people have to care for infants and nearly born fetuses that could survive outside the womb. In other words, an ethics of care tries to nurture the best of human impulses, if possible, rather than impelling compliance with some legal or philosophical principle. If the objective is for parents to care well for any born baby, then it seems obvious to me that a care ethic is the only appropriate approach to the issue of abortion and fetal viability.

If one takes seriously the ethicality of emotions in caretaking, then a relational and contextual approach to abortion ethics is important. The morality of a decision like abortion should be based not on abstract principles but, rather, on a relational process of assessing many needs and trying to act on one's best impulses of caring—the outcome of which cannot be determined in advance or apart from each situation. Pregnancy is a very intimate and individual form of caring that can elicit the most profound devotion from the mother, but when nothing about the pregnancy elicits from the woman a decision to want to birth and care for a child, it is an unwanted pregnancy. A pregnant woman deciding not to gestate her fetus is not an abdication of caring; it is her assessment—explicit or inchoate—that the caregiving tasks of gestation and mothering are beyond her capacities at that moment in her life. Thus, I endorse a paradigm of gestational hospitality that nurtures the impulse to care while safeguarding the relational and contextual nature of abortion decisions.

Fairness and Embodied Self-Gifting

Beyond the commonplace claim that people who give of themselves to others have bodies, some giving entails the actual donation of one's body parts—that is, live organ donation—with possible long-term health ramifications. If fairness and justice apply morally and legally to self-gifting in live organ donation, then fairness and justice should also apply to gestational self-gifting, Patricia Jung argues. For Jung, gestation and organ donation are "morally analogous in significant ways" because, despite their differences, they both entail the giving of special, if not extraordinary, bodily life support to another, which can affect the donor's own health.[86] Jung emphasizes that while live organ donation is seen by most if not all ethicists as discretionary, pregnancy is not. Jung wishes to change this perception by arguing that organ donation

86. Patricia Beattie Jung, "Abortion and Organ Donation: Christian Reflections on Bodily Life Support," *Journal of Religious Ethics* 16, no. 2 (1988): 281.

and gestation are bodily gifts, and when offered under difficult circumstances, should be seen as "supererogatory."[87]

Jung acknowledges that the most "formidable objection" to her argument is from fellow Roman Catholic ethicist Lisa Cahill, and it is twofold. First, according to Jung, Cahill claims that pregnancy is an intrinsic, natural good, hence not analogous to organ donation, which is "pathological or biologically nonnormative."[88] Second, for Cahill, there is "*some* kind of responsibility to maintain all intrinsically good states of affair," such as gestation. Jung does not dispute that pregnancy, as a "gift of a womb," is a good that implies some responsibility; however, she disputes Cahill's depiction of gestation as a "*prima facie* duty."[89] Jung insists that pregnancy, as a unique "*bodily* form of life support," should not be grouped with other ethical duties but should be seen as an extraordinary gift.[90] I agree and add that while pregnancy is not pathological, neither is it free of burdens and significant health risks for the woman. The claim that the recipient of this gift—the fetus—has a right to use that womb simply because it needs it for the good of life has troubling ramifications, which are exposed when one applies the same logic to live organ donation. That logic would imply that a compatible live donor would have a duty to give up, say, a kidney to someone who needs it to survive. No one seriously makes living organ donation, even to a close family member, a moral requirement or tries to mandate it legislatively. Indeed, a health directive from the U.S. Conference of Bishops explicitly states that in the case of live organ transplant, "the freedom of the prospective donor must be respected."[91] Pro-life proponents argue that because a pregnant woman is the only one able to keep her fetus alive, she is obligated to do so. Jung invokes a fairness principle to argue precisely the inverse. Because the pregnant woman is the only one who could gestate, "it is blatantly unfair to ask her to carry the full burden of life support."[92] If a

---

87. Jung, "Abortion and Organ Donation," 277. See Ann Mongoven, "Sharing Our Body and Blood: Organ Donation and Feminist Critiques of Sacrifice," *Journal of Medicine and Philosophy* 28, no. 1 (2003): 89–114.

88. Jung, "Abortion and Organ Donation," 279. Here Jung discusses a conference paper by Cahill that was eventually published as Lisa Sowle Cahill, "Abortion and Argument by Analogy," *Horizons* 9, no. 2 (1982): 271–87. For my extended discussion of L. Cahill's views, see chap. 5 above.

89. Jung, "Abortion and Organ Donation," 280.

90. Jung, "Abortion and Organ Donation," 284.

91. United States Conference of Catholic Bishops, *Ethical and Religious Directives for Catholic Health Care Services*, 5th ed. (2009), http://www.usccb.org/issues-and-action/human-life-and-dignity/health-care/upload/Ethical-Religious-Directives-Catholic-Health-Care-Services-fifth-edition-2009.pdf. Even in cadaver organ donation, hospitals have strict guidelines to respect the bodily integrity of the deceased person and refrain from pressuring the family for consent. See Mongoven, "Organ Donation," 92.

92. Jung, "Abortion and Organ Donation," 289.

lifesaving responsibility cannot be "equitably distributed," it should be discretionary, not obligatory.[93]

Jung is aware that sacrifice and self-giving are deeply rooted in the Christian tradition, but these noble values have been distorted by patriarchal bias.[94] Sacrificing and serving are enjoined for Christian women, but the church is mostly silent on the risks of pregnancy and how the burdens of caring for others inordinately fall on women, to the detriment of their well-being and that of their dependents—usually children. Thus, when the giving is of a very extraordinary, embodied type, such as live organ donation or gestation, the proper ethical impulse should be toward fairness—all the more so when the pregnancy is unwanted. Thus, I endorse a paradigm of gestational hospitality that insists on fairness in the ethics of corporeal self-gifting—specifically, the protections and freedom of choice afforded to live organ donors should be afforded to pregnant women as well.

Jewish Ethics and Pregnant Women's Needs

Jung argues for fairness and legal protections regarding pregnancy by means of an analogy to organ donation, in part, because there is little in the Christian tradition to offset its central message about sacrifice for others, which has historically been used in gender-biased, oppressive ways. Women have been excluded from positions of authority, relegated to service roles, and exploited under the guise of sacrificial neighbor love. Theologians and ethicists would do well to take a lesson from Jewish ethics, which are informed by the same Scriptures about neighbor love. Rabbinic Judaism, which arose concurrently with the advent of Christianity, codified some principles delineating limits of self-sacrifice, generally, and extending specific protections for pregnant women, including the right to a lifesaving therapeutic abortion. Subsequent Jewish ethicists have interpreted this protection not as an exception to the practice of neighbor love but as one of its important manifestations.

Jewish ethical thought insists on the duty to help one's neighbor. This duty is expressed in biblical texts from the times of ancient Israel, such as the command in Leviticus 19:16, "You shall not stand idle while your neighbor

---

93. Jung, "Abortion and Organ Donation," 280.

94. See Jung, "Abortion and Organ Donation," 294–95. Mary Sommers questions Jung's premise that pregnancy can be analogized to organ donation, which Sommers sees as a greater sacrifice than gestation. That is, once an organ is donated, it is gone, whereas gestation and breastfeeding use "renewable" bodily products that are "easily shared and replaced." Mary Catherine Sommers, "Living Together: Burdensome Pregnancy and the Hospitable Self," in *Abortion: A New Generation of Catholic Responses*, ed. Stephen J. Heaney (Braintree, MA: Pope John Center, 1992), 259. Sommers thus gives a version of the pro-life argument I criticized in the previous chapter—namely, that pregnancy is obligatory because it is not that much of a burden.

bleeds."[95] An ethical commitment to the neighbor was exemplified in the comment by the early second-century CE Talmudist Rabbi Akiba who stated that the Leviticus 19:18 command, "You shall love your neighbor as yourself," was "the supreme rule of the Torah."[96] While the duty for neighbor love is a shared concept in both Judaism and Christianity, I argue that Judaism has a better ethical understanding of how it should be applied to abortion because of the way that duty is governed by certain Jewish ethical and legal principles. First, giving help is required but heroism is not; second, women have no halakic requirement to procreate; and third, there is a halakic requirement to intervene to save a birthing mother in distress.

Jewish ethics specifies "an unwavering obligation to help all those in distress, even when doing so might endanger the rescuer";[97] however, Jewish legal writings do not require heroic neighbor aid at the risk of lethal or even nonlethal injury to the giver. Indeed, respect for one's own body, created "in the image of God," is required.[98] Requiring respect for one's own body has two important ethical implications. Self-sacrificial acts, while admirable, should not be sought out and pursued without serious self-reflection. Second, surviving is not blameworthy, even if it necessitates withholding aid to one's neighbor such that the neighbor dies.[99]

What if the risk of severe injury or death to the good Samaritan is not high? A majority of halakic opinion specifies that when the risk of lethal injury to the Samaritan is not likely, giving assistance is required.[100] However, since helping one's neighbor is not a virtue but a command, that help logically must have the possibility for any member of the community to be capable of offering it. No one person or group of persons should take on all the risks of helping needy neighbors, and there is no halakic expectation of extraordinary or heroic acts. This view plays out in a range of opinions on, for example, live organ donation, which most rabbis today see as a "mitzvah" (good deed) to be encouraged but not required.[101] Thus, Jewish bioethical views of Samaritan

---

95. Tanakh translation quoted in Daniel Schiff, *Abortion in Judaism* (Cambridge: Cambridge University Press, 2002), 59 n. 3.

96. Michael N. Rader, "The 'Good Samaritan' in Jewish Law: Lessons for Physicians, Attorneys and Laypeople," *Journal of Legal Medicine* 22, no. 3 (2001): 381.

97. Rader, "The 'Good Samaritan' in Jewish Law," 375. This viewpoint about the obligation for Samaritanism reflects some Muslim perspectives as well. See Mohammed Ali Al-Bar and Hassan Chamsi-Pasha, "Beneficence," in *Contemporary Bioethics* (Springer Open, 2015), 129–39; doi 10.1007/978-3-319-18428-9.

98. Rader, "The 'Good Samaritan' in Jewish Law," 379.

99. See Rader, "The 'Good Samaritan' in Jewish Law," 383. In 382 n. 40 Rader references Jews who survived Nazi concentration camps.

100. See Rader, "The 'Good Samaritan' in Jewish Law," 382–83.

101. Richard V. Grazi and Joel B. Wolowelsky, "Nonaltruistic Kidney Donations in Contemporary Jewish Law and Ethics," *Transplantation* 75, no. 2 (2003): 252.

organ donation cohere with Jung's contention that live organ donation is discretionary and supererogatory.

Second, Jewish men are required halakically to try to have children, based on the Genesis 1:28 mandate to "be fruitful and multiply"; however, the requirement to bring children into the world is not incumbent on Jewish women, in large part, because of "the risk or suffering associated with pregnancy and birth."[102] Moreover, gestation should not be seen as woman's primary duty: "As one rabbi explained, a woman is not a field that nourishes any seed planted in it."[103] Hence, she has no halakic obligation to bear children or attempt with every act of intercourse to conceive—even if cultural expectations for large families are enormous in many traditional Jewish communities.[104]

Third, rabbinic abortion ethics are governed by the principle that until birth, the mother's life comes before that of the fetus, based on a ruling ensconced in the Mishnah, the authoritative early third-century CE codification of Jewish law. As in Christianity, debates exist on abortion in Judaism. Ultra-Orthodox Judaism argues that Jewish law precludes most abortion, yet much of Orthodox and Conservative Judaism allows for abortion if the woman expresses a serious need.[105] All rabbinic *poskim* (scholars authorized to make legal rulings) accept as authoritative the Mishnaic principle that a fetus may be killed in a therapeutic abortion, if necessary to save the mother, "because her life comes before the fetus's life."[106] There is no analogous consensus in Christianity. In chapter 5, I briefly discussed Maimonides's interpretation of this passage from the Mishnah and his ruling that the woman is allowed to defend herself against the fetus when it is seen as *"rodef,"* a threat to her life.[107]

---

102. See Y. Michael Barilan, "Abortion in Jewish Religious Law: Neighborly Love, *Imago Dei*, and a Hypothesis on the Medieval Blood Libel," *Review of Rabbinic Judaism* 8, no. 1–2 (2005): 13.

103. Y. Michael Barilan, "From *Imago Dei* in the Jewish-Christian Traditions to Human Dignity in Contemporary Jewish Law," *Kennedy Institute of Ethics Journal* 19, no. 3 (2009): 238.

104. See Rebecca Alpert, "Sometimes the Law Is Cruel: The Construction of a Jewish Anti-abortion Position in the Writings of Immanuel Jakobovits," *Journal of Feminist Studies in Religion* 11, no. 2 (1995): 28.

105. See Melanie Mordhorst-Mayer, Nitzan Rimon-Zarfaty, and Mark Schweda, "'Perspectivism' in the Halakhic Debate on Abortion between Moshe Feinstein and Eliezer Waldenberg—Relations between Jewish Medical Ethics and Socio-Cultural Contexts," *Women in Judaism* 10, no. 2 (2013): 1–35. Halakah is case-study-based law in which rulings on specific cases then become precedent and form principles for further judgments.

106. Mishnah *Ohalot* 7:6, as quoted in Alan Jotkowitz, "Abortion and Maternal Need: A Response to Ronit Irshai," *Nashim: A Journal of Jewish Women's Studies & Gender Issues* 21, no. 1 (2011): 99. Ultra-Orthodox Jewish rabbis respect this principle from the Mishnah, though they insist that the danger must be medically certified as "certain" and "immediate." See Mordhorst-Mayer et al., "'Perspectivism' in the Halakhic Debate," 7.

107. See Schiff, *Abortion in Judaism*, 49–52. While therapeutic abortion for the sake of the mother's life is deemed permissible in Muslim ethics, it is not based on the notion of the fetus as an aggressor. See Kamyar M. Hedayat, P. Shooshtarizadeh, and Mohsin Raza, "Therapeutic

The *rodef* concept connects halakah on abortion to the neighbor care instruction in Leviticus 19—namely, one has an obligation to help one's neighbor who is injured and bleeding as a result of attack by an aggressor—in this case, the fetal aggressor.[108] Unlike conservative Christian pro-life views, in Jewish ethics, if a pregnancy poses a serious threat to the life or, arguably, the general well-being of the mother, the pregnancy can be lawfully terminated. Indeed, some Jewish scholars suggest that the *rodef* principle implies a positive command—meaning, "killing the fetus to save the life of the mother is not an optional possibility, but rather a Torah-based demand" in light of the Leviticus command not to stand idly by while one's neighbor (the pregnant woman) bleeds.[109] My Samaritan allegory earlier in this chapter was informed by this Jewish understanding of the pregnant woman as the neighbor in need.

Attending to Jewish views of neighbor love—which formed the context for Jesus' parable of the good Samaritan[110]—exposes, by comparison, the lacunae in Christian pro-life interpretations of neighbor love. Samaritanism in Christian pro-life ethics implies that gestation is a pregnant woman's absolute or at least expected Christian duty, and there are no provisions or protections for pregnant women. Jewish ethics, on the other hand, includes such provisions and protections. While halakah imposes the duty to procreate on men, it refrains from imposing it on women because pregnancy is a hardship and women are not required to gestate heroically. Pro-life Christians think primarily of the fetal neighbor, as if the woman's body is expendable. In most Jewish ethics, the burdens and dangers of pregnancy are taken as a given; until emergence at birth, fetal life cannot be given precedence over the mother's life; and protecting the gestating and birthing mother from pain and suffering is not just halakically allowable, it is also mandated. The eminently practical nature of Jewish ethics is evidenced by the fact that these principles are implemented in legal and medical practices regarding abortion in the State of Israel.[111] While neighbor love is a shared ethical principle in both Christianity and Judaism, based on shared biblical texts, Judaism wisely has in place legal (halakic) principles that provide at least some safeguards for pregnant women's needs and well-being. Thus, I endorse a pro-choice paradigm of

Abortion in Islam: Contemporary Views of Muslim Shiite Scholars and Effect of Recent Iranian Legislation," *Journal of Medical Ethics* 32, no. 11 (2006): 652–57. See also Jonathan Brockopp, ed., *Islamic Ethics of Life: Abortion, War, and Euthanasia* (Columbia: University of South Carolina Press, 2003), chaps. 2–4.

108. See Schiff, *Abortion in Judaism*, 59, 145.

109. Schiff, *Abortion in Judaism*, 145.

110. See Berel Dov Lerner, "Samaritans, Jews and Philosophers," *Expository Times* 113 (2002): 152–56.

111. Israeli law requires that women provide appropriate reasons before an abortion is granted; however, nearly 97 percent are granted. See Y. Michael Barilan, "Her Pain Prevails and Her Judgment Respected—Abortion in Judaism," *Journal of Law and Religion* 25, no. 1 (2009): 177.

gestational hospitality that includes a (halakically informed) view of neighbor love that refrains from directing pregnant women toward heroic Samaritanism and mandates that their lives be protected.

Infinite Responsibility to the Fetal Other without Coercion

Even within a contextual ethics of care, where gestation is seen as an act of discretionary self-giving and heroism is not expected, the question still arises: Is there an ethical call to offer hospitality to the fetal neighbor? Philosophers like Emmanuel Levinas might say "Yes." Levinas's notion of "infinite" ethical responsibility is central to the work of a number of feminist philosophers, who take seriously Levinas's notion that the "face" of the "Other" makes an ethical demand without limit, including and especially in pregnancy and mothering.[112] Analyzing Lisa Guenther's and Sarah LaChance Adams's critical feminist interactions with Levinas's ethics lead us to a fifth aspect of a pro-choice paradigm of gestation hospitality: because the ethical demand of the (fetal) Other is infinite, a woman's gestation response must be legally protected and free from coercion.

For Lisa Guenther, Levinasian ethical responsibility means an obligation that is demanded of me not because of a "universal moral law," much less legal statutes, but because of the always, everywhere presence of the "Other," the neighbor, the wounded stranger.[113] The neediness of the neighbor is a boundless responsibility, issuing from "an infinite command, a command that grows larger in proportion to my response."[114] A principal metaphor used by Levinas to illustrate hospitality is the "maternal body," which symbolizes the all-encompassing, self-giving welcome that should be offered to the stranger at the door.[115] The maternal body is also, Guenther insists, the literal body of a pregnant woman faced with a situation where "the Other invites me to 'mak[e] a gift of my own skin.'"[116] Sarah Adams agrees with Guenther that something rings true in Levinas's writings about the call of the "face" of the

112. Lisa Guenther, *The Gift of the Other: Levinas and the Politics of Reproduction* (Albany: State University of New York Press, 2006), 5 and passim.

113. Guenther, *The Gift of the Other*, 6. Guenther does not focus on the religious concept of neighbor love in Levinas; however, other scholars do. See Jaime Ferreira, *Love's Grateful Striving: A Commentary on Kierkegaard's Works of Love* (Oxford: Oxford University Press, 2001), 48–50; Lawrence Vogel, "Emmanuel Levinas and the Judaism of the Good Samaritan," *Levinas Studies* 3 (2008): 193–208.

114. Guenther, *The Gift of the Other*, 65; see also 151, 142.

115. Guenther, *The Gift of the Other*, 98. This metaphorical maternal responsibility can be seen as incumbent on any caregiver, no matter their gender identity; see Guenther, *The Gift of the Other*, 7.

116. Guenther, *The Gift of the Other*, 102, quoting Levinas.

Other.[117] The ethical obligation to the Other seems to begin before one has even consented to it, and Adams offers anecdotes of women recounting how seeing the face of their newborn instantly evoked in them feelings of nurturance and protectiveness that they did not expect to feel.[118]

Maternal hospitality, however, is not without ambivalence, and both Adams and Guenther criticize Levinas for idealizing actual maternal giving. Adams's research exposes how mothers are capable of heroic sacrifices but can also be pushed to the edge and find themselves overcome with violent thoughts toward their children. Loving, ordinary mothers, not just so-called bad ones, can experience a range of ambivalent emotions in their attempts to do right by their children, whose needs can be great.[119] Maternal ideals, Adams worries, can dangerously overwhelm mothers to the point that they "feel guilty, angry, worthless, ashamed, depressed, and fearful of the judgment of others."[120] Guenther likewise objects to Levinas's praise for the suffering, maternal giving person, which could be seen as echoing "the patriarchal image of the Good Mother [as] a quiet and patient martyr."[121]

In addition to concerns about ideals of female self-sacrifice in Levinas's ethics, Guenther and Adams are concerned with the lack of sociopolitical awareness in his discussions of maternal giving. Guenther affirms the experience of pregnancy as a powerful, ethical labor of hospitality but insists on attentiveness to what she describes as "the long history in which women have been coerced, both directly and indirectly, to produce children."[122] The reality of unwanted pregnancies in cultural contexts where women's rights and resources are minimal brings us to the limits of Levinasian thought for prochoice ethics or, at least, one must turn to other resources, which for Adams includes Simone de Beauvoir.[123] For resources regarding maternal ethics, Adams turns in particular to de Beauvoir's *The Ethics of Ambiguity*.[124] Beyond the commonplace notion that some women may have ambiguous feelings

---

117. Sarah LaChance Adams, *Mad Mothers, Bad Mothers, and What a "Good" Mother Would Do: The Ethics of Ambivalence* (New York: Columbia University Press, 2014), 94.

118. Adams, *Mad Mothers, Bad Mothers*, 97.

119. See Adams, *Mad Mothers, Bad Mothers*, 100.

120. Adams, *Mad Mothers, Bad Mothers*, 102.

121. Guenther, *The Gift of the Other*, 111. She notes "Levinas's own notorious comments about the nobility of women dying in childbirth" (142).

122. Guenther, *The Gift of the Other*, 140.

123. De Beauvoir is known for her outspoken advocacy of legalizing abortion in France, and she commented negatively on Levinas's work in the late 1940s. See Diane Perpich, "From the Caress to the Word"; and Sonia Sikka, "The Delightful Other: Portraits of the Feminine in Kierkegaard, Nietzsche, and Levinas"—both in *Feminist Interpretations of Emmanuel Levinas*, ed. Tina Chanter (University Park: Pennsylvania State University Press, 2001), 28–29 and 96–97, respectively.

124. For an extended discussion of de Beauvoir's notion of ambiguity, see Sonia Kruks, *Simone de Beauvoir and the Politics of Ambiguity* (New York: Oxford University Press, 2012).

toward an unintended pregnancy and that mothering is a lifelong, arduous, and difficult-to-do-well endeavor, Adam emphasizes de Beauvoir's existentialist view that ambiguity is a sign of our authenticity as free individuals. Only the metaphorical devoted servant, de Beauvoir stated, lives without ambiguity: "The master is hungry and thirsty; the devoted slave desires only to be the dish that he prepares and the glass of water that he brings to appease the hunger and thirst."[125] For the servant, there is no ambiguity, just the master's need. The woman, however—qua free individual—is engaged in the project of authentic selfhood, which entails ambiguity. For de Beauvoir, human existence is ambiguous, humans are finite, and thus ethical failures are unavoidable in the exercise of human freedom. As de Beauvoir wrote, "One does not propose ethics to a god."[126] Adams applies de Beauvoir's ethics of ambiguity to reproductive decisions, commenting that "sometimes it is simply not possible for a mother to provide for a child's well-being. Ending a new life, instead of leaving it to an existence of pain, may be the most ethical choice."[127] Adams's stance on abortion echoes views of many other feminists who see abortion not as a celebration of women's control over their bodies but as a serious, difficult, and perhaps sometimes tragic choice, because it is a finite woman's attempt to meet her overall commitments in a world of ambiguity. Unless a woman is free to make that choice, it cannot be an ethical one.

While Adams balances Levinasian ethics with resources in Beauvoir's ethics of ambiguity, Guenther turns to the work of feminist political philosopher Drucilla Cornell for notions of justice. Guenther draws from Cornell's writings the idea that a woman's project of developing her own "personhood" happens within a "social imaginary" that is open to manipulation by cultural discourses of "women as mothers, saints, whores," and, if she has an abortion, discourses of "a mother murdering her baby." It is imperative, Guenther believes, that women have the cultural space to construct their own discursive imaginary, "in which the meanings of woman and mother can be reinvented."[128] To enable such endeavors, women need legal protections: "the function of law is to hold open the space" for women's project of personhood which may or may not include gestation and motherhood.[129] Reproductive rights and "the political demand for justice and equality" help ensure that the corporeal self-giving to the fetal Other will not become a "persecution, trauma" or "slavery."[130] Guenther affirms the ethical demands of the fetal

---

125. Adams, *Mad Mothers, Bad Mothers*, 178, quoting de Beauvoir.
126. Adams, *Mad Mothers, Bad Mothers*, 157, quoting de Beauvoir.
127. Adams, *Mad Mothers, Bad Mothers*, 105.
128. Guenther, *The Gift of the Other*, 143, 145.
129. Guenther, *The Gift of the Other*, 145.
130. Guenther, *The Gift of the Other*, 142–43.

Other but also specifies what must be in place, politically, for hospitality not to be an oppression for women—namely, legal choice.

Guenther and Adams give us a number of weighty philosophical notions to ponder. To be human is to respond to the "face" of the Other whose demand is infinite and always at my door. The fetal Other is a being who also makes an ethical demand. However, people are finite and society is unjust; the reality of finitude and life's ambiguities means that it is not possible always to respond to every fetal neighbor. Abortion, even if tragic, may be the best choice a woman can make. To protect the ethicality of her decision, legal protections must be in place. If we accept that women are neither gods nor servants, then a feminist pro-choice paradigm of hospitality must insist that a woman's gestational response to the fetal Other be legally protected and uncoerced.

CONCLUSION

Believers looking for guidance on abortion need a morally serious understanding of gestational hospitality that is more realistic and thoughtful than what is currently available in Christian pro-life writings. As pastoral theologians, bioethicists, rabbis, and feminist philosophers insist, an ethical approach to abortion must be cognizant of real-life complexities surrounding unplanned pregnancies, the health risks of pregnancy, and how gender, racial and other injustices trap many women in exploitative and unhealthy caretaking roles. Pro-life appeals to Samaritanism and neighbor love downplay these complexities, risks, and injustices by suggesting that pregnancy is not that much of a hardship and, even if it is, gestating her fetus is a pregnant woman's biblical or sacramental Christian duty. Pro-life pleas to churches to help women with crisis pregnancies, while well intentioned, convey a dangerously idealistic understanding of hospitality. Moreover, their appeals to Jesus' parable fall flat because the Samaritan's generosity is not even closely analogous to the demands and life-changing realities women face with pregnancy, birthing a baby, and the lifetime of mothering demands that follow.

I have developed a pro-choice paradigm of gestational hospitality that combines the wisdom of (1) pastoral theology, (2) feminist care ethics, (3) the bioethics of bodily self-gifting, (4) Jewish ethics, and (5) feminist philosophy in an effort to construct a paradigm of gestational hospitality that is equal to the reality of gestating a fetus—knowing that what lies ahead is birthing and mothering. Feminist and womanist pastoral theologians hope that women will be empowered to avoid unhealthy Samaritan self-sacrifice and commit themselves to finishing their journey. This pastoral advice is all the more important when one factors in disparities and injustices under which many women suffer based on race, nationality, economic status, and so on. Feminist care ethicists (like Noddings) advocate for nurturing our best impulses of care and empathy but also supporting women's contextual decisions about an unwanted pregnancy. Bioethicists (like Jung) remind us that pregnancy is an act of extraordinary bodily hospitality that should be seen as ethically discretionary, analogous to live organ donation. Jewish ethics of neighbor love have something important to say for Christian abortion debates today, especially regarding safeguards against compelling a woman to sacrifice herself to bring every pregnancy to birth. No matter how observant a Jewish man is, in no case would he find a halakic provision indicating that his pregnant wife should be allowed to die in an attempt to save their baby. Feminist philosophers who find something compelling in the Levinasian notion of the infinite demand of the Other insist on recognizing human finitude and the need for legal protections for reproductive rights.

If there is a moral to this chapter for women with unwanted pregnancies, it might be summed up as this: it is good to help the needy fetal neighbor in your womb, but make sure you can finish your journey. Some women with unwanted pregnancies turn out to be splendid Samaritans who go above and beyond what they thought they could. Other pregnant women end up being more like the beast in the parable, coerced to carry a burden with no real choice of their own. The approach to gestational hospitality I have proposed would militate especially against the latter situation coming to pass. If there is a moral to this chapter for pro-life Christians, it might be summed up as this: it is good to value children, but make sure you are not a judgmental passerby, who would never listen and respond to the needs voiced by a wounded neighbor with an unwanted pregnancy. This chapter hopefully points a way for pro-life Christians to think more deeply about the troubling moral and spiritual aspects of impelling—ethically or legally—a fellow Christian or any neighbor to be a gestational Samaritan against her wishes.[131]

Even if this chapter has succeeded in convincing some readers to think in a different Samaritan way about women with unwanted pregnancies, it still is possible to conclude that I have done no more than to present competing interpretations to the Samaritan parable, which turn out to be the hermeneutical equivalent of the stalled debate over conflicting fetal and maternal rights. The difference between pro-life and pro-choice allegories of the Samaritan parable is that the former envision a wounded fetus on the road rescued by a compassionate pro-life Samaritan (preferably the mother herself), and

---

131. Rebecca Peters has forcefully claimed that "coerced pregnancy under any circumstances . . . is a fundamentally immoral act." Rebecca Todd Peters, *Trust Women: A Progressive Christian Argument for Reproductive Justice* (Boston: Beacon Press, 2018), 175.

the latter envision a pregnant woman rescued by compassionate pro-choice Samaritans, who support her with whatever abortion decision she feels she must make (as in my allegory). My multifaceted pro-choice paradigm of gestational hospitality is essentially an ethical guide aiming to ensure that pregnant women will never be treated as mere beasts of burden without a choice.

Perhaps the paradigm I have proposed achieves the necessary minimum for a pro-choice ethics of abortion, but the theological task is not yet complete. In this book my objective is not just to refute pro-life Christian claims but to propose alternative interpretations of the Christian tradition in support of women's reproductive self-determination. Returning one last time to the Samaritan parable gives us an indication of a crucial theological theme that has yet to be addressed for a sufficiently comprehensive Christian pro-choice position. Thus far in this chapter, I have focused on contemporary understandings of the parable, but premodern allegorical interpretations of the good Samaritan parable cast the story's symbolism in a completely different light. Historically, the Samaritan parable was not primarily interpreted in terms of ethics. For the fathers of the early church, the wounded man represented Adam and his sinful descendants; the Samaritan was Christ. The story was used to exhort the listener "to assume the perspective of the beaten man," not primarily to go out and do good deeds.[132] The early church shared the view that the proper understanding of love of God and love of neighbor would not develop unless Christians "recognized themselves in the robbed man who was left half-dead along the road to Jericho."[133] In the sixteenth century Martin Luther still followed this line of interpretation: "This Samaritan of course is our Lord Jesus Christ himself [who] . . . lifts the wounded man on his beast. This beast is Christ the Lord himself."[134] In other words, a classically theological understanding of the parable is a christological one that speaks to the most central claim of Christianity: God so loved the wounded world that God gave the Son for its salvation.

For my pro-choice paradigm of gestational hospitality to be Christian, it is not enough that Christians implement any or all of the five elements of my paradigm presented above (though doing that, in and of itself, will contribute vastly to the well-being of women and their children). In addition, the paradigm would need to be grounded christologically. To put it another way, unless one can envision Christ the Samaritan stopping to help the wounded

132. Patrick M. Clark, "Reversing the Ethical Perspective: What the Allegorical Interpretation of the Good Samaritan Parable Can Still Teach Us," *Theology Today* 71, no. 3 (2014): 308.

133. Riemer Roukema, "The Good Samaritan in Ancient Christianity," *Vigiliae Christianae* 58, no. 1 (2004): 73.

134. Martin Luther, *Sermons of Martin Luther*, vol. 5, ed. and trans. John Nicholas Lenker (Grand Rapids: Baker, 1983), 17, 19.

pregnant woman on the road, accepting her decision that her pregnancy is unwanted, and standing next to her and comforting her as she is undergoing an abortion, then my pro-choice proposal falls short of being a Christian theological one. The final chapter of this book addresses how women's consent to pregnancy, gestational decision making, and act of terminating an unwanted pregnancy—all these aspects of women's reproductive lives can be encompassed in the hospitality of God.

7

Motherhood Choices, Abortion Death, and the Womb of God

The chapters in this book have taken a stand against pro-life claims for fetal personhood and have offered arguments for a pro-choice understanding of maternal authority, fetal value, and gestational hospitality. The final task is, in many ways, the most challenging because we face the theologically and existentially fraught question: Can a woman choose Christianly to terminate her pregnancy? The question brings us face-to-face with how central Christian symbols contribute to expectations about motherhood and to the stigmatizing of believing women who abort or who even deem their pregnancy unwanted. The first step toward answering this question entails making a convincing case that the Christian tradition can be read as affirming motherhood as a choice and as validating women's decision to pursue callings other than gestating and mothering each time they find themselves pregnant. Only then is there a basis for arguing how a woman's choice not to continue gestating— and thus to cause abortion death—is not a sinful negation of mothering. This chapter offers specifically theological reasons against labeling abortion as sin and, beyond that, offers reasons for seeing the difficult choice of abortion as encompassed by God's compassion.

The maternal self-understandings of Christian women, and those living in Christianized cultures, are arguably influenced by the symbol of the Virgin Mary, which has been used both to inspire women's spiritual vocations but also to heap guilt upon the heads of women who fall short of Marian virtues. Mary's exclamation to the angel Gabriel, "*Fiat mihi*" (Luke 1:38, Vulgate), is often invoked as a symbol of obedient maternity, which makes the very notion of unwanted pregnancy theological anathema. When pro-life writers pose the rhetorical question "What if Mary had chosen abortion?" the question is meant to shame pregnant women into thinking that they might be aborting a potentially important person.[1] The idea of a young first-century Jewish peasant girl having access to abortion is anachronistic, and no woman should be shamed into motherhood. There are more appropriate questions to pose about Mary: Did Mary choose motherhood? If so, what was entailed in her decision making?

In response, I offer an interpretation of the birth narrative in Luke's Gospel that sees Mary's choice as the result of a period of decision making while she wrestled with an unintended pregnancy. This message, more than a traditional Christian message of Mary's obedience before the angel, arguably speaks more strongly to the decision making that women facing an unplanned pregnancy actually go through. Seeing Mary face difficult choices allows us then to ask: Should women be able to choose against motherhood and still consider themselves as upholding a Marian spirituality? In answer to this question, I discuss a surprisingly candid story of unwanted pregnancy drawn from the spiritual autobiography of Margery Kempe, medieval mystic and reluctant mother of fourteen children, who chose to follow Mary into a spiritual vocation other than motherhood. My interpretations of Mary and Margery Kempe contribute to the pro-choice task of providing a basis within the Christian tradition for motherhood choices, reducing the stigma of unplanned pregnancies, and affirming women who do not want to continue gestating because they have other callings in life.

Christian women with unwanted pregnancies, who do go ahead and terminate a pregnancy, are even more strongly stigmatized—as sinners who have committed murder, rebelled against God, and rejected the message of sacrifice exemplified by Christ on the cross. I offer theological rebuttals to all of these stigmatizing claims. I argue that abortion should be seen as a morally serious, sometimes tragic choice but not as ipso facto sin, and that the crucifixion, properly understood, does not obligate women to sacrifice their own bodies to gestate an unwanted pregnancy. Finally, I propose a Christian view of death, seen through the prism of a mothering God, which allows one to imagine how reproductive losses, including abortion deaths, are taken up into the womb of the Trinitarian God and healed. This chapter begins what will, no doubt, be an ongoing pro-choice theological process of deconstructing and reconstructing Christian symbols. My hope is that believing pregnant women can find in their tradition new spiritual resources for reproductive decision making and callings other than motherhood and, most importantly,

---

1. See Jennifer LeClaire, "What If Mary Had Chosen Abortion?," *CharismNews* (December 18, 2015), http://www.charismanews.com/opinion/watchman-on-the-wall/53920-what-if-mary -had-chosen-abortion.

a view of God other than as a Father-who-turns-away from a sinful woman who aborts.

UNWANTED PREGNANCY AND THE VIRGIN MARY

The foundational plank in pro-life uses of Mary is her consent in the Annunciation scene (Luke 1:26–38). Many pro-life proponents interpret this passage in support of women's God-given maternal vocation. Feminist scholars dispute this interpretation of Mary and propose their own liberationist, womanist, and other counternarratives. While these feminist Mariologies are powerful in many ways, I do not think they can decenter the pro-life appropriation of Mary's motherhood. These Mariologies do not interrogate the pro-life claim that because Mary said "yes" immediately to motherhood and never looked back, so to speak, all pregnant women should follow her example. I argue that the Annunciation, when contextualized in light of pregnancy in first-century Palestine, reveals Mary's situation as one of medical and social vulnerability. In this light, Mary's initial consent can be seen as much more tentative than traditionally understood. Christian women struggling with an unintended pregnancy can see Mary struggling with and deciding over a period of time about her situation as well. Christian women can also recognize that Mary had the promise of miraculous succor to see her through her unintended pregnancy; yet women today face their unintended and unwanted pregnancies mostly on their own. If Mary was allowed to choose motherhood, how much more so should ordinary women.

Eve and Mary

In order to understand how the story of the Virgin Mary's consent to pregnancy might speak to the situation of unwanted pregnancy today, we have to take into account historical and contemporary theological appeals to Mary. There are two prevalent views of Mary in Christian thought historically: as redeemer of Eve and as handmaid consenting to motherhood. Feminist scholars have long worked to expose aspects of the symbol of the Virgin Mary as a patriarchal construct that imposes impossible standards of sexual purity and maternal duty on women; however, we must probe deeper to see how the Eve-Mary binary and the symbol of Mary accepting to bear God's Son affects attitudes toward women with unwanted pregnancies. Unless the Eve-Mary binary is deconstructed, then a woman who even voices that her pregnancy is unwelcome—whether she terminates it or carries the fetus reluctantly to term—will always be an Eve falling short of the ideal of Mary. The gestational self-understanding of women in Christianized cultures falls under the shadow of this Eve-Mary contrast, according to which the very notion of unwanted pregnancy is theological anathema. Mary's consent to be God's handmaid, ironically, is a valued trope in feminist theological writings as well as in pro-life writings, though for different reasons. I will argue, contrary to the claims of both groups, for a picture of Mary's response at the Annunciation as tentative, even ambiguous, followed by a period of decision making—a picture that I believe is truer to the biblical text and to the reality of what women experience with unintended pregnancies.

Seeing Mary as the antitype to Eve is deeply rooted in church discourse and iconography, having its origins in the theology of recapitulation promoted in the patristic era.[2] The Virgin Mary was pronounced—pervasively and authoritatively from the patristic era onward—as the redeemer of Eve, and not just of Eve but all of Eve's daughters, who share in her fallen condition. Of the various ways the church fathers depicted Mary in contrast with Eve, the most prominent theme was disobedience versus obedience. Eve listened disobediently to the serpent, whereas Mary listened obediently to the angel. For most of the early church theologians, both Eve (in the garden) and Mary were assumed to be virgins. What separated them was not their sexuality but their obedience. Justin Martyr, a second-century theologian, wrote: "Eve, while a virgin incorrupt, conceived the word which proceeded from the serpent, and brought forth disobedience and death. But the Virgin Mary was filled with faith."[3]

This typology continues to be affirmed today by pro-life theologians such as Monica Migliorino Miller. Reiterating the trope that "the knot of Eve's disobedience was loosed by the obedience of Mary" is useful for Miller's efforts to argue that Mary completes women's task begun by the fallen Eve[4]—namely, the uniquely female-bodied task of maternally producing life: "Woman, even after the Fall, is still 'source of life.'"[5] While not every woman will achieve biological reproduction, her divinely given female essence is receptivity to male initiative and maternal nurturing of life.[6] According to Miller, women achieve their fullest "feminine authority" in the church to the extent that they

---

2. See Benjamin H. Dunning, "Virgin Earth, Virgin Birth: Creation, Sexual Difference, and Recapitulation in Irenaeus of Lyons," *Journal of Religion* 89, no. 1 (2009): 57–88.

3. Justin Martyr, *Dialogue with Trypho* 100, quoted in Maurice Hamington, *Hail Mary? The Struggle for Ultimate Womanhood in Catholicism* (New York: Routledge, 2014), 134.

4. Irenaeus, *Against Heresies* 3, 22:4, as quoted in Monica Migliorino Miller, *Sexuality and Authority in the Catholic Church* (Scranton: University of Scranton Press, 1995), 117. Miller is a professor and prominent Roman Catholic pro-life activist. She is director of Citizens for a Prolife Society, whose mission is "sidewalk counseling" in front of abortion clinics. See their Web page: http://www.prolifesociety.net/pages/AboutUs/standard/aboutus.aspx.

5. M. Miller, *Sexuality and Authority in the Catholic Church*, 125.

6. See M. Miller, *Sexuality and Authority in the Catholic Church*, 176, 182.

freely accept their role, as Mary did, as giver and protector of life.[7] Miller makes the pro-life connection, asserting that abortion is not only the unjust taking of a fetal life; the act also reverberates by severing the woman from her powerful feminine life-giving essence. Miller's pro-life argument thus hinges on an interpretation of Mary as first among many other women who assent to and cooperate with the particular kind of maternal empowerment that is uniquely theirs as female.

Feminist theologians have pushed back against this kind of interpretation of Mary. Tina Beattie disagrees with Monica Miller's essentialist claim that receptivity and maternal care are the core of women's divinely ordained being (and I suspect many feminist theologians would echo Beattie's critique).[8] Beattie herself offers a feminist reinterpretation of the Eve-Mary typology that attempts to recast Eve in such a way that she will no longer be denigrated in comparison with Mary's sexual purity and maternal exaltation. According to Beattie, to say that "Eve is woman redeemed in Mary" means that the two women are not in opposition but together in solidarity.[9] Beattie presents an image of Eve as a kind of "patron saint of battered wives, victims of rape, women whose fertility is a misery and a trap."[10] Beattie's rehabilitation of the Eve-Mary relationship lays the groundwork for a "protest" Mariology that would rail against all injustice, interpersonal violence, and social inequities that have rendered maternity an affliction and a serious health risk.[11] Beattie's proposal goes far to reorient issues of sexuality and maternity in the Eve-Mary typology. However, unless these new images are supplemented by a critical interrogation of how Eve and Mary are used in anti-abortion writings, Christian women will continue to live under the shadow of the "sanctification of biological motherhood."[12] This typology has bequeathed to Christendom an entrenched binary that casts women who fall short of Mary's obedient acceptance of motherhood in a negative light, even when their sexual activity is licit and maternally focused.

7. M. Miller, *Sexuality and Authority in the Catholic Church*, 123. Miller voices a viewpoint common in Catholic teachings. See Joseph Cardinal Ratzinger and Hans Urs von Balthasar, *Mary: The Church at the Source*, trans. Adrian Walker (San Francisco: Ignatius Press, 2005), 175.

8. See Tina Beattie, "Review of Monica Migliorino Miller, *Sexuality and Authority in the Catholic Church*," *Theology & Sexuality* 6 (1997): 112–13; Natalie Knödel, "The Church as a Woman or Women Being Church? Ecclesiology and Theological Anthropology in Feminist Dialogue," *Theology & Sexuality* 7 (1997): 106–16.

9. Tina Beattie, *God's Mother, Eve's Advocate* (New York: Continuum, 2002), 172. Other feminist attempts to rehabilitate Eve include Judith Plaskow, "The Coming of Lilith: Toward a Feminist Theology (1972)," in Judith Plaskow, *The Coming of Lilith: Essays on Feminism, Judaism, and Sexual Ethics, 1972–2003* (Boston: Beacon Press, 2015); and Deborah Sawyer, "Hidden Subjects: Rereading Eve and Mary," *Theology & Sexuality* 14, no. 3 (2008): 305–20.

10. Beattie, *God's Mother, Eve's Advocate*, 173.

11. Beattie, *God's Mother, Eve's Advocate*, 103.

12. Beattie, *God's Mother, Eve's Advocate*, 77.

Fiat Mihi and Mary's Decision Making

Pro-life proponents extol Mary's exemplary acceptance in faith to be God's handmaid when she utters the words "Be it unto me" (Luke 1:38 KJV), *fiat mihi* (Vulgate). Pro-life advocates use Mary's words insistently to encourage women to follow her example, and they strategically direct their comments to women with unwanted and difficult pregnancies. One priest on a popular pro-life Web site urges his readers to see Mary as someone who "can identify with every pregnant mother in a difficult pregnancy. . . . True devotion to Mary means imitating her virtues—her faith, her trust and her willingness to make sacrifices."[13] The pro-life use of the message of Mary's trusting acceptance of pregnancy under difficult circumstances is ubiquitous on Catholic pro-life Web sites, but it can be found on Protestant evangelical ones as well, often with the provocative trope mentioned above, "What if Mary had chosen abortion?"[14]

It is not surprising that feminist theologians would also turn to Mary's *fiat* as authoritative, though their message is not that of unquestioning acceptance of motherhood but rather of autonomy, empowerment, and liberation from oppression.[15] Elizabeth Johnson references multiple global Christian feminist interpretations of Mary to paint a picture of Mary, whose "consent is a free and responsible act"—namely, an act free from all male authority, which contributed to her "partnering with God in the work of redemption."[16] Johnson recuperates Mary as the "*compañera*" of grassroots Latin American communities or a "womanish" woman of color who is relatable to African American believers—in short, a mother of the people.[17] Johnson does not make an explicit connection to reproductive choice, but she could be taken as obliquely gesturing in a pro-choice direction with her emphatic conclusion: "Mary was

13. Fr. Peter West, "A Reflection on Mary and the Birth of Christ," *Priests for Life*, http://www .priestsforlife.org/preaching/frpeteradvent.htm.

14. See LeClaire, "What If Mary Had Chosen Abortion?"; see also Rev. Mark H. Creech, "What If Mary Had Known about Abortion?," *Christian Post* (December 17, 2012), http://www .christianpost.com/news/what-if-mary-had-known-about-abortion-86736/. Ironically, some Catholic theological writings preclude that Mary could have ever chosen otherwise. Mary's *fiat* is seen as a graced decision that could only have been in accordance with God's will. See Aaron Riches, "Deconstructing the Linearity of Grace: The Risk and Reflexive Paradox of Mary's Immaculate *Fiat*," *International Journal of Systematic Theology* 10, no. 2 (2008): 183–85. This interpretation secures the immaculate, obedient motherhood of Mary but undercuts any claim that hers was "a condition of utter vulnerability" (187).

15. Feminist treatments of Mary are numerous and diverse. For an excellent overview essay, see Kilian McDonnell, "Feminist Mariologies: Heteronomy/Subordination and the Scandal of Christology," *Theological Studies* 66, no. 3 (September 2005): 527–67. For Protestant perspectives, see Beverly Roberts Gaventa and Cynthia L. Rigby, eds., *Blessed One: Protestant Perspectives on Mary* (Louisville, KY: Westminster John Knox Press, 2002).

16. Elizabeth A. Johnson, *Truly Our Sister: A Theology of Mary in the Communion of Saints* (New York: Continuum, 2004), 256.

17. E. Johnson, *Truly Our Sister*, 13–14. "Womanish" is borrowed from womanist theologian Diana Hayes.

not *forced* to bear the Messiah. Acting as a responsible moral agent, she made her own choice."[18] Beattie also reads Mary's *fiat* as agential, insisting that Mary should not be seen as "a passive object to be appropriated by the divine will" but rather as someone who "co-operates in her own redemption."[19] Beattie explicitly addresses reproductive issues and, in doing so, draws a strong distinction between Mary and ordinary women, arguing that Mary, although a powerful "eschatological symbol of Christian hope," cannot be a role model for the reproductive decision making of women today.[20] Recall that Beattie's stance on abortion is based on the notion that women in early pregnancy often have not experienced an "awakening of maternal consciousness," and thus they are justified in terminating an unwanted pregnancy (given, in addition, that the fetus is barely developed).[21] Beattie reads Luke's account as suggesting that Mary's maternal consciousness was immediate and perfect at the Annunciation. Mary's consent to maternity was unique and, thus, should not be obligatory for ordinary women. In other words, Beattie, who sees negative ramifications of Mary's *fiat* for women facing unwanted pregnancy, drives a wedge between Mary's gestational self-consciousness and that of women today in order to secure a space for women's reproductive choice in early pregnancy.

I see the feminist advantages, in different contexts, of both invoking Mary as empowered to partner with God (Elizabeth Johnson) as well as distancing her maternal consciousness at conception from that of ordinary women (Tina Beattie). However, I agree with those exegetes who see Mary as, at first, not fully comprehending that to which she was consenting.[22] I propose a reading of the story that does not focus on a single moment of consent, or on the outcome of Mary's decision, but on her lived experience of difficult decision making regarding motherhood. It is that process of decision making that can be a relevant model for ordinary women today facing an unintended pregnancy.

In Luke's narrative, Mary first negotiated about being "overshadowed" by God's power before she gave a positive response.[23] We can surmise, based on

---

18. E. Johnson, *Truly Our Sister*, 257.
19. Beattie, *God's Mother, Eve's Advocate*, 174, 182.
20. Tina Beattie, "Catholicism, Choice and Consciousness: A Feminist Theological Perspective on Abortion," *International Journal of Public Theology* 4, no. 1 (2010): 74.
21. Beattie, "Catholicism, Choice and Consciousness," 73. See my discussion of Beattie's views in chap. 5 above.
22. See Beverly Roberts Gaventa, *Mary: Glimpses of the Mother of Jesus* (Minneapolis: Fortress Press, 1999). Mary "consents to what is not fully understood." Gaventa, *Mary*, 55.
23. "The angel said to her, '. . . The power of the Most High will overshadow you'" (Luke 1:35). My former student Anita Peebles remarked in a class essay: "There is a tentative nature to the way Gabriel announces God's will for Mary, almost as if others had said 'no' and he was waiting for a 'yes.'"

the Gospel accounts, that Mary was not planning to become pregnant at that time. Pregnancy could only have been unintended for Mary and, given her unmarried state, she must have felt trepidation. After this encounter with the angel, Mary sought out a trusted confidante, her cousin Elizabeth, who helped her accept that bearing a child was a positive thing. Only after Elizabeth's exclamation "Blessed is the fruit of your womb" (Luke 1:42) does Mary break out in the song of praise referred to as the Magnificat (Luke 1:46–55). Up until this point, there is no textual evidence that Mary welcomed her pregnancy or even fully understood that being overshadowed by the Holy Spirit was connected with conceiving a child.[24] Indeed, Luke's story does not specifically say that Mary had conceived in the angel's presence, as compared with how Hebrew Bible specifies, for example, that Abraham "went in to Hagar, and she conceived" (Gen. 16:4). We do not see Mary actually verbalizing reproductive comprehension other than in the most basic way (Luke 1:34); whereas, one can find much more sexually explicit reproductive discourse used by her Jewish ancestresses of old.[25] At the Annunciation, we see her "much perplexed" (Luke 1:29) and pondering deeply. After Jesus' birth, the text again describes Mary as pondering (Luke 2:19), an act Bonnie Miller-McLemore associates with what Sara Ruddick famously called "maternal thinking."[26] Focusing too much on Mary's *fiat* invests that moment with a definitiveness that is not supported by the narrative and that obscures Mary's process of tentative maternal pondering in the midst of uncertainty and precariousness. For Mary to be mobilized fully in a pro-choice manner, she needs to be seen not merely as giving a single act of consent to bear a child but rather as engaging in a process of deciding to gestate and accepting motherhood; otherwise, her initial agreement to become impregnated becomes a morally problematic moment. Given her precariousness as a betrothed but unmarried, possibly reproductively naive young woman, her consent can barely be seen as fully informed.[27]

24. I do not see any basis for assuming that Mary "proceeds 'with haste' to Elizabeth's side out of eagerness, not fear or anxiety," since the text does not present Mary as eager about her pregnancy, and there are ample historical reasons for her to have been anxious. David T. Landry, "Narrative Logic in the Annunciation to Mary (Luke 1:26–38)," *Journal of Biblical Literature* 114, no. 1 (1995): 77.

25. Sarah makes arrangements with Abraham so that "it may be that I shall obtain children" through Hagar (Gen. 16:2); Leah announces to Jacob that he must have a conjugal visit with her: "You must come in to me" (Gen. 30:16); Ruth approaches Boaz in the middle of the night and solicits sexual relations with him, saying, "Spread your cloak over your servant, for you are next-of-kin" (Ruth 3:9).

26. Bonnie J. Miller-McLemore, "'Pondering All These Things': Mary and Motherhood," in Beverly Roberts Gaventa and Cynthia L. Rigby, eds., *Blessed One: Protestant Perspectives on Mary* (Louisville, KY: Westminster John Knox Press, 2002), 106.

27. Mary Daly famously referred to Mary as a rape victim, though I see no narrative evidence of it (see the discussion in McDonnell, "Feminist Mariologies," 532). Certainly rape, sexual abuse, forced marriages, unwanted pregnancies, and dangerous births are in evidence elsewhere in the

Pregnancy and birthing in first-century Palestine were dangerous endeavors. In Jesus' day, the risk of death in childbirth was high.[28] Christ's birth is a narrative of miracles but also must be seen as an event of extreme vulnerability. Upon becoming pregnant, notwithstanding the angel's prophecies, Mary would have seen her future as uncertain and risky—socially and medically. Unless one wants to posit that God miraculously removed from Mary's consciousness beforehand any thoughts of unwanted pregnancy or any normal fear of birthing, then one has to conclude that the incarnation was an unintended pregnancy that became—with God's empowering grace and Mary's choice—a wanted and safe pregnancy. All well and good. But what about other women, who do not experience a spiritual overshadowing sufficient to transmute an unplanned pregnancy into a wanted one?

In a wanted pregnancy, the mother accepts with fear and trembling her condition of vulnerability, often finding those feelings changed into hope about the unknown future. In an unintended pregnancy, vulnerability is magnified. Although medical interventions have vastly improved for women since ancient times, pregnant women today still die in disturbing numbers from pregnancy or birth-related problems, even in the developed world.[29] God, for reasons of infinite mystery, deemed that pregnancy should remain a vulnerable, uncertain condition to which God, nevertheless, willed to be present in the incarnation.[30] The idea that God is intimately present in the vulnerability of unintended or unwanted pregnancy might give some women the fortitude to consent to pregnancy. Some women may be inspired by the fact that Mary did finally fully understand and accept to bear a child under adverse conditions. However, there is a significant difference between Mary's situation and that of all other women facing an unintended pregnancy. The outcome of Mary's unintended pregnancy was ensured by the protective care of divine power and the ministry of angels. Hers was a difficult decision but one aided by divine prophecy and promise. However, there have been and always will be pregnant women who deem that pregnancy and birth are not feasible for their life at that moment. The reading of Mary's story that I have proposed can be seen as affirming women's decision making about their troubled pregnancies, in light of the fact that they cannot count on an angelic visitation to assure them of the outcome of their gestation and birthing.

Bible in troubling ways. See Susanne Scholz, *Sacred Witness: Rape in the Hebrew Bible* (Minneapolis: Fortress Press, 2010).

28. See T. Heyne, "Tertullian and Obstetrics," *Studia Patristica* 53 (2013): 419.

29. See Priya Agrawal, "Maternal Mortality and Morbidity in the United States of America," *Bulletin of the World Health Organization* 93, no. 3 (2015): 135.

30. For a different view about the vulnerability of pregnancy and birth, see Elizabeth O'Donnell Gandolfo, "A Truly Human Incarnation: Recovering a Place for Nativity in Contemporary Christology," *Theology Today* 70, no. 4 (2014): 382–93.

Without extensive sociological studies, one cannot know which images of Mary hold sway with Christians worldwide and how those images inform actual pregnant women's decision making, but one cannot rule out that believing women turn to Mary as someone who "helps them in areas of life of which she supposedly did not know anything: sexuality, abortion, violence, ordinary motherhood."[31] Feminists hope for a liberating Mary who is free to choose, but even a liberationist *fiat mihi* may not speak directly enough to the struggles of women today who face not only unintended but also unwanted pregnancies and who lack the assurances of an angel and a miraculously pregnant, supportive cousin. Christian women facing a crisis pregnancy need examples of Marian spirituality where thoughts of unwanted pregnancy may be honestly expressed and accepted by God. The section that follows turns to the rich history of Christian women's mystical writings and, in particular, one woman's surprisingly personal narrative, where following the example of Mary entailed not wanting to be pregnant so that she could answer other spiritual callings.

UNWANTED PREGNANCY AND *IMITATIO MARIAE* IN THE LIFE OF MARGERY KEMPE

In the mid-1500s, a devout middle-aged English woman, Margery Kempe—married and the mother of thirteen—found herself in deep despair over becoming pregnant again. She prayed and, miraculously, Christ appeared to her in a vision. She bemoaned her condition, saying, "Lord, how shall I then do for keeping of my child? . . . It is to me a great pain and great distress."[32] If ever there was a declaration of unwanted pregnancy, this is one. We can find in her spiritual autobiography, *The Book of Margery Kempe*, a surprisingly candid interrogation of maternity. Margery's story suggests two important themes relevant to Christian women's reproductive decision making today: first, consent to both sex and gestation are not just desiderata but the right and responsibility of every woman; second, motherhood is not the only virtuous way for a believing pregnant woman to honor Mary, the mother of Christ.

Margery's spiritual visions began when she was newly married, following her first traumatic experience with childbirth. From that point onward, she

---

31. Elina Vuola, "Seriously Harmful for Your Health? Religion, Feminism and Sexuality in Latin America," in *Liberation Theology and Sexuality*, ed. Marcella Althaus-Reid (Aldershot, UK: Ashgate, 2006), 154.

32. *The Book of Margery Kempe*, trans. and ed. Lynn Staley (New York: Norton, 2001), 36 (chap. 21). I note in parentheses the chapters in book I of her text where the quoted material may be found.

apparently felt a lack of desire to mother her own children and, instead, felt called to the role of spiritually mothering others, which she saw as a mode of emulating the Virgin Mary.[33] Scholars of medieval Christianity explain that rituals of devotion to Mary, or *imitatio Mariae*, consisted of various attitudes and practices whereby mystics, often guided by visions, experienced a kind of spiritual closeness with the Virgin Mary. These mystics, usually women, shared aspects of Mary's life, such as experiencing a vision of Mary as the *Mater Dolorosa* at the cross, or had dreams of nursing or caring for the Christ child. The tradition of *imitatio Mariae* usually was practiced by consecrated nuns.[34] Despite the fact that she was married and many times a mother, Margery yearned for a celibate life of Marian devotion and experienced such an affinity with the Virgin Mary that, according to her accounts, "she begins to exceed Mary as a spiritual mother and intercessor."[35] Margery's devotion to spiritual motherhood affected all aspects of her life, and her *Book* contains many surprisingly candid references to her attempts to control her reproductive sexuality. She mentioned being "in bed with her husband" and discussing their "fleshly commoning" (chap. 3) and how long it had been since the last time they had had sex (chap. 11).[36] For many years Margery reluctantly submitted to conjugal obligations, all the while importuning her husband to allow her to live chastely devoted to God. Finally, after much arguing, she received her husband's promise that he would no longer "meddle with" her—meaning, have intercourse (chap. 11).[37] Her desire to have no more children was confirmed when Christ appeared to her and said that "she should bear no more children" (chap. 17).[38] At one point, Margery's desire to live a chaste married life was tested by ecclesial authorities, and she was asked the meaning of the Genesis (1:22, Vulgate) biblical mandate, "Crescite et multiplicamini" (be fruitful and multiply). She responded that the phrase does not only mean "begetting of bodily children physically, but also for the purchasing of virtue" (chap. 51).[39]

Indeed, the belief of some medieval women mystics that their spiritual calling took precedence over maternal duty led to words and actions that are as

33. See Liz Herbert McAvoy, *Authority and the Female Body in the Writings of Julian of Norwich and Margery Kempe* (Cambridge: D. S. Brewer, 2004), 34–38.

34. See Rosemary Hale, "*Imitatio Mariae*: Motherhood Motifs in Devotional Memoirs," *Mystics Quarterly* 16, no. 4 (1990): 199.

35. Tara Williams, "Manipulating Mary: Maternal, Sexual, and Textual Authority in *The Book of Margery Kempe*," *Modern Philology* 107, no. 4 (2010): 546.

36. Staley, *The Book of Margery Kempe*, 18.

37. Staley, *The Book of Margery Kempe*, 18, 20.

38. Staley, *The Book of Margery Kempe*, 29. Margery cannot be said to have had a pathological aversion to her children since her *Book* does mention involvement in the life of a grown son (see McAvoy, *Authority and the Female Body*, 33).

39. Staley, *The Book of Margery Kempe*, 89.

shocking today as they would have been then. Medieval historian Barbara Newman notes that the fourteenth-century mystic Saint Birgitta wrote that if all her children "cried for bread," she would give it first to Christ; Elizabeth of Hungary abandoned her three small children for "a life of charity."[40] Similarly, Margery's spiritual devotion entailed her literally leaving her children— even one newly born—so that she could cultivate her spirituality by visiting holy people and places far from home.[41] Some scholars read Kempe's life as a rejection of traditional family life,[42] though this claim does not capture the complexity of her life. As historian Laura Howes calculates: "If all fourteen children were carried full term, Margery would have been pregnant for a total of 126 months out of 240 months, or just over half of the time between her twentieth and fortieth birthdays."[43] I read Margery not as abandoning her family or her title as wife but as struggling to negotiate how to be a wife and mother on her own reproductive terms in light of her own spiritual calling to imitate Mary.

While Margery's medieval story cannot be said to exemplify contemporary sexual ethics or family planning, it nevertheless can be read today as strongly suggesting that a woman should, as much as she is able, insist upon a sexual relationship where she has voice to negotiate her reproductive and mothering preferences. Given the historical context in which Margery lived, her consenting to sexual intercourse was all the more vital because there were few safe or reliable resources for contraception, so an unwanted pregnancy could have followed any instance of sexual intercourse.[44] Although Margery and her husband eventually agreed upon a celibate marriage, a late pregnancy still did occur after embarking on her career as a pilgrim and lay spiritual counselor. This pregnancy appears to have been a failure of the couple's abstinence while traveling together and not some illicit sexual encounter. Nevertheless, even though the pregnancy was licit (because she was still married to her husband), she was tormented by the fact. In the vision mentioned above, Christ assured

40. Barbara Newman, *From Virile Woman to WomanChrist: Studies in Medieval Religion and Literature* (Philadelphia: University of Pennsylvania Press, 1995), 83–84, 86.

41. God commands her to leave her newborn in order to visit a holy man 40 miles away (see Staley, *The Book of Margery Kempe*, 29). Some historians suggest that Kempe fictionalized her own biography. See Lynn Staley, *Margery Kempe's Dissenting Fictions* (University Park: Pennsylvania State University Press, 1994). Whether fictional or historical, the themes in Kempe's account are still relevant for reflecting on spirituality and unwanted pregnancy.

42. See David Aers, *Community, Gender, and Individual Identity: English Writing, 1360–1430* (London: Routledge, 1988), 99.

43. Laura L. Howes, "On the Birth of Margery Kempe's Last Child," *Modern Philology* 90, no. 2 (1992): 224 n. 12.

44. For a discussion of fertility control in the Middle Ages, see Monica H. Green, "Gendering the History of Women's Healthcare," *Gender & History* 20, no. 3 (2008): 487–518.

her that he still loved her—pregnant though she was—as if she were "like a virgin."[45] The text does not say that Christ instructed her to change her attitude and welcome the child; rather, the text implies that getting pregnant was something that Christ would overlook in order to see her as an honorary maiden. To this end, Christ himself would arrange for a "keeper" for the child (chap. 21), so that Margery would be free to continue her spiritual vocation, which apparently did not include mothering her children.[46]

Margery, a mother many times over, rejected traditional motherhood as a virtuous calling for herself. For Margery, having another child was an unwelcome interruption of her spiritual calling, and her attitude struck her contemporaries (and maybe even strikes readers today) as a little indecent; nevertheless, she chose to be "despised" in the world for the love of God (chap. 22).[47] Despite the condemnation Margery may have received, the theme of deciding against motherhood as being an acceptable mode of Marian devotion is found elsewhere in the medieval period. In the words of one sixth-century Spanish bishop to an order of nuns, marriage is rife with dangers such as "corruption, disgust over corruption, the weight of a pregnant womb, the birth pangs, very often leading to a risk of death," and that a "crown of righteousness" awaits those who emulate Mary, "the mother of incorruption."[48] It is doubtful that Margery knew of this text, but the words seem to capture her sense that not wanting to be pregnant was a way to imitate Mary. There is even a hagiographical literature of saints who miraculously end problematic pregnancies, especially of consecrated virgins. One nun confessed her sin of fornication to a saint, who then "blessed her womb, and at once the baby . . . in her womb disappeared as if it did not exist."[49] Also included in this literature is the notion of restored virginity for nuns who had their pregnancies miraculously removed or those who gave birth after illicit sexual activity.[50] Both of these examples cohere with Margery's desire not be pregnant and her claim that Christ viewed her as a maiden despite becoming pregnant again.

45. For a discussion of Margery being "like a virgin," see Sarah Salih's chapter "White Clothes," in *Versions of Virginity in Late Medieval England* (Woodbridge, Suffolk, UK: D. S. Brewer, 2001), 217–23.

46. Staley, *The Book of Margery Kempe*, 36. Howes conjectures that Margery gave birth to this last child in Venice, while awaiting boat passage to the Holy Land; see Howes, "On the Birth of Margery Kempe's Last Child," 222.

47. Staley, *The Book of Margery Kempe*, 39.

48. John R. C. Martyn, ed. and trans., *Saint Leander, Archbishop of Seville: A Book on the Teaching of Nuns and a Homily in Praise of the Church* (Lanham, MD: Lexington, 2009), 78, 72.

49. St. Áed quoted in Maeve B. Callan, "Of Vanishing Fetuses and Maidens Made-Again: Abortion, Restored Virginity, and Similar Scenarios in Medieval Irish Hagiography and Penitentials," *Journal of the History of Sexuality* 21, no. 2 (2012): 290–91.

50. See Callan, "Of Vanishing Fetuses," 294.

One cannot say that Margery's desire not to be pregnant came from igno-rance about what it meant to gestate and give birth. Had she lived today, Mar-gery would not have needed to submit to some legally mandated ultrasound to prove to her that she was indeed gestating a life when she got pregnant for at least the fourteenth time. She knew how she got pregnant, and she knew what was entailed with being pregnant and giving birth (no doubt more so than the young Mary of Nazareth at the Annunciation). Margery's conclusion that her pregnancy was unwanted was reproductively knowledgeable. For Margery, having children and mothering interrupted her spiritual calling. She saw her *imitatio Mariae* as a graced state; she felt herself to be authorized by God to commit herself to a vocation where not wanting to get pregnant and not wanting to remain pregnant were not only grudgingly accepted attitudes but also praiseworthy ones.

Margery's story, even with its distant medieval setting, allows us to see how Christian spirituality—including but not restricted to the symbol of the Virgin Mary—can be creatively accessed in a transgressive way that speaks to contemporary women's reproductive and spiritual needs. I suggest that Christians might benefit by a new, modern *imitatio Mariae*, so that if a woman deems her pregnancy unwanted, she can see herself as spiritually authorized to make a maternal evaluation to continue mothering gestationally or not. Religious women should be able to envision their rejection of gestation as a manifestation of a desire for other life choices—choices that have as much possibility of being welcomed by God as the choice to give birth. Indeed, to assume without question that carrying every pregnancy to birth is God's will would be to abdicate one's responsibility to listen for divine guidance. For Margery, that guidance came through mystical visions. I am not suggesting that an abortion is only justified if the woman has received a vision of Christ or heard a voice of an angel. For Christian women today facing an unwanted pregnancy, guidance may come in the form of a quiet, biblically informed sense of assurance that it is right "to rely on '. . . a sound mind' that God had given me," as one evangelical woman facing an abortion choice put it.[51]

Considering a pregnancy unwanted should not be deemed theological anathema. A woman who does not want to gestate should not be relegated to the category of a daughter of Eve but should be empowered to see herself in the company of foremothers like Margery Kempe, a mother who received Christ's blessing to deem her pregnancy unwanted. Whether her gestational decision making is religiously contemplated or not, a woman with an unwanted pregnancy shoulders the unique maternal obligation to ponder her situation

---

51. Anne Eggebroten, ed., *Abortion—My Choice, God's Grace: Christian Women Tell Their Sto-ries* (Pasadena, CA: New Paradigm Books, 1994), 32.

and has the unique authority to make a mothering decision. Christian women no longer need to see their abortion decision as alienation from the religious symbols they honor, such as Mary's story. Religious women should be able to envision their rejection of gestation not as a negation of motherhood but as a manifestation of a desire for other life callings to which they wish to say *fiat mihi*.

Margery's story plausibly validates the spiritual impulse of not wanting to be pregnant and not wanting to commit oneself only to mothering born children. Margery did not have a practical option of abortion, which in her day would have endangered her own life, and we cannot even speculate about what she might have requested from one of the supposed abortionist saints of medieval Ireland, if she ever heard of or crossed paths with one of them. Margery's story tells us about a Marian spirituality of not wanting to be pregnant; it does not recount attempting to end a pregnancy. To answer the question of whether a woman can choose *Christianly* to terminate that pregnancy, I need to offer theological rebuttals to the pro-life claims that abortion is a sin and that it is a believing woman's place to bear the cross of an unintended or unwanted pregnancy. In addition, I discuss how a pro-choice theological position on abortion death may be situated within a larger Christian theology of death.

SIN, SACRIFICE, AND DEATH IN THE WOMB OF GOD

I have proposed how Mary and Margery Kempe can be read as validating women's sense of vulnerability in facing an unplanned pregnancy and as alleviating some of the stigma of deeming their pregnancy as unwanted. Still to be addressed is the theological basis for a woman actually terminating her unwanted pregnancy. There are two major obstacles to thinking of abortion as a woman's Christian option: the pro-life claim that abortion is a heinous sin and the claim that Jesus' sacrifice on the cross means that believing women should, likewise, take up their cross and carry an unwanted pregnancy. Not only do such notions stigmatize and shame Christian women who have had abortions, but, I argue, they are theologically mistaken. In order to counteract the acids of these pro-life discourses in women's lives, I make the theological case that abortion should not be seen as ipso facto sin and that the symbol of the cross does not obligate pregnant women to sacrifice their bodies in order to gestate. I conclude with a discussion of women's reproductive loss, including abortion loss, which many women experience as death within their womb. I offer a Trinitarian way of thinking about the crucifixion event that enables one to imagine how all reproductive losses, including abortion deaths, are taken up into the womb of a compassionate God and healed.

Contesting Abortion as Sin

In some way, shape, or form, pro-life proponents see abortion as sinful. At the most compassionate side, if one can call it that, there is a discourse about "abortive moms" as sinners, but partially victimized ones[52]—coerced into abortion by selfish partners or angry parents, manipulated by unscrupulous abortion providers, and then traumatized by regret. There are a number of pro-life writers who promote these views, such as self-described psychologist David Reardon and Eastern Orthodox writer Frederica Mathewes-Green, who focus on issues such as the psychological and spiritual trauma that "post-abortive women" experience. On the latter point, Reardon writes: "One could argue that the harm that the woman suffers is greater since her soul is damaged by abortion, while the child only suffers physical death and remains spiritually untouched."[53] Mathewes-Green has been a strong advocate of showing compassion to these post-abortive women because doing so, she believes, will produce genuine repentance that will prevent any future abortions. By interviewing women recruited from pro-life postabortion counseling groups (which is not a random sampling), Mathewes-Green finds data in support of this compassion-oriented approach. As one woman said, speaking retrospectively about her abortion, "I also realized that, even though I did this terrible thing, God loves me; he loved me even before I said, 'I'm sorry, it was wrong.'"[54] This type of pro-life advocacy supports organizations that have ministries to serve women with counseling and retreats where they can repent of the wrong they have done and ask forgiveness from God and from their aborted fetus.

At the other end of the pro-life spectrum are those voices criticizing the trope of the victimized postabortion woman who needs compassion. One sees these arguments from scholars such as Francis Beckwith, who criticizes the pro-life strategy of "appealing to the pregnant woman's self-interest to persuade her not to have an abortion." Beckwith argues that this so-called softball strategy "may result in nurturing . . . a philosophical mindset that is consistent with abortion's moral permissibility,"[55] because it does not insist on calling abortion "unjustified homicide."[56] More politically extreme versions of Beckwith's rigorist call-a-sin-a-sin viewpoint can be found in the writings of

52. Frederica Mathewes-Green, *Real Choices: Offering Practical Life-Affirming Alternatives to Abortion* (Sisters, OR: Multnomah Books, 1994), 124.
53. David C. Reardon, "A Defense of the Neglected Rhetorical Strategy (NRS)," *Ethics & Medicine* 18, no. 2 (2002): 25.
54. Mathewes-Green, *Real Choices*, 125.
55. Francis J. Beckwith, "Taking Abortion Seriously: A Philosophical Critique of the New Anti-Abortion Rhetorical Shift," *Ethics & Medicine* 17, no. 3 (2001): 161.
56. Beckwith, "Taking Abortion Seriously, 162. Beckwith's views on abortion as murder are discussed in chap. 4 above.

militant anti-abortion activists. Some radical anti-abortion proponents claim that women who abort are guilty of "premeditated murder."[57] Extremist anti-abortion groups support penalizing women who abort and even using violence against abortion clinics and abortion providers. One ultra-right-wing Christian Web site states more baldly what Beckwith says indirectly: "The 'pro-life movement' in this nation has made the woman into a victim. That's right—they actually want us to believe that the woman who hires a paid assassin to murder her own child is in fact a victim herself."[58] There are a number of assumptions grounding this kind of rhetoric, whether scholarly or extremist: the two central ones are the claim that the fetus is a person, not just analogous to a born child but actually substantially equivalent to a born child; and the claim that the fetus needs to be protected (via strict abortion bans) from its gestating mother. My critique of the fallacies of these assumptions and their thinly veiled misogyny is given in chapter 4 (above).

Pro-choice proponents reject calling abortion sin—mostly invoking the notion of tragedy. There is a realistic basis for this viewpoint, if one thinks about the human condition—its brutishness and precariousness, especially for vulnerable classes of people—and the fact that, short of the eschaton, the believer has only partial knowledge of God's ways and sees only as if "through a glass, darkly" (1 Cor. 13:12 KJV). When human finitude combines with the inability to see how to move forward with an unintended pregnancy, one has the recipe for a tragic choice. That said, I disagree with Daniel Maguire's claim that "abortion is always tragic."[59] Calling all abortions tragic could imply that gestating fetal life is a pregnant woman's intrinsic moral obligation, but life circumstances tragically make it impossible for her to follow through. I have already argued against the viewpoint of the intrinsic good of maintaining a fetal life in pregnancy and the relatively light burden of pregnancy.[60] Instead, I insist on recognizing pregnancy as a risky and significant demand. In discussing gestational hospitality in chapter 6, I pressed for seeing pregnancy as

---

57. Michael Bray, *A Time to Kill: A Study concerning the Use of Force and Abortion* (Portland, OR: Advocates for Life, 1994), 21.

58. Matthew Trewhella, "Should Women Be Punished for Murdering Their Own Son or Daughter by Abortion?" *Army of God* (n.d.), https://www.armyofgod.com/MatthewTrewhella WomenPunishedAbortion.html. For more on this group, see Jennifer Jefferis, *Armed for Life: The Army of God and Anti-Abortion Terror in the United States* (Santa Barbara, CA: Praeger, 2011). This type of extreme language was even recently used by Pope Francis: see Philip Pullella, "Pope Compares Having an Abortion to 'Hiring a Hit Man,'" *Reuters* (October 10, 2018), https://www .reuters.com/article/us-pope-abortion/pope-compares-having-an-abortion-to-hiring-a-hit-man -idUSKCN1MK1E7.

59. Daniel C. Maguire, "Abortion: A Question of Catholic Honesty," *Christian Century* 100, no. 26 (1983): 805.

60. This viewpoint is argued by Lisa Cahill, who claims that nurturing fetal life is an intrinsic good supported by the natural process of pregnancy that, normally, is not onerous or a pathological condition. See chap. 5 above.

discretionary embodied self-giving, analogous to organ donation, as Patricia Jung perceptively argues. If a woman decides not to continue her pregnancy because she has already committed herself to other obligations, that decision should not be spoken of as tragic, any more than one would call tragic a person's decision not to be a live organ donor. No physician would ever say to the potential donor, "You must avert the tragedy of my patient dying and give him your kidney" or "It's a tragedy that you are not opting to be a kidney donor." Some women's abortions are felt by them as tragic since they wish they could have had more options to be able to do otherwise, but not all abortions should be categorized as such.

Pro-choice scholars invoke the notion of tragedy, in part, to garner sympathy for women with unwanted pregnancies, and I agree that sympathy is in order; however, the category of tragedy can inadvertently mask the fact that abortion is a decision—to my mind, a maternal decision—that a gestating women has the responsibility and the authority to make. In chapter 5 (above), I insisted on the necessity of seeing abortion as a woman's morally serious maternal decision that there be no child born to whom she would have further mothering obligations. If one takes the position that abortion is a woman's decision, and not just a calamity that befalls her, then one has to face head on, theologically, the pro-life charge that abortion is an intentional sin.

There are at least four reasons why a choice for abortion should not be seen as ipso facto intentional sin. First, there is no clear theological basis for declaring that abortion is a sin of murder, because that judgment can only be made within a mind-set that has already predetermined that abortion is the intentional and unwarranted killing of a person. Part 1 of this book offered a sustained critique of the many ways pro-life proponents try, and fail, to establish that a fetus is a person. Historically, deeming abortion to be homicide was largely a canon law development linked to the criminalization of abortion in the Middle Ages; even then, the crime did not apply to the unformed fetus but only to the ensouled, formed fetus—that is, a legal person.[61] Pro-life proponents today reject the unformed/formed conceptuality but try to sustain the charge of homicide with a variety of biblical, theological, and philosophical arguments. I have shown the instability and confusion of pro-life claims to fetal personhood from conception (based on genetics, the *imago Dei*, biblical descriptions of life in the womb, probabilism, and so on). In my discussion of the status of the fetus in chapter 5, I suggested that the term "person"—whose commonplace meaning is an embodied, born individual—cannot be said to apply unambiguously to a human being existing contingently and contiguously to its mother's body. A fetus, thus understood, is neither innocent

61. See chap. 1 above.

nor an aggressor, neither mere human tissue nor preborn baby. Its death, by miscarriage or abortion, is not negligible, as women's own words attest. One cannot say that a fetus is a nonperson. Neither can one say that abortion of a still-developing fetus is the murder of a person in any commonplace meaning of the word. Abortion is undeniably the demise of a developing human being, but because pregnancy is a sui generis type of human experience, abortion death is a sui generis type of death. Abortion is the only situation in which one human agent causes the death of a human being developing within her own body. It is death that is not accidental, but it is death without malice. The one who dies is not a nonperson but not a person either. Hence, abortion cannot be said to constitute the sin of murder.

Second, even if someone concedes that "murder" is not an appropriate word for abortion, the argument could still be made that the destruction of uterine life constitutes a sinful denial of its value. I agree with the premise about uterine life having value but disagree that its destruction should be necessarily seen as denying its value, no matter how paradoxical that sounds. I have argued for seeing value as inhering at every emergent stage of a human organism for multiple reasons: it is genetically human, developing toward personhood, and intimately existing contingently and contiguously to its ges-tating mother.[62] If the discourse of women who abort is any indication, a pregnant woman's "no" to further gestation is rarely a denial of the value of life in her womb; indeed, many women speak of aborting their "baby." Even feminist philosophers invoke Levinas's notions of the ethical demand of the "face" of the Other, including the fetal Other.[63] A woman's "no" to gesta-tional hospitality may be expressed as an immediate desire simply not to be pregnant anymore, and that desire is valid, in and of itself, for all the reasons I have given about the burdens and risks of pregnancy. In addition, abortion decisions can be seen as an acknowledgment that the woman feels unable to take on the caring relationship of nurturing, birthing, and being the mother of this baby—whether she uses those words or not. Instances of frivolous abortion do not negate the ethicality of how most women terminate their pregnancies.[64] Pro-life accusations that women who abort are callous and, hence, sinful do not even cohere with their own research data, which docu-ments some women as admitting anguish over their abortion.[65] To pro-life

---

62. See chap. 5 above.

63. For my discussion of this Levinasian point, see chap. 6 above.

64. I mentioned the occurrence of abortion-doping in some competitive sports in chap. 5 above.

65. See David C. Reardon, "Women Who Abort: Their Reflections on Abortion," *Post-Abortion Review* 4, no. 1 (1996), http://afterabortion.org/1996/women-who-abort-their-reflections-on-abortion/. I have criticized Reardon's research and credentials elsewhere. See Margaret D. Kamitsuka, "Feminist Scholarship and Its Relevance for Political Engagement: The Test Case of Abortion in the U.S.," *Religion and Gender* 1, no. 1 (2011): 26.

proponents, women's admission of anguish is proof of sin; I take it as proof of a moral conscience and, hence, a tacit acknowledgment of fetal value. As such, abortion cannot be said to be an ipso facto sin of denying fetal value.

Third, even if one accepts that abortion is not a sin against a fetal person and not a denial of fetal value, it could still be a sin against God. Most theologians would agree that sin is a relational category including so-called horizontal relationships among humans in the world and the vertical God-human relationship. A pro-choice theologian cannot rule out that a woman may be sinning against God, in some way, in her act of abortion, if one accepts the aptness of the biblical assertion "all have sinned and fall short of the glory of God" (Rom. 3:23). However, this biblical assertion about sin cuts both ways: if a woman might sin in her abortion, so might pro-life protesters in their self-righteous and judgmental attitudes.[66] If, when, and the degree to which any abortion (or any judgment about that abortion) involves alienation from God—that can only be determined by the individual's own conscience, *coram Deo*, since God alone will "test the mind and search the heart" (Jer. 17:10). There is no objective way to know if, or the extent to which, a particular act of abortion death has damaged a woman's relationship with God, and thus there is no justifiable theological reason for assuming that a woman's act of abortion has automatically alienated her from God.

Abortion cannot be judged, from the outside, to be a sin against God simply because a death has occurred. Theologically, if God is acknowledged as the "maker of all things both seen and unseen" (Nicene Creed), then to destroy any part of God's creation—including fetal life, however one views it—could be a sin against the Creator. However, God has chosen to wrap uterine life in a veil of obscurity: "Just as you do not know how the breath comes to the bones in the mother's womb, so you do not know the work of God, who makes everything" (Eccl. 11:5). There is no definitive theological or biblical teaching, or even a preponderance thereof, to establish that every fetus is ordained by God for life on earth. Impregnation should not be taken as an indubitable sign of God's providential will that a child should be gestated and born (as I argued in chap. 2). For this reason, a woman's decision not to continue to gestate her fetus until birth cannot be deemed ipso facto sin against God. On the other hand, compelling a woman to gestate a fetus against her will strikes me as a callous act and an act of hubris, even if done with the best intentions toward the fetus.

A fourth reason for why one should not call abortion a sin is supplemented by feminist analyses about women surviving under conditions of patriarchy and other oppressions. It is not a sin to survive. As Asian American feminist

66. I discussed this point in chap. 5.

theologian Rita Nakashima Brock has so perceptively explained, women, who for so long were praised for being obedient and passive, must learn another mode of existing in order to survive and build a decent future for themselves and their families. Brock, who has worked to bring the issue of domestic violence and sexual abuse into the sphere of theological reflection, argues that one of the most destructive aspects of the Christian tradition is its privileging of notions such as Christ's purity and obedience unto death. For those people who experience various forms of abuse, and the resulting internalized shame, these ideals of obedience and purity are devastating. Brock suggests that marginalized groups, such as Asian American women like herself, struggle analogously from the exploitation that falls upon them as a result of "seeking to be good or clinging to trust in the power of others." To all these marginalized survivors, Brock says: "We must lose innocence in order to gain hope." Instead of innocence, Brock prefers the category of wisdom, which she associates with being "strong, strategically smart, skeptical, cunning, caring, . . . politically savvy"—attributes that she believes fit Jesus of the Gospel narratives.[67] Those who abandon romantic notions of purity may be labeled as sinners, in part because taking the path of wise survival may involve acts of moral ambiguity.

I find Brock's category of being wise, rather than obedient, as aptly applicable to many women who face difficult reproductive decisions. This category further shows that it may not be appropriate to call every abortion a tragedy. It is not a tragedy for a woman to survive. To put this idea into a biblical key, we might say that *fiat mihi* may be an obedient, trusting response to an unplanned pregnancy but may not always be the wise and feasible response. In some situations, what a woman deems as necessary for her survival (whether physical, economic, emotional, or something else) may mean she loses her so-called innocence in lieu of a wise course of action. This kind of survival cannot be appropriately labeled sin.

The Cross and Gestational Sacrifice

The pro-life theme that gestation is an acceptable and not too onerous burden for women has been discussed and criticized at several points in this book. Some pro-life writers, however, do recognize that pregnancy is a great sacrifice, and the cross is invoked in various ways in this regard to justify obligating a woman to make sacrifices in order to gestate her fetus. An extreme example

---

67. Rita Nakashima Brock, "Losing Your Innocence but Not Your Hope," in *Reconstructing the Christ Symbol: Essays in Feminist Christology,* ed. Maryanne Stevens (Mahwah, NJ: Paulist Press, 1993), 40, 42–43.

of this kind of discourse is found in one Roman Catholic "Stations of the Cross" liturgy on the popular pro-life Web site "Priests for Life." The prayer exhorts women to submit to pregnancy as a kind of crucifixion: "And have mercy on all pregnant mothers who are overwhelmed by anxieties over their pregnancy; may they, through the example and prayers of our Blessed Mother, have the grace and courage to accept crucifixion with their baby rather than try to escape the cross by aborting their baby."[68] This prayer does not soften the message of the sacrifice entailed in an unwanted pregnancy; indeed, it seems to emphasize the suffering, with the caveat that it will be made bearable by the intercessions of Mary. A more nuanced message that encourages pregnant believers to forge ahead to give birth is found in an essay by Catholic philosophy professor Mary Sommers on hospitality and pregnancy. Sommers sees in gestation a unique situation of embodied hospitality that does entail sacrifice. She differs from the stations of the cross perspective above, however, and insists that gestation should not be thought of as "a commitment to crucifixion. The cross is not an explanation, in that sense, of why the Christian woman should complete a burdensome pregnancy." Sommers neither paints the woman as a "Christ-like" savior to her fetus nor gives a rosy picture of unplanned pregnancy. She even acknowledges the risk, perhaps even the inevitability, that the woman "may be left alone to bear the full burden" without help from others. Nevertheless, she affirms that the commitment to the Christian life may, and perhaps mostly does, lead the believer "to the cross."[69] Thus, whether extreme or more theologically nuanced, both pro-life invocations of the cross present Christ's crucifixion as an example of self-sacrifice that the pro-life proponent may appropriately apply to induce or encourage self-sacrificial behavior from the pregnant believer with a crisis pregnancy.

I have already discussed the pastoral theological critique of encouraging women toward self-sacrificial caretaking and mothering in the previous chapter. Here it is important to note that womanist scholars and feminist theologians of many types have for decades spoken emphatically about problematic aspects of crucifixion metaphors and atonement theories, arguing that the notion of redemptive suffering on the cross smacks of "divine child abuse" and has been used to justify the exploitation and surrogacy of African American women.[70] These scholars have justifiable concerns about gruesome sacrificial

68. Fr. Cletus Healy, S.J., "Stations of the Cross for Victims of Abortion," *Priests for Life*, http://www.priestsforlife.org/prayers/stations-victims-of-abortion.htm.

69. Mary Catherine Sommers, "Living Together: Burdensome Pregnancy and the Hospitable Self," in *Abortion: A New Generation of Catholic Responses*, ed. Stephen J. Heaney (Braintree, MA: Pope John Center, 1992), 259. Sommers's essay criticizes Patricia Jung's analogy between pregnancy and live organ donation, discussed in chap. 6

70. Joan Carlson Brown and Rebecca Parker, "For God So Loved the World?," in *Christianity, Patriarchy, and Abuse: A Feminist Critique*, ed. Joan Carlson Brown and Carol R. Bohn (New York:

imagery related to the atonement, and it is understandable how some theologians would simply abandon any reference to the redemptive aspect of self-sacrificial acts, including those of Christ on the cross. However, I suggest that the crucifixion, seen in the context of the incarnation as Christ's processive, emergent deification (as presented in chap. 3), has the possibility of not only avoiding these damaging entailments but also offering a more appropriate religious message (compared to the pro-life rhetoric above) for women who chose to abort.

In a processive, emergent deification approach to the incarnation, the union of Christ's divine and human natures is not spoken of as achieved in an instant at his conception in Mary's womb, which is what pro-life theologians assert as the only true Chalcedonian interpretation.[71] The divinization of Christ's humanity may be understood as an emergent process throughout his whole life—a life where he shared in and was affected by the real human conditions of birth, frailty, temptation, and death. That Jesus faced a real death is decisive for this view of the incarnation, which posits that his deification was not fully achieved until he had passed through death and reached the "final glorification of Jesus' humanity" in the resurrection.[72] Jesus' crucifixion is definitive not because that is how a redemptive transaction took place, paid for in blood, but because Jesus' process of divinization could not bypass the event of death (which all humans face) and still be salvific. The soteriological principle this view of deification aims to fulfill is articulated in the Cappadocian theological axiom that what is not assumed is not healed. Jesus lived a human life on earth, so that in the cross and resurrection event, all sin and suffering in the human condition would be "drawn up into the life of the Trinity as its final destiny."[73] Not only is sin thus addressed, by making available to each person the possibility of a Spirit-guided life journey toward divinization, but in addition, death is addressed with the promise that when humans die, they "do not die into nothingness but into the mystery of the triune God."[74] The sacrifice that Christ makes on the cross is the sacrifice of setting aside divinity and assuming the final and most definitive aspect of the human condition—death—in order to heal it.

Pilgrim Press, 1989), 2; see Brock, "Losing Your Innocence but Not Your Hope," 38. See Delores S. Williams, *Sisters in the Wilderness: The Challenge of Womanist God-Talk* (Maryknoll, NY: Orbis Books, 1993), 161–67. For a longer discussion of these issues see Margaret D. Kamitsuka, *Feminist Theology and the Challenge of Difference* (Oxford: Oxford University Press, 2007), 98–105.

71. For a fuller presentation of a processive, emergent view of the incarnation and how it provides a Chalcedonian alternative to pro-life views, see chap. 3.

72. Kathryn Tanner, *Jesus, Humanity and the Trinity: A Brief Systematic Theology* (Minneapolis: Fortress Press, 2001), 52.

73. Henry L. Novello, *Death as Transformation: A Contemporary Theology of Death* (Farnham, Surrey, UK: Ashgate, 2013), 210.

74. Novello, *Death as Transformation*, 203.

A processive, emergent approach thus sees the cross as a sacrificial, saving death, but properly understood, Jesus' crucifixion is not meant to endorse or encourage sacrifice or surrogacy from the believer. The cross is "the sacrifice that ends sacrifice," because the second person of the Trinity offered himself, and no further offering is needed.[75] If the cross is seen in this way, we can begin to understand another aspect of how abortion is not sin. Because the cross is the definitive end to all further sacrifice, a pregnant woman does not sin by refusing to make a maternal self-offering of her body on behalf of her fetus. Such a sacrifice is not required of her toward God, since after the cross "humans are not to offer sacrifices to God."[76] To sacrifice one's life voluntarily on behalf of another is heroic, and a "decisionally capable" pregnant woman has the right to make that sacrifice if she chooses, as much as, for example, soldiers do on the battlefield to save their comrades.[77] Nevertheless, it is morally dubious to promote women sacrificing their body, even to the point of literally dying from the effort to gestate a fetus until it can be safely born, as a religious virtue to which pregnant women should aspire.[78] Even if there is no immediate threat to her life, it is not a sin for a pregnant woman to refrain, if she feels she must, from the extreme bodily gift of gestation and birthing.

Pro-life, pro-choice, and clinical pastoral accounts of Christian women's abortion decisions indicate that few believing women simply brush off an abortion decision.[79] However, giving one's body to gestate and birth and then giving years of one's time and energy to raise the child (because a woman will most likely not be able to relinquish that child for adoption) should be seen, as I argued in the preceding chapter, as a supererogatory embodied gift, not a Christian woman's Samaritan obligation. Christ's offering of his body was a unique salvific event that should not be presented as a template the pregnant believer is required or urged to imitate. Moreover, it would be

75. Kathryn Tanner, *Christ the Key* (Cambridge: Cambridge University Press, 2010), 271.

76. Tanner, *Christ the Key*, 272.

77. See Committee on Ethics, "Refusal of Medically Recommended Treatment during Pregnancy," *American College of Obstetricians and Gynecologists*, no. 664 (June 2016), https://www.acog .org/Clinical-Guidance-and-Publications/Committee-Opinions/Committee-on-Ethics/Refusal -of-Medically-Recommended-Treatment-During-Pregnancy?

78. Pro-life proponents extol Gianna Molla and Chiara Corbella, who each refused cancer treatments to protect her unborn child and as a result died after the birth. See Marie Meaney, "Chiara Corbella: A Witness to Joy," *Crisis Magazine* (April 16, 2014), https://www.crisismagazine.com /2014/chiara-corbella-a-witness-to-joy. For a critical assessment of Molla's canonization, see Michael W. Higgins, *Stalking the Holy: The Pursuit of Saint Making* (Toronto: House of Anansi, 2006), 68–72.

79. See Mathewes-Green, *Real Choices*; Eggebroten, *Abortion—My Choice, God's Grace*; Roy R. Jeal and Linda A. West, "Rolling Away the Stone: Post-Abortion Women in the Christian Community," *Journal of Pastoral Care & Counseling* 57, no. 1 (2003): 53–64.

aberrant to suggest that Christ's sacrifice on the cross is the theological basis for coerced or forced gestation and motherhood, which raises the specter of abusive surrogacy that womanist theologians and others have so trenchantly criticized.

Death in the Womb and Death in God

Death on the cross is unavoidably a central Christian symbol—whether one sees that symbol as inspiring, doctrinally normative, or pastorally troubling. Sadly, death and pregnancy have always been close companions in diverse and often tragic ways. When a child is wanted, any demise—whether early or late—is a gut-wrenching loss. Women speak of these reproductive experiences, and their discourses of loss, including abortion death, are theologically relevant. These discourses reveal a profoundly intimate exposure to death—including experiencing the death of one's own child within one's body. Theologians are only just beginning to see the implications of this phenomenon for understanding the meaning of the incarnation, the cross event, and even a doctrine of God.

Serene Jones has noted how women's experiences of miscarriage cause us to rethink loss, maternalness, and the divine. Jones describes the experience of one friend of hers, "Wendy," who suffered a miscarriage and was overtaken with the physicality of the experience: "I find myself walking around my kitchen bleeding away a life." Many such women are overwhelmed by a cascade of emotions of grief and guilt: "'What did I do to make this happen?' they ask. 'Was it that cigarette I smoked last Saturday?' . . . 'Is God punishing me?'"[80] In particular Jones notes how her friend spoke about the strange feeling she had of experiencing death within her body: "It fills her, a final death, and yet she lives to remember not a death diverted but a death accomplished and completed in her loins. . . . What does it mean to . . . have death quite literally inside you?"[81] Womanist theologian Monica Coleman's description of her experience of miscarriage as the helpless bleeding away of a life is similar to that of Wendy. The similarity of discourse indicates a tragic experience that in some ways binds women together across various racial and cultural boundaries—and yet, maybe not, since "while miscarriage is not particular to African American women, they do experience miscarriage at a rate of 1.5

---

80. Serene Jones, "Hope Deferred: Theological Reflections on Reproductive Loss," in *Trauma and Grace: Theology in a Ruptured World* (Louisville, KY: Westminster John Knox Press, 2009), 135. Originally published as "Hope Deferred: Theological Reflections on Reproductive Loss (Infertility, Stillbirth, Miscarriage)," *Modern Theology* 17, no. 2 (2001): 227–45.

81. S. Jones, "Hope Deferred," 138.

to two times the rate of their White counterparts." Moreover, an African American woman's loss of her unborn child can be haunted by the ghosts of "enslaved African American mothers [who] often had their children sold away from them."[82] Thus, there is no single type of miscarriage experience.

Janice Thompson describes a very different loss, a stillbirth or death of a neonate, and how women who have suffered this indescribable experience feel emotions and perform rituals that may not make sense to the outside observer. One woman whose infant died is compelled by a maternal protectiveness to "put a baby blanket and a tarp on her daughter's grave" when it rains.[83] Among the many Web sites devoted to support for infant loss, one can find a range of religious beliefs. Some parents mourning reproductive loss find solace in their faith. One grieving mother thinks of her miscarried babies as having been "born into heaven" where, she believes, they are aware of her ongoing motherly love for them.[84] These expressions of grief and faith show believers struggling with personal tragedy. Some are graced with a comforting certitude about their child being in heaven, while others come only slowly to "eschatological hope."[85]

The feminist literature and personal accounts of miscarriage and neonatal death often speak about how little understood these kinds of reproductive loss are. Women whose lives have been devastated by neonatal death or stillbirth "describe the way the silence of the birth seems to extend into the silence of hospital personnel, friends, and family who avoid mentioning the death, and even avoid the mother herself."[86] Similarly, miscarriage has been called a "silent sorrow" because it often happens without even friends, family, and sometimes even one's spouse or partner being aware.[87] The voices of women who have undergone these experiences deserve to be heard, as theologians ponder the relevance of Jesus' death to experiences of fetal or neonatal death. How should one speak theologically about these inexpressible experiences of miscarriage or having an infant die?

Let me say first how these types of women's experiences and discourses should *not* be referenced. First and foremost, those in positions of theological or ecclesial authority should not manipulate these kinds of images and

---

82. Monica A. Coleman, "Sacrifice, Surrogacy and Salvation: Womanist Reflections on Motherhood and Work," *Black Theology* 12, no. 3 (2014): 205.

83. Janice Allison Thompson, "Making Room for the Other: Maternal Mourning and Eschatological Hope," *Modern Theology* 27, no. 3 (2011): 401. Thompson gives a moving account of her own loss of a newborn baby girl.

84. Blog by Jessica (October 4, 2013), *The Humbled Homemaker*, https://thehumbledhomemaker.com/baby-born-into-heaven-via-miscarriage-or-stillbirth/.

85. Thompson, "Making Room for the Other," 401.

86. Thompson, "Making Room for the Other," 404.

87. See Ingrid Kohn, Perry-Lynn Moffitt, with Isabelle A. Wilkins, *A Silent Sorrow: Pregnancy Loss; Guidance and Support for You and Your Family*, 2nd ed. (New York: Routledge, 2013).

emotions for purposes of anti-abortion preaching or public policy cam-paigns.[88] I also reject making an abortion rights argument based on the claim that fetal death is not significant because embryos and fetuses who die will enjoy eternal life with God.[89] I particularly object to interpreting women's grief about reproductive loss as a tacit admission that a preborn baby died, implying that "women should be held accountable for their pregnancies" and that "the state has a right to take some kind of action" against women who harm or kill their fetuses.[90] Instead, I encourage theologians and other schol-ars to take seriously maternal grief over reproductive death without imposing an outsider's judgment.[91]

If understanding how to speak appropriately about even miscarriage and stillbirth have eluded theologians, how much more so do women's experi-ences of abortion death strike many theologians as unintelligible. It is human to recoil from that which one cannot comprehend. Pro-life proponents find abortion incomprehensible and often lash out in condemnations that contrib-ute to the stigma of abortion and have little theological grounding. (Some women find that even pro-choice theologians fall short regarding how to speak about miscarriage and abortion death.)[92] The idea that God could sanc-tion a believer choosing to take the life of another human being is a wide ditch that many believers have difficulty crossing.

Some feminist theologians and ethicists argue that the ditch is not so wide at some points in a pregnancy—meaning, some fetuses in early pregnancy are more morally negligible than later on. I have already explained why I do not think we should cross the ethical ditch of abortion in this way because it both undercuts the mother's authority to decide how to manage her preg-nancy and also does not credit fetal value early in a pregnancy.[93] A pro-choice claim that an early abortion is a pre-mothering decision does not address the stigma of abortion as a negation of motherhood but, rather, avoids address-ing the stigma. I believe the stigma can only be lessened by insisting that the

88. See "Heaven and the Eternal Destiny of Preborn Infants," *Focus on the Family* (2011), https://www.focusonthefamily.com/family-q-and-a/faith/heaven-and-the-eternal-destiny-of -preborn-infants.

89. An odd argument is made along these lines in Kenneth Einar Himma, "No Harm, No Foul: Abortion and the Implications of Fetal Innocence," *Faith and Philosophy* 19, no. 2 (2002): 172–94.

90. Stephen H. Webb, "Response to L. Serene Jones, Hope Deferred," *Modern Theology* 17, no. 4 (2001): 510.

91. See also Linda L. Layne, *Motherhood Lost: A Feminist Account of Pregnancy Loss in America* (New York: Routledge, 2003); Kate Parsons, "Feminist Reflections on Miscarriage, in Light of Abortion," *International Journal of Feminist Approaches to Bioethics* 3, no. 1 (2010): 1–22.

92. Janice Thompson, for example, in light of her own experience of neonatal loss, finds something too "abstract" in Rosemary Ruether's healing ritual after miscarriage or abortion. See Thompson, "Making Room for the Other," 403, 412 n. 47.

93. See chap. 5 above.

pregnancy outcome be seen as a decision that a pregnant woman has the obligation and authority to make, and it is a maternal decision—as confirmed by ordinary women's discourses about their aborted "baby." How do the themes, doctrines, or symbols of Christian faith support the notion of abortion as a mothering decision, which the pregnant woman has the authority to make?

Any death that a woman brings into her own body in an abortion cannot be a trivial event, no matter how sure she may be that it is necessary. For the Christian woman, life and death have been given a particular meaning because of the life, death, and resurrection of God incarnate. If abortion is to be seen as Christianly understandable, then the cross-resurrection event must be seen to speak to abortion death in a way that presents God as not turning away from the woman who aborts. I am asking, to use again the Levinasian term, what "face" does God show to the woman who brings death into her own body? If the image one has in mind is the stern visage of a patriarchal God seated upon his celestial throne and wondering how to keep the "daughters of humankind . . . bringing forth children in sorrow and living in subjugation" (to borrow from Rosemary Ruether's famous "Kenosis of the Father"), then one can only conclude that God turns his face away from a woman unwilling to reproduce.[94]

However, when I think of women in reproductive distress, including abortion, I do not see such a God—if I keep in mind the meaning of the incarnation in its proper Trinitarian perspective. I am moved by the image Serene Jones gives for how God might be imagined as comforting her friend who miscarried: "I imagine [God] holding Wendy, curling Her own ruptured body around Wendy and rocking her. 'I know,' [God] says. 'I know.'"[95] In this context of miscarriage and stillbirth, God is envisaged as compassionate Mother, because God also suffered the death of her own Son. I submit that this same image of a mothering, suffering God could also speak to abortion. I imagine a woman having an abortion and, between the painful dilation and cramping, uttering a prayer to God: "Shekhinah, in the darkness of your womb we find protection and comfort!"[96] For the stigma of abortion to be overcome, one needs to imagine this prayer being heard by a mothering God

---

94. Rosemary Radford Ruether, *Sexism and God-Talk: Toward a Feminist Theology*, with a new introduction (Boston: Beacon Press, 1993), 1.

95. S. Jones, "Hope Deferred," 148, 149. Jones points to Jürgen Moltmann's work in this regard.

96. Words of a Jewish feminist liturgy quoted in Melissa Raphael, *The Female Face of God in Auschwitz: A Jewish Feminist Theology of the Holocaust* (London: Routledge, 2003), 119. The Shekhinah is a female-gendered concept from Jewish mystical writings, meaning the emanation of the divine in the world who accompanies Israel through catastrophe and exile. See Raphael, *The Female Face of God*, 148–50. Jewish feminists like Raphael retrieve the concept to reimagine God's maternal presence among those who suffer.

who turns her face not away but toward such a woman and feels compassion for the death that the woman brings into her own womb.[97] When I invoke the notion of compassion, I am not positing a God, as described by some moderate pro-life writers, who welcomes back into the fold sinful women who repent of their abortion. There are (especially conservative Christian) women who do believe they sinned in their abortion. However, I am making a different theological point here. I suggest that God sends God's Spirit of comfort not just to repentant women but also to women who believe they made the best or at least the only feasible choice available to them—whether their abortion choice is experienced by them as tragic, a survival tactic, or a response to other callings. What theological basis is there for thinking of God as looking with compassion upon such a mother and for the woman to image God standing compassionately by her side at her abortion?

Answering this question brings us to the most inscrutable aspect of the doctrine of the Trinitarian God—namely, how the Trinity encompasses the death of the second person of the Trinity. Many aspects of Christ's passion and crucifixion are mysterious and even disturbing: Jesus' cry of abandonment on the cross, the silence of God for the hours of Jesus' tormented dying, the enigma of suffering within the Godhead—these and other profound and impenetrable themes remain perennially open theological questions. I do not suggest I can definitively clarify these complicated themes and thereby completely settle the theological challenge posed by abortion death. However, I can gesture toward how the Trinitarian event of the crucifixion speaks to abortion with the implication that God does not turn away from the woman who aborts.

In the processive, emergent interpretation of the incarnation that I have endorsed in this book, the climax of the incarnation is not Jesus' conception in Mary's womb but occurs when Jesus, after dying, is taken up into the Godhead. This image of the cross and resurrection event allows one to affirm that all death, including fetal deaths, reverberate into the divine; nothing is lost to God, as Jürgen Moltmann has said.[98] I think Henry Novello and Serene Jones are correct to turn to Moltmann as one resource for understanding the complexity of death on the cross. His groundbreaking book *The Crucified God* probes the issue of death, abandonment, fatherhood, and love in the crucifixion as a Trinitarian event: "The Father who abandons [Christ] and delivers him up suffers the death of the Son in the infinite grief of love."[99]

---

97. My comments about a mother God channel decades if not centuries of feminist and proto-feminist writing. See Elizabeth Johnson, *She Who Is: The Mystery of God in Feminist Theological Discourse* (New York: Crossroad, 1995), especially 254–55.

98. See Novello, *Death as Transformation*, 155.

99. Jürgen Moltmann, *The Crucified God: The Cross of Christ as the Foundation and Criticism of Christian Theology*, trans. R. A. Wilson and John Bowden (Minneapolis: Fortress Press, 1993), 243.

Moltmann here captures the perichoresis (*perichōrēsis*) of lethal abandonment and living love within the being of God. Feminists have not often turned to this complicated imagery, which seems to contradict the metaphor of a nurturing, mothering God.[100] It would grate against most people's ears to restate Moltmann's words in terms of a mother God: "The Mother who abandons [Christ] and delivers him up suffers the death of the Son." Yet it is important to see a "female face of God," to use Melissa Raphael's term, in the crucifixion event. Moltmann jars his readers with seeing suffering and death within the Godhead; I am extending this image so that we can reflect on the seemingly antimaternal aspect of a mothering God. The mothering Trinitarian God is able to forsake the Son unto death on a cross yet still extend life-giving "boundless love" to the Son, who is received back into the Trinity.[101] Even if one's image of God is governed by metaphors of maternal care, in the crucifixion there is a subtext whereby God, in an unfathomable way, is implicated in the death of the Son, making it "a rupturing, antimaternal tale."[102]

Abortion is also, in some ways, a rupturing, antimaternal tale: a pregnant woman decides not to mother her fetus any longer, causing its death. The juxtaposition I am making between the God who abandons the Son and the woman who aborts is not meant as a claim that abortion is analogous to the crucifixion or that the woman should be seen as having divine power: just the opposite. The woman who aborts does so precisely because she is not a god. In her finitude, she makes the best decision she can. The woman does not have the power to lose her child and yet have it back in a perichoresis of divine love. Therefore, the crucified God understands and has compassion on the pain of the woman who aborts. God understands the loss of a child and the infinite joy of receiving him back again—a joy denied to a woman who does not have the power to take back her aborted child again. That fetus will always only be the woman's "child-who-was not."[103]

Reading the Trinitarian event of Christ's death and resurrection through the prism of women's reproductive loss reveals not just a begetting Father of

---

100. The patristic term "perichoresis" (Greek: *perichōrēsis*) is often used to suggest the dynamic circle of communal love within the Trinity. See Jürgen Moltmann, *The Trinity and the Kingdom*, with new preface (Minneapolis: Fortress Press, 1993), 174–77. For a different discussion of God in terms of the maternal womb metaphor, see Gloria Schaab, *The Creative Suffering of the Triune God: An Evolutionary Theology* (Oxford: Oxford University Press, 2007), 166.

101. Moltmann, *The Crucified God*, 245. Moltmann does not speak of the cross in terms of reproductive loss. Moltmann calls an in-utero being a "human life" (not a person) who should be protected but concedes that pregnancy termination may be allowed in the "tragic situation" when the mother's life is endangered, a position espoused by many moderate pro-life proponents. Jürgen Moltmann, *Ethics of Hope*, trans. Margaret Kohl (Minneapolis: Fortress Press, 2012), 81, 85.

102. S. Jones, "Hope Deferred," 149.

103. Karen Houle, *Responsibility, Complexity, and Abortion: Toward a New Image of Ethical Thought* (Lanham, MD: Lexington Books, 2014), 220.

the creeds who might be seen as turning away from a woman considering or having an abortion. This Trinitarian approach allows—even compels—one to imagine a divine Mother who suffers the death of her child. If one can imagine a mothering God who forsakes the Son, grieves his death, and receives him back into her divine womb, then one can begin to comprehend—not just intellectually but more viscerally—how all reproductive events that bring death are encompassed by and gathered up into the womb of God and compassionately healed. Believing women who abort are released from the stigma for not having chosen to gestate and give birth; they can be comforted that God understands their suffering and irretrievable loss from abortion. God does not turn her face away. More than that, the incarnation vouchsafes that God has given these women the Spirit, who calls them not to cower in shame and self-recrimination but to go forward and grow in wisdom.[104]

The death of abortion is not desired by women. As Mathewes-Green famously said: "No one wants an abortion as she wants an ice-cream cone or a Porsche. She wants an abortion as an animal, caught in a trap, wants to gnaw off its own leg."[105] It is a strong image and may not capture all women's experience of abortion, but it does capture the anguish for some—perhaps especially for Christian women. For these women, especially, I offer a theological final word:

A Credo for a Woman Who Has Had an Abortion

I believe God became flesh
  in the vulnerability and uncertainty of human existence.
I believe that because Mary hesitated, vulnerable before the angel,
  the stigma of unwanted pregnancy has been assumed and healed.
I believe that because Christ passed from embryo to personhood to forsakenness unto death,
  all unborn dying is taken up into the infinite love of the dark womb of God.
I believe that when a pregnant woman chooses no longer to gestate,
  the Spirit remains beside her with "sighs too deep for words,"[106]
  and, afterward, empowers her to go on living toward the mystery of God.

---

104. Some abortion discourses invoke the notion that a fetus is in heaven with God. The Christian tradition would affirm in hope that God the creator welcomes all such creatures, whatever their bodily form (even Augustine said as much, as discussed chap. 1). On this topic, however, one may need to resort to the category that Sarah Coakley describes as apophatic belief (see chap. 3).

105. Mathewes-Green, *Real Choices*, 11.

106. Rom. 8:26.

Selected Bibliography

Aasgaard, Reidar. "Paul as a Child: Children and Childhood in the Letters of the Apostle." *Journal of Biblical Literature* 126, no. 1 (2007): 129–59.

Adams, Sarah LaChance. *Mad Mothers, Bad Mothers, and What a "Good" Mother Would Do: The Ethics of Ambivalence.* New York: Columbia University Press, 2014.

Agrawal, Priya. "Maternal Mortality and Morbidity in the United States of America." *Bulletin of the World Health Organization* 93, no. 3 (2015): 135. https://doi.org/10.2471/BLT.14.148627.

Allen, Pauline. "Sophronius and His *Synodical Letter*." In *Sophronius of Jerusalem and Seventh-Century Heresy: The Synodical Letter and Other Documents,* edited and translated by Pauline Allen, 3–64. Oxford: Oxford University Press, 2006.

Alpert, Rebecca T. "Sometimes the Law Is Cruel: The Construction of a Jewish Anti-abortion Position in the Writings of Immanuel Jakobovits." *Journal of Feminist Studies in Religion* 11, no. 2 (1995): 27–37.

Alton, Althea K. "Staying within an 'Understanding Distance': One Feminist's Scientific and Theological Reflections on Pregnancy and Abortion." In *Interdisciplinary Views on Abortion: Essays from Philosophical, Sociological, Anthropological, Political, Health and Other Perspectives,* edited by Susan A. Martinelli-Fernandez, Lori Baker-Sperry, and Heather McIlvaine-Newsad, 122–40. Jefferson, NC: McFarland, 2009.

American College of Obstetricians and Gynecologists. "Increasing Access to Abortion: Committee Opinion No. 613." *Obstetrics & Gynecology* 124, no. 5 (2014): 1060–65.

Amnesty International. *The Total Abortion Ban in Nicaragua.* London: Amnesty International, 2009. https://www.amnestyusa.org/pdfs/amr430012009en.pdf.

Anthony, Paul. "Sex, Sin and the Soul: How Galen's Philosophical Speculation Became Augustine's Theological Assumptions." *Conversations: A Graduate Student Journal of the Humanities, Social Sciences, and Theology* 1, no. 1 (2013): 1–18.

Augustine. *Confessions and Enchiridion.* Translated by Albert C. Outler. Philadelphia: Westminster Press, 1955.

Barilan, Y. Michael. "Abortion in Jewish Religious Law: Neighborly Love, *Imago Dei,* and a Hypothesis on the Medieval Blood Libel." *Review of Rabbinic Judaism* 8, nos. 1–2 (2005): 1–34.

———. "From *Imago Dei* in the Jewish-Christian Traditions to Human Dignity in Contemporary Jewish Law." *Kennedy Institute of Ethics Journal* 19, no. 3 (2009): 231–59.

———. "Her Pain Prevails and Her Judgment Respected—Abortion in Judaism." *Journal of Law and Religion* 25, no. 1 (2009): 97–186.

Barr, Julian. *Tertullian and the Unborn Child: Christian and Pagan Attitudes in Historical Perspective*. London: Routledge, 2017.

Bauerschmidt, Frederick Christian. "Being Baptized: Bodies and Abortion." In *The Blackwell Companion to Christian Ethics*, edited by Stanley Hauerwas and Samuel Wells, 250–62. Malden, MA: Blackwell, 2004.

Beattie, Tina. "Catholicism, Choice and Consciousness: A Feminist Theological Perspective on Abortion." *International Journal of Public Theology* 4, no. 1 (2010): 51–75.

———. *God's Mother, Eve's Advocate*. New York: Continuum, 2002.

———. "Review of Monica Migliorino Miller, *Sexuality and Authority in the Catholic Church*." *Theology & Sexuality* 4, no. 6 (1997): 112–13.

Bechtel, Daniel R. "Women, Choice, and Abortion: Another Look at Biblical Traditions." *Prism* 8, no. 1 (1993): 74–89.

Beckwith, Francis J. "Answering the Arguments for Abortion Rights (Part One): The Appeal to Pity." *Christian Research Journal* 13, no. 2 (1990): 1–9. http://www.equip .org/article/abortion-rights-answering-the-arguments-for-abortion-rights/.

———. "Answering the Arguments for Abortion Rights (Part Two): Arguments from Pity, Tolerance, and Ad Hominem." *Christian Research Journal* 13, no. 3 (1991): 1–10. http://www.equip.org/article/ad-hominem-attacks-the-ad-hominem -argument-for-abortion/.

———. "Brave New Bible: A Reply to the Moderate Evangelical Position on Abortion." *Journal of the Evangelical Theological Society* 33, no. 4 (1990): 489–508.

———. "A Critical Appraisal of Theological Arguments for Abortion Rights." *Bibliotheca Sacra* 148, no. 591 (1991): 337–55.

———. "The Explanatory Power of the Substance View of Persons." *Christian Bioethics* 10, no. 1 (2004): 33–54.

———. "Taking Abortion Seriously: A Philosophical Critique of the New Anti-Abortion Rhetorical Shift." *Ethics & Medicine* 17, no. 3 (2001): 155–66.

Bellinger, Charles K. *Jesus v. Abortion: They Know Not What They Do*. Eugene, OR: Cascade Books, 2016.

Benedict, Hans Urs von Balthasar, and Adrian J. Walker. *Mary: The Church at the Source*. San Francisco: Ignatius Press, 2005.

Berg, Jessica. "Owning Persons: The Application of Property Theory to Embryos and Fetuses." *Wake Forest Law Review* 40, no. 1 (2005): 159–217.

Biggs, M. A., U. D. Upadhyay, C. E. McCulloch, and D. G. Foster. "Women's Mental Health and Well-Being 5 Years after Receiving or Being Denied an Abortion: A Prospective, Longitudinal Cohort Study." *JAMA Psychiatry* 74, no. 2 (2017): 169–78.

Blackwell, Benjamin C. "You Are Filled in Him: *Theosis* and Colossians 2–3." *Journal of Theological Interpretation* 8, no. 1 (2014): 103–23.

Blanchard, Dallas A., and Terry J. Prewitt. *Religious Violence and Abortion*. Gainesville: University Press of Florida, 1993.

Blowers, Paul M., and Robert Louis Wilken. *On the Cosmic Mystery of Jesus Christ: Selected Writings from St. Maximus the Confessor*. Crestwood, NY: St. Vladimir's Seminary, 2003.

Bray, Michael. *A Time to Kill*. Portland, OR: Advocates for Life, 1994.

Brock, Rita Nakashima. "Losing Your Innocence but Not Your Hope." In *Reconstructing the Christ Symbol: Essays in Feminist Christology*, edited by Maryanne Stevens, 30–53. Mahwah, NJ: Paulist Press, 1993.

Brockopp, Jonathan E. *Islamic Ethics of Life: Abortion, War, and Euthanasia*. Columbia: University of South Carolina Press, 2003.

Brown, Joan Carlson, and Rebecca Parker. "For God So Loved the World?" In *Christianity, Patriarchy, and Abuse: A Feminist Critique*, edited by Joan Carlson Brown and Carol R. Bohn, 1–30. New York: Pilgrim Press, 1989.

Butler, Judith. *Frames of War: When Is Life Grievable?* London: Verso, 2009.

Cahill, Courtney Megan. "Abortion and Disgust." *Harvard Civil Rights-Civil Liberties Law Review* 48, no. 2 (2013): 409–56.

Cahill, Lisa Sowle. "Abortion and Argument by Analogy." *Horizons* 9, no. 2 (1982): 271–87.

———. "Abortion, Sex and Gender: The Church's Public Voice." *America* 168, no. 18 (1993): 6–11.

Calhoun, Samuel W. "Valuing Intrauterine Life." *Regent University Law Review* 8 (1997): 69–81.

Callahan, Sidney. "Abortion and the Sexual Agenda: The Case for Pro-life Feminism (1986)." In *The Ethics of Abortion: Pro-life vs. Pro-choice*, edited by Robert M. Baird and Stuart E. Rosenbaum, 167–78. Buffalo, NY: Prometheus Books, 2001.

Callan, Maeve B. "Of Vanishing Fetuses and Maidens Made-Again: Abortion, Restored Virginity, and Similar Scenarios in Medieval Irish Hagiography and Penitentials." *Journal of the History of Sexuality* 21, no. 2 (2012): 282–96.

Carol, Juniper B. "The Absolute Predestination of the Blessed Virgin Mary." *Marian Studies* 31, no. 1 (1979): 172–238.

Case-Winters, Anna. "Rethinking the Image of God." *Zygon* 39, no. 4 (2004): 813–26.

Cassidy, Keith. "A Convenient Untruth: The Pro-Choice Invention of an Era of Abortion Freedom." In *Catholicism and Historical Narrative: A Catholic Engagement with Historical Scholarship*, edited by Kevin Schmiesing, 73–101. Lanham, MD: Rowman & Littlefield, 2014.

Cavanaugh, Thomas A. "Double-Effect Reasoning, Craniotomy, and Vital Conflicts: A Case of Contemporary Catholic Casuistry." *The National Catholic Bioethics Quarterly* 11, no. 3 (2011): 443–53.

Centers for Disease Control and Prevention. "Pregnancy Mortality Surveillance System." Division of Reproductive Health, National Center for Chronic Disease Prevention and Health Promotion, 2016. https://www.cdc.gov/reproductive health/maternalinfanthealth/pregnancy-mortality-surveillance-system.htm.

Chadwick, Henry. *The Early Church*. London: Penguin Books, 1993.

"Chalcedon." In *Decrees of the Ecumenical Councils*, vol. 1, *Nicaea I to Lateran V*, edited by Norman Tanner, SJ, translated by Robert Butterworth, 75–103. Washington, DC: Georgetown University Press, 1990.

Charney, Evan. "Cytoplasmic Inheritance Redux." In *Advances in Child Development and Behavior* 44 (2013): 225–55. doi.org/10.1016/B978-0-12-397947-6.00008-8.

Chervenak, Frank A., and Laurence B. McCullough. "An Ethically Justified, Clinically Comprehensive Management Strategy for Third-Trimester Pregnancies Complicated by Fetal Anomalies." *Obstetrics and Gynecology* 75, no. 3 (1990): 311–16.

———. "An Ethically Justified Practical Approach to Offering, Recommending, Performing, and Referring for Induced Abortion and Feticide." *American Journal of Obstetrics and Gynecology* 201, no. 6 (2009): 560e1–60e6.

Cilliers, Louise. "Roman North Africa in the 4th Century AD: Its Role in the Preservation and Transmission of Medical Knowledge." *Acta Classica: Proceedings of the Classical Association of South Africa*, Supplement 2 (2008): 49–63.

Clark, Patrick M. "Reversing the Ethical Perspective: What the Allegorical Interpretation of the Good Samaritan Parable Can Still Teach Us." *Theology Today* 71, no. 3 (2014): 300–309.

Clarke, Peter D. "Canon Law." In *The Routledge History of Medieval Christianity, 1050–1500*, edited by R. N. Swanson, 77–90. London: Routledge, 2015.

Coakley, Sarah. "What Does Chalcedon Solve and What Does It Not?" In *The Incarnation: An Interdisciplinary Symposium on the Incarnation of the Son of God*, edited by Stephen T. Davis, Daniel Kendall, and Gerald O'Collins, 143–63. Oxford: Oxford University Press, 2002.

Coleman, Monica A. "Sacrifice, Surrogacy and Salvation: Womanist Reflections on Motherhood and Work." *Black Theology* 12, no. 3 (2014): 200–212.

Colker, Ruth. "Feminism, Theology, and Abortion: Toward Love, Compassion, and Wisdom." *California Law Review* 77, no. 5 (1989): 1011–75.

Collins, Nina L. "Notes on the Text of Exodus XXI 22." *Vetus Testamentum* 43, no. 3 (1993): 289–301.

Congregation for the Doctrine of the Faith. "Declaration on Procured Abortion." The Vatican, November 19, 1974. http://www.vatican.va/roman_curia/congregations /cfaith/documents/rc_con_cfaith_doc_19741118_declaration-abortion_en.html.

———. "*Donum Vitae*: Instruction on Respect for Human Life in its Origin and on the Dignity of Procreation." The Vatican, February 22, 1987. http://www.vatican .va/roman_curia/congregations/cfaith/documents/rc_con_cfaith_doc_19870222 _respect-for-human-life_en.html.

———. "Instruction *Dignitas Personae* on Certain Bioethical Questions." The Vatican, September 8, 2008. http://www.vatican.va/roman_curia/congregations/cfaith /documents/rc_con_cfaith_doc_20081208_dignitas-personae_en.html.

Cooper, Adam G. *The Body in St Maximus the Confessor: Holy Flesh, Wholly Deified.* Oxford: Oxford University Press, 2005.

Creech, Mark H. "What If Mary Had Known about Abortion?" *Christian Post*, 2005. http://www.christianpost.com/news/what-if-mary-had-known-about-abortion -86736/ (December 17, 2012).

Crisp, Oliver D. *Divinity and Humanity: The Incarnation Reconsidered.* Cambridge: Cambridge University Press, 2007.

———. *God Incarnate: Explorations in Christology.* London: T&T Clark, 2009.

———. "Is Ransom Enough?" *Journal of Analytic Theology* 3 (2015): 1–16.

———. *The Word Enfleshed: Exploring the Person and Work of Christ.* Grand Rapids: Baker Academic, 2016.

Cunningham, Mary B. "'All-Holy Infant': Byzantine and Western Views on the Conception of the Virgin Mary." *Saint Vladimir's Theological Quarterly* 50, nos. 1/2 (2006): 127.

Davis, John Jefferson. *Abortion and the Christian: What Every Believer Should Know.* Phillipsburg, NJ: Presbyterian & Reformed, 1984.

De Simone, Michael. "Birth Mother Loss: Contributing Factors to Unresolved Grief." *Clinical Social Work Journal* 24, no. 1 (1996): 65–76.

Devolder, Katrien, and John Harris. "The Ambiguity of the Embryo: Ethical Inconsistency in the Human Embryonic Stem Cell Debate." *Metaphilosophy* 38, nos. 2–3 (2007): 153–69.

Disney, Lindsey, and Larry Poston. "The Breath of Life: Christian Perspectives on Conception and Ensoulment." *Anglican Theological Review* 92, no. 2 (2010): 271–95.

Dombrowski, Daniel A., and Robert John Deltete. *A Brief, Liberal, Catholic Defense of Abortion.* Urbana: University of Illinois Press, 2000.

Douglas, Kelly Brown. "To Reflect the Image of God: A Womanist Perspective on Right Relationship." In *Living the Intersection: Womanism and Afrocentrism in Theology*, edited by Cheryl Sanders, 67–77. Minneapolis: Fortress Press, 1995.

Dunn, Geoffrey D. "Mary's Virginity *in partu* and Tertullian's Anti-Docetism in *De Carne Christi* Reconsidered." *Journal of Theological Studies* 58, no. 2 (2007): 467–84.

Dunning, Benjamin H. "Virgin Earth, Virgin Birth: Creation, Sexual Difference, and Recapitulation in Irenaeus of Lyons." *Journal of Religion* 89, no. 1 (2009): 57–88.

Eggebroten, Anne, ed. *Abortion—My Choice, God's Grace: Christian Women Tell Their Stories*. Pasadena, CA: New Paradigm Books, 1994.

Ellison, Linda. "Abortion and the Politics of God: Patient Narratives and Public Rhetoric in the American Abortion Debate." ThD diss., Harvard Divinity School, 2008.

Elsakkers, Marianne J. "Reading between the Lines: Old Germanic and Early Christian Views on Abortion." PhD diss., University of Amsterdam, 2010. https://pure.uva.nl/ws/files/1578588/76065_00_a_officiele_titelpagina.pdf.

Fergusson, David. "Humans Created according to the *Imago Dei*: An Alternative Proposal." *Zygon* 48, no. 2 (2013): 439–53.

———. "The Theology of Providence." *Theology Today* 67, no. 3 (2010): 261–78.

Frishman, Michele Kurs. "Wisconsin Act 110: When an Infant Survives an Abortion." *Wisconsin Women's Law Journal* 20, no. 1 (2005): 101–36.

Fowler, Anne, Nicki Nichols Gamble, Frances X. Hogan, Melissa Kogut, Madeline McCommish, and Barbara Thorp. "Talking with the Enemy." *Boston Globe*, January 28, 2001. https://www.feminist.com/resources/artspeech/genwom/talkingwith.html.

Gambero, Luigi. *Mary and the Fathers of the Church: The Blessed Virgin Mary in Patristic Thought*. Translated by Thomas Buffer. San Francisco: Ignatius Press, 1999.

Gandolfo, Elizabeth O'Donnell. "A Truly Human Incarnation: Recovering a Place for Nativity in Contemporary Christology." *Theology Today* 70, no. 4 (2014): 382–93.

Gaventa, Beverly Roberts. *Mary: Glimpses of the Mother of Jesus*. Minneapolis: Fortress Press, 1999.

Gaventa, Beverly Roberts, and Cynthia L. Rigby, eds. *Blessed One: Protestant Perspectives on Mary*. Louisville, KY: Westminster John Knox Press, 2002.

George, Timothy. "The Blessed Virgin Mary in Evangelical Perspective." In *Mary, Mother of God*, edited by Carl E. Braaten and Robert W. Jenson, 100–121. Grand Rapids: Wm. B. Eerdmans Publishing Co., 2004.

Gieniusz, Andrzej. "'As a Miscarriage': The Meaning and Function of the Metaphor in 1 Cor 15:1–11 in Light of Num 12:12 (LXX)." *Biblical Annals* 60, no. 1 (2013): 93–107.

Gilbert, Scott F. "When 'Personhood' Begins in the Embryo: Avoiding a Syllabus of Errors." *Birth Defects Research* 84, no. 2 (2008): 164–73.

Gonzalez, Michelle A. *Created in God's Image: An Introduction to Feminist Theological Anthropology*. Maryknoll, NY: Orbis Books, 2014.

Gorman, Michael J. *Abortion and the Early Church: Christian, Jewish and Pagan Attitudes in the Greco-Roman World*. Eugene, OR: Wipf & Stock, 1998.

———. "Scripture, History, and Authority in a Christian View of Abortion: A Response to Paul Simmons." *Christian Bioethics* 2, no. 1 (1996): 83–96.

———. "Why Is the New Testament Silent about Abortion?" *Christianity Today* 37, no. 1 (1993): 27–29.

Gottschall, Jonathan A., and Tiffani A. Gottschall. "Are Per-Incident Rape-Pregnancy Rates Higher than Per-Incident Consensual Pregnancy Rates?" *Human Nature* 14, no. 1 (2003): 1–20.

Gottstein, Alon Goshen. "The Body as Image of God in Rabbinic Literature." *Harvard Theological Review* 87, no. 2 (1994): 171–95.

Gray, Frances. "Original Habitation: Pregnant Flesh as Absolute Hospitality." In *Coming to Life: Philosophies of Pregnancy, Childbirth, and Mothering*, edited by Sarah LaChance Adams and Caroline R. Lundquist, 71–87. New York: Fordham University Press, 2013.

Green, Lisa C. "New Survey: Women Go Silently from Church to Abortion Clinic." *Care-Net*, November 23, 2015. https://www.care-net.org/churches-blog/new-survey-women-go-silently-from-church-to-abortion-clinic.

Green, Monica H. "Gendering the History of Women's Healthcare." *Gender & History* 20, no. 3 (2008): 487–518.

Grimes, David A. "The Continuing Need for Late Abortions." *JAMA* 280, no. 8 (1998): 747–50.

Gudorf, Christine E. "Encountering the Other: The Modern Papacy on Women." *Social Compass* 36, no. 3 (1989): 295–310.

Guenther, Lisa. *The Gift of the Other: Levinas and the Politics of Reproduction*. Albany: State University of New York Press, 2006.

Gushee, David P. *The Sacredness of Human Life: Why an Ancient Biblical Vision Is Key to the World's Future*. Grand Rapids: Wm. B. Eerdmans Publishing Co., 2013.

———. *Still Christian: Following Jesus out of American Evangelicalism*. Louisville, KY: Westminster John Knox Press, 2017.

Guterman, Kai. "Unintended Pregnancy as a Predictor of Child Maltreatment." *Child Abuse & Neglect* 48 (2015): 160–69.

Guttmacher Institute. "Abortion Bans in Cases of Sex or Race Selection or Genetic Anomaly." October 1, 2018. https://www.guttmacher.org/state-policy/explore/abortion-bans-cases-sex-or-race-selection-or-genetic-anomaly. Updated.

———. "Induced Abortion in the United States." January 2018. https://www.guttmacher.org/fact-sheet/induced-abortion-united-states.

———. "Later Abortion." January 20, 2017. https://www.guttmacher.org/print/evidence-you-can-use/later-abortion.

———. "State Policies in Brief: Requirements for Ultrasound." October 1, 2018. https://www.guttmacher.org/sites/default/files/pdfs/spibs/spib_RFU.pdf.

———. "Unintended Pregnancy in the United States." September 2016. https://www.guttmacher.org/fact-sheet/unintended-pregnancy-united-states.

Haldane, John, and Patrick Lee. "Aquinas on Human Ensoulment, Abortion and the Value of Life." *Philosophy* 78, no. 2 (2003): 255–78.

Hale, Rosemary. "*Imitatio Mariae*: Motherhood Motifs in Devotional Memoirs." *Mystics Quarterly* 16, no. 4 (1990): 193–203.

Hamington, Maurice. *Hail Mary? The Struggle for Ultimate Womanhood in Catholicism*. New York: Routledge, 2014.

Hanigsberg, Julia E. "Homologizing Pregnancy and Motherhood: A Consideration of Abortion." *Michigan Law Review* 94, no. 2 (1995): 371–418.

Hanson, Ann. "Roman Medicine." In *A Companion to the Roman Empire*, edited by David S. Potter, 492–523. Malden, MA: Blackwell, 2006.

Harris, Mark. "When Jesus Lost His Soul: Fourth-Century Christology and Modern Neuroscience." *Scottish Journal of Theology* 70, no. 1 (2017): 74–92.

Harrison, Beverly Wildung. *Our Right to Choose: Toward a New Ethic of Abortion*. Boston: Beacon Press, 1983.

Hauerwas, Stanley. "Abortion Theologically Understood (1991)." In *The Hauerwas Reader*, edited by John Berkman and Michael Cartwright, 603–22. Durham, NC: Duke University Press, 2001.

Hays, Richard B. *The Moral Vision of the New Testament: Community, Cross, New Creation; A Contemporary Introduction to New Testament Ethics*. San Francisco: HarperSanFrancisco, 1996.

Healy, Cletus, SJ. "Stations of the Cross for Victims of Abortion." *Priests for Life*. n.d. http://www.priestsforlife.org/prayers/stations-victims-of-abortion.htm.

Heaney, Stephen J. "Aquinas and the Presence of the Human Rational Soul in the Early Embryo." *The Thomist: A Speculative Quarterly Review* 56, no. 1 (1992): 19–48.

Hedayat, Kamyar M., P. Shooshtarizadeh, and Mohsin Raza. "Therapeutic Abortion in Islam: Contemporary Views of Muslim Shiite Scholars and Effect of Recent Iranian Legislation." *Journal of Medical Ethics* 32, no. 11 (2006): 652–57.

Heyne, Thomas F. "Tertullian and Obstetrics." *Studia Patristica* 53 (2013): 419–33.

Himma, Kenneth Einar. "No Harm, No Foul: Abortion and the Implications of Fetal Innocence." *Faith and Philosophy* 19, no. 2 (2002): 172–94.

Hollander, Harm, and Gijsbert E. van der Hout. "The Apostle Paul Calling Himself an Abortion: 1 Cor. 15:8 within the Context of 1 Cor. 15:8–10." *Novum Testamentum* 38, no. 3 (1996): 224–36.

Houle, Karen. "Abortion as the Work of Mourning." *Symposium* 11, no. 1 (2007): 141–66.

———. *Responsibility, Complexity, and Abortion: Toward a New Image of Ethical Thought*. Lanham, MD: Lexington Books, 2013.

Howes, Laura L. "On the Birth of Margery Kempe's Last Child." *Modern Philology* 90, no. 2 (1992): 220–25.

Huby, Pamela M. "Soul, Life, Sense, Intellect: Some Thirteenth-Century Problems." In *The Human Embryo: Aristotle and the Arabic and European Traditions*, edited by G. R. Dunstan, 113–22. Exeter, Devon, UK: University of Exeter Press, 1990.

Hurst, Jane. *The History of Abortion in the Catholic Church: The Untold Story*. Washington, DC: Catholics for a Free Choice, 1983.

Irshai, Ronit. "Response to Alan Jotkowitz." *Nashim: A Journal of Jewish Women's Studies & Gender Issues* 21, no. 1 (2011): 110–13.

Jeal, Roy R., and Linda A. West. "Rolling Away the Stone: Post-Abortion Women in the Christian Community." *Journal of Pastoral Care & Counseling* 57, no. 1 (2003): 53–64.

Jefferis, Jennifer L. *Armed for Life: The Army of God and Anti-Abortion Terror in the United States*. Santa Barbara, CA: Praeger, 2011.

Jerman, Jenna, Rachel K. Jones, and Tsuyoshi Onda. "Characteristics of U.S. Abortion Patients in 2014 and Changes since 2008." Guttmacher Institute. May 2016. https://www.guttmacher.org/sites/default/files/report_pdf/characteristics-us-abortion-patients-2014.pdf.

John Paul II, Pope. *Evangelium vitae*. The Vatican, March 25, 1995. http://w2.vatican.va/content/john-paul-ii/en/encyclicals/documents/hf_jp-ii_enc_25031995_evangelium-vitae.html.

———. *Mulieris dignitatem*. The Vatican, August 15, 1988. http://w2.vatican.va/content/john-paul-ii/en/apost_letters/1988/documents/hf_jp-ii_apl_19880815_mulieris-dignitatem.html.

Johnson, Elizabeth A. *She Who Is: The Mystery of God in Feminist Theological Discourse*. New York: Crossroad, 1995.

———. *Truly Our Sister: A Theology of Mary in the Communion of Saints*. New York: Continuum, 2004.

Johnson, Mark. "Delayed Hominization: Reflections on Some Recent Catholic Claims for Delayed Hominization." *Theological Studies* 56, no. 4 (1995): 743–63.

Jones, David Albert. *The Soul of the Embryo: An Enquiry into the Status of the Human Embryo in the Christian Tradition.* London: Continuum, 2004.

Jones, Rachel K., Lori F. Frohwirth, and Ann M. Moore. "'I Would Want to Give My Child, Like, Everything in the World': How Issues of Motherhood Influence Women Who have Abortions." *Journal of Family Issues* 29, no. 1 (2008): 79–99.

Jones, Rachel K., and Megan L. Kavanaugh. "Changes in Abortion Rates between 2000 and 2008 and Lifetime Incidence of Abortion." *Obstetrics & Gynecology* 117, no. 6 (2011): 1358–66.

Jones, Serene. "Hope Deferred: Theological Reflections on Reproductive Loss." In *Trauma and Grace: Theology in a Ruptured World*, edited by Serene Jones, 127–50. Louisville, KY: Westminster John Knox Press, 2009.

Jotkowitz, Alan. "Abortion and Maternal Need: A Response to Ronit Irshai." *Nashim: A Journal of Jewish Women's Studies & Gender Issues* 21 (2011): 97–109.

Jung, Patricia Beattie. "Abortion and Organ Donation: Christian Reflections on Bodily Life Support." *Journal of Religious Ethics* 16, no. 2 (1988): 273–305.

Kaczor, Christopher. *The Ethics of Abortion: Women's Rights, Human Life, and the Question of Justice.* New York: Routledge, 2014.

———. "The Ethics of Ectopic Pregnancy: A Critical Reconsideration of Salpingostomy and Methotrexate." *The Linacre Quarterly* 76, no. 3 (2009): 265–82.

———. "In Defense of Live Action." *Public Discourse*, February 11, 2011. http://www.thepublicdiscourse.com/2011/02/2538/.

Kamitsuka, Margaret D. "Feminist Scholarship and Its Relevance for Political Engagement: The Test Case of Abortion in the U.S." *Religion and Gender* 1, no. 1 (2011): 18–43.

———. *Feminist Theology and the Challenge of Difference.* Oxford: Oxford University Press, 2007.

Kaye, Julia, Brigitte Amiri, Louise Melling, and Jennifer Dalven. "Health Care Denied: Patients and Physicians Speak Out about Catholic Hospitals and the Threat to Women's Health and Lives." American Civil Liberties Union, 2016. https://www.aclu.org/sites/default/files/field_document/healthcaredenied.pdf.

Kelsey, David H. *Eccentric Existence: A Theological Anthropology.* 2 vols. Louisville, KY: Westminster John Knox Press, 2009.

Kimport, Katrina, J. Parker Dockray, and Shelly Dodson. "What Women Seek from a Pregnancy Resource Center." *Contraception* 94, no. 2 (2016): 168–72.

Kitzler, Petr. "Tertullian and Ancient Embryology in *De carne Christi* 4,1 and 19,3–4." *Zeitschrift für Antikes Christentum / Journal of Ancient Christianity* 18, no. 2 (2014): 204–9.

Kohn, Ingrid, Perry-Lynn Moffitt, and Isabelle A. Wilkins. *A Silent Sorrow: Pregnancy Loss; Guidance and Support for You and Your Family.* 2nd ed. New York: Routledge, 2013.

Kurz, William S. "Genesis and Abortion: An Exegetical Test of a Biblical Warrant in Ethics." *Theological Studies* 47, no. 4 (1986): 668–80.

Ladner, Gerhart B. "The Philosophical Anthropology of Saint Gregory of Nyssa." *Dumbarton Oaks Papers* 12 (1958): 59–94.

Landry, David T. "Narrative Logic in the Annunciation to Mary (Luke 1:26–38)." *Journal of Biblical Literature* 114, no. 1 (1995): 65–79.

Layne, Linda L. *Motherhood Lost: A Feminist Account of Pregnancy Loss in America.* New York: Routledge, 2003.

Leath, Jennifer. "(Out of) Places, Please! Demystifying Opposition to Procreative Choice in Afro-Diasporic Communities in the United States." *Journal of Feminist Studies in Religion* 30, no. 1 (2014): 156–65.

Lee, Patrick. *Abortion & Unborn Human Life.* 2nd ed. Washington, DC: Catholic University of America Press, 2010.

———. "A Christian Philosopher's View of Recent Directions in the Abortion Debate." *Christian Bioethics* 10, no. 1 (2004): 7–31.

———. "The Pro-Life Argument from Substantial Identity: A Defence." *Bioethics* 18, no. 3 (2004): 249–63.

Lee, Susan J., Henry J. Peter Ralston, Eleanor A. Drey, John Colin Partridge, and Mark A. Rosen. "Fetal Pain: A Systematic Multidisciplinary Review of the Evidence." *JAMA* 294, no. 8 (2005): 947–54.

Leftow, Brian. "A Timeless God Incarnate." In *The Incarnation: An Interdisciplinary Symposium on the Incarnation of the Son of God,* edited by Stephen T. Davis, Daniel Kendall, and Gerald O'Collins, 273–99. Oxford: Oxford University Press, 2002.

Lerner, Berel Dov. "Samaritans, Jews and Philosophers." *Expository Times* 113, no. 5 (2002): 152–56.

Lillis, Julia Kelto. "Paradox *in Partu*: Verifying Virginity in the *Protevangelium of James*." *Journal of Early Christian Studies* 24, no. 1 (2016): 1–28.

Little, Margaret Olivia. "Abortion and the Margins of Personhood." *Rutgers Law Journal* 39, no. 2 (2007): 331–48.

———. "Abortion, Intimacy, and the Duty to Gestate." *Ethical Theory and Moral Practice* 2, no. 3 (1999): 295–312.

Logan, Janette. "Birth Mothers and Their Mental Health: Uncharted Territory." *British Journal of Social Work* 26, no. 5 (1996): 609–25.

Longenecker, Dwight, and David Gustafson. *Mary: A Catholic-Evangelical Debate.* Grand Rapids: Brazos Press, 2003.

Ludlow, Jeannie. "Sometimes, It's a Child and a Choice: Toward an Embodied Abortion Praxis." *NWSA Journal* 20, no. 1 (2008): 26–50.

———. "The Things We Cannot Say: Witnessing the Trauma-tization of Abortion in the United States." *Women's Studies Quarterly* 36, nos. 1/2 (2008): 28–41.

Lugosi, Charles I. "When Abortion Was a Crime: A Historical Perspective." *University of Detroit Mercy Law Review* 83, no. 2 (2006): 51–69.

Lymer, Jane. *The Phenomenology of Gravidity: Reframing Pregnancy and the Maternal through Merleau-Ponty, Levinas and Derrida.* London: Rowman & Littlefield, 2016.

MacKellar, Calum. *The Image of God, Personhood and the Embryo.* London: SCM Press, 2017.

Mackenzie, Catriona. "Abortion and Embodiment." *Australasian Journal of Philosophy* 70, no. 2 (1992): 136–55.

Maguire, Daniel C. "Abortion: A Question of Catholic Honesty." *Christian Century* 100, no. 26 (1983): 803–7.

Maguire, Marjorie Reiley. "Can Technology Solve the Abortion Dilemma?" *Christian Century* 93, no. 34 (1976): 918–19.

———. "Personhood, Covenant, and Abortion." *American Journal of Theology & Philosophy* 6, no. 1 (1985): 28–46.

Mahkorn, Sandra. "Life Matters: Pregnancy from Rape." U.S. Conference of Catholic Bishops, 2013. http://www.usccb.org/about/pro-life-activities/respect-life-program/2013/upload/2013-Life-Matters-Pregnancy-From-Rape-secured.pdf.

Mahowald, Mary. "As If There Were Fetuses without Women: A Remedial Essay." In *Reproduction, Ethics, and the Law: Feminist Perspectives*, edited by Joan C. Callahan, 199–218. Bloomington: Indiana University Press, 1995.

Manninen, Bertha Alvarez. "The Value of Choice and the Choice to Value: Expanding the Discussion about Fetal Life within Prochoice Advocacy." *Hypatia* 28, no. 3 (2013): 663–83.

Mathewes-Green, Frederica. *Real Choices: Offering Practical Life-Affirming Alternatives to Abortion*. Sisters, OR: Multnomah Books, 1994.

McAvoy, Liz Herbert. *Authority and the Female Body in the Writings of Julian of Norwich and Margery Kempe*. Cambridge: D. S. Brewer, 2004.

———. "Spiritual Virgin to Virgin Mother: The Confessions of Margery Kempe." *Parergon* 17, no. 1 (1999): 9–44.

McDonagh, Eileen. "Adding Consent to Choice in the Abortion Debate." *Society* 42, no. 5 (2005): 18–26.

———. *Breaking the Abortion Deadlock: From Choice to Consent*. New York: Oxford University Press, 1996.

McDonnell, Kilian. "Feminist Mariologies: Heteronomy/Subordination and the Scandal of Christology." *Theological Studies* 66, no. 3 (2005): 527–67.

Meyer, John R. "Embryonic Personhood, Human Nature, and Rational Ensoulment." *Heythrop Journal* 47, no. 2 (2006): 206–25.

———. "The Ontological Status of Pre-Implantation Embryos." In *Contemporary Controversies in Catholic Bioethics*, edited by Jason T. Eberl, 17–34. Cham, Switzerland: Springer, 2017.

Middleton, J. Richard. *The Liberating Image: The* Imago Dei *in Genesis 1*. Grand Rapids: Brazos Press, 2005.

Miller, Monica Migliorino. *Sexuality and Authority in the Catholic Church*. Scranton: University of Scranton Press, 1995.

Miller, Patricia. *Good Catholics: The Battle over Abortion in the Catholic Church*. Berkeley: University of California Press, 2014.

Miller-McLemore, Bonnie. "'Pondering All These Things': Mary and Motherhood." In *Blessed One: Protestant Perspectives on Mary*, edited by Beverly Roberts Gaventa and Cynthia L. Rigby, 97–114. Louisville, KY: Westminster John Knox Press, 2002.

Mistry, Zubin. *Abortion in the Early Middle Ages, C. 500–900*. Woodbridge, Suffolk: York Medieval, 2015.

Mitchell, Matthew W. "Reexamining the 'Aborted Apostle': An Exploration of Paul's Self-Description in 1 Corinthians 15.8." *Journal for the Study of the New Testament* 25, no. 4 (2003): 469–85.

Moloney, Anastasia. "Abortion Ban Leads to More Maternal Deaths in Nicaragua." *The Lancet* 374, no. 9691 (2009): 677. https://www.thelancet.com/journals/lancet/article/PIIS0140-6736(09)61545-2/fulltext.

Moltmann, Jürgen. *The Crucified God: The Cross of Christ as the Foundation and Criticism of Christian Theology*. Translated by R. A. Wilson and John Bowden. Minneapolis: Fortress Press, 1993.

———. *Ethics of Hope*. Translated by Margaret Kohl. Minneapolis: Fortress Press, 2012.

Mongoven, A. "Sharing Our Body and Blood: Organ Donation and Feminist Critiques of Sacrifice." *Journal of Medicine and Philosophy* 28, no. 1 (2003): 89–114.

Mordhorst-Mayer, Melanie, Nitzan Rimon-Zarfaty, and Mark Schweda. "'Perspectivism' in the Halakhic Debate on Abortion between Moshe Feinstein and Eliezer Waldenberg—Relations between Jewish Medical Ethics and Socio-Cultural

Contexts." *Women in Judaism* 10, no. 2 (2013): 1–35. https://wjudaism.library
.utoronto.ca/index.php/wjudaism/article/view/20905.

Moreland, J. P., and Scott B. Rae. *Body & Soul: Human Nature & the Crisis in Ethics.*
Downers Grove, IL: InterVarsity Press, 2000.

Morgan, Lynn M. "Fetal Relationality in Feminist Philosophy: An Anthropological
Critique." *Hypatia* 11, no. 3 (1996): 47–70.

———. "The Potentiality Principle from Aristotle to Abortion." *Current Anthropology*
54, no. 57 (2013): S15–S25.

Muehlenberg, Bill. "Abortion and the Good Samaritan." *Culture Watch*, August 6, 2015.
https://billmuehlenberg.com/2015/08/06/abortion-and-the-good-samaritan/.

———. "Abortion, Prosecution, Ethics and the Law." *Culture Watch*, May 19, 2016.
https://billmuehlenberg.com/2016/05/19/abortion-prosecution-ethics-law/.

Müller, Wolfgang. *The Criminalization of Abortion in the West: Its Origins in Medieval
Law.* Ithaca: Cornell University Press, 2012.

Mumford, James. *Ethics at the Beginning of Life: A Phenomenological Critique.* Oxford:
Oxford University Press, 2013.

Murphy, Nancey. "Nonreductive Physicalism." In *In Search of the Soul: Perspectives on
the Mind-Body Problem*, edited by Joel B. Green, 115–52. Downers Grove, IL:
InterVarsity Press, 2005.

Musallam, Basim. "The Human Embryo in Arabic Scientific and Religious Thought."
In *The Human Embryo, Aristotle and the Arabic and European Traditions*, edited by
G. R. Dunstan, 32–46. Exeter, UK: University of Exeter Press, 1990.

Nelson, Ted. "Traducianism? Creationism? What Has an Ancient Debate to Do with
the Modern Debate over Abortion?" *Denison Journal of Religion* 13, no. 1 (2014):
1–15.

"Nestorius of Constantinople." In *The Westminster Handbook to Patristic Theology*,
edited by John Anthony McGuckin, 237–38. Louisville, KY: Westminster John
Knox Press, 2004.

Neuger, Christie Cozad. "The Challenge of Abortion." In *Pastoral Care and Social
Conflict*, edited by Pamela D. Couture and Rodney J. Hunter, 125–40. Nashville: Abingdon Press, 1995.

Newman, Barbara. *From Virile Woman to WomanChrist: Studies in Medieval Religion and
Literature.* Philadelphia: University of Pennsylvania Press, 1995.

Nicholson, Susan T. *Abortion and the Roman Catholic Church.* Knoxville, TN: Religious
Ethics, 1978.

Nixon, Laura. "The Right to (Trans) Parent: A Reproductive Justice Approach to
Reproductive Rights, Fertility, and Family-Building Issues Facing Transgender
People." *William and Mary Journal of Women and the Law* 20 (2013): 73–103.

Noddings, Nel. *Caring: A Relational Approach to Ethics and Moral Education.* 2nd ed.
Berkeley: University of California Press, 2013.

———. *Starting at Home: Caring and Social Policy.* Berkeley: University of California
Press, 2002.

———. *Women and Evil.* Berkeley: University of California Press, 1989.

Noonan, John T., Jr. "Abortion and the Catholic Church: A Summary History." *Natural Law Forum* 12 (1967): 85–131.

———. "An Almost Absolute Value in History." In *The Morality of Abortion: Legal and
Historical Perspectives*, edited by John T. Noonan Jr., 1–59. Cambridge, MA:
Harvard University Press, 1970.

Norris, Richard A., Jr. "Chalcedon Revisited: A Historical and Theological Reflection."
In *New Perspectives in Historical Theology: Essays in Memory of John Meyendorff,*

edited by Bradley Nassif, 140–58. Grand Rapids: Wm. B. Eerdmans Publishing Co., 1996.

————, ed. and trans. *The Christological Controversy*. Philadelphia: Fortress Press, 1980.

Novello, Henry L. *Death as Transformation: A Contemporary Theology of Death*. Farnham, Surrey, UK: Ashgate, 2011.

————. "Integral Salvation in the Risen Christ: The New 'Emergent Whole.'" *Pacifica* 17, no. 1 (2004): 34–54.

Nutton, Vivian. "The Fatal Embrace: Galen and the History of Ancient Medicine." *Science in Context* 18, no. 1 (2005): 111–21.

Oakes, Edward T. "Predestination and Mary's Immaculate Conception: An Evangelically Catholic Interpretation." *Pro Ecclesia* 21, no. 3 (2012): 281–98.

O'Connor, June. "Ritual Recognition of Abortion: Japanese Buddhist Practices and U.S. Jewish and Christian Proposals." In *Embodiment, Morality, and Medicine*, edited by Lisa S. Cahill and Margaret Farley, 93–111. Dordrecht: Kluwer Academic Publishers, 1995.

Olasky, Marvin N. *Abortion Rites: A History of Abortion in America*. Wheaton, IL: Crossway Books, 1992.

Olson, Roger E. "Deification in Contemporary Theology." *Theology Today* 64, no. 2 (2007): 186–200.

O'Mathuna, Donal. "The Bible and Abortion: What of the 'Image of God'?" In *Bioethics and the Future of Medicine*, edited by John Frederic Kilner, David L. Schiedermayer, and Nigel M. De S. Cameron, 199–211. Grand Rapids: Wm. B. Eerdmans Publishing Co., 1995.

Ott, Kate M. "From Politics to Theology: Responding to Roman Catholic Ecclesial Control of Reproductive Ethics." *Journal of Feminist Studies in Religion* 30, no. 1 (2014): 138–47.

Otten, Willemien. "Christ's Birth of a Virgin Who Became a Wife: Flesh and Speech in Tertullian's *De carne Christi*." *Vigiliae Christianae* 51, no. 3 (1997): 247–60.

Outka, Gene. "The Ethics of Love and the Problem of Abortion." In *Church, Society, and the Christian Common Good: Essays in Conversation with Philip Turner*, edited by Ephraim Radner, 146–67. Eugene, OR: Wipf & Stock, 2017.

Parsons, Kate. "Feminist Reflections on Miscarriage, in Light of Abortion." *International Journal of Feminist Approaches to Bioethics* 3, no. 1 (2010): 1–22.

Pasnau, Robert. *Thomas Aquinas on Human Nature: A Philosophical Study of* Summa Theologiae, *1a 75–89*. Cambridge: Cambridge University Press, 2002.

Pennington, Keith. "Corpus iuris canonici." In *The Oxford Dictionary of the Middle Ages*, edited by Robert E. Bjork. Oxford: Oxford University Press online, 2010. http://www.oxfordreference.com/view/10.1093/acref/9780198662624.001.0001/acref-9780198662624-e-1567.

Perez-Gil, Maria Mar. "Mary and the Carnal Maternal Genealogy: Towards a Mariology of the Body." *Literature and Theology* 25, no. 3 (2011): 297–311.

Petchesky, Rosalind Pollack. "Fetal Images: The Power of Visual Culture in the Politics of Reproduction." *Feminist Studies* 13, no. 2 (1987): 292.

Peters, Rebecca Todd. *Trust Women: A Progressive Christian Argument for Reproductive Justice*. Boston: Beacon Press, 2018.

Pew Research Center. "Worldwide Abortion Policies." October 5, 2015. http://www.pewresearch.org/interactives/global-abortion/.

Porter, Jean. "Individuality, Personal Identity, and the Moral Status of the Preembryo: A Response to Mark Johnson." *Theological Studies* 56, no. 4 (1995): 763–70.

Price, Kimala. "What Is Reproductive Justice? How Women of Color Activists Are Redefining the Pro-Choice Paradigm." *Meridians: Feminism, Race, Transnationalism* 10, no. 2 (2010): 42–65.

Price, Richard, and Michael Gaddis, trans. and eds. *The Acts of the Council of Chalcedon.* Vol. 1. Liverpool: Liverpool University Press, 2005.

Prusak, Bernard G. "Double Effect, All Over Again: The Case of Sister Margaret McBride." *Theoretical Medicine and Bioethics* 32, no. 4 (2011): 271–83.

Purvis, Sally B. "Mothers, Neighbors and Strangers: Another Look at Agape." *Journal of Feminist Studies in Religion* 7, no. 1 (1991): 19–34.

Rader, Michael N. "The 'Good Samaritan' in Jewish Law." *Journal of Legal Medicine* 22, no. 3 (2001): 375–99.

Rankin, John. "The Corporeal Reality of *Nepeš* and the Status of the Unborn." *Journal of the Evangelical Theological Society* 31, no. 2 (1988): 153–60.

Raphael, Melissa. *The Female Face of God in Auschwitz: A Jewish Feminist Theology of the Holocaust.* London: Routledge, 2003.

Raz, Yosefa. "Jeremiah 'Before the Womb': On Fathers, Sons, and the Telos of Redaction in Jeremiah 1." In *Prophecy and Power: Jeremiah in Feminist and Postcolonial Perspective*, edited by Christl M. Maier and Carolyn J. Sharp, 86–100. London: Bloomsbury, 2014.

Reader, Soran. "Abortion, Killing, and Maternal Moral Authority." *Hypatia* 23, no. 1 (2008): 132–49.

Reagan, Leslie J. *When Abortion Was a Crime: Women, Medicine, and Law in the United States, 1867–1973.* Berkeley: University of California Press, 1997.

Reardon, David C. "A Defense of the Neglected Rhetorical Strategy (NRS)." *Ethics & Medicine: A Christian Perspective on Issues in Bioethics* 18, no. 2 (2002): 23–32.

———. "Women Who Abort: Their Reflections on Abortion." *Post-Abortion Review* 4, no. 1 (1996). http://afterabortion.org/1996/women-who-abort-their-reflections -on-abortion/.

Reid, Shelley Annette. "The First Dispensation of Christ Is Medicinal: Augustine and Roman Medical Culture." PhD diss., University of British Columbia, 2008.

Riches, Aaron. "Deconstructing the Linearity of Grace: The Risk and Reflexive Paradox of Mary's Immaculate *Fiat*." *International Journal of Systematic Theology* 10, no. 2 (2008): 179–94.

Robinson, Michael. "Divine Image, Human Dignity and Human Potentiality." *Perspectives in Religious Studies* 41, no. 2 (2014): 65–77.

Ross, Susan A. "Joys and Hopes, Griefs and Anxieties: Catholic Women since Vatican II." *New Theology Review* 25, no. 2 (2013): 30–38.

Roukema, Riemer. "The Good Samaritan in Ancient Christianity." *Vigiliae Christianae* 58, no. 1 (2004): 56–97.

Ruether, Rosemary Radford. *Sexism and God-Talk: Toward a Feminist Theology.* With a new introduction. Boston: Beacon Press, 1993.

———. *Women and Redemption: A Theological History.* Minneapolis: Fortress Press, 2011.

———. "Women, Reproductive Rights and the Catholic Church." *Feminist Theology* 16, no. 2 (2008): 184–93.

Rzepka, Jane Ranney. "Counseling the Abortion Patient: A Pastoral Perspective." *Pastoral Psychology* 28, no. 3 (1980): 168–80.

Salih, Sarah. *Versions of Virginity in Late Medieval England.* Woodbridge, Suffolk, UK: D. S. Brewer, 2001.

Saward, John. *Redeemer in the Womb: Jesus Living in Mary*. San Francisco: Ignatius Press, 1993.

Sawyer, Deborah. "Hidden Subjects: Rereading Eve and Mary." *Theology & Sexuality* 14, no. 3 (2008): 305–20.

Schaab, Gloria L. *The Creative Suffering of the Triune God: An Evolutionary Theology*. New York: Oxford University Press, 2007.

Schiff, Daniel. *Abortion in Judaism*. Cambridge: Cambridge University Press, 2002.

Schlesinger, Eugene R. "From Rights to Rites: A Eucharistic Reframing of the Abortion Debate." *Anglican Theological Review* 94, no. 1 (2012): 37–57.

Schlesinger, Kira. *Pro-Choice and Christian: Reconciling Faith, Politics, and Justice*. Louisville, KY: Westminster John Knox Press, 2017.

Schlossberg, Terry. "Abortion Matters: Abortion as a Challenge to Christian Orthodoxy." *Touchstone* 8, no. 2 (1995): 30–32.

Shannon, Thomas A., and Allan B. Wolter. "Reflections on the Moral Status of the Pre-Embryo." *Theological Studies* 51, no. 4 (1990): 603–26.

Shanzer, Danuta. "Voices and Bodies: The Afterlife of the Unborn." *Numen* 56, nos. 2–3 (2009): 326–65.

Shults, F. LeRon. *Christology and Science*. Hampshire, UK: Ashgate, 2008.

———. *Reforming Theological Anthropology: After the Philosophical Turn to Relationality*. Grand Rapids: Wm. B. Eerdmans Publishing Co., 2003.

Sider, Ronald J. *Completely Pro-Life: Building a Consistent Stance*. Downers Grove, IL: InterVarsity Press, 1989.

Simmons, Paul D. "Biblical Authority and the Not-So Strange Silence of Scripture about Abortion." *Christian Bioethics* 2, no. 1 (1996): 66–82.

Slusser, Michael. "The Issues in the Definition of the Council of Chalcedon." *Toronto Journal of Theology* 6, no. 1 (1990): 63–69.

Smith, Andrea. "Beyond Pro-Choice versus Pro-Life: Women of Color and Reproductive Justice." *NWSA Journal* 17, no. 1 (2005): 119–40.

Sommers, Mary Catherine. "Living Together: Burdensome Pregnancy and the Hospitable Self." In *Abortion: A New Generation of Catholic Responses*, edited by Stephen J. Heaney, 243–61. Braintree, MA: Pope John Center, 1992.

Staley, Lynn, trans. *The Book of Margery Kempe: A New Translation, Contexts, Criticism*. New York: Norton, 2001.

Steffen, Lloyd H. *Life/Choice: The Theory of Just Abortion*. Cleveland: Pilgrim Press, 1994.

Stevenson-Moessner, Jeanne. "From Samaritan to Samaritan: Journey Mercies." In *Through the Eyes of Women: Insights for Pastoral Care*, edited by Jeanne Stevenson Moessner, 322–32. Minneapolis: Fortress Press, 1996.

———. "The Road to Perfection: An Interpretation of Suffering in Hebrews." *Interpretation: A Journal of Bible and Theology* 57, no. 3 (2003): 280–90.

Sullivan, Francis A. "The Development of Doctrine about Infants Who Die Unbaptized." *Theological Studies* 72, no. 1 (2011): 3–14.

———. "The Doctrinal Weight of *Evangelium vitae*." *Theological Studies* 56, no. 3 (1995): 560–65.

Tanner, Kathryn. *Christ the Key*. Cambridge: Cambridge University Press, 2010.

———. *Jesus, Humanity and the Trinity: A Brief Systematic Theology*. Minneapolis: Fortress Press, 2001.

Tasioulas, Jacqueline. "'Heaven and Earth in Little Space': The Foetal Existence of Christ in Medieval Literature and Thought." *Medium Aevum* 76, no. 1 (2007): 24–48.

Tauer, Carol A. "Abortion: Embodiment and Prenatal Development." In *Embodiment, Morality, and Medicine*, edited by Lisa S. Cahill and Margaret Farley, 75–92. Dordrecht: Kluwer Academic Publishers, 1995.

———. "Personhood and Human Embryos and Fetuses." *Journal of Medicine and Philosophy* 10, no. 3 (1985): 253–66.

———. "The Tradition of Probabilism and the Moral Status of the Early Embryo." *Theological Studies* 45, no. 1 (1984): 3–33.

Temkin, Owsei. *Hippocrates in a World of Pagans and Christians*. Baltimore: Johns Hopkins University Press, 1991.

———, trans. *Soranus' Gynecology*. Baltimore: Johns Hopkins University Press, 1991.

Tertullian. "A Treatise on the Soul." In *Ante-Nicene Fathers*. Translated by D. D. Holmes, edited by Alexander Roberts and James Donaldson. Vol. 3. New York: Scribner's, 1899.

Thakkilapati, Sri Devi. "Better Mothers, Good Daughters and Blessed Women: Gender Performance in the Context of Abortion." PhD diss., Ohio State University, 2009.

Thomas Aquinas. *Summa Theologica*. Translated by the Fathers of the Eastern Dominican Province. New York: Benzinger, 1947.

Thompson, Janice Allison. "Making Room for the Other: Maternal Mourning and Eschatological Hope." *Modern Theology* 27, no. 3 (2011): 395–413.

Thomson, Judith Jarvis. "A Defense of Abortion." *Philosophy & Public Affairs* 1, no. 1 (1971): 47–66.

Tomson, Peter J. *Paul and the Jewish Law: Halakha in the Letters of the Apostle to the Gentiles*. Assen, Netherlands: Van Gorcum, 1990.

Torrance, T. F. *The Soul and Person of the Unborn Child*. Edinburgh: Handsel Press, 1999.

Toulouse, Mark G. "Perspectives on Abortion in the Christian Community from the 1950s to the Early 1990s." *Encounter* 62, no. 4 (2001): 327–403.

Townes, Emilie M. "Ethics as an Art of Doing the Work Our Souls Must Have." In *Womanist Theological Ethics: A Reader*, edited by Katie Geneva Cannon, Emilie M. Townes, and Angela D. Sims, 35–50. Louisville, KY: Westminster John Knox, 2011.

Traina, Cristina L. H. "Papal Ideals, Marital Realities: One View from the Ground." In *Sexual Diversity and Catholicism: Toward the Development of Moral Theology*, edited by Patricia Beattie Jung with Joseph Andrew Coray, 269–88. Collegeville, MN: Liturgical Press, 2001.

Trewhella, Matthew. "Should Women Be Punished for Murdering Their Own Son or Daughter by Abortion?" *Army of God*. n.d. https://www.armyofgod.com/MatthewTrewhellaWomenPunishedAbortion.html.

Tu, Stephen. *Pro-Life Pulpit: Preaching and the Challenge of Abortion*. Eugene, OR: Wipf & Stock, 2011.

Turner, Max. "Approaching Personhood in the New Testament, with Special Reference to Ephesians." *Evangelical Quarterly* 77, no. 3 (July 2005): 211–34.

U.S. Department of Health and Human Services. "Voluntary Relinquishment for Adoption." Child Welfare Information Gateway, March 2005. https://www.childwelfare.gov/pubPDFs/s_place.pdf.

Van Huyssteen, Wentzel. "Fallen Angels or Rising Beasts? Theological Perspectives on Human Uniqueness." *Theology and Science* 1, no. 2 (2003): 161–78.

Vorster, Nico. "The Value of Human Life." *The Ecumenical Review* 59, nos. 2–3 (2007): 363–83.

Vuola, Elina. "Seriously Harmful for Your Health? Religion, Feminism and Sexuality in Latin America." *Liberation Theology and Sexuality*, edited by Marcella Althaus-Reid, 137–62. Aldershot, UK: Ashgate, 2006.

Wade, Francis C. "Potentiality in the Abortion Discussion." *The Review of Metaphysics* 29, no. 2 (1975): 239–55.

Walker-Barnes, Chanequa. *Too Heavy a Yoke: Black Women and the Burden of Strength*. Eugene, OR: Cascade Books, 2014.

Waltke, Bruce K. "Reflections from the Old Testament on Abortion." *Journal of the Evangelical Theological Society* 19, no. 1 (1976): 3–13.

Ward, Bernadette Waterman. "Abortion as a Sacrament: Mimetic Desire and Sacrifice in Sexual Politics." *Contagion: Journal of Violence, Mimesis, and Culture* 7, no. 1 (2000): 18–35.

Warren, Mary Anne. "On the Moral and Legal Status of Abortion." *The Monist* 57, no. 4 (1973): 43–61.

Webb, Stephen H. "Response to L. Serene Jones, Hope Deferred." *Modern Theology* 17, no. 4 (2001): 509–11.

Welz, Claudia. "Imago Dei: References to the Invisible." *Studia Theologica—Nordic Journal of Theology* 65, no. 1 (2011): 74–91.

Wennberg, Robert N. *Life in the Balance: Exploring the Abortion Controversy*. Grand Rapids: Wm. B. Eerdmans Publishing Co., 1985.

West, Fr. Peter. "A Reflection on Mary and the Birth of Christ." *Priests for Life*. n.d. http://www.priestsforlife.org/preaching/frpeteradvent.htm.

West, Robin L. "Liberalism and Abortion." *Georgetown University Law Journal* 87 (1999): 2117–47.

"What Does the Bible Say about Abortion?" *American Right to Life*. n.d. http://americanrtl.org/what-does-the-bible-say-about-abortion.

White, Andrew A. "The Corporeal Aspect and Procreative Function of the *Imago Dei* and Abortion." *Journal of Biblical Ethics in Medicine* 6, no. 1 (1992): 15–20.

Williams, Tara. "Manipulating Mary: Maternal, Sexual, and Textual Authority in *The Book of Margery Kempe*." *Modern Philology* 107, no. 4 (2010): 528–55.

Witte, John, Jr., and Robert M. Kingdon. *Sex, Marriage, and Family in John Calvin's Geneva: Courtship, Engagement, and Marriage*. Grand Rapids: Wm. B. Eerdmans Publishing Co., 2005.

Wolf-Devine, Celia. "Abortion and the 'Feminine Voice.'" *Public Affairs Quarterly* 3, no. 3 (1989): 81–97.

———. "Postscript to 'Abortion and the "Feminine Voice"': The Gutting of the Ethics of Care by Carol Gilligan and Nel Noddings." *Life and Learning III: Proceedings of the Faculty for Life Conference*. 1993. http://www.celiawolfdevine.com/pdf/Postscript-to-Abortion-and-the-Feminine-Voice-1993.pdf.

Young, Iris Marion. "Pregnant Embodiment: Subjectivity and Alienation." *The Journal of Medicine and Philosophy* 9, no. 1 (1984): 45–62.

Index

Aasgaard, Reidar, 29n53
abnormality, fetal, 179
abortifacients, 22, 30–31, 35n85,
    130n86
abortion
    "abortion-as-killing," 130
    botched, 158, 160
    clinics, 6, 107n35, 159, 196n4, 209
    coerced/forced, 131n40, 208
    criminalization of, 24, 32–36, 47,
        210
    as difficult decision, 3, 13, 87, 128,
        154, 156, 166, 188, 193, 213
    ektrōma, 25, 27–29
    elective, 143–44
    frivolous, 136, 211
    history of, 17–47
    as mothering/maternal decision, 10,
        122, 124, 127–38, 153, 207, 210,
        220
    "partial birth abortion," 42
    as pre-mothering decision, 125–27,
        134, 219
    providers, 56, 159–160, 161n17,
        208–9
    and sin, 11, 23, 30, 34, 65, 73, 112,
        136, 193–94, 207–13, 216
    stigma and, 3, 6n15, 11, 73, 122,
        193–94, 207, 219–20, 223
    therapeutic, 8, 19, 27–28, 36–37, 39,
        44–45, 182, 184
    as tragic, 47, 135, 188–89, 194,
        209–10, 221, 222n101
    U.S., rate in, 3
    women's maternal discourse of,
        145–46

    See also consent to pregnancy;
        pro-choice stance; pro-life stance;
        specific topics and descriptions, e.g.,
        coercion; first trimester; waiting
        period, mandatory
abortion bans, 9–10, 117, 179n81, 209
"Abortion Conversation Projects," 6n15
abortion doping, 136n57
Abortion and the Early Church (Gorman),
    17
abortion procedures, 25, 36, 42–43,
    132–33, 143n95
abortion rights, 121, 123–24, 138,
    144, 148, 178, 219. *See also*
    reproductive rights; *Roe v. Wade*
abortion stigma, 3, 6n15, 11, 73, 122,
    193–94, 207, 219–20, 223. *See also*
    shame/shaming
abuse, 217
    child, 214
    sexual, 200n27, 213
    See also exploitation; incest; rape
Adam-and-Eve story, 53–54, 56–59, 61
Adams, Sarah LaChance, 186–89
adoption, 130, 132, 159, 168–70, 216
adultery, 22–23, 31
African American women, 5, 130n36,
    137n58, 167, 169, 173–75, 198,
    214, 217–18
afterlife, 39n103, 130. *See also* heaven
agency, 61, 64, 69, 142
    women as rational moral agents, 2,
        10, 13, 102, 127, 136, 138, 151
Akiba, Rabbi, 183
Alexandrine theology, 74
Alton, Althea K., 104–5

241

ambiguity, ethics of, 187–88
American Medical Association, 45
Anglican, 71, 161
Annunciation, 1, 83, 195–96, 199–200, 206
anomaly, fetal, 179. *See also* disability
anti-abortion, the term, 4n10
anti-abortion activity, 47, 160n10, 209
    as domestic terrorism, 3–4, 209
    vigilante, 107n35
    See also violence: anti-abortion
anti-abortion discourse, 3, 17–18, 20–25, 29, 31, 36, 39, 45, 47, 56, 58, 107–8, 160–61. *See also* law/ laws: anti-abortion lobbying for
Antiochene theology, 74
antisexuality, 19, 21–23, 77–78, 84, 92, 114
Apollinarianism, 74, 90–93
Apollinaris of Laodicea, 74
apophatic approach to doctrine, 88, 90, 95, 223n104
Aquinas, Thomas. *See* Thomas Aquinas
Arendt, Hannah, 152n129
Aristotle, 37–38, 78–79
Asian American women, 212–13
atonement, 214–15
Augustine of Hippo, 38–41, 43n127, 223n104
authority
    and Christian textual sources, 2, 19, 73, 76, 89, 198
    church/ecclesial, 20, 22, 31–34, 110n46, 203, 218–19
    and Jewish textual sources, 27n48, 123, 184
    maternal, 10, 13, 98, 121–54
    state/legal, 33, 133
    of women, 2, 10, 13, 98, 117
autonomy, 62, 104–5, 115, 140, 179, 198

baby/babies
    embryo or fetus as called, 6, 12, 25, 58, 122, 128–29, 153
    newborn, 40, 105, 140–41, 187
    See also children; neonates; unborn
baptism, 165
Barilan, Y. Michael, 26nn38–42
Barr, Julian, 42n121, 44

Barth, Karl, 50–51
Basil of Caesarea, 82
Bauerschmidt, Frederick Christian, 161, 165
Beattie, Tina, 114, 125–26, 134–35, 138, 142–44, 197–99
Beckwith, Francis J., 62n62, 99–100, 105–8, 208–9
be fruitful and multiply, 27, 55, 184, 203
begetting, 66, 203, 222. *See also* procreation
Bellinger, Charles K., 160–61, 168, 171
Benedict XVI, Pope, 110
Beyond Pro-Life and Pro-Choice: Moral Diversity in the Abortion Debate (Rudy), 2, 4
Bible. *See* Hebrew Bible; New Testament; Old Testament
biological determinism, 50, 63, 67, 69
Birgitta, Saint, 204
birth. *See* childbirth
birth control. *See* contraception
birth narratives, Gospels, 11, 59n41, 63, 193–95, 199–200
black women. *See* African American women
blastocyst, 91, 102
Boaz, 200n25
bodily integrity, 123, 134n51, 175, 181n91
bodily self-giving, 11, 172, 174–75, 180–82, 186, 188–89, 210
body-soul paradigm, 8, 71–73, 79, 86, 90, 92, 95–96
bonding in pregnancy, 126, 137
botched abortion, 158, 160
brain activity/waves, 142–43
Brief, Liberal, Catholic Defense of Abortion, A (Dombrowski and Deltete), 2
Brock, Rita Nakashima, 213
Brooks, Gwendolyn, 131
burden, pregnancy as, 107, 156–57, 159, 161–62, 166, 181, 182n94, 190, 209, 213–14
Butler, Judith, 146n101

Caesarius of Arles, 21
Cahill, Courtney Megan, 178n77

Cahill, Lisa Sowle, 146–51, 181,
     209n60
Calhoun, Samuel W., 133n50
calling
     from the womb, 65, 67
     prophetic, 29, 67
     spiritual 11, 193–94, 202–5, 221
     See also vocation
Calvin, John, 20
canon law, 8, 24, 31–36, 47, 109, 210
     Corpus iuris canonici, 32
care ethics, 175–80, 189
caretaking roles, 11, 172–74, 180, 189,
     214
Cassidy, Keith, 35n86, 44n130
celibacy, 21, 77, 203–4
Centers for Disease Control and
     Prevention, 149
Chalcedon, Council of, 8–9, 71–96, 215
     regulative doctrinal approach to,
          88–90, 96
child abuse, 214
child-bearing years, women of, 2–3, 150
     childbirth
     cost of, self-pay (U.S.), 168n51
     death in, 46, 107, 187n121, 190, 201
     difficult, 27, 37, 42
     obstructed, 28, 42, 44, 46–47, 123
     premature, 106, 132n44
     See also gestation; Jesus Christ: birth
          narratives; *specific topics, e.g.,* risks
child/children
     born, 10, 104, 108, 111, 114, 129,
          133, 151, 177, 207, 209
     "future child," 127, 131
     innocent, 7, 20, 47, 99–100, 158, 160
     See also baby/babies; procreation;
          teen pregnancy
China, 131n40
     choice/motherhood choices,
          193–223 (*see also* consent to
          pregnancy; decision-making;
          pro-choice stance; reproductive
          rights)
Christ. *See* Jesus Christ
Christianity/Christian faith, 1–4, 57, 73,
     155, 182–85, 191, 203
     abortion history in, 17–47
     authoritative textual sources, 2, 19,
          73, 76, 89, 198
     choice and, 2, 4, 8, 46–47, 191, 207
     creeds of, 1, 8, 82, 88–89, 223
     orthodoxy, 8, 71–72, 80, 88, 92,
          95–96
     See also church/churches; Protestant
          tradition/perspectives; Roman
          Catholic tradition/perpectives;
          specific topics, e.g., symbols
Christian women, 3, 6, 11–13, 18, 66,
     68, 135–37, 155, 161–64, 172,
     182, 193–95, 197, 202, 206–7,
     214, 216, 220–21, 223
     and choice, 4, 47, 207
     conservative, 6, 129, 136, 163, 221
Christology, 59–62, 71–76, 81–86,
     191. *See also* hypostatic union,
     incarnation.
Chrysostom, John, 23
church/churches, 156, 164, 170–72,
     189
     and "bearing the burdens," 161–62
     church history, 1, 4, 7–8, 21, 24–47,
          50, 69
     separation of church and state,
          35–36
     See also Christianity/Christian faith;
          Protestant tradition/perspectives;
          Roman Catholic tradition/
          perpectives; *specific topics, e.g.,*
          authority: church/ecclesial
civil disobedience, 107n35
class, socioeconomic, 164n33, 190
Coakley, Sarah, 88–90, 95, 223n104
coercion
     coerced/forced abortion, 131n40,
          208
     coerced gestation/motherhood, 47,
          68, 117, 122, 150, 152, 156, 162,
          167, 169, 172, 175, 186–90, 208,
          212, 217
     See also exploitation
Coleman, Monica A., 217–18
Colker, Ruth, 132n44
common good, 12, 148, 150, 154
compassion, 8, 18–20, 31–32, 46,
     53n17, 65–66, 148, 156, 158,
     161–62, 164, 166, 171, 174, 189–
     91, 193, 207–8, 220–23
     care ethics, 175–80, 189
     See also love

conception
    and God's will, 8, 64–65, 68
    and personhood, 1, 7–10, 23, 30,
        34–50, 54n20, 63, 72, 76, 96,
        101
    See also specific topics, e.g.,
        contraception; ensoulment
Congregation for the Doctrine of the
    Faith, 111
conscience, 2, 114–15, 128, 136–37,
    166, 212
consciousness, maternal/self-
    consciousness of motherhood,
    86, 122, 125–26, 135, 144, 199
consecrated virgins, 21, 203, 205–7
consent to pregnancy, 11, 13, 108,
    123–24, 139, 148–50, 187, 192,
    202, 204
    Mary and, 195–96, 198–201
conservative Christians, 55, 185
    women, 6, 129, 136, 163, 221
Constantinople, Third Council of
    (680), 76
Constitution, U.S., 66, 121, 123–24,
    132
    Equal Protection Clause, 124
contraception, 21, 23, 31, 33, 106
Corbella, Chiara, 216n78
Corinthians, epistles to the, 25–27,
    60
Cornell, Drucilla, 188
Corpus iuris canonici, 32
    councils, ecumenical, 32
    Council of Chalcedon (451), 8–9,
        71–96, 215
    Council of Elvira (fourth century),
        22
    Council of Ephesus (431), 75
    Council of Nicaea (325), 73–74
    Third Council of Constantinople
        (680), 76
    Third Council of Toledo (589), 31
counseling
    pastoral care/advice, 173, 175,
        189–90
    pro-life, 196n4, 208
creation, 1, 8, 25–26, 40, 49–60, 63–64,
    68, 87, 212. *See also* image of
    God/*imago Dei*
creationism, 58–59

creationist view of soul, 40–41
creeds of the church, 1, 8, 82, 88–89,
    223
criminalization of abortion, 24, 32–36,
    47, 210
crisis pregnancies, 137, 156, 161, 163–
    66, 168, 171, 189, 202, 214
crisis pregnancy centers, 137, 164n34,
    170–71
Crisp, Oliver D., 71–72, 79–80, 83–84,
    88n83, 90–92
cross/crucifixion, 11–12, 167n49, 194,
    203, 207, 214–16, 219–22
    and gestational sacrifice, 213–17
Crucified God, The (Moltmann), 221
Cyril of Alexandria, 75

Daly, Mary, 200n27
David, 56–57, 66
Davis, John Jefferson, 53n18, 57n36,
    65–66
death, 87, 207–23
    abortion and, 193–223
    in childbirth, 200–201
    in trinitarian God, 217, 221–23
    natural, 110, 116
    See also cross/crucifixion;
        resurrection
de Beauvoir, Simone, 187–88
decision-making
    abortion as mothering/maternal
        decision, 10, 122, 124, 127–38,
        153, 207, 210, 220
    abortion as pre-mothering decision,
        125–27, 134, 219
    difficulty of abortion decisions, 2,
        13, 87, 128, 154, 156, 164–66,
        188, 193, 213, 222
    fiat mihi and Mary's, 198–202
    See also choice; conscience;
        pro-choice stance
Declaration on Procured Abortion
    (1974), 112
Decretum (Gratian), 32
deification/divinization, 61, 72, 84
    of Jesus, 85, 91, 93, 96, 215, 221
    See also emergent, processive
        paradigm/emergentism; Jesus
        Christ
Deltete, Robert John, 2, 39, 143n93

determinism
    biologically deterministic theology,
        50, 63, 67, 69
    "genetic," 105
Didache, 17, 25
Dignitas personae (2008), 109–12
dignity, human, 9, 52, 94, 100, 102,
        109–14, 162, 165
disability, 5, 51, 152n128, 166, 179
discipleship, 50, 59–63
divine nature of Christ, 83, 90–91, 93.
        See also Christology
DNA, 79–80, 101, 104–5
Docetism, 79–82
doctrine, 10, 13
    apophatic approach to, 88, 90, 95,
        223n104
    of election, 50, 63, 65, 67–69
    of God, 217
    of the incarnation, 1, 8–9, 110, 201,
        215, 217, 220–21, 223
    of Mary's perpetual virginity, 80, 82
    of original sin, 20, 56–58, 82, 101,
        136–37
    propositionalist view of, 88–90
    of providence, 49–50, 63–69, 95, 212
    regulative view of, 88–90, 96
    of the Trinity, 12, 71, 87, 194, 207,
        215–16, 220–23
Dombrowski, Daniel A., 2, 39, 143n93
Donum vitae (1987), 110–11
double effect ethics principle, 133n46,
        143–44n95
Down syndrome, 166
duty, 181
    and gestation, 13, 69, 138, 146–50,
        157, 167n49, 170, 181, 184, 189,
        195, 203–4, 209
    Jewish ethics and, 84–85
    See also responsibility; *specific topics,*
        e.g., neighbor love
dying violinist analogy (Thomson), 148,
        156

Eastern Orthodox tradition/
        perspectives, 61, 80, 84, 208
ectopic pregnancy, 151n127, 159, 170
ecumenical councils, 32. *See also*
        specific councils, e.g., Chalcedon,
        Council of

Effraenatam (Sixtus V, papal bull), 35
ektrōma, 25, 27–29. *See also* Paul,
        apostle: reference to self as
        "abortion"
election, 50, 63, 65, 67–69. *See also*
        predestination; providence, divine
elective abortion, 143–44
Elizabeth (Mary's cousin), 59n41, 95,
        200
Elizabeth of Hungary, 204
Ellison, Linda, 129, 135, 137n58, 163
Elsakkers, Marianne J., 32
Elvira, Council of (fourth century), 22
embodied self-giving, 180–82
embryo
    as baby, 6, 12
    bearing image of God, 8, 57, 62
    Christ as, 8, 72, 84, 95, 223
    ensouled, 23, 36, 40–41, 79, 88, 91,
        109
    personhood of, 97–103, 106, 109–
        113, 116, 143
    predestined, 50, 67
    preembryo, 101, 103n21
    as sacred, 17n3, 93–94
    sinful, 58
    the term, 151n127
    totipotency of, 103, 106
    See also "prenate"; unborn; zygote;
        specific topics, e.g., ensoulment
embryology, 41, 45, 78–79, 102, 105
embryotomy, 42–45
emergent, processive paradigm/
        emergentism, 9, 72–73, 84–87,
        90–96
emotions, 107, 129, 131, 136, 146, 149,
        168, 171, 176, 178 180, 187, 213,
        217–19
empowerment, 74, 137, 189, 197–99,
        201, 206, 223
encyclicals, Catholic, 100, 108–11
endangerment view of pregnancy,
        122–24
ensoulment, 8, 20, 23, 30, 36, 38–43,
        46–47, 71, 76–79, 83–84, 88,
        91–93, 101–3, 107–13, 210
Ephesians, epistle to the, 61
Ephesus, Council of (431), 75
Equal Protection Clause, 124
Esau, 65

eschatology/eschatological, 51, 199,
    218
ethics, 154, 188
    of ambiguity (de Beauvoir), 187–88
    bioethics and self-gifting, 156, 189
    of care, 175–80, 189
    double effect principle, 133n46,
        143–44n95
    feminist, 2, 5, 6, 19, 130, 172
    Jewish, 182–86
    probabilism in moral reasoning, 9,
        108–17
    supererogatory, 148, 159, 181, 184
    See also fairness; justice; morality
ethnography, 5, 145
Eucharist, 161–62
eugenics, 45n136
evangelicals/evangelicalism, 53–54, 80,
    129n31, 145, 198, 206
Evangelium vitae (John Paul II,
    encyclical), 109
Eve
    Mary and, 195–97
    See also Adam-and-Eve story
evil, 18, 23, 31, 108. See also sin
evolution, 56n29, 58, 72, 85–87, 95
    anti-evolutionary creationism,
        58–59
excommunication, 35, 45, 109n42
Exodus, book of, 27
exploitation, 114, 131n40, 162, 172–73,
    182, 189, 213–14. See also abuse;
    coercion; oppression; specific
    topics, e.g., slavery/enslavement

fairness, 10–11, 180–82
faith, 198, 218
    deposit of, 89
    sensus fidelium, 46
    sola fide, 61
    See also Christianity/Christian faith
fathers, 18, 34–35, 39n103, 134n51,
    139
feminist thought/theology
    as challenging pro-life reading of
        church history, 7–8, 19–23
    ethics/ethicists, 2, 6, 19, 130, 172
    feminist philosophy/philosophers,
        5–6, 122, 155, 186, 189–90,
        211

    on sexism and antisexuality, 19–23
    See also womanist thought/theology
Fergusson, David, 52, 68
fertility, 22, 55, 66n70, 197, 204n44
fertilization, 36, 64, 67–68, 98, 101–3,
    110n45, 143. See also conception
fetal anomaly, 179. See also disability
fetal Other, responsibility to, 186–89
fetal personhood, 1, 3, 8–9, 36, 38–39,
    49–50, 52–53 55, 58–59, 62n55,
    63, 68–68, 153, 162n19, 166,
    175, 210
    and Christ's incarnation, 71–96
    feminist developmental view of,
        140–44
    feminist relational view of, 138–140
    not a person/not a nonperson, 10,
        122, 144–46, 153–54, 211
    probabilist view of, 108–13
    substantialist view of, 9, 97–108
    See also fetal value; person/
        personhood
fetal value, 10, 13, 43, 130, 211
    and grievability, 146
    in terms of four material realities,
        151–53
    maternal authority and, 121–54
fetus
    contingent/contiguous existence of,
        10, 151–53, 210–11
    not a person/not a nonperson, 10,
        122, 144–46, 153–54, 211
    and predestination, 63–69
    preresponsive, 176
    the term, 151n127, 153, 210–11
    viability of, 132, 139–41, 152–54,
        178–80
    See also fetal personhood; "prenate";
        specific topics, e.g., imago Dei
fiat mihi, 193, 198–200, 202, 207, 213.
    See also Mary/the Mary story
first trimester, 127, 138, 142, 149. See
    also pregnancy, early
flesh, 79, 91–92, 125–26, 223
forced abortion, 131n40
forced gestation/motherhood, 47, 117,
    122, 150, 152, 156, 162, 167, 169,
    172, 175, 186–90, 208, 212, 217
forced sterilization, 5
forgiveness, 129, 208

fornication, 23n29, 30–31
foster parenting, 167, 169
Francis, Pope, 209n58
Frei, Hans, 86n71
"future child," 127, 131

Gabriel (angel), 82, 193–96, 202, 223
  the Annunciation, 1, 83, 195–96,
    199–200, 206
Gaddis, Michael, 75n15
Galen of Pergamum, 37–38, 41
Gaventa, Beverly Roberts, 199n22
gender bias, 113, 182
generosity, 82n56, 167–68, 172, 189.
  See also Good Samaritan parable/
    Samaritanism; self-giving,
    embodied
Genesis, book of, 8, 26, 49–61, 69, 139,
  184, 203
genetics, 36, 54n20, 91, 97, 99, 103–5,
  116–17, 151, 210
genome, 103–5, 108, 151
gestation
  as developmental, 104–5, 125–26,
    134, 139–44, 152
  duty and, 13, 69, 84–85, 138,
    146–50, 157, 167n49, 170, 181,
    184, 189, 195, 203–4, 209
  forced, 12, 69, 107, 117, 122,
    149–50, 152, 212, 217
  and grace period to decide, 134,
    143–44
  as stage of mothering, 127–28
  as punishment, 149–50
  See also consent to pregnancy;
    pregnancy; specific topics, e.g.,
    surrogacy
gestational hospitality, 11, 13, 155–92
  pro-choice paradigm for, 172–89
gestational realism, 80–84
Gilbert, Scott F., 102n19, 105
God
  coram Deo (in the presence of God),
    69, 212
  as Creator, 50, 54n20, 60–61, 212,
    223n104
  inscrutability of, 13
  as mothering, 12, 194, 220–23
  and providence, 49–50, 63–69, 95,
    212

  will of, 8, 13, 64–65, 68, 69, 198n14,
    199n23, 206
  womb of, 207–23
  See also imago Dei; Trinity; specific
    topics, e.g., creation; love; mystery
good/goodness
  "intrinsic goodness," 148
  mitzvah (good deed), 183
  See also common good; virtues
"Good Mother" ideal, 122, 187
Good Samaritan parable/Samaritanism,
  1, 11, 155–92
  extreme anti-abortion Samaritanism,
    158–61
  Jewish interpretations of, 183–85
  moderate pro-life Samaritanism,
    161–69
  as not heroic, 171, 183, 186
  pastoral theological interpretations
    of, 172–75
  premodern allegories of, 191–92
  "Splendid Samaritan," 157, 190
Gorman, Michael J., 17–18, 23–25,
  27n48, 29n55, 36–37, 39, 41,
  44–45
Gosnell, Kenneth, 160n14
Gospels, 86, 213
  birth narratives, 11, 59n 41, 63,
    193–95, 199–200
  "history-like," 86n71
  See also Luke, Gospel of; Matthew,
    Gospel of
grace, divine, 25, 61, 85–86, 198n14,
  201, 206
Gratian, 32
gravidity, 126
Gray, Frances, 125–26
Greco-Roman period, 19, 27, 29n55,
  36–38, 44–45, 81. See also
  Hellenistic Judaism; patristic
  theology
Green, Monica H., 37n93, 204n44
Gregory IX, Pope, 34
Gregory of Nazianzus, 74
Gregory of Nyssa, 81–82
Gregory XIII, Pope, 32
grief, 130n33, 146, 179, 217–19, 221,
  223
Guenther, Lisa, 186–89
guilt, 30, 32, 129, 132, 187, 193, 217

Gushee, David P., 52–55, 57–60,
    94n103

Hagar, 200
hagiography, 205
halakah, 26–29, 37n94, 122–23, 156,
    183–86, 190
Haldane, John, 46n137, 101–2, 107,
    116n65
Harrison, Beverly Wildung, 19–23, 33,
    114, 138, 140–41, 143, 146–47
Hauerwas, Stanley, 161–69, 171
Hays, Richard B., 60n44, 161, 166–69
Heaney, Stephen J., 103
heaven, 61, 82, 218–19, 223n104
Hebrew Bible, 26, 28–29, 50, 52, 60,
    63, 200
    the Septuagint, 28
    See also Old Testament
Held, Virginia, 145
Hellenistic Judaism, 8, 26–29, 60
herbal abortifacients, 30–31
heresy, 35, 67, 74, 91–93
hermeneutics, 8, 49, 51, 52–59, 63–64,
    79, 166, 190
    of suspicion, 89
Heyne, Thomas F., 43n125
Himma, Kenneth Einar, 219n89
Hippocrates, 27–28, 37–38, 40, 42n124
Hippocratic Oath, 36
history
    of abortion, 17–47
    church/Christian, 1, 4, 7, 21, 24–47,
        50, 69
    "history-like" Gospels, 86
Holocaust, the, 161n17, 220n96
Holy Spirit, 21, 61–62, 79–80, 86–87,
    94, 165, 200. See also Trinity
homicide, 21, 24, 33–35, 38–42, 46, 66,
    107, 159, 208, 210
    fetal, issue of, 18, 27, 34–35, 56
    "honorable," 33
    See also killing; murder; violence
homunculus, 94
hospitality. See gestational hospitality
Houle, Karen, 6–7
Howes, Laura L., 204–5
human being, 52–53, 60, 78, 92, 108,
    210–11, 137, 151, 154, 219

at conception, 23, 36, 66. 72, 77,
    102–3, 110n45
as developing/emergent, processive,
    91, 106, 126n19, 130, 134, 140,
    143, 152–53
in womb, 10, 39, 41, 54, 99–100
See also imago Dei; person/
    personhood
human condition, 86–87, 209, 215
human dignity. See dignity, human
human life. See life, human
human nature, 9, 56–57, 60–61, 72, 74,
    76–79, 81, 84–87, 90
    of Christ, 85, 90–93, 96, 215
human race, 54, 59n42
human reproduction, 50, 63, 67. See also
    sexual intercourse
human rights, 54, 58, 100, 109, 115,
    141
hylomorphic persons, 79
hypostasis, 89
hypostatic union, 72, 74–80, 82–84,
    86–94, 96. See also Christology;
    incarnation

idealism, pro-life, 162–63, 165, 167,
    169, 189
image of Christ/imago Christi, 59,
    61–62
image of God/imago Dei, 1, 7–8, 25–29,
    49–64, 69, 110, 139, 143, 183,
    210, 222
    fetuses and, 50–63
    hermeneutical leaps in pro-life
        appeals to, 52–59
    in the New Testament, 59–63
imitatio Mariae, 202–7
incarnation, 1, 8–9, 110, 201, 215, 217,
    220–21, 223
    fetal personhood and, 71–96
    a processive, emergent view of,
        84–96
    See also Chalcedon, Council of;
        Christology; hypostatic union
incest, 18, 35, 46, 106–8, 115
infancy narratives. See birth narratives,
    Gospels
infanticide, 25, 45, 130n36
infants. See baby/babies

infinite responsibility to the fetal
    Other, 186–89
injustice, 145, 162, 189, 197. *See also*
    justice
innocence, 213
    fetal, 7, 20, 47, 97, 99–100, 108, 117,
        158, 160–61, 210, 211, 219n89
    of Jesus, 160
    wisdom and, 213
intercourse, sexual. *See* sexual
    intercourse
Internet. *See* Web sites
"intrinsic goodness," 148
in vitro fertilization, 143n94, 151n127
Ireland, 29, 207
irresponsibility, and sex, 136–37,
    149–50

Jacob, 65, 200n25
Jeremiah, 66
Jerome, 81
Jesus Christ, 8–9, 59
    birth narratives, 11, 59n 41, 63,
        193–95, 199–200
    death and resurrection of, 91,
        220–23
    divine and human natures of
        (hypostatic union), 9, 72, 74–80,
        82–94, 96, 215
    emergent, processive deification/
        divinization of, 85, 91, 93, 96,
        215, 221
    Logos, 74, 85, 91
    sinlessness of, 82n56
    theōsis in, 61
    See also cross/crucifixion;
        incarnation; Trinity
Jews. *See* Judaism
John Chrysostom, 23
John Paul II, Pope, 111–14
Johnson, Elizabeth A., 198–99
Johnson, Mark, 101–3
John the Baptist, 58, 63, 95
Jones, David Albert, 17–19, 23, 31, 33,
    35–38, 41–42, 44, 71, 75–79, 83,
    90, 93
Jones, Serene, 217, 220–21
Judaism
    Conservative, 184

halakah, 26–29, 37n94, 122–23, 156,
    183–86, 190
Hellenistic, 8, 26–29, 60
the Holocaust, 161n17
Jewish ethics, 182–86
Mary as Jewish, 194
Orthodox, 184
Paul's Hellenistic Jewish
    background, 8, 26n36, 28–29, 60
rabbinic, 26–28, 123, 155, 182, 184
Shekhinah, 220
Ultra-Orthodox, 184
See also Mishnah
judging others/being judgmental, 136,
    153, 156, 164–65, 187, 190, 212,
    219. *See also* shame/shaming
judgment, God's, 55n23, 161n17
judgment, moral/judgment calls, 10,
    89, 130. *See also* conscience;
    decision-making
Jung, Patricia Beattie, 180–84, 190,
    210, 214n69
justice, 10–11, 180–82
    reproductive, 2–3n3, 5
    social, 5, 51
    See also injustice
justifiable abortion, 2, 47, 125, 142–44
Justin Martyr, 196

Kaczor, Christopher, 159–60, 168–69
Kawaguchi, Yuriko, 132n43
Kelsey, David H., 60, 162n19
Kempe, Margery. *See* Margery Kempe
"Kenosis of the Father" (Ruether),
    220
killing, 23, 25, 27, 31, 34, 46–47, 55,
    58, 65–66, 95 107, 111, 128
    "abortion-as-killing," 130
    "direct" versus "indirect," 133
    and fetal value, 130, 211
    See also death; homicide; murder;
        violence
Kitzler, Petr, 40n110, 41n112
Kurz, William S., 64–65

late/third trimester abortion, 138,
    143–44, 154, 160n14, 178–79
Latin America, 115–16, 198
Latina feminist theologians, 51

law/laws
  abortion bans, 9–10, 179n81, 209
  anti-abortion lobbying for, 116,
    137, 161, 168
  criminalization of abortion, 24,
    32–36, 47, 210
  global abortion laws, 115–16
  Jewish, 37n94, 184
  natural/universal, 151, 186
  and public policy, 115n62, 163,
    219
  See also canon law; reproductive
    rights; Roe v. Wade; ultrasounds,
    prenatal; waiting period,
    mandatory
Leah, 200n25
Lee, Patrick, 46n137, 99–103, 107,
    116n65
Levinas, Emmanuel, 186–87, 190, 211,
    220
Leviticus, book of, 182
liberation, 173–74, 195, 198, 202
life, human, 20, 85, 91–94, 110–16,
    138–40, 188, 215, 222–23
  contingency/contiguousness of fetal
    existence, 10, 151–53, 210–11
  right to life, 1, 5, 51, 56, 100,
    115–16, 177
  sanctity of, 17, 37n94, 46, 60, 177
  "short and brutish," 87
  women's lives in Greco-Roman
    world, 36–47
  See also person/personhood
Lindbeck, George, 88–90
Little, Margaret Olivia, 149–51,
    153n130
Logos, 74, 85, 91. See also Word of
    God
love
  divine, 110, 173, 199, 208, 221–23
  mother-love, 174
  self-love, 173
  See also compassion; neighbor love
Ludlow, Jeannie, 6–7
Luke, Gospel of
  Mary's story in, 11, 24, 63, 95,
    193–95, 198–200
  See also Good Samaritan parable
Luther, Martin, 191
Lymer, Jane, 126

MacKellar, Calum, 17n3, 64n60,
    93n101
Mackenzie, Catriona, 128n30, 131
Magnificat, 200
Maguire, Daniel C., 209
Maguire, Marjorie Reiley, 138–40
Maimonides, Moses, 123
Manninen, Bertha Alvarez, 145
Marcionites, 81
Margery Kempe, 11, 194, 202–7
Marian spirituality, 11, 194, 202, 204,
    206–7
Marian symbols
  obedient handmaid, 193, 195–96,
    198–200, 202, 207, 213
  redeemer of sinful Eve, 195–97
Mariology, 81–83, 195–98, 200n27
marriage, 21–23, 34, 47, 68, 77, 106,
    114
  forced, 200n27
martyrdom, 187
Mary/the Mary story, 193–207
  the Annunciation, 1, 83, 195–96,
    199–200, 206
  birth narratives, Gospels, 11, 59n 41,
    63, 193–95
  and Elizabeth, 59n41, 95, 200
  and Eve, 195–97
  feminist interpretations of, 198
  fiat mihi, 193, 195–96, 198–200, 202,
    207, 213
  imitatio Mariae, 202–7
  in Luke's Gospel, 24, 63, 95, 193–
    95, 198–200
  the Magnificat, 200
  Mater Dolorosa, 203
  obedience, 193, 195–96, 198–200
  perpetual virginity of, 80, 82
  sinlessness of, 82n56
  Theotokos, 75, 82, 93
  unwanted pregnancy and, 195–202
  the Virgin, 71–83, 90n88, 126n15,
    193, 195–202
  as vulnerable, 198n14, 200–201, 223
  womb of, 80–84
  See also Marian spirituality; Marian
    symbols; Mariology
Mater Dolorosa, 203
maternal authority. See authority:
    maternal

"maternal consciousness," 125, 144, 199
maternal hospitality, 126, 187. *See also*
    gestational hospitality
maternal decision-making
    responsibility, 128–131, 134–36
"maternal thinking" (Ruddick), 200
maternity, 109, 115, 126n19, 193, 197,
    199, 202. *See also* motherhood
Mathewes-Green, Frederica, 208, 223
Matthew, Gospel of, 95
Maximus the Confessor, 76–78, 84, 89,
    92
McDonagh, Eileen, 123–24
McDonnell, Kilian, 198n15
medical science/procedures, 134n51,
    141, 179, 185, 201
    abortion procedures, 25, 36, 42–43,
        132–33, 143–44n95
    American Medical Association, 45
    Greco-Roman, 19, 24, 28, 36–47
    See also obstetric medicine; *specific
        topics and descriptions*, e.g., late/
        third trimester abortion
menstruation, 38, 143
Merleau-Ponty, Maurice, 125–26
metaphysics, 9, 81, 89, 99–100, 102. *See
    also* ontology
Meyer, John R., 101, 103
Middle Ages, 8, 11, 18–19, 24, 30–37,
    46–47, 79–80, 123, 194, 203,
    210. *See also* penance: penitential
    manuals, medieval
Miller, Monica Migliorino, 196–97
Miller, Patricia, 139n61
Miller-McLemore, Bonnie, 200
miracles, 79, 82–83, 87, 95, 134, 151,
    195, 201–2, 205
Miriam, 28
miscarriage, 27–28, 34–35, 38, 41, 47,
    64n62, 68, 127, 133n48, 211,
    217–20
    in book of Exodus, 27–28, 41
    punishment for causing, 18, 27, 34,
        56, 109n42
    as "silent sorrow," 218
    See also reproductive loss
Mishnah, 27–28, 123, 184. *See also*
    Judaism
misogyny, 10, 21, 23, 47, 107, 153, 209
Mistry, Zubin, 30–32

Molla, Gianna, 216n78
Moltmann, Jürgen, 87, 220–22
Moral Vision of the New Testament, The
    (Hays), 166
morality, 9–10
    of abortion, 45, 127, 146–47, 153–
        54, 180
    emotions as important moral
        indicator, 178
    legalistic approach, 32–33, 47
    pregnant women as rational moral
        agents, 2, 10, 13, 69, 127, 206
    See also authority: moral; ethics
moral status of embryo/fetus, 125,
    142–44
Moreland, J. P., 99
Morgan, Lynn M., 102n16
Moses, 28, 56
"mother," the term, 126n19
motherhood, 113–14
    "Good Mother" ideal, 122, 187
    and Marian devotion, 202, 205, 207
    responsibility of, 137, 188
    sanctification of biological
        motherhood, 197
    self-consciousness of, 86, 125–26,
        135, 142, 144, 199
    See also forced gestation/
        motherhood; maternity
mothering, 5, 10, 12, 121–37, 174, 186,
    188–89, 203–7, 214
    abortion as mothering/maternal
        decision, 10, 122, 124, 127–38,
        153, 207, 210, 220
    abortion as pre-mothering decision,
        125–27, 134, 219
    gestational, 127–28
    imposed, 150
    a mothering God, 12, 194, 220–23
    spiritually mothering others, 203–7
Muehlenberg, Bill, 158–59, 161, 168
Mulieris dignitatem (John Paul II,
    apostolic letter), 112–14
Müller, Wolfgang, 33–35
Mumford, James, 149n119
murder
    abortion as, 9, 11, 23, 25, 30, 35, 41
        45, 47, 56, 58, 72, 96, 98, 111–12,
        157, 159–60, 188, 194, 209–11
    of Dr. George Tiller, 161n17

murder (*continued*)
and fetal value, 130, 211
women as murderers, 3, 56, 157,
168, 171, 188, 209
See also homicide; killing; violence
Muslim ethics, 183n97, 184–85n107
mystery, 13, 69, 87, 201, 215, 221, 223
mystics/mysticism, 11, 194, 202–7,
220n96. *See also* Margery Kempe
myth, 8, 19, 94

natalism. *See* pro-natalism
natality/natal personhood, 106, 152–53
Native women, 5
natural/universal law, 15, 186
neighbor love, 11, 155–56, 161, 166,
170–71, 174–75, 182–86, 189–90.
See also Good Samaritan parable/
Samaritanism
neonates/ newborn babies, 40, 105,
106, 140–41, 187, 218. *See also*
baby/babies
Nestorianism, 74–76, 90–93
Nestorius of Constantinople, 74–75
Newman, Barbara, 204
New Testament
birth narratives in, 11, 59n 41, 63,
193–95, 199–200
imago Dei and *imago Christi* in,
59–63
See also Gospels; *specific topics, e.g.,*
Good Samaritan parable
Nicaea, Council of (325), 73–74, 89
Nicaragua, 115
Nicene Creed, 212
Noddings, Nel, 130–31, 175–78, 190
Noonan, John T., Jr., 7, 17–20, 23–24,
34–35, 44–46
Novello, Henry L., 72, 84–87, 90–93,
221
Numbers, book of, 28
nuns/consecrated virgins, 21, 203,
205–7

obstetric medicine, 36–37, 40, 42, 54,
134, 143n94, 179. *See also*
medical science/procedures
obstructed birth, 28, 42, 44, 46–47,
123
Olasky, Marvin, 19n7, 45n136

Old Testament, 56–57, 59–60. *See also*
Hebrew Bible; *specific books, e.g.,*
Genesis, book of
ontology, 50–51, 55, 59–63, 86, 89, 94,
97, 99–100, 103, 105, 108, 116
oppression, 117, 135, 155, 162, 174,
182, 189, 198, 212. *See also*
exploitation; slavery/enslavement;
specific descriptions, e.g., patriarchy
organ donation, 156, 180–84, 190, 210,
214n69
Origen, 67
original sin, 20, 56–58, 82, 101,
136–37
Other, the fetal, 186–89
*Our Right to Choose: Toward a New Ethic
of Abortion* (Harrison), 2. *See also*
Harrison, Beverly Wildung
Outka, Gene, 12n24

pagans, 19, 37, 44–46
Palestine, 195, 201
parable of the Good Samaritan. *See*
Good Samaritan parable
parent, the term 127n24
parent, gestational, 129, 133. *See also*
motherhood
"partial birth abortion," 42. *See also*
late/third trimester abortion
Pasnau, Robert, 79n40
pastoral theology, 172–75
patriarchy, 20–21, 45n136, 114, 135,
182, 187, 195, 212, 220
patristic theology, 71, 91, 196
pro-life misuses of, 8, 72–73, 75–81,
84–85, 89, 96
Paul, apostle, 24–29
Hellenistic Jewish background of, 8,
26n36, 28–29, 60
reference to self as "abortion,"
27–29
Pavone, Frank, Fr., 132n41
Peebles, Anita, 199n23
penance, 18, 46
penitential manuals, medieval,
24–32, 34
perichoresis, 222. *See also* Trinity
person/personhood, 52–54, 57, 116,
140, 147, 210
biblical arguments for, 49–69

body-soul paradigm, 8, 71–73, 79, 86, 90, 92, 95–96
covenant/relational paradigm, 139
emergent, processive paradigm, 86–87, 90–96, 211, 215
fetal value and, 144–54
hylomorphic, 79
natal, 106, 152–53
potential, 52, 102n16, 142, 162n19
See also conception: and personhood; ensoulment; fetal personhood
"perversity position," 23n29
pessaries, 36. *See also* contraception
Peters, Rebecca Todd, 2, 45n136, 126n19, 139n63, 190n131
Phenomenology of Gravidity (Lymer), 126
Philo, 26–27
philosophy
    Christian, and fetal personhood, 97–117
    feminist, 5–6, 122, 155, 186, 189–90, 211
Pius IX, Pope, 35, 109
Planned Parenthood, 160n10, 170
Plaskow, Judith, 197n9
pleasure, sexual, 23, 47, 77
Porter, Jean, 103n21, 147n105
postabortion rituals, 7
"postabortion stress syndrome," 179
poverty, 18, 30–32, 46, 131n40, 159n6, 164n33
power, divine, 199, 201, 222. *See also* authority; empowerment
predestination, 8, 50, 63–69
preembryo, 101, 103n21
pregnancy, 84, 126, 181
    as condition of vulnerability, 201, 207
    difficult, 167, 198
    ectopic, 151n127, 159, 170
    as endangerment, 122–24
    gestation as developmental, 104–5, 125–26, 134, 139–44, 152
    intrinsic goodness of, 148, 150–51, 181, 209n60
    materiality of, 146–54
    pregnant women as rational moral agents, 2, 10, 13, 69, 127, 206
    as "primitive hospitality," 125
    as punishment, 149–50

    risks of/as risky, 3, 11, 134, 146, 149–52, 169, 178, 181–84, 189, 197, 201, 205, 209, 211, 214
    second trimester, 143
    as stage of mothering, 127–28
    as sui generis relationality, 146–47, 151–52, 211
    third trimester, 143, 179
    wanted/planned, 12, 168, 201
    See also consent to pregnancy; gestation; gestational hospitality; *specific topics and descriptions, e.g.,* crisis pregnancies
pregnancy, early, 122, 125–27, 134, 144, 176, 199, 219
    pre-motherhood state in, 125–27
    See also first trimester
pregnancy, unplanned, 11, 24, 137, 150, 169, 176, 189, 194, 201, 207, 213–14
    churches and "bearing the burdens," 161–62
pregnancy, unwanted
    as anathema, 11, 193, 196, 206
    in life of Margery Kempe, 202–7
    mother/maternal decision-making for, 10, 122, 124, 127–38, 153, 207, 210, 220
    proving neighbor to women with, 170–71
    and the Virgin Mary, 195–202
premarital sex, 23n29, 30–31
pre-maternal state, 126–27, 135
premature birth, 106, 132n44
pre-mothering decision, abortion as, 125–27, 134, 219
"prenate" (Peters) 126n19, 139n63. *See also* embryo; fetal personhood; fetus; unborn
"primitive hospitality," 125
privacy argument (*Roe v. Wade*), 124
probabilism/probabilist moral arguments, 9, 97, 108–13, 210
pro-choice stance, 2, 4–5, 10–12, 121–223
    care ethics, 175–80
    Christian, 2, 4, 8, 46–47, 191, 207
    constructive pro-choice proposals, 11–12, 121–223
    pro-choice, the term, 4–5

pro-choice stance (*continued*)
  See also abortion rights; decision-
    making: abortion as mothering/
    maternal decision; justifiable
    abortion; *specific topics, e.g.,* fetal
    value; gestational hospitality
procreation, 8, 20–24, 26, 31, 38, 47,
  55–57, 59, 64, 77, 183
  be fruitful and multiply, 27, 55, 184,
    203
  Jewish ethics and, 84–85
pro-life stance, 1, 4, 7–10
  critique of pro-life arguments, 7–10,
    17–117
  extreme, 3, 4n10, 158–61, 170,
    208–9, 214
  moderate, 3, 4n10, 161–71, 221,
    222n101
  probabilist moral arguments, 108–13
  pro-life, the term, 4–5
  substantialist pro-life arguments,
    97–108
  See also anti-abortion discourse;
    fetal personhood; pro-natalism;
    specific topics, e.g., Good Samaritan
    parable/Samaritanism; Web sites
pro-natalism, 8, 19–23, 29, 38, 40,
  45n136
propositionalist view of doctrine,
  88–90
Protestant tradition/perspectives, 12,
  61, 137n58, 174n61
  Luther, 191
  the Reformation, 20–21, 80
  Reformed/Calvinist, 20, 56–57, 65,
    71
  views of Mary, 80, 83, 198
  See also specific descriptions, e.g.,
    evangelicals/evangelicalism;
    specific topics, e.g., sola gratia/sola
    fide
providence, divine, 8, 50, 63, 67–69
public policy, 115n62, 163, 219
punishment
  for causing miscarriage, 18, 27, 34,
    56, 109n42
  forced pregnancy as, 149–50
Purvis, Sally B., 174–75

"quickening," 95, 126

rabbinic Judaism, 26–28, 123, 155, 182,
  184. *See also* Judaism
race, 5, 54, 141n81, 174, 189–90, 217
racism, 173
Rader, Michael N., 183nn97–99
Rae, Scott B., 99
Rahner, Karl, 87n76
rape, 30, 65–66, 106–8, 115, 166–67,
  197, 200n27
  statutory, 167
Raphael, Melissa, 220n96, 222
rational moral agents, pregnant women
  as, 2, 10, 13, 69, 127, 206
Reader, Soran, 128–30, 133–34
Reagan, Leslie J., 19n7, 45n136
Reardon, David C., 208, 211n65
recapitulation, theology of, 196
redemption, 59, 85, 136, 198–99,
  214–15
Reformation, Protestant, 20–21, 80
Reformed/Calvinist tradition, 20,
  56–57, 65, 71
regulative view of doctrine, 88–90, 96
repentance, 30, 208, 221
reproduction, human, 50, 63, 67
reproductive justice, 2–3n3, 5
reproductive loss, 6, 12, 84, 87, 194,
  207, 217–19, 222. *See also*
  abortion; miscarriage
reproductive rights, 1–3, 5, 10, 98, 135,
  141, 146n101, 175–76, 188, 190.
  See also abortion rights; *Roe v.*
  Wade
responsibility
  covenant/relational, 139
  to the fetal Other, 186–89
  maternal responsibility principle,
    128–131, 134, 137, 186n115
  See also duty; irresponsibility;
    decision-making
resurrection
  of Christ, 85, 91, 215, 220–23
  fetuses and final resurrection, 38
right to life, 1, 5, 51, 56, 100, 115–16,
  177
risks
  of abortion, 25, 36, 111–12
  of pregnancy, 3, 11, 134, 146, 149–
    52, 169, 178, 181–84, 189, 197,
    201, 205, 209, 211, 214

rodef ("pursurer"), 123, 184–5
Roe v. Wade, 5, 124, 132, 135, 142, 178
Roman Catholic tradition/perpectives,
  2, 9, 17, 20, 32, 34, 61, 80, 86n66,
  99nn1–2, 101nn13–14, 135, 125,
  138, 181, 196n4, 214
  Catholic hospitals, 133, 144n95, 170
  Catholics for a Free Choice (CFFC),
    138
  double effect ethics principle,
    133n46, 143–44n95
  probabilism in moral reasoning, 9,
    108–13
  See also canon law; Marian
    spirituality; *individual popes; specific
    apostolic letters, councils, papal bulls,
    and encyclicals*
Roman Empire, 37–38. *See also* Greco-
  Roman period
Ruddick, Sara, 200
Rudy, Kathy, 2, 4
Ruether, Rosemary Radford, 21,
  219n92, 220
Ruth, 200n25

sacrament, 156, 161–62, 165, 169, 189.
  See also baptism; Eucharist
sacredness, ascribed, 59
sacrifice, 152, 156, 162, 167, 172–75,
  182, 187, 189–90, 194
  gestational, 213–17
  martyrdom, 187
  self-sacrifice, 156, 162, 172–74,
    182–83, 187, 189, 214–15
  See also cross/crucifixion; self-giving,
    embodied
Salih, Sarah, 205n45
salvation, 66, 74, 85–87, 95, 191,
  215–16
Samaritanism. *See* Good Samaritan
  parable/Samaritanism
sanctification, 50, 59, 67n78, 83–84, 86,
  93, 95
"sanctification of biological
  motherhood," 197
sanctity of human life. *See* life, human:
  sanctity of
Sarah, 200
Saward, John, 71–72, 76–80, 82–84, 90,
  93–95

Schaab, Gloria, 222n100
Schlesinger, Eugene R., 161–62, 165
Schlesinger, Kira, 2
Scholz, Susanne, 200–1n27
science, 36–38, 40, 42, 45, 56n29, 79,
  80, 85, 91
  embryological, 102, 105, 108, 111
  See also evolution; medical science/
    procedures
Scripture. *See* Bible
secrecy, 3, 163. *See also* shame/
  shaming
self-consciousness of motherhood, 86,
  125–26, 135, 142, 199
self-giving, embodied, 11, 156, 172,
  174–75, 180–82, 186, 188–89,
  210
selfishness, 6, 122, 136–37, 150, 177,
  179–80, 208
self-love, 173
self-righteousness, 212
self-sacrifice, 156, 162, 172–74, 182–83,
  187, 189, 214–15. *See also*
  sacrifice; self-giving, embodied
semen/male "seed," 38, 41, 64, 79, 103,
  184
sensus fidelium, 46
separation of church and state, 35–36
Septuagint, 28
sexism, 19–23, 47, 173
sexual abuse, 200n27, 213. *See also*
  incest; rape
sexual intercourse, 40, 66n70, 77,
  90n88, 109, 139, 184, 202–4
  consent, importance of, 202, 204
sexual intercourse, nonconsensual, 117.
  See also rape
sexuality, 4, 18, 21–23, 38, 55, 72–73,
  77–78, 196–97, 202–3. *See also*
  antisexuality
sexual pleasure, 23, 47, 77
shame/shaming, 3, 7, 167n48, 187, 194,
  207, 213
Shanzer, Danuta, 39n103
Shekhinah, 220
Sherman, Susan, 145
Shults, F. LeRon, 61, 74–75, 83
Sider, Ronald J., 53n18, 54n20
sin, 136, 207–23
  call-a-sin-a-sin viewpoint, 208–9

sin (*continued*)
  contesting abortion as, 11, 73,
    208–13
  sexual, 20, 22, 31
  sinlessness of Christ, 83
  sinlessness of Mary, 82n56
  See also original sin; *related topics, e.g.,*
    penance
Sixtus V, Pope, 35
slavery/enslavement, 5, 130n36,
  173n58, 175, 188, 218
Smith, Andrea, 5
sola gratia/sola fide, 61
Sommers, Mary Catherine, 182n94, 214
sonography. *See* ultrasounds, prenatal/
  ultrasound legislation
Sophronius, patriarch of Jerusalem, 76
Soranus of Ephesus, 40–45
sorcery, 31
soteriology, 74, 78, 87, 215
soul, 67, 91–92, 102n18, 110–11, 208
  Aquinas's view, 78–79
  creationist view, 40
  from conception, 36, 39, 76–77, 139
  rational, 38, 71, 74, 77, 79
  traducian view, 39–41, 43, 57–59
  See also body-soul paradigm;
    ensoulment
Soul of the Embryo, The (Jones), 17
spirituality/spiritual aspects, 21, 77,
  194, 201
  Christian, 4, 6–7, 11, 13, 172, 206
  in New Testament, 62
  spiritually mothering others, 203–7
  visions, 202–3
  See also Marian spirituality
spontaneous abortion, 127. *See also*
  miscarriage
separation of church and state, 35–36
State of Israel, 185
statutory rape, 167. *See also* teen
  pregnancy
Steffen, Lloyd H., 139n65
sterilization, forced, 5
Stevenson-Moessner, Jeanne, 172–75
stillbirth, 28, 133n48, 218–20
Storer, Horatio, 45n136
subjectivity, 121–22, 125–27, 134, 142,
  153, 176
  pregnant woman's, 122–37

substantialist view, pro-life, 97–108
suffering, 91, 107, 135, 170, 174–75,
  184–85, 187, 214–15, 220–23.
  See also care ethics; cross/
    crucifixion; *specific topics, e.g.,*
    poverty; rape
sui generis context of gestation/
  pregnancy, 146–47, 151–52, 211
Sullivan, Francis A., 110n46
supererogatory acts, 148, 159, 181, 184
surrogacy, 131n40, 173n58, 175n65,
  214, 216–17
survival, 107, 183, 212–13, 221
symbols, 171, 186, 191
  Christian, 1, 4, 193, 207, 217
  of the Virgin Mary, 193–95, 199,
    206–7
syngamy, 9, 88, 104n27, 108, 151

Taggard, Genevieve, 147
Tanner, Kathryn, 61n50, 61n52, 72,
  84–87, 90–93, 96n109
Tauer, Carol A., 109, 111–13, 138,
  142–43
teen pregnancy, 11, 98, 107, 115n64,
  163–64, 167–69.
temptation, 21, 85, 91, 215
Tertullian, 18, 36, 39–47, 81
theology, 25, 49–50, 52, 60, 73, 84, 92,
  196
  of death, 12, 207
  deification-oriented, 84
  deterministic, 50, 63, 67, 69
  of motherhood, Roman Catholic,
    114–15
  pastoral, 172–75, 189
  processive, emergent-oriented, 9,
    72–73, 86–87, 90–96, 215–16
  sacramental, 156, 165
  two schools of (Alexandrine and
    Antiochene), 74
  See also doctrine; *specific descriptions,*
    e.g., feminist thought/theology;
    patristic theology
theōsis in Christ, 61
Theotokos, 75, 82, 93
therapeutic abortion. *See* abortion:
  therapeutic
Thomas Aquinas, 67, 78–79, 86, 89
Thompson, Janice Allison, 218–19

Thomson, Judith Jarvis, 140, 148, 156–57, 159, 165
Tiller, Dr. George, 161n17
Toledo, Third Council of (589), 31
Tomson, Peter, 28n54
Torah, 183, 185. *See also* Judaism
Torrance, T. F., 102n18
Townes, Emilie M., 175n65
traducianism, 39, 41, 43, 57–59
transgender, 2–3n3, 127n24
Trinity, 12, 71, 87, 194, 207, 215–16, 220–23
Trust Women: A Progressive Christian Argument for Reproductive Justice (Peters), 2, 45n136, 126n19, 139n63, 190n131
truth, 57, 76, 88–90, 113, 160n10
Turner, Max, 62
twentieth century, 17, 19n7
twins, 102–3, 152n128

ultrasounds, prenatal/ultrasound legislation, 54, 58, 127n23, 137, 146, 152, 168n50, 170, 206
unborn, 1, 6, 25, 28, 31, 44–45, 100n6, 107n35, 145, 147, 216n78, 218, 223
    Christ, 83
    as divinized, 93–94
    and *imago Dei*, 51–52, 58
    as innocent, 7, 20,
    as predestined, 63, 66–67
    See also fetus; "prenate"
United States, 1, 3, 164n33, 168n51
    abortion rate in, 3
    Constitution of, 66, 121, 123–24, 132
    cost of childbirth in, self-pay, 168n51
    pregnancy health complication rate, 149
    See also specific topics, e.g., *Roe v. Wade*
unplanned pregnancy. *See* pregnancy, unplanned
unwanted pregnancy. *See* pregnancy, unwanted
uterus/uterine, 8, 42–43, 82, 105–6, 108, 113, 126, 131, 151–52, 159n8

viability of fetus, 132, 139–41, 152–54, 178–80
violence, 160, 187, 197, 202
    and abortion, 18, 43, 44n129, 108, 135, 166
    anti-abortion, 47, 58, 159–61, 166–67, 209
    domestic, 213
    See also murder; rape
violinist analogy (Thomson), 148, 156
virginity
    consecrated, 21, 203, 205–7
    of Eve, 196
    See also Mary: the Virgin
virtues, 13, 150, 155, 162, 165, 183, 193, 198, 203
vocation, 21, 68, 114–15, 133, 193–95, 205–6. *See also* calling
Vorster, Nico, 65
vulnerable/vulnerability, 134, 165, 209, 223
    fetuses as, 11, 51, 158, 170
    Mary as, 198n14, 200–201, 223
    pregnancy as, 201, 207

waiting period, mandatory, 137, 168
Walker-Barnes, Chanequa, 173–75
Waltke, Bruce K., 56–59, 64n59
Warren, Mary Anne, 5–6, 145
Web sites
    for infant loss, 218
    pro-life/anti-abortion, 56–58, 66, 105, 108, 132, 198, 209, 214
Welz, Claudia, 60
White, Andrew A., 54–57, 59
white women, 169, 175n64
will, 125
    gestation against a woman's, 107, 122, 149–50, 152, 212, 217
    of God, 8, 13, 64–65, 68, 69, 198n14, 199n23, 206
wisdom, 22, 213, 223
Wolf-Devine, Celia, 176–77
womanist thought/theology, 5, 51, 173–75, 189, 195, 214, 217–18
woman/women
    African American, 5, 130n36, 137n58, 167, 169, 173–75, 198, 214, 217–18

woman/women (*continued*)
  Asian American, 212–13
  of child-bearing age, 2–3, 150
  in Greco-Roman world, 36–47
  Mulieris dignitatem, 112–14
  Native, 5
  as rational moral agents, 2, 10, 13,
    69, 127, 206
  the term, 2n3
  white, 12, 169, 175n64
  young women and girls, 11, 98, 107,
    115n64, 129, 163–64, 166–69,
    200
  See also specific descriptions, e.g.,
    Christian women; *specific topics,*
    e.g., bodily integrity; caretaking

    roles; misogyny; reproductive
    rights
womb
  of God, 207–23
  of Mary, 80–84
  See also uterus/uterine
women of color, 131n40, 198. *See also*
    African American women; Asian
    American women; Native women
Word of God, 8, 75, 82–84, 90n88, 92,
    94. *See also* Logos

Young, Iris Marion, 147

zygote, 15n41, 62, 64, 101–4, 110,
    113n56. *See also* embryo

CPSIA information can be obtained
at www.ICGtesting.com
Printed in the USA
FSHW021910081019
62822FS

9 780664 265687